PRINCES TO ACT

Princes to Act

Royal Audience
and Royal Performance,
1578–1792

~

MATTHEW H. WIKANDER

THE JOHNS HOPKINS UNIVERSITY PRESS   BALTIMORE AND LONDON

The Johns Hopkins University Press
2715 North Charles Street
Baltimore, Maryland 21218-4319
The Johns Hopkins Press Ltd., London

LIBRARY OF CONGRESS CATALOGING-IN-PUBLICATION DATA
Wikander, Matthew H.
Princes to act : royal audience and royal performance, 1578–1792 /
Matthew H. Wikander.
p.   cm.
Includes bibliographical references and index.
ISBN 0-8018-4428-2
1. Theater—Europe—History.   2. Theater—Great Britain—History.
3. Theater—Political aspects—Europe.   4. Theater—Political aspects—
Great Britain.   5. European drama—History and criticism.   6. English
drama—History and criticism.   7. Masques—History and criticism.
8. Europe—Court and courtiers.   9. Great Britain—Court and courtiers.
I. Title.
PN2570.W55   1993
792'.094—dc20   92-351

A catalog record for this book is available from the British Library.

To Christine

Contents

Acknowledgments

This study has received generous institutional support from the Columbia University Division of Arts and Sciences, the Columbia Council for Research in the Humanities, and the University of Toledo Faculty Research Fellowships Program. I am grateful to the Visiting Scholars Program of the Horace H. Rackham School of Graduate Studies at the University of Michigan and to Robert Weisbuch, chair of the Department of English, and his assistant, Rebecca Sizemore, for successive appointments as a visiting scholar at the University of Michigan.

A grant-in-aid from the American Council of Learned Societies made it possible for me to travel to do research in Sweden. A summer stipend from the National Endowment for the Humanities enabled me to devote two months to uninterrupted work on the project.

Among libraries whose librarians have made me welcome are: the Columbia University Library, the University of Toledo Library, the Harlan Hatcher Graduate Library of the University of Michigan, the Cleveland Public Library, the Cambridge University Library, the Drott-

ningholm Theater Collection, and Kungliga Biblioteket, the Swedish
Royal Library.

The debt I owe to colleagues who have read parts of the manuscript
and offered their counsel and support is great. Martin Meisel, Herbert
Lindenberger, J. L. Styan, David Bevington, and Birgitta Steene have
all been unstintingly generous in their help. My gratitude to Michael
Manheim extends far beyond thanks for his careful reading and
thoughtful comments on an early version of the manuscript. Portions
of this book have been presented at meetings of the Shakespeare Association of America (1987 and 1991), the Ohio Shakespeare Conference
(1988), the Midwest Modern Language Association (1989), and the
conference on New Languages for the Stage at the University of Kan-
sas in 1988. The anonymous readers for the Johns Hopkins University
Press have contributed greatly to the final shape of this book through
their critiques and recommendations; Eric Halpern of the Press has
been a model editor from the very beginning.

PRINCES TO ACT

1

Royal Performance,
A Midsummer Night's Dream,
and a Royal Progress

~

I

"A kingdom for a stage, princes to act / And monarchs to be-hold the swelling scene": this, the prologue to Shakespeare's *Henry V* wistfully suggests, is an ideal confluence of theater, audience, and performer, and one impossible for the English public stage.[1] Shakespeare's professional actors cannot show their audience of "gentles" the "warlike Harry, like himself." What the prologue apologizes for is both a social and a mimetic problem. Actors are not kings, and the act of playing the king is presumptuous in at least two ways. If an actor is successful in the role, the risk is that of showing that the role of king is playable by a common player; if the actor fails to make the warlike Harry like himself, then social decorum has been preserved but at the cost of the whole point of going to the theater.

Baldesar Castiglione frames the problem in the opposite way. His courtiers discuss the difficulty that might occur should Shakespeare's impossible vision prove possible, and the king play himself:

Therefore it were not meete in such pastimes and open shewes, where they take up counterfeiting of false visages, a prince should take upon him to bee like a prince in deede, because in so doing, the pleasure that the lookers on receive at the noveltie of the matter shoulde want a great deale, for it is no noveltie at all to any man for a prince to bee a prince. And when it is perceyved that beside his being a prince, he will also beare the shape of a prince, he loseth the libertie to doe all those things that are out of the dignitie of a prince.

First of all, the dissatisfaction would be aesthetic. There is no novelty to the prince playing the prince: this suggests that when an actor plays the role of prince, part of the excitement for an audience comes from the very incongruity of social roles placed in juxtaposition. But Castiglione's Sir Fredericke goes on to make a second, more dangerous, point. In the event that weapons might be used in such pastimes, the prince might be thought to remain in his role to avoid being hurt: "beside that, doing in sporte the verie same he should doe in good earnest when neede required, it would take away his authoritie in deede, and would appeare in like case to be play also." If a prince were to play the prince, and do "in sporte" what he must do "in good earnest when neede required," the risk is apparently one of demystification. His authority in actual moments of crisis would be lessened; reality might appear to be "play also." Better, the courtier concludes, that a prince should take the role of a social inferior. Precisely this kind of feigning will reveal his greater worth: among his inferiors, but still recognizable, the masquing prince will display a worth based upon ability rather than station.[2]

In both the *Henry V* prologue and the moment cited from *The Courtier,* the problem is the playability of the royal role. So dressed in the metaphor of the stage is the idea of kingship that there is always the possibility of the metaphor literalizing itself, of the kingdom becoming a stage. The most famous instance of this occurs in Andrew Marvell's "An Horatian Ode upon Cromwel's Return from Ireland," in which Charles I, "the *Royal Actor,*" mounts the scaffold at Whitehall and plays his death scene to perfection. Marvell captured a sense, far from uniquely his, that player and role had fused in that instant. Drawing its legal basis from a contorted reading of the medieval doctrine of the king's two bodies, the British regicide was also an assault upon theater. Charles Stuart was merely a man, separable from his role, just as the professional players had been separated from theirs by Parliament seven years before the regicide. Yet the attempt of the High Court of Justice to find precedent for their unprecedented act in common law showed an anxiety that would later be vindicated: playing the role of martyred king to perfection, Charles rejuvenated the mystique of royalty. Paradoxically, in the court masques in which he and his queen had appeared in the 1630s and 1640s, with their glorification of the royal mystique, he had vindicated Castiglione's anxiety, and trivialized greatness.[3]

This study of court drama in the seventeenth and eighteenth centuries is haunted by regicide. The British regicide punctuates its middle, just as the Swedish regicide, the assassination of Gustav III in 1792, punctuates its end. The trial and execution of Louis XVI in 1793 waits in the wings. While the death of Gustav III was an assassination "in the old style," the French and British regicides were "double executions," as Michael Walzer has put it, in which "the principle of monarchy or monarchy itself was done to death along with the king." Charles I and Louis XVI, Walzer continues, "died as they had tried to live, as bodies simultaneously politic and natural, symbols of a regime, gods incarnate: greater justice could not have been done them."[4] Walzer here recognizes the paradox that Marvell celebrated in his "Horatian Ode," that the British regicides had despite themselves been forced to honor the royal mystique.

"A king is a thing men have made for their own sakes, for quietness' sake," John Selden remarked in his table talk. "Just as in a family one man is appointed to buy the meat."[5] Selden's blunt remark has an antitheatrical as well as an antimonarchical dimension. Kings had never been, as Selden surely knew, "appointed" in this way, any more than actors could be said to perform a social function as useful as buying meat. Neither phenomenon can be seen in the light of this functional analogy. By stressing function here, Selden heretically portrays kingship as a job like any other. But, like the actor's job, the monarch's is not, properly speaking, a job at all.

There is a profound intersection between antitheatrical and antimonarchical sentiments in the seventeenth and eighteenth centuries, as Selden's own particular advocacies testify. But the problem of regicide reveals an even more fundamental theatrical concern: the role of king, as understood in the seventeenth and eighteenth century, was an impossible, an unplayable one. As Franco Moretti has put it, "the sovereign is the missing person, the impossible being in Shakespearean tragedy," because "the 'Christian prince,' wholly Christian and wholly a prince, does not exist," cannot exist: the role itself, of a being whose equilibrium of self "provides the point of equilibrium for the social body," is an unplayable vacancy.[6] The ideal cannot be realized.

This is a secret shared by actor and prince. The period punctuated by the British, Swedish, and French regicides is also the period of extraordinary interdependence of the royal court and the professional stage. With the accession of King James in 1603, the English theater companies came under direct royal patronage, each adopted by a member of the royal family. French actors, in a legal paradox that Voltaire would later deplore, were excommunicated by virtue of their profession, but ordered to take the stage at royal command. Trained to act the roles of kings and princes, the actors played these parts before audiences made up of kings and princes. The covert agreement in such royal performances is that neither party to the occasion, neither actor nor king, will reveal his private knowledge of the impossibility of the role.

Playing the king and being the king are not essentially different activities, for the thing itself is as much an imagined construct as any part a playwright might sketch out for a player. The king is a type: like a pantaloon, a braggart soldier, or a parasite. This conclusion is the demystification which Castiglione's courtier warns against. And, of course, it is both true and untrue. For the king does hold absolute power over the actor, whether the king functions within the rules of an explicitly absolutist system of government, like Louis XIV's France, or within the shifting rules of English common law. As the drama's patron—and, increasingly over the seventeenth century, its only patron—the monarch has a hold over actors that exceeds his grasp over courtiers or commoners. The actor has no profession save by royal license: the profession's dependence is absolute. But the continuing sponsorship of actors by royalty reveals a contrary dependence: the king requires the actor's gifts in service to the royal mystique. For a prince to play the prince is to run the risk of erasing difference. For an actor to play the prince, under the king's sponsorship and watchful eye, however, is an act of gratitude that reinforces difference. By how closely the actor approaches the idea of royalty, he evokes about the king his own power and glory. By how far he falls short of perfection, of an impossible condition of being that which he seems, the actor highlights and celebrates royalty.

Actor and king share a doctrine of two bodies. The king inhabits a body politic and a body physical; he speaks as both when he uses the royal *we*. As Ernst Kantorowicz has proved, the political doctrine of the king's two bodies derives from the theology of Christ's mystic body in the Church. Through this analogy, the king becomes a type of Christ, a divinity on earth, but also his people's sacrifice. Married to his people as Christ is to his Church, he can also expect martyrdom: in this way, the deaths of Charles I and Louis XVI could be seen by royalists as fulfillments of the doctrine.[7] The analogy works on a natural level as well: the realm figures as a body with only one head, the king. With two heads, the body is monstrous, and a king can be a monster, too, if his two bodies are not in harmony. "What am I else," complains the king in William Davenant's *The Fair Favourite* "that still beneath / Two bodies groan, the natural and the politic?"[8] His problem, as we shall see, is the reconciliation of his public responsibilities with his private desires, and it is especially in this aspect of the doctrine of two bodies that the actor's problems coincide with the king's.

Onstage, the actor is both self and other, exposing what is private to the public gaze. Actor and monarch each exist in a mortal body that betokens a role that is immortal, indefinitely replayable. Where this is a political doctrine for the king, its roots are in ideas of ritual substitution and replacement that are perilously close to the roots of drama. Both actor and king take on a godlike power to be double, to endure sacrifice, to suffer a people's crimes as a scapegoat.[9] Anne Barton cautiously notices these parallel origins in ritual: "The resemblances between the actor and the true king might seem, at first, to be only superficial. There are certain flaws, however, in the nature of the king symbol itself which tend to bring reality closer to illusion. The king is an abstraction, the representation of an eternal ideal, but he is also mortal. As a man, he must die, and his death destroys that unity of individual and ideal which the king's life had proclaimed. It is an imperfection in the king symbol by which people have always been troubled."[10] One way people in the seventeenth and eighteenth centuries found of working out this trouble was to kill kings. Actors and playwrights, one feature of whose employment was to entertain kings with plays about the deaths of kings, had to find less violent ways of working out the imperfection in the symbol.

The playwright's difficulties here are special: his is a double dependence. The playwright must avoid writing a script that will give offense, and must also worry about the actor's performance giving offense, belying the innocent text's intentions. Like Blanche Dubois, playwrights rely upon the kindness of strangers. Playwrights who are actors can shorten the odds; Shakespeare, whose only recorded role is that of Tiberius in Ben Jonson's *Sejanus,* seems to have played the royal part at least once. Molière could safely parody absolutism's weaknesses and excesses in the guise of foolish bourgeois patriarchs. But for the most part, playwrights function like Peter Quince in *A Midsummer Night's Dream,* fearful lest ineptitude and misinterpretation on the part of the actors will lead to disastrous misinterpretation and offense on the part of the royal audience.

This study takes *A Midsummer Night's Dream* as its starting place because of that play's intense interest in the problems inherent in entertaining royalty. The anxieties among actors and playwrights that it dramatizes epitomize the strains of royal performance. As a kind of control, this first chapter also examines a narrative account of a royal progress, Thomas Churchyard's *A Discourse of the Queenes Maiesties entertainement in Suffolk and Norfolk: with a description of many things then presently seene* (1578). Both *A Midsummer Night's Dream* and Churchyard's *Discourse* allude to the central problem of royal performance: what is of primary interest is not the show itself, but the reaction of the monarch to the show. That reaction is itself a kind of performance, as the monarch is required to respond to the gesture of love and service that a dramatic performance represents. According to Duke Theseus, the mechanicals' "nothing" becomes something because he permits it to do so; Churchyard's lame efforts testify to Elizabeth's greatness because she thanked him for them. In both instances, the royal audience has the power, like Egeus's power over Hermia, "to leave the figure, or disfigure it" (I.i.51). What makes the play different from the progress is of course its complexity: that is, the multiple ironies of Pyramus and Thisbe, like the multiple possible facets of Elizabeth, are fully dramatized. The multiple ironies of the progress to Norwich, on the other hand, only become apparent as Churchyard struggles to demonstrate his prince's greatness by documenting his own love and duty.

The Elizabethan progress and the court performance mocked in the play-within-the-play in *A Midsummer Night's Dream* offer a starting point because both Elizabeth and Theseus seem so comfortable with themselves, so easy in the royal role. Chapter 2 moves on to a less comfortable fit. Here Shakespeare's *Measure for Measure* offers a way to characterize the Jacobean royal audience. Whether or not it was especially designed for court performance, *Measure for Measure* was performed before King James I on December 26, 1604. Attempts to determine whether the duke in this play allegorizes James or divine providence or Hapsburg ambitions are somehow beside the point, for what the play metatheatrically sets up is a conflict between the duke and Lucio over its very meaning. In his enforced idleness, his closeness to the stews, his mocking pretention to private knowledge of the duke's habits of rule, Lucio seems to embody the professional theater. Its frequent visits to court and its actors' expert portrayal of state affairs lie as restlessly with its Bankside roots as Lucio with Kate Keepdown. "For the imported play at court and for court theatricals," Keith Sturgess reminds us, "the King . . . was not only the chief spectator but a rival performance."[11] The rivalry between the duke and Lucio over the duke's reputation dramatizes some of the implications of that rival performance.

Court masque was the proper genre in which to praise the Jacobean monarch, and *Measure for Measure* refuses the royal theophany of masque. The plays of Beaumont and Fletcher examined in the latter part of chapter 2 incorporate within themselves the language of masque, in the case of *Philaster* and *A King and No King,* and a masque-within-a-play, in *The Maid's Tragedy.* Masque functions in this chapter much as Churchyard's progress functions in chapter 1, as a control, an instance of royal entertainment that is not a play. Editors of Shakespeare's late plays have long desired to see *Henry VIII* on the list of plays that the King's Men performed at court on the occasion of Princess Elizabeth's wedding to Frederick, the Elector Palatine. The list survives, however, and is resistant to such hopes. The royal wedding party saw twenty plays over the holiday season of 1612–13: *Philaster* twice, *The Maid's Tragedy,* and *A King and No King* among them.[12] Ironic in their treatment of masque's cosmic transformations, these plays seem far less appropriate to the occasion than *Henry VIII* would have been. Rather than delighting in panegyric, the Jacobean courtiers found themselves confronting riddling treatments of the pitfalls and dangers of court life.

If kings have two bodies, so too do plays, in that they consist of texts capable of idealization and performances capable of repetition.

Chapter 3 concentrates on the phenomenon of revival and replaying on the court stages of Charles I. William Davenant's plays, written for the professional theater, are complex revisions of Beaumont and Fletcher originals, and they seem to assume their audience's familiarity with the repertoire. Celebrated by Davenant in the court masques of the reign, royal marriage becomes problematic in such plays as *The Platonic Lovers, The Unfortunate Lovers,* and *The Fair Favourite.* These plays, a comedy, a tragedy, and a tragicomedy, run the gamut of genres in which Davenant was expert: all are written with an eye to a particular royal audience, Davenant's patron, Queen Henrietta Maria. Her intense involvement in theater at court encouraged amateur dramatists as well. The chapter continues by looking at two plays by amateur playwrights that received reprise performances at court. William Cartwright's *The Royal Slave* was performed before the king and queen at Oxford by members of the university; later the queen requested that the sets, machines, and costumes of this production be moved to Hampton Court so that the professional players could act the play. The play, to Cartwright's confusion, necessarily became something quite different the second time around. Sir John Suckling rewrote his play *Aglaura*. After it was performed once as a tragedy, he adapted it to court taste and had it played with a revised ending as a tragicomedy. A special effort to please the queen, no doubt: but both texts of the play hark back to the multiple ironies of Beaumont and Fletcher's presentations of court life. Charles and Henrietta Maria appeared together in apotheosis in Davenant's court masques. The plays they saw, however, scrutinized royal marriages and found a source of anxiety in the figure of the king in love.

Charles's royal performances culminated in the prize of a "martyr's crown."[13] Louis XIV also appeared in apotheosis before his court and also presented himself as a royal martyr. Early in his career, he danced as Apollo or as Jupiter in splendid entertainments at Versailles. Later in his career, the king acted out his royal sacrifice, his isolation as the only truly Christian king among the crowned heads of Europe. Chapter 4 traces the identification of Louis XIV with an ideal of absolutist self-mastery, through Corneille's *Cinna* (written in the reign of Louis XIII, but the single most frequently performed play at the court of Louis XIV), Molière's *Tartuffe,* and Racine's *Esther. Tartuffe* dramatizes its own story of suppression and royal patronage; its *rex ex machina* ending is not flattery but a recognition of the king's godlike (and fickle) power over the creations of the players, his creatures. *Esther* finds Louis presiding over a reformed stage, on which convent girls innocently act out a story drawn from the Bible. Yet the play also celebrates Madame de Maintenon's dominance over the king: intentionally or not, Racine had written a play that was perceived as scandalous allegory by a large number of courtiers.

But Louis, central as he was to the performances of *Esther* in 1689, was not the play's only royal audience. King James II of Britain, newly replaced by his daughter Mary and her husband, William of Orange, his nephew, was in exile at Saint-Germain and also attended the play with his queen. A French *Esther* and a British *Esther* materialized on this instant. For all of the play's praise of the godlike triumphs of Louis XIV, the presence of his sullen cousin, a king without a kingdom, suggested that the king's two bodies do not easily remain one.

Esther at Saint-Cyr was not professional theater. As in the England of Charles I, amateur performances came to compete with the visits of professionals to the court. The vogue for private, amateur theaters— *théâtres de société*—overtook the court in France in the eighteenth century. Madame de Pompadour established a theater company that played in the Petits Cabinets, in the king's private quarters, at Louis XV's Versailles. Chapter 5 follows Voltaire as he seeks to win a position as court poet, like that of Racine in the court of Louis XIV. Voltaire's tragedy *Alzire* was performed in Madame de Pompadour's theater February 28 and March 6, 1750: the king's response to this performance, and the circumstances surrounding the performance, help to explain Voltaire's decision to leave France and attach himself to the court of Frederick the Great at Potsdam. There we can watch Voltaire take the stage himself as an actor, playing the role of Cicéron in his own *Rome sauvée* on a number of occasions in September and October 1750. No more than his playwriting did Voltaire's acting earn him the position of intimate at court that he craved. Finally he established theaters at his estates near the Swiss border in France, where he settled after his ignominious departure from Prussia. At Ferney he functioned as an impresario, directing and acting in productions of his own plays: with no one but himself to please, he became his own royal audience.

If Voltaire's visitors frequently found his dramatic productions absurd and his manner overbearing, he was wealthy, prestigious, and old enough to disregard them. His theater epitomized his independence. Louis XV and Frederick had interfered with his quest for independence by insisting on their prerogatives as kings. Gustav III of Sweden, in chapter 6, also sought total control over all aspects of theatrical activity at his court, as Voltaire did at Ferney; but he was a king. As an actor, Gustav played before his court roles characterized by energy and excess of passion. Like Bottom, he preferred the role of tyrant to that of lover. We will visit the court at Gripsholm castle over the Christmas holidays of 1775–76, where Gustav played five major tragic roles from the French classical repertoire, appearing twice in the title role of *Cinna,* and five leading roles in comic afterpieces, in the space of two weeks. Advised after this to quit the stage by conservative courtiers and the French ambassador, Gustav then became a playwright, drafting (with the help of various court poets) a number of plays on Swedish history, to be performed in Swedish by his courtiers. *Gustav Vasa,* an opera based upon a scenario by Gustav, became his greatest triumph. When it appeared in 1786, in the opera house that Gustav himself had constructed, performed by the professional opera company of which he was patron, he supervised every detail of production. Gustav Vasa's apotheosis, staged in the opera, became a vindication of Gustav III's policies as well as of his art.

As over Charles I, historians have often waxed ironic over Gustav III, who was assassinated as he left a masked ball at the opera house in 1792. His assassination became the stuff of a libretto by Scribe and an opera by Verdi. But where Charles, as Marvell's royal actor, transcended his mortal weakness in that final moment, Gustav's theatricality seems to highlight his vulnerability. Contrary to its representation in opera, the manner of his death was horribly undignified. His assassin, Jacob Anckarström, mentally unstable and possibly a former lover, had charged his pistol with rusty nails, and the king died of peritonitis three days after he was shot. Anckarström had been encouraged by factions hostile to the king, but his public execution by drawing and quartering was equally horrible. Both deaths, the king's and his assassin's, demonstrated the ruthless power of the aristocratic party offended by Gustav's absolutist reforms.

In the theater, Gustav had sought applause, not immortality. He aspired to the condition of the actor, and delighted in praise as a playwright. In his theatrical career, this king was willing to change places with the player. Not in order to play himself; that would be no novelty. Gustav's favorite role was Corneille's Cinna, a would-be assassin unmasked by a clement emperor. It is to this final paradox that royal role-playing, at least in the seventeenth- and eighteenth-century courts of Europe, comes. *Cinna*'s vision of absolutist self-sufficiency dominates the final three chapters. Gustav delighted in the role, and Voltaire, his rival Crébillon, and his patron Frederick the Great all borrowed from and imitated Corneille's play. Playing the conspirator rather than the emperor, Gustav wholly adopted the persona of the actor: he chose not the royal role, but the best part.

Louis XVI's death on the guillotine in 1793 was meant to be mechanized, impersonal, the death of the criminal Louis Capet, not the death of a king. The intention of the revolutionary council was that it be no different from any other guillotine death. But the place became sacred anyway. Spectators dipped their handkerchiefs in the king's blood.[14] Gustav's death, some months before, anticipates this demonstration of the persistence of the royal mystique and its paradoxical dependence upon the actor. With the end of personal rule in England, with the end of the *ancien régime* in France, with the end of Gustav's unique progressive absolutism in Sweden, comes also an end to direct royal sponsorship of theater. And an end to tragedy: at least to tragedy as understood by the Renaissance, "the high and excellent Tragedy," as Sir Philip Sidney put it, "that openeth the greatest wounds, and showeth forth the ulcers that are covered with tissue; that maketh kings fear to be tyrants, and tyrants manifest their tyrannical humours; that, with stirring the affects of admiration and commiseration, teacheth the uncertainty of this world, and upon how weak foundations gilden roofs are builded."[15]

As we watch Gustav playing Gengis-Kan in Voltaire's *L'Orphelin de la Chine,* the royal player merges with and disengages from the tyrannical role. This appears to fulfill the dream of *Henry V*'s prologue: here is a prince who acts. But when we finally do see a monarch who acts, a king who manifests tyrannical humours, we are forced to disbelieve what we see. Gustav cannot play the tyrant without somehow threatening to become one. The king who acts still remains the king. What Gustav did instead was to play the actor. Many in the courtly audience were of Castiglione's mind: such playacting cheapened the dignity of the monarchy. As impresario, Gustav could reclaim some degree of royalty: but it is a kind of royalty that can be measured alongside Voltaire's. At Gripsholm and Drottningholm, he was like Voltaire at Ferney or Tournay, host to a select gathering. Even at the opera, he took pleasure in the crowd's applause. Unlike the duke in *Measure for*

Measure, he felt no discomfort at the people's "aves vehement."

When a king can conceive of himself as an actor, playwright, and director,[16] and take pleasure in doing so, he challenges the sense of difference that Shakespeare and Castiglione seek to maintain (even by wittily challenging it, as Shakespeare does). The irony in Marvell's praise of the royal actor is that the mystique Charles reclaimed on the scaffold was the mystique he had lost by participating in court masques (masques whose purpose was to glorify his mystique). Along with the mystique of royalty, the old form of tragedy—and the old way of defining it—persisted through the eighteenth century, not because of the French Academy's imposition of rules, but because the royal role remained fascinating. Voltaire, the most popular and respected dramatist of the age, challenged the rules by introducing scenic effects, ghosts, and medieval costumes to the French stage. But he continued to work within the classic tragic form, and one of his favorite roles was that of Lusignan in *Zaïre,* last king in a long line of crusader kings of Jerusalem. It is an index, perhaps, of the degree to which the idea of monarchy was demystified by the European revolutions of the seventeenth and eighteenth century that Voltaire's drama now holds none of the prestige it once enjoyed. But that Voltaire, energetic demystifier that he was, should have had such a weakness for kings, as his niece put it, that he actively sought out his humiliations by Louis and Frederick, testifies to a contrary persistence of the mystique. There is something in it yet.

The new form of serious drama without kings that developed in Europe in the mid-eighteenth century (sentimental comedy, bourgeois tragedy, *comédie larmoyante, bürgerliche Trauerspiel*—call it what you will) was not ruled out in the royal courts. Voltaire wrote some plays of this sort, and Madame de Pompadour played in one of them, *L'Enfant prodigue,* at the Petits Cabinets. Beaumarchais's *Le Mariage de Figaro,* a play whose reputation for subversiveness is familiar, was performed by Marie Antoinette and her society theater company at the Petit Trianon before Louis XVI, with Beaumarchais invited to attend in the audience.[17] Gustav III had enjoyed the play, although he disapproved of its antimonarchical tone. But he also wrote serious comedies in the new form. The precursor of modern dramatic realism coexisted through the eighteenth century with the final vestiges of Renaissance tragedy.

This book is not a narrative of the death of tragedy or of the rise of modern drama: rather, it sets out to be a complicating counterpoint to such narratives, whose evolutionary paradigms invite suspicion.[18] By tracing the persistence of the royal mystique and by characterizing the relationship of actor and king as one of interdependence rather than subversion and ultimate displacement, we can blur some distinctions between periods and styles which have always seemed arbitrary. A Renaissance culture of emulation animates Gustavian performance in the late eighteenth century; Voltaire, despite his progressive ideas, works contentedly within the old classical forms, and wins fame and universal acceptance to an extent unheard of by earlier playwrights. As the regicides remind us, to notice such coexistence is not in any way to claim that there is an unbroken continuity to be found in the idea of royal performance from Elizabeth to Gustav. But the major social changes of the seventeenth and eighteenth centuries did not bring instant and utter change to the court theaters; changes in the institution of theater came slowly.

Not all the European kings who enjoyed theater and indulged in acting or dancing died at their people's hands. Louis XIV, whose pious reform was often described in theatrical terms, certainly did not. Frederick the Great, who played the flute like a virtuoso and delighted in Italian-style comedy, was by no means perceived by his contemporaries as frivolous, or living in a fantasy world. Theatrical as their recreations may have been, Charles I, Louis XVI, and Gustav III devoted considerable attention to the serious business of being kings: and costly wars, arbitrary taxation, and the agendas of powerful factions were factors weightier than antitheatrical sentiment in bringing them down. To oppose the king is not necessarily to oppose the actor: yet the institutional imbrication of theater with monarchy in early modern Europe led revolutionary movements to identify themselves with ideas of theatrical reform. But kings could also dream of a reformed theater, and Voltaire could attack the practices of his professional rivals and still be ambitious to succeed at court.

Antitheatrical thinkers of the period, like William Prynne and Jean-Jacques Rousseau, emphasized, more than defenders of theater did, its power to effect real psychic and political transformations. To them, the actor is indeed "terrific," in Michael Goldman's sense of the word, capable of uprooting from his place on the stage the most deeply and privately held sense of self in each member of the audience, capable of turning a well-ordered group into a raging mob.[19] Royal patronage of playing suggests by distant analogy royal subversion of private self-hood, of the new subjectivity of the age. Rousseau certainly makes this connection, praising republican Geneva for its lack of a professional theater in his letter to d'Alembert. Rousseau looks forward to romanticism and democracy. The actor and the king do not: they are neither of them sincere, nor are they equals. Rousseau's ideals of sincerity and equality are alien to both. As they must be. The actor who plays the king can do so precisely because he is not royal, because he poses no threat. The king who plays the actor is a novelty because he is permitting himself to slide down the social scale, but he puts off none of his power as he puts on his costume.

The decorums of court performance work to reinforce royal difference at the same time that they call attention to the royal audience as rival performer. Colley Cibber, in a familiar account of his own performances at Hampton Court before King George I in 1717, reminds us that English actors, after the Revolution of 1688, after the last Stuart monarch, still paid special attention to the king as they played before him. Cibber begins his anecdote with a flourish:

> But I have done with my Digression, and now return to our the-atre at *Hampton-Court,* where I am not sure the Reader, be he ever so wise, will meet with any thing more worth his notice: However, if he happens to read, as I happen to write, for want of something better to do, he will go on; and perhaps wonder when I tell him that
>
> A Play presented at Court, or acted on a publick Stage, seem to their different Auditors a different Entertainment. Now hear my Reason for it. In the common Theatre the Guests are at home, where the politer Forms of Good-breeding are not so nicely regarded: Every one there falls to, and likes or finds fault according to his natural Taste or Appetite. At Court, where the Prince gives the Treat, and honours the Table with his own Presence, the Audience is under the Restraint of a Circle, where Laughter or Applause rais'd higher than a Whisper would be star'd at. At a publick Play, they are both let loose, even 'till the Actor is sometimes pleas'd with his not being able to be heard for the Clamour of them. But this Coldness or Decency of Attention at Court I observ'd had but a melancholy Effect upon the Vanity of some of our Actors, who seem'd inconsolable when their flashy Endeav-

ours to please had pass'd unheeded: Their not considering where they were quite disconcerted them; nor could they recover their Spirits 'till from the lowest Rank of the Audience some gaping *John* or *Joan,* in the fullness of their Hearts, roar'd out their Approbation: And, indeed, such a natural Instance of honest Simplicity a Prince himself, whose indulgence knows where to make Allowances, might reasonably smile at, and perhaps not think it the worst part of his Entertainment.[20]

Certainly one needs no stronger evidence of the demystification of royalty than Cibber's identification of a court performance with a formal dinner party. His whole sphere of reference is domestic, with the audience at the public theater falling to greedily, while the court audience worries about the right fork. The actors themselves feel inhibited, "inconsolable" at the lack of loud laughter or applause. It is only when the court begins to feel like the public playhouse, and the gaping John or Joan begins to roar, that the actors begin to feel at home. The king is to be praised for his indulgence of the "honest simplicity" of the lower ranks. The king is a gracious host: so, too, as we shall see, does Theseus in *A Midsummer Night's Dream* present himself as he indulges the rude mechanicals' performance at his court.

For Cibber on these occasions, as for any actor on a similar occasion, it is important to watch the king's response: "But, however, as we were not here itinerant Adventurers, and had properly but one Royal Auditor to please, after that Honour was attain'd to, the rest of our Ambition had little to look after: And that the King was often pleas'd, we were not only assur'd by those who had the Honour to be near him; but could see it, from the frequent Satisfaction in his Looks at particular Scenes and Passages." Playing at court offers to the actor the special advantage of having only "one Royal Auditor to please"; this contrasts favorably to the give-and-take business of daily paid performances, with their attendant risk. But there is some anxiety hidden in Cibber's account, for the actors need to be "assur'd" of the king's enjoyment by other audience members, and to keep a close eye on his "Looks." Cibber goes on to record a specific moment, in which, playing Cardinal Wolsey in Shakespeare's *Henry VIII,* he subtly claims credit for a new policy of tax relief. This double-dealing on the part of a powerful minister "seem'd to raise the King into something more than a Smile whenever that Play came before him," Cibber confides:

"And I had a more distinct Occasion to observe this Effect, because my proper Stand on the Stage when I spoke the Lines required me to be near the Box where the King usually sate." Here the reader of the *Apology* is treated to a glimpse of Cibber watching the king watching Cibber. The king's smile is not private: it signals to the auditors not only a naive pleasure at Cibber's performance, but also a rueful awareness of the deviousness of the ministers whom kings must trust.

If Cibber's language of dinner parties evokes the domestic, the private, the demystified version of royalty, his watchful eye suggests that the "Royal Auditor" still enjoys extraordinary power over the actor. The eighteenth century saw increasing social status for the actor, and it saw the royal courts move toward smaller theaters and private entertainments. But it did not see theaters wholly free of royal patronage, exclusively commercial adventures in which actors, in all the dignity of their craft, performed before paying audiences of social equals. Cibber's distinction between those occasions when the actors were "itinerant Adventurers," dependent upon fickle Johns and Joans, and the relative security of the court, where only one audience member needs to be pleased, is reminiscent of the institutional structure of the English companies under King James I. Those actors, too, served two masters: public theater audiences who paid for regular performances, and the king, upon whose patronage they depended. Nor were their demands, any more than in Cibber's time, always congruent.

This is a story, then, of uneasy survival and of incipient but incomplete change. Its method is to look at particular instances of royal performance closely. The plays here were all performed at courts, before royal audiences. The evidence for this is sometimes overwhelming, sometimes sketchy. More importantly, these are plays that incorporate within their own structures the dynamics of royal performance. These are plays in which the actor, like Cibber as Cardinal Wolsey, has to keep a close eye on the monarch in the audience. The playwright has to keep an eye on the royal audience as well, and where anecdotes of performance can reveal the actor's anxiety, the playwright's heightened awareness of the royal audience lurks in the tensions and conflicts of the texts themselves. Such especially intense "stage fright," as Herbert Blau reminds us, "was surely a serious question and hardly a minor matter in an age when the playwright and the actor had reason to be wary, as Ben Jonson knew, since the one who gave audience also had the power to cut off their ears."[21]

Playwrights in royally sponsored companies knew that their plays always stood a good chance of being performed before the monarch. Sometimes they knew this with full certainty, on the basis of a particular commission: more frequently, however, it seems to have been a matter of some uncertainty. This uncertainty is programmatic in plays that had to succeed on both the commercial and the court stage. Some court drama is specifically occasional and free of commercial constraint. Writing *Esther,* Racine knew precisely for what kind of event he was supplying the script. Writing *Alzire* in 1736, Voltaire could expect the Comédie Française to act the play at court after its Paris premiere, but he could not know precisely when; and he could in no way have anticipated that Madame de Pompadour would perform the role before the king in 1750. Shakespeare, too, must have been aware that any play he wrote as a member of the King's Men could be performed on short notice at court; but his plays, like Voltaire's, also had to make their own way before the paying audiences of the town.

Much of the excitement of royal performance can be traced to this particular problem of playwriting. For the professional playwright, like Colley Cibber at Hampton Court, is well aware of the different demands from his different constituencies. A play that will be commercially successful might not be one that would please the king. But to write plays displeasing to the king would be to threaten the playwright's livelihood and expose actor, playwright, and company to harsh retribution. Shakespeare dramatizes this tension within his plays themselves: their strong metatheatrical dimension heightens our awareness of their complex institutional status. At the other end of the spectrum, with Voltaire, that tension is revealed primarily in the playwright's letters and complaints to his friends, and in anecdotes of rehearsal and performance. The plays themselves offer models of virtuous behavior that only inadvertently become ambiguous in the context of what we know about the particular conditions of their performance.

Voltaire wrote for posterity; Shakespeare wrote for his company. But the conventional distinction between Voltaire as a man of letters and Shakespeare as a man of the theater breaks down. Voltaire took extraordinary pains to prepare his plays for production, as his detailed letters to his representatives in Paris, the d'Argentals, and to actors such as Mademoiselle Clairon and Lekain demonstrate. And Shakespeare's company presented his works to posterity with the command, "Reade him, therefore, and againe, and againe."[22] The rich anecdotal evidence shows that Voltaire was in constant negotiation with the play-ers. In Shakespeare's case, the anecdotal record is almost nonexistent, but the plays themselves dramatize similar negotiations. Uncertainty about the status of the actor animates much Renaissance drama; Molière shows the same anxieties as Shakespeare. Voltaire struggled against an entrenched bureaucracy in his battles with the Comédie Française; he took more satisfaction finally in sponsoring the playing of his plays himself.

The focus of this book shifts from attention to texts to attention to circumstances of production, as the narrative moves from Renaissance to eighteenth-century drama. This is due partly to the availability of evidence, but mostly to the greater degree of self-consciousness in Renaissance texts. Nonetheless, criticism of drama must reflect the demands of the form itself. While text-oriented dramatic criticism tends to privilege an idea of the play over the limiting constraints of performance, performance-oriented criticism, except at its best, as practiced by J. L. Styan, tends to denigrate the idea of a transcendent text.[23] If plays can be said to exist only as blueprints or orchestral scores to be fully realized in performance, they nonetheless do exist in that form. There is something for the interpreter to interpret. But dra-matic texts differ from texts in other literary genres in the way they make their claims of transcendence: playwrights have always known that their production is mediate, indeterminate, and negotiable. To Ben Jonson, railing at the "loathèd stage," the playwright's depen-dence upon others is sordid bondage. As John G. Sweeney and Tim-othy Murray have pointed out, Jonson turned to print for vindication or legitimation of his endeavors.[24] All playwrights feel pulled in this direction; but successful playwrights find themselves, like kings, in a curious mutual dependence with the actors whose bodies defy their texts' transcendent claims. For James Calderwood, this is a paradox at the very edge of life: "the play dies every night," but by dint of subse-quent performances it can be "miraculously reborn." "The play out-lives all its mortal performances and thus lays claim to a kind of platonic immortality," Calderwood continues. "Yet though the play outlives its performances, it can have no life without them."[25]

It may be impossible to resolve this paradox or at least to strike a balance: to convey the immediacy and urgency of performance with-out denigrating the play's claim to independent existence, to acknowl-edge playwrights' claims of authority without eliding the institutional constraints under which they operate.[26] Authors exist and have intentions (no one who knows writers can say otherwise): but no mechanism for transmitting those intentions can be less reliable, more distorting, more assertive of its own institutional prerogatives, than the theater. I have attempted throughout to respect the rights of playwrights and actors, to pay attention both to performance and to publication as means by which drama reaches audiences, to recognize that on different occasions before different audiences the same play can carry different meanings. This has led to a curious methodology, no doubt already apparent. I call it "conjectural theater history": where records are lacking, I have not hestitated to flesh out a monarch's or an actor's or a playwright's secret fear. Such conjecture is not in itself ahistorical: especially if we construe history, with Lynn Hunt, as "an ongoing tension between stories that have been told and stories that might be told."[27] Rather, it is a way of narrowing down the astonishing multiplicity of meanings that plays can generate when contemplated as dramatic poems, existing outside time and space.

The plays and the occasions I have selected offer striking examples of the dynamics of royal performance. My emphasis on repeat performances in many instances illustrates an important principle: the same play never means the same thing twice. While my method has been to look closely at the plays' texts, placing these texts in different contexts reveals sharp differences of potential meaning: Gustav III as Cinna discovers dimensions of that play unimagined by its author or its original actors. I hope to complicate traditional theater history by multiplying the voices in the texts of plays, by recognizing the persistence of texts through multiple performances, and by insisting upon the constant renewal of plays' complicity in their social and institutional context.

At the end of the eighteenth century, playwrights could achieve the dignity of authors, actors could achieve the dignity of Christian burial, and kings could not invoke their special difference from actors without some degree of irony.[28] Renaissance plays, well before such changes could take effect, entertained the possibility of these freedoms with extraordinary self-awareness. Plays take liberties. "Each age will have its own image of the simultaneously appalling and appealing stance, of the occupation or preoccupation that elevates and exposes, of the power that puts its wielder into jeopardy," Michael Goldman proposes.[29] Thomas Rymer, in *The Tragedies of the Last Age Consider'd,* professes to be amazed at the liberties taken in English Renaissance drama:

> Some have remark'd, that *Athens* being a *Democracy,* the Poets,
> in favour of their Government, expos'd Kings and made them
> unfortunate. But certainly, examin the Kings of their *Tragedies,*
> they appear all *Heroes,* and ours but *Dogs,* in comparison of
> them. So respectful they seem to Kings, in their *Democracy,* and
> so unthinking and unpolitick are our *Poets* under a *Monarchy*
> . . . . They made the Kings *unfortunate,* we made them *wicked:*
> they made them to be *pittied,* we made them to be *curst* and
> *abhorr'd.*[30]

In Rymer's own age, after the Revolution of 1688, royalty had come
commonly to be dramatized as an unfortunate condition, worthy of
pity; it had ceased to appall.[31] Under strong monarchies, like the age
of the early Stuarts here invoked by Rymer, and like that of Louis
XIV, the role of king, developed toward either of its complementary
extremes, tyranny and clemency, continued to appall and appeal to a
series of ages usually seen as discrete.

Renaissance England, Classical France, and Enlightenment Europe
are categories that suggest different social, religious, and epistemological worlds. They constitute, for Michel Foucault, three separate and
distinct "epistemes." But the court theaters of these worlds share not
only a similar architectural style, developed from the Italian perspective stages of the sixteenth century, but also a preoccupation with the
nature of the royal role.[32] We witness this preoccupation in the plays'
awareness of their royal audiences, an awareness that can be found
both in surviving texts and in anecdotes of particular occasions. Plays
performed at court are acutely conscious of their status as rival performances, as interlopers. Yet as interlopers, they claim and take freedoms that the political order would yield only grudgingly.

Shakespeare constitutes a beginning for this study, because his
drama epitomizes the dynamic of royal performance. His theater is
charged with awareness of its volatile status, its utter dependency and
its radical freedom, its ability to take liberties, to cause offense and
emerge unpunished. Shakespeare's seeming impunity in a time of increasing governmental control of theater derives from the complexity
of his drama: his plays abound in a multiplicity of voices.[33] In *A Midsummer Night's Dream,* Shakespeare sets into action three voices that
will be of central importance to this study of royal performance. The
playwright's voice can be heard in the anxious Peter Quince; the actor's

in Bottom and in Puck; and Duke Theseus speaks with the unmistakable voice of the king.

II

"Say, what abridgement have you for this evening?" Duke Theseus asks Philostrate, his master of revels; "What masque? what music? How shall we beguile / The lazy time, if not with some delight?" (V.i. 39–41). With his impatient urgings, Theseus returns *A Midsummer Night's Dream* to the mood of its beginning, when he eagerly prodded Philostrate to "Stir up the Athenian youth to merriments" (I.i.13). At his next appearance, Theseus and his bride are hunting in the forest outside Athens; this is a monarch who likes to spend his time in royal recreations. He demands to be entertained. On her annual summer progresses to the great houses of the nobility and to the large corporate towns, Queen Elizabeth I was also a guest for whom revels, hunts, and shows had to be provided. "Sartyrs and Wild Men lurked behind every tree, ready to address her in Poulter's Measure," Jean Wilson puts it; "Shepherds and Shepherdesses infested the hills, singing pastoral ditties, and demanding that she arbitrate in their disputes."[34] Nor was the queen reluctant to play her part in these pageants, adjudicating disputes and accepting gifts. During a royal progress, shows were presented to the monarch while at the same time the monarch was presented to her people. The play-within-the-play in *A Midsummer Night's Dream* functions in the same way as these royal performances: a monarch—Duke Theseus or Queen Elizabeth—cannot watch a play without being watched. Spectators and actors alike key their responses and performances to the royal smile or frown. *A Midsummer Night's Dream* and Thomas Churchyard's narrative of a royal progress, *A Discourse of the Queenes Maiesties entertainement in Suffolk and Norfolke,* characterize a particularly Elizabethan kind of royal performance. They share a common language and project a similar image of the ruler as gracious audience, piecing out imperfections and taking in the proper spirit what might otherwise be mistaken as offense.

Theseus has a certain amount of trouble getting the entertainment he wants: neither the merriments proposed by Theseus in the play's first scene nor the hunt in the fourth act ever takes place. And at the play's end, Philostrate presents Theseus with a bill of fare of inappropriate entertainments. "Not sorting with a nuptial ceremony," Theseus complains of a satirical piece, but the same could be said also for "the battle with the Centaurs" or "the riot of the tipsy Bacchanals" (V.i.44–55). Over the objections of Philostrate (who does not seem to have done his job very well—in this he resembles Thomas Churchyard, as we shall see) and of his new bride, Hippolyta, the duke selects the rude mechanicals' play of Pyramus and Thisbe: "very tragical mirth" (57). Theseus overrules opposition. "Egeus, I will overbear your will," he announced in accepting the new arrangement of lovers after the night in the woods (IV.i.178). There he brushed aside the "ancient privilege of Athens" (I.i.41) in favor of the comic institution of marriage; here he brushes aside the qualms of his court with what can be seen as an expression of the exquisite generosity of a noble audience in permitting social inferiors to perform before it.

"He says they can do nothing in this kind," Hippolyta points out (V.i.88); for her and for Philostrate, observing ineptitude is embarrassing. But for Theseus, bad drama offers an opportunity for the display of noblesse oblige. "The kinder we, to give them thanks for nothing," he quips, and embarks upon a famous speech:

> Our sport shall be to take what they mistake;
> And what poor duty cannot do, noble respect
> Takes it in might, not merit.
> Where I have come, great clerks have purposed
> To greet me with premeditated welcomes;
> Where I have seen them shiver and look pale,
> Make periods in the midst of sentences,
> Throttle their practised accent in their fears,
> And in conclusion, dumbly have broke off,
> Not paying me a welcome. Trust me, sweet,
> Out of this silence yet I picked a welcome,
> And in the modesty of fearful duty
> I read as much as from the rattling tongue
> Of saucy and audacious eloquence.
> Love, therefore, and tongue-tied simplicity
> In least speak most, to my capacity.
>
> (89–105)

In light of Theseus's almost universal enshrinement in criticism as a "mirror of the model ruler and wise man,"[35] this speech deserves some special scrutiny. The rationalist Theseus seems to be suggesting that a charitable act of the imagination, a faculty he deplores, can "read" the love that motivates a stumbling speech and pick a welcome from silence. Thus we might be tempted to see here a Theseus who has somehow changed from his first act alignment with forces hostile to love—he exits from the first scene accompanied by the querulous Egeus and the "spotted and inconstant" Demetrius—to an alignment not only with lovers and courtly graciousness but also with charity and grace. A royal audience can creatively "amend" bad plays with "imagination" (210): a generous monarch can see his subjects as "excellent men" ("if we imagine no worse of them than they of themselves" [213–14]). The rude mechanicals' incompetent playing, like the "great clerks'" throttled mumbling, betokens a subject's love; the monarch's charitable apprehension of that love embodies a reciprocal gesture of generosity.

But throughout Theseus's endorsement of this principle we sense the hostility to imagination that animated his repudiation of lunatics, lovers, and poets and charged his endorsement of Egeus's complaints— "rhymes" and "love tokens" constitute Lysander's dangerous charms— at the play's outset. Theseus's condescension, like the word *condescension* itself, is double-edged. He generously lowers himself to entertain the theatrical offering of his underlings, and at the same time he envelops himself in a sort of smugness. His first remark—"The kinder we, to give them thanks for nothing"—pulls both ways. It would be "kind," in the most powerful archaic sense of this word so charged in Shakespeare's usage, to receive the laborers' offering with charity: *kind* being in this sense humble, generous, gentle (precisely what the jejune lordlings of *Love's Labour's Lost* are not when they scoff at the pageant of the Nine Worthies). Furthermore, the quibble on Hippolyta's remark (she uses *kind* to refer to the species of endeavor the mechanicals have embarked upon) suggests a craft morality here: although the amateur actors are hampered by not performing in a trade they know, the monarch is fulfilling the obligation of his "kind" by accepting their performance kindly. The more so, Theseus says, because it will not merely be bad, but, because the craftsmen are operating outside their crafts, it will be "nothing." Theseus's generous condescension is coupled with contemptuous dismissal. In his republic, as in Plato's, tradesmen who adopt the craft of acting negate their claim to social status; unlike Plato, Theseus plans to forgive them.

There is enough in that word *nothing* to make us feel that the rude mechanicals' fears of giving offense as they puzzled over the problems of presenting Lion to the ladies of the court ("that were enough to hang us all" [I.ii.70]) were not utterly unfounded. But Theseus's speech generates more disturbing overtones yet: "Our sport shall be to take what they mistake." Fair enough: we (as royal audience) will enjoy ourselves by virtue of our superior understanding of something the actors do not understand. But *sport* sounds slightly mocking. The actors do "mistake" in the sense that they are not masters of the craft of acting as they are of weaving, joining, and bellows mending, their true trades. Incorporated in the word *mistake* there is also the sense that in presenting a play at all they are committing a gross breach of etiquette. To be taken in a mistake suggests not merely embarrassment but arrest.

Theseus, however, continues to announce his princely forbearance. "And what poor duty cannot do, noble respect / Takes it in might, not merit" (92): editors worry over this troublesome phrasing. Again, what Theseus is saying seems to be double-edged: "noble respect"— the generous condescension of the educated audience—accepts the intention for the deed. But the generosity sounds violent. The fact that Theseus has a mythological history as a rapist and "wooed" Hippolyta with his "sword" (I.i.16) troubles feminist readers of the play; here he seems to be proposing a "taking" of the mechanicals' play that is no less troublesome. Whether the play is good or not does not matter; merit has nothing to do with it. Nothing matters but power: "might, not merit" determines what "poor duty" can or cannot do. We might say, like the critics who endorse Theseus's rational rule, that subduing the Amazon is (if only iconologically) a good thing to do, and that subduing a bad play by enjoying it without regard to its badness is a good thing too. Or we might feel that Theseus's announcement of his plan to enjoy whatever he sees because he has the power to "take" it as good is uncomfortably blunt in its announcement of the dynamics of court drama. And if the rude mechanicals' intentions are good, what makes their duty "poor"?

The example Theseus goes on to give of his noble behavior in "taking" his subjects' intentions for deeds is an awkward and inappropriate one in this context. He does not display himself acknowledging a bungled play. Rather, he moves into a context more explicitly political—and, given his new subject, a royal progress, more explicitly Elizabethan. Instead of clumsy tradesmen, the bunglers are "great clerks." The shift is important, because up to now we have understood Theseus to be talking about the play he is soon to see performed, and we have understood the problem to be the craftsmen's ineptitude in what is not, after all, their craft. But the clerks' responsibilities must include that of greeting their ruler "with premeditated welcomes" (94); the throttling of these by fear is analogous to the stumbling of the poor players only in so far as Theseus is fearsome. The Prologue to "Pyramus and Thisbe" does exactly what the "great clerks" in Theseus's story do — he "doth not stand upon the points," Theseus notices (118). This suggests an identity between stage fright and the fear inspired by the monarch. Given the inherent theatricality of the royal progress, this identity is not altogether surprising.

What is more surprising is Theseus's attitude to the "rattling tongue / Of saucy and audacious eloquence" (102–3). Apparently he prefers his subjects to be struck dumb by his presence: speech he treats as slightly seditious — "rattling," "saucy," "audacious." Theseus has moved from the speech's beginning, in which he decides graciously to accept the players' "nothing" as a testament to their "simpleness and duty" (83), to a total repudiation of eloquence. In this, as in his dismissal of imagination, he reminds us of less pleasant aspects of the Platonic philosopher-king. He prefers bad performance — or tongue-tied greetings — because the badness insists that what he is seeing is performance. Good performance could be dangerous: "noble respect" might have trouble distinguishing matter from manner where the two are harmonious. "How shall we find concord of this discord?" Theseus wonders at the oxymoronic title of the Pyramus and Thisbe play and its promise of "very tragical mirth" (60, 57). The point his speech hints at, obliquely, is that the finding of concord is the ruler's prerogative. Harmonious art, which bodies forth the shape not of things unknown (as Theseus would have it) but of things known, in which the rational borderlines of appearance and reality blur, cannot offer the monarch this advantage. Just as he prefers inarticulateness among his courtiers, Theseus prefers art that does not look like life. Like Don Quixote, he prefers lies that look like lies; the lies that look like truth are too confusing. Theseus enjoys "Pyramus and Thisbe" because it is easy to see that it is a play; poor performance subverts the tragic theme. Its deaths generate no authentic emotional response. But he would not enjoy *A Midsummer Night's Dream*.

Or perhaps he would: because Theseus cannot tell the difference between good art and bad (and takes some pride in not doing so), whether he enjoys a play or not depends entirely on his "might." "The best in this kind are but shadows," he says; "and the worst are no worse, if imagination amend them" (V.i.209–10). The echoes here of the beginning of his long speech ("the kinder we") and of his famous debate about imagination with Hippolyta at the beginning of the act draw attention here to Theseus's hard-line Platonism. The kindness of his "thanks for nothing" is summed up here as his dismissal of a whole species of human endeavor as worthless. Plays are obnoxious to Plato as "shadows," imitations at a third remove from the Idea, dangerously exciting distractions from the unchanging, the stable, the real. Philosophically, this is Theseus's position: his rejection of the lovers' stories as "more strange than true" (2) insists upon the distorting function of imagination. Poets in Plato are dangerous because they describe techniques they are not masters of: Homer was not a soldier, so his descriptions of warcraft are suspect; we can use a carpenter's imitation of the Idea of chair, but not a poet's. (This Platonic notion is ironically figured here in the bungling tradesmen, whose craft is not poetry.) For Theseus the question is not that poets are ignorant of what they imitate or that they lie: like Sidney, he would agree that poets do not lie because they do not affirm. Thus they imitate not the brazen world we live in but a golden world; dismissively, Theseus sees this as "airy nothing" (16).[36] Accepting what poets offer, either good or bad, is thus a matter without epistemological import. Plato finds plays, good or bad, epistemologically confusing and therefore risky; Theseus knows that plays are without substance. Less troubled than a philosopher might be, the duke may not know much about art, but he knows what he likes.

Theseus's dismissal of plays as "shadows" follows upon Hippolyta's confirmation of her embarrassment: "This is the silliest stuff that ever I heard" (208). As the person who finds "something of great constancy" (26) in the lovers' story, Hippolyta has trouble with the play. Her inchoate sense that "antic fables" and "fairy toys" (as Theseus calls them [3]) can be carriers of meaning leads her to reject the rude mechanicals' play on the grounds of its incompetent performance. This is disturbing in a way different from Theseus's ironclad complacency: for Hippolyta, who does seem to take the lovers' story seriously, to miss the rather obvious connection — a connection on the level of plot, no less—between the Pyramus and Thisbe sketch and "the story of the night told over" (23) lets us down with a thud. She has disagreed with Theseus in this scene on philosophical grounds (in finding "something" in the lovers' story) and on ethical grounds (in finding his desire to see a poorly presented play embarrassing). But she seems unable to get past the imperfect representation presented by the poor players to the thematic nub of their play. "Beshrew my heart but I pity the man," she remarks of Pyramus' speech of dreadful dole (283). Whether she pities the character in his sufferings or Bottom in his rapture of bad acting is not clear.

Hippolyta's response has wide repercussions in terms of her function as Theseus's consort in the play. In her very first appearance, she is clearly identified with the moon as Diana the huntress ("like to a silver bow / New bent in heaven" [I.i.9–10]). Her importance to the first scene is more obvious in performance than in reading: after Egeus's interruption she does not speak for the scene's remaining 125 lines. A reader may forget her existence, but audiences must watch her as Theseus defends patriarchy ("To you your father should be as a god" [47]) and spills contempt on the nuns who "master . . . their blood" and spend their lives in chaste female communities "chanting faint hymns to the cold fruitless moon" (74, 73).[37] The nun and the Amazon represent women who live without men, as do the "vot'ress" of Titania's "order" (II.i.123) who gives birth to the changeling boy with Titania in the role of husband and the "fair vestal" (158) whose immunity to "Cupid's fiery shaft" (161) is guaranteed by the moon.

An important agenda in the play is thus the reconciliation of these elements to the social imperatives of patriarchy and the formal imperatives of comedy. The world must be peopled, and the unassimilated Hippolyta of the first scene makes this a problem. So too do the confusions of the lovers, who resist the social imperatives of marriage even as they move toward the comic fulfillment of the institution. When Theseus "overbears" Egeus in the fourth act, the lovers are no longer a problem: their comic plot is at an end. In formal terms, the play has achieved its goal at that point: the philosophical tone of the debate between Theseus and Hippolyta raises the stakes considerably. For in discussing the merits of the lovers' story in philosophical terms, they are forcing us to question seriously the formal resolution of the comedy itself.

As a comedy, *A Midsummer Night's Dream* engages with explicitness comedy's traditional social agenda: the incorporation of passion into the power structure by means of the institution of marriage. Comedy's celebration of lovers' triumphs over parents is founded on society's need for new generations of parents. Thus the debate about plays (bad or good) in the first scene of the fifth act is really a reflection of large speculation about the institutional validity of comedy. The images of the Amazon, the nun, the "vot'ress," the "fair vestal," the female court of Titania, the girlhood "union in partition" (III.ii. 210) of Helena and Hermia, all combine to resist comedy's push toward marriage. But it is a push which the play itself dramatizes as irresistible. "I know not by what power I am made bold," confesses Hermia as she confronts the duke (I.i.59). The pun on *maid* and the bawdy sense of *bold* are especially revealing in retrospect, as we recall Hermia's subsequent portrayal as the more prudish of the two girls. Hermia sees the beginning of love as a kind of fall: Lysander "hath turned a heaven into a hell" (207). Similarly Helena sees herself as erring and afflicted: "as he errs," she says of Demetrius, "doting on Hermia's eyes, / So I, admiring of his qualities" (230–31). Falling in love is as inevitable as human fallenness. Marriage stabilizes the human condition; passion necessitates social organization.

The "very tragical mirth" of "Pyramus and Thisbe" reflects the other side of the comic agenda: passion excluded from society, erring, misconceiving, results in death. Without the fairies' intervention, the play as a whole suggests, it could have happened here. Thus Hippolyta's dismissal of the mechanicals' play as "the silliest stuff that ever I heard" shows a failure to recognize the "stuff" of the larger play's critique of the comic agenda—a critique which she has, through her Amazonian isolation and Aristotelian opposition to Theseus's tyrannical Platonism, embodied. Her remark accompanies the exit of Wall, the rude mechanicals' inadvertently brilliant dramatization of the comic principle of futile social resistance to the force of passion. Since it is her wedding night, Wall's departure can also metonymically suggest the loss of her inviolate status, her incorporation into the round of procreation that the fairies celebrate at the end of the play proper. "I am aweary of this moon. Would he would change!" she cries (V.i.245) in her next interruption of "Pyramus and Thisbe", here she sounds like the impatient Theseus of the first scene.

The incorporation of the Aristotelian Amazon into Platonic patriarchal Athens is thus a *concordia discors* analogous to the oxymoronic promises of the tradesmen's "tragical mirth." "Hippolyta is gently tugging at Theseus' sleeve," says René Girard, "but Theseus hears nothing. Posterity hears nothing." Girard's identification of Theseus with posterity, with the "impressive scaffoldings of Degree," reflects his own critique of the tradition in criticism of the play that enshrines Theseus's rationalism as carrier of the play's meaning.[38] What validates Theseus's rationalism is his power; he takes what the rude mechanicals mistake; he wins Hippolyta's love doing her injuries. Wall is brought down. Hippolyta's criticism of the silliness of the style of the play before her has the social status of a "gentle tug." The difference between the wifely nudge and the splendid isolation of the first scene is striking.

In such a reading of the play as tyrannically patriarchal, the play's message becomes identical to that of the Earl of Leicester's pageant at Kenilworth in 1575, in which the woods echoed with his unrequited love for Queen Elizabeth, and which was to conclude with a play proving "how necesserie were for worthy Queenes to wed." No gentle tug here, however: Elizabeth fell into a sulk at Leicester's impertinent wooing, and the final play was never performed.[39] Neither as wife nor as Amazon does Hippolyta fully figure Queen Elizabeth; as the veteran of numerous awkward greetings on royal progresses, Theseus reminds us of the queen, but again not fully. As a couple, seated before us, watching a play, differing and agreeing, Theseus and Hippolyta embody a harmony of discords that has been achieved by means of marriage; Leicester could ruefully testify that such a speaking picture might not be expected best to delight his queen.

III

Thomas Churchyard was invited to Norfolk to prepare a series of shows to commemorate the queen's visit in 1578. Recording some of his unanticipated difficulties, his narrative throughout pays tribute to the queen's forbearance at his clumsy shows. The account, like the plays he presented to the queen, is characterized by a tone of ingratiating ineptitude, and like the Theseus of the "great clerks" speech, Elizabeth found herself confronted by a series of shows that must have put her forbearance and imaginative sympathy for her subjects to the test. Churchyard ingenuously records the difficulties he encountered during his stint as producer of the civic entertainments presented to the queen, "whose gratious inclination is suche," he notes hopefully, "as will not have anye thing duetifully offred to passe unregarded."[40] "If you mislike, our griefes do grow on heape," intoned a boy in prologue to the week's activities; "But knowing that your goodnesse takes things well / That well are meant, we boldly did proceed." (C1v).

"If we offend, it is with our good will," blurts the Prologue to the Pyramus and Thisbe play; the clumsy attempts at courtly disclaimer in Churchyard's pageants and in the rude mechanicals' play-within-the-play speak a similar language of "wretchedness o'ercharged, / And duty in his service perishing," as Hippolyta puts it, in her attempt to evade witnessing the craftsmen's play (85–86). Churchyard's descriptions of his eager service to his queen at Norwich link up with *A Midsummer Night's Dream* principally in this way: the combination of embarrassment and noble condescension that Shakespeare splits into the characters of Theseus and Hippolyta infuses the character of Queen Elizabeth that Churchyard's narrative evokes.

"The ruler's task is to *comprehend*—to understand and to encompass—the energies and motives, the diverse, unstable, and potentially subversive *apprehensions* of the ruled," Louis Adrian Montrose has declared of Theseus's role in *A Midsummer Night's Dream*. In performing this task as he views the mechanicals' play, Theseus becomes "not so much Queen Elizabeth's *masculine* antithesis as he is her *princely* surrogate." Yet just as Theseus and Hippolyta form a concord of their discordant attitudes toward art and life by sharing the stage together in comic marriage, they also embody aspects of Elizabeth herself that may seem contradictory; indeed, in Montrose's words again, "as the female ruler of what was, at least in theory, a patriarchal society, Elizabeth incarnated a contradiction at the very center of the Elizabethan sex/gender system."[41] This is a contradiction that led to some peculiar distortions of allegory in the conventional praise lavished upon her. The virgin queen with the "heart and stomach of a king," as she herself put it, Elizabeth comes perilously close to matching the play's paradigm of unassimilated, unmastered, un-"distilled" maidenhead that comedy must win over into marriage: with a sword, if necessary.

Thus there is something uniquely Elizabethan in the rude mechanicals' worries about the squeamishness of the "ladies" confronted with Lion. The reduction to conventional cliché that this shows—they cannot be utterly unaware that their ruler's fiancée was herself a war hero—shows itself too in the awkwardness of Churchyard's sketches. "I will boldly hold on my matter which I have penned," Churchyard declares, "for those people that dwell farre off the Court, that they may see with what maiestie a Prince raigneth, and with what obedience and love good Subiectes do receive hir" (A3v). The far from spontaneous outpourings of duty choreographed by Churchyard are then published by Churchyard as evidence of the majesty of Elizabeth's reign. For audience of his narrative, Churchyard addresses himself to those who "dwell farre off the Court," but also to those who missed seeing the spectacles at Norwich (including Londoners who might be thought to be insufficiently enthusiastic because too familiar with sights of the court). But the record itself is a record of mistakes: of spectacles "hir Highness sawe not, by meanes of evill weather" (A3v), of "crossing causes in the Citie" (C4v), of a pageant that "hovered on the water three long houres," waiting for the queen to pass by, until darkness fell and "we were faine to withdraw oure selves and goe homeward, trusting for a better time and occasion" (E3r). Churchyard's praise for his prince, then, consists not only in the words of welcome he penned for his boy performers, but also in his depiction of her "gratious thankes" (A3v). Elizabeth, like Theseus, sees her duty as taking what the inept producer mistakes; just as Theseus declares this duty in a speech in his own praise, Churchyard describes his failed shows as well as his successes in order to reflect greater glory on his prince.

Both *A Midsummer Night's Dream* and Churchyard's *Discourse* generate an ideal of royal performance, in which what is of primary interest is the reaction of the monarch to the show. Performer and audience become confused. Theseus permits the mechanicals' "nothing" to become something; Elizabeth's thanks convey status upon Churchyard's lame efforts. Churchyard flatters his prince by recounting her generous response to his dismal shows. Shakespeare, too, represents royal performance as disaster: *A Midsummer Night's Dream* offers the "'worst case' for theater," as Alvin Kernan puts it; but it does so in such a way as "to defend plays in a most subtle fashion."[42] Churchyard, on the other hand, struggling to demonstrate his prince's greatness by documenting his own love and duty, ends up sounding a lot like Peter Quince.

Like Quince and his fellows, Churchyard is eager not to give offence, and like them, he then proceeds to effusions that offend "with our good will." No more than poets of higher repute in his age, Churchyard had some difficulty praising Elizabeth without straying too far in the wrong directions. In his Tuesday show, Chastitie presented the bow of Cupid to the queen: its possession, she says, is "more fitte for such a one / In fleshly forme, that bears a heart of stone / That none can wound, nor pearce by any meane" (D3v). Bearing in mind that the language here is all utterly conventional (and therefore that the question of influence is diffuse), it is nonetheless tantalizing to notice the way Shakespeare has incorporated this language into his play. While the moon is "like to a stepdame or a dowager" to the impatient Theseus of the first scene (I.i.5), to Hippolyta it is "like to a silver bow" (9). The Amazon queen, from the first, coopts the bow: the weapon is chaste Diana's, not blind Cupid's. Cupid's archery gone awry as he aims at the "imperial vot'ress" (II.i.163) empurples the white flower "with love's wound" (167), but Churchyard's "heart of stone" has been replaced by the more satisfactory "maiden meditation, fancy-free" (164). Churchyard's clumsy praise is elegantly rephrased; yet the pierced and wounded heart recurs throughout the play—in Hermia's dream ("Methought a serpent eat my heart away," she cries [II.ii.149]), in Helena's image of the "double cherry," one heart rent asunder "to join with men" (209–16), and most suggestively of all in the broached breasts of Pyramus and Thisbe. What for Churchyard is a tactical problem becomes for Shakespeare a central factor in his play's drive toward concord.

The whole structure of A Midsummer Night's Dream suggests that the way the civic poet, Churchyard, confronted his difficulties in entertaining Elizabeth is not dissimilar to the way the professional playwright, Shakespeare, had to confront the same problem. Without raising the issue of Elizabeth's actual presence at specific performances of A Midsummer Night's Dream, critics are agreed that the play abounds in the particular language associated with Elizabeth, and it treats with unusual explicitness the dynamics of court performance.[43] The published account of the queen's progress to Norwich— that city of weavers—offered to Shakespeare's view a panorama of poorly executed royal entertainment that his professional company could happily spoof, and that his creative imagination could apprehend and comprehend.

The first show of any royal progress would be a mass greeting of the monarch: "Two hundred yong gentlemen," were assembled, writes

Churchyard, "cladde all in white velvet, and three hundred of the graver sorte apparelled in blacke velvet coates, and fair chaynes, all ready at the one instant and place, with fifteene hundred serving men more on Horsebvack well and bravely mounted in good order, ready to receyve the Queenes highnesse into Suffolke, which surly was a comely troupe, and a noble sight to beholde" (B3r). The polarity here between the "yong gentlemen" in white and the "graver sorte" in black anticipates the disruptions that interrupt Theseus's solemnities in the first scene of the play: "full of vexation," grave Egeus invokes his right to dispose of his child. The terms of dispute about the moon's phase during the time of the play are equally black and white: Theseus and Hippolyta await the new moon—noticeable for its darkness—while Oberon meets Titania by moonlight, and the rude mechanicals "find out moonshine" in the almanac. The greeting of Elizabeth on the way to Norwich was an embodiment of concordant discord—white youth, black age, bravely mounted serving men. Dark and light, youth and age confront each other too at the start of Shakespeare's play.

"Methinks I see these things with parted eye," Hermia muses of her night's experiences (IV.i.188–89), "When everything seems double." "O Norwich, heere the well-spring runnes / whose vertue still doth floe," ran the song as Elizabeth entered the city, "And loe this day doth shine two Sunnes, / within thy walles also" (C1r). The multiple moons of Shakespeare's play find anticipatory echo in Norwich's two suns. Shakespeare's psyche "assembled around and responded to polarity, doubling negations, structures of distributive reciprocity," Joel Fineman has said. It appears that Churchyard's did too—or perhaps that the paradox of Elizabeth encouraged all poets to think in terms of paradoxical pairs.[44]

An "excellent Boy" with a scarf "folded on the Turkish fashion about his browes" made the obligatory apologies at Norwich: "If you mislike, our griefes do grow on heape" (C1v). The dispute that vexes the weather in A Midsummer Night's Dream has its source, too, in a "lovely boy," who, crowned with flowers, attends upon the fairy queen. What is a gesture of courtesy in Churchyard's pageant of greeting—the presentation to Gloriana of a boy attendant—provokes in the fairy world of the play jealousy and marital strife. Oberon's mastery over his wayward wife necessitates her bondage to erotic infatuation; her love for a monster lets him recapture the boy, reassert patriarchal dominance. Churchyard's slightly exotic hostage to the queen's courtesy is a pawn too—a pledge for the success of his show.

These greetings took place on a Saturday, when the queen also was greeted with a pageant on weaving and one made up of heroic ladies; on Sunday, as Churchyard informs us, the queen spent her day in prayer and contemplation. Monday's show began with the arrival of Mercury in a coach; the divine messenger's rod was especially equipped with "two wriggling or scrawling Serpentes, which seemed to have life when the rodde was moved or shaken" (C4r). Norfolk, before the queen's arrival, has been a world disturbed by strange creatures:

> The Satyres wilde, in forme and shape of man,
> Crept through the woodes, and thickets full of breeres,
> The water Nymphes, and Feyries streight appeares
> In uncouth formes, and fashion strange to view.
>
> (C3r)

The queen's role in this situation is clear enough: "plant perfite peace, and roote up all debate" (C3v). In Churchyard's nightmare Norfolk, the graves have opened and yielded their dead; "Now is the time of night," sings Shakespeare's Puck with his broom at the end of the play,

> That the graves, all gaping wide,
> Every one lets forth his sprite,
> In the churchway paths to glide.
>
> (V.i.368–71)

In Churchyard's spectacle, the queen is asked to subdue such wayward spirits and return them to their proper places.

The casting of the royal audience, in shows presented during a progress, as a judge confronted with rival claimants continued the next day. On Tuesday, Churchyard's company intercepted the queen as she went riding with the play we have already mentioned in which Chastitie, after beating Cupid, presented the queen with his bow. In his first entrance, Cupid recalls a debate he has just endured with a Philosopher. The Philosopher's attitude toward love is definitely of the "graver sorte": like Egeus he decries "feigning verses of feigning love" (I.i.31). Cupid quotes his "thundering words" on the subject:

> A leawd delight, a flying fancie light,
> A shadow fonde, that beares no shape, but name,

The whole abuse of each good witte or wight,
An idle ground, whereon vayne Poets walke.

(D2r)

Churchyard's Philosopher moves beyond conventional Elizabethan praise of chastity to a Platonism as harsh as Theseus's dismissal of lovers, lunatics, and poets. In the pageant's version of Plato, Cupid

Is neyther God nor Man in forme, nor monster as you see
But such a kind of shade, as can no substance shoe,
Begot by braynelesse blind delight, and nurst with natures foe,
Fed up with faithlesse food, and trayned in trifling toyes,
Awakt with vice and luld asleep agayne with yrkesome ioyes.

(D4r)

The finest joke about the love-juice in *A Midsummer Night's Dream* is that it makes those under its influence talk like philosophers, and in awakening and rejecting his love for Hermia, Demetrius—the only lover still under the influence—talks like Churchyard's Philosopher himself, describing his love to Hermia as an "idle gaud," an unnatural sickness, and Helena as his "natural taste," a wholesome food (IV.i. 165–75). Lewd life, Churchyard's show insists, must be "Found out and pointed at, / A monster of the mind, / A canckred worme, that conscience eates, / And strikes cleere senses blind" (E2r). Titania's humiliation, as staged by Oberon, consists in just such a finding out and pointing at: "There lies your love" (IV.i.77).

Mastering the monster of lust (like taming the Amazon) is, Paul Olson reminds us, characteristic of the Renaissance Theseus; in the presence of his chaste monarch, Churchyard's Philosopher can reduce Cupid to despair. "Nay *Cupid* will, go hang himself I trow," he moans, "Much better were, to fall on point of knife, / Than from rich state, to leade a begger's life" (E1r). Passion leads to "point of knife" in the Pyramus and Thisbe play, and, like Peter Quince, the Philosopher is quick to make his teaching explicit. "Gentles, perchance you wonder at this show," says Quince as Prologue, "But wonder on, till truth make all things plain" (V.i.126–27). Churchyard's Platonic Philosopher likewise worries that the wonders of his show have distracted its audience's attention from its truth: "We stay, save that, some Musicke commes, to knitte in order due / The substance of this sillie Shew, that we present to you," he tells the queen as he introduces the final dance (E1r). Elizabeth apparently stayed to see this show; Theseus and the young lovers decide to forgo that epilogue in which Bottom will reveal the depths of his dream. Both the play and the progress toy with the question of substance and shadow. The conflict in the play of Chastitie and Cupid becomes central to the scrutiny of show and theater in *A Midsummer Night's Dream*. The moral clarity of Cupid's despair is undercut by the tragical mirth of Pyramus and Thisbe's bloody suicides.

On Wednesday, Churchyard hoped to offer to the queen another such moral debate, entitled "Manhode and Dezart." With his pageant he waited until dark and then was forced to withdraw, "trusting for a better time and occasion, which indeed was offred the next day after by the Queenes Maiesties owne good motion who told me she woulde see what pastimes were prepared" (E3r). When he addressed the queen on Monday, Mercury had promised a show each day "if time doth serve and weather waxeth faire" (C3v); on Thursday it rained. "It was a greater pastime to see us looke like drowned Rattes," confessed Churchyard, "than to have beheld to the uttermost of the Shewes rehearsed. Thus you see, a Shew in the open fielde is always subiect to the sudden change of the weather, and a number of more inconveniences than I expresse" (E4v). Peter Quince might have said the same about his outdoor rehearsal for "Pyramus and Thisbe"; no amount of looking in the almanac could prepare a troupe of civic actors for the inconvenient transformation of Bottom.

With Quince-like earnestness, Churchyard beseeches his readers to piece out the imperfections of his pageant with their imaginations: "And first and foremost you must conceive, that the shew of *Manhode* was invented to be playde in a Garden, or where soever had been found a convenient place, the Prince then being in presence" (F1r). "Here's a marvellous convenient place for our rehearsal," Quince enthuses as his troupe approaches the cradle of the fairy queen, unaware of the presence of Titania. His mind is on the presence, not here in the convenient place, but at court: "This green plot shall be our stage, this hawthorn brake our tiring house, and we will do it in action as we will do it before the Duke" (III.i.2–5). Enumerating the items in the play that will not please, Bottom, too, keeps his mind's eye fixed on the court at Athens. Bottom's translation reminds us that the green plot is a stage populated, like an Elizabethan court entertainment, by monsters.

Puck is able to transform himself into a "headless bear" (99), while Churchyard, "fearing that all my labour should be lost, devised to convert the Nimphes of the water, to the Fairies of the land" (F1r). Nonetheless, he provides a printed text of the play of Manhode, which again casts the queen in the role of judge. Here the rival claimants are, at first, Manhode and Good Favour; like Demetrius and Lysander, each claims a right to Beauty. Manhode's verbal assault on Good Favour again takes up the language of idle gauds and nosegays:

> A snare for witte, a bayte for wanton youth,
> A false conceyte, an error of the mind,
> A fond delight, wherein there is no truth,
> A poysoned dish, that doth the reason blind.
> A colour cast on things that are but bace,
> A glorious shewe, to shrowde a homely part,
> A rule to runne, a leawd and retchlesse race,
> A deep deceyte which daunteth oft the heart.
>
> (F2v)

This speech is almost a list of the iterative images in *A Midsummer Night's Dream*. Helena characterizes love as an error of the mind: "Love looks not with the eyes but with the mind / And therefore is winged Cupid painted blind," she muses (I.i.234–35). Lysander, rejecting Hermia in the fullness of his passion for Helena, discards her as a noisome food, and later reviles her as not precisely a "poysoned dish," but a "loathèd med'cine," a "hated potion" (III.ii.264).

More intriguing is Churchyard's identification of love with "a glorious shewe, to shrowde a homely part." This is antitheatrical language, anticipating Theseus's dismissive linkage of lunatics, lovers, and poets. What Churchyard worries about is love's transformative, theatrical power. "Things base and vile, holding no quantity, / Love can transform to form and dignity," Helena concludes, pondering her infatuation with Demetrius and his with Hermia (I.i.232–33). Theater can do this as well, transforming the classless vagabond, the actor, into the monarch by means of glorious show. The play responds to the homiletic antitheatricality of Churchyard's homiletic skits on the dangers of passion. Bottom's transformation makes Helena's image concrete; a vile thing with an ass's head, he entrances the fairy queen with his "fair virtue's force" (III.i.127). His transformation is explicitly theatrical: it takes place in the "tiring house," both figuratively, as

Peter Quince has defined the hawthorn brake, and literally. The actor playing Bottom must retire to the actual tiring house, get his ass head, and put it on before making his next entry, a little late for his cue in Quince's play, but right on time in Shakespeare's. Alone of the lovers, Helena is aware of the theatrical snares passion sets for reason. When the young men, like Titania under the influence of the love-juice, confidently declare the triumph of reason and higher love as they woo her, she feels herself the victim of a malicious play, a "confederacy" of "false sport." "Ay, do," she charges the actors: "Persever, counterfeit sad looks" (III.ii.192, 194, 237).

Shakespeare, vindicating the power of love in his play, also then vindicates the power of theater: the young men's infatuation, under the love-juice, is no less real than their infatuations without chemical aid. But Churchyard, like the rude mechanicals, is less interested in the complex interplay of the passions he represents than in the royal audience to whom he presents his show. Therefore in the play of Manhode and Dezart, Dezart in his own defense carefully flatters the monarch:

> The Gods accepts, our dutie in good part,
> The Prince rewards, the billes of our request,
> The greatest men, consider but the heart,
> The friendly meanes, can tame the wildest beast.

> (F4r)

Dezart proposes the kind of kindness that Shakespeare's Theseus has claimed he embodies. As designed for Elizabeth, though, Churchyard's show reaches a point of difficulty when Beauty must finally be awarded to one of the claimants, Manhode, Good Favour, or Dezart. The issue is finessed, as Fortune enters and, in effect, kidnaps her. There would have been quite a battle if the play had been performed, Churchyard enthused, "in which time was legges and armes of men (well and lively wrought) to be let fall in numbers on the grounde, as bloudy as mighte be" (E4v). One kind of offense is thus avoided: Beauty does not have to choose a mate, nor does the virgin judge have to choose one for her. Churchyard lets destiny do the dirty work. Thus in one way, Churchyard dodges the issue: Fortune will decide the fate of Beauty. But in another, the allegory, like Theseus's allegory of the rose distilled, suggests that Beauty's destiny is possession.

Shakespeare's play, too, in spite of its evocation of visions of female solidarity and impregnability, must end with a vision of married fertility.[45] The multiple identities associated with Elizabeth in the play—Hippolyta, Theseus, Titania, Oberon, Hermia, Helena, the liveried nun, the imperial vot'ress—help Shakespeare to elide any sort of direct allegorical reference. The embarrassment of a clumsy plot device like Fortune's abduction of Beauty is avoided, but the reliance upon comic plot to deliver the proper harmony of contraries is itself an embarrassment. The play's closing, from the tragical mirth of Pyramus and Thisbe through to Puck's epilogue, makes it clear that Shakespeare is acutely aware of this. The fairies, who have dominated the otherworldly middle, "dream" portion of the play, return to assert if not control at least a high degree of authority over the play's nominally "real" world, Theseus's orderly Athens. The fantastic engineers of the confusions of the night trip to the "best bride-bed" (V.i.392) and bless its fortunate issue. This is, to say the least, a stinging qualification of Theseus's rejection of "fairy toys" (3): the fairies slip into the most secret mysteries of his own marriage bed.

Churchyard, too, concluded his royal entertainment with a dance of fairies. As one of the water-nymphs in the pageant of Manhode describes them, these fairies are Puckish, not Oberon's "spirits of another sort" (III.ii.388):

The *Phayries* are another kind, of elfes that daunce in darke,
Yet can light Candles in the night, and vanish like a sparke,
And make a noyse and rumbling great among the dishes oft,
And wake the sleepie, sluggish Maydes that lies in Kitchen loft.
And when in field, they treade the grasse, from water we repayre,
And hoppe and skippe, with them sometimes, as weather waxeth fayre.

(G2r)

"Are not you he / That frights the maidens of the villagery?" the fairy asks Puck on his first entrance (II.i.35). Puck's mischief is inextricably intertwined with Oberon's restorations of correct amorous alignments, a restoration that involves the humbling of Titania and an assertion of paternal dominance over the changeling boy. Shakespeare's fairies can seem free, unfettered, natural—or they can seem to be the agents of a tyrannical male order enforcing its control over wayward females. The fairies seem to inhabit a variety of worlds: in a world of pagan mythology, they can see Cupid's arrow drop harmless to the ground, and in an English country world they can frighten maidens and curdle cream.

Just as uncertainty about what to make of the fairies vexes criticism of the *Dream,* so too does uncertainty about what the fairies should look like vex productions of the play. A striking solution to the problem was proposed by William Ringler: that the four fairies in Shakespeare's original cast would have been "played by the same large lumbering adult actors who take the part of the rude mechanicals."[46] This enhances the idea that Titania's fairies are hard-handed craftsmen of their own kind. Churchyard, transforming his water-nymphs into fairies for the Friday of the queen's visit, likewise fuses what in his proposed Thursday play would have been two different sorts of beings.

When Churchyard sought out a convenient place for his Friday play: "chose I a ground, by which the Queene must passe, enclosing my company in the corner of a field, being defenced with high and thicke bushes" (G2r). As the queen passed, seven boys would "passe through a hedge" and speak: "And these Boyes (you must understand) were dressed like Nimphes of the water, and were to play by a device and degrees the *Phayries* and to daunce (as neere as could be imagined) like the *Phayries.* Their attire, and comming so strangely out, I know made the Queenes highnesse smyle and laugh withal" (G2r). Churchyard here makes a virtue of his economy. Although the boys still wore the water-nymph costumes that had been destined for the play that Elizabeth missed, here the costumes become the occasion of another transformation. The last fairy offered Churchyard's own epilogue to the queen's visit to Norwich, referring back to the pageants of Saturday and Monday:

> With Gods, yea Kings & Quenes, began your entrie to this place,
> With gentle Gosts & merrie Sprites, we mind to end the cace.
> So in good signe of happie chance, to thee O sacred Queene,
> To knit up all, we meane to daunce with Timbrels on this greene.
> And then farewell, we can no more, salute thee in our gise,
> All that is done, by great good will, is offred to the wise.
>
> (G3r)

Churchyard's fairies dance "to knit up all"; so do Shakespeare's. The queen's visit began with a spectacle of harmonious discord, youth and age, black and white, and moved through a series of plays and shows in which disruptive, passional presences were defused by the monarch's presence. In Shakespeare's play the conflicts are more complex, for the disruptive passional presences inhabit the rationalist Theseus himself, both lover and tyrant, and the stage is filled with images of female self-sufficiency that this patriarchal comedy cannot abide. More so perhaps than Churchyard's (or Peter Quince's) lame but well-meant shows, *A Midsummer Night's Dream* must at last throw itself upon the gracious mercy of its audience.

The play is constantly aware, not simply in the debates of the rude mechanicals, of the unpredictability of royal audiences. Self-identified as a youthful lover, an impatient heir resentful of (female) age withering out his revenue, Theseus sides with (male) age, parental authority, and social stability from the very first. The Athenian youth of the play must experience much before being called to mirth. Theseus commands mirth and then rejects it unreflectively in the first scene. By giving to Theseus himself the choice of pastimes, by putting into his mouth the invocation of courtly generosity and noblesse oblige by which the play in court becomes a loving expression of duty, Shakespeare puts the royal audience on stage. He foregrounds the problem of offense *and* elides it. Churchyard does so too, in print: where his clumsy celebrations of reason's control over the passions and his curious selection of Fortune as Beauty's mate tread close to offense, his descriptions of the queen's gracious thanks, her "owne good motion" to see whatever was offered, and her smiles and laughter at the fairy dance, allow him also to control the monarch's response.

Whatever might have been the conditions of its first performance, however, *A Midsummer Night's Dream* does not, like Chruchyard's playlets, rest at being a royal entertainment. The very fact that it depicts royal entertainment so specifically marks important differences: the rude mechanicals' play for the duke is civic entertainment, performed by craftsmen out of their craft, amateur actors, as an expression of love and duty. It hints at the darker side of Theseus's legislative distaste for passion out of ineptitude, not out of subversive purpose. It offends with good will. But the play in which it appears is written for public performance: the institution that will present it, the public theater, is a constant source of displeasure to the civic authorities who indite and present pageants; its craftsmen are professionals of the acting trade; and as their skills in dissembling are commensurately far more developed than those of weavers, their love and duty is less easy (for Theseus or for Elizabeth) to read. The play, in Puck's epilogue, reaches out to its audience, as Churchyard's opening speeches did to Queen Elizabeth, to apologize for offense.

If *A Midsummer Night's Dream* was acted at court, Shakespeare's professional actors, who can mock the ineptitude of unskilled craftsmen from their stage, find themselves, as Annabel Patterson has pointed out, in another sort of bind. Here he and his players would be interlopers:

> Shakespeare's own situation as a member of the Chamberlain's company would situate him somewhere *between* the court and amateur popular theatricals, with the occasional 'command performance' bringing him closer to Bottom and his colleagues than to those, frequently themselves aristocrats, who created the royal entertainments. The artisanal hope of being 'made men,' with 'sixpence a day for life,' is a parodic version of that discontinuous patronage relation; but the play speaks more to its uneasiness than to its rewards, as well as to Shakespeare's self-consciousness about how the popular theatrical impulse was in danger of being appropriated to hegemonic ends.[47]

The play, dramatizing its own "uneasiness," does not equate the expertise of its players with that of Bottom. The social gulf between the players and their noble audience is analogous to the gulf between Bottom and Theseus. But Shakespeare's actors would never descend to the level of Bottom's presumptuous attempts to explain the conventions of drama to his auditors. Whether the play's audience is to be imagined as the popular audience at the professional playhouse or the courtly audience of royal performance, the play expects it to understand its conventions. Only through full participation in its conventions can the full range of the play's challenge to simplistic distinctions between dream and reality, true love and false love, Plato and Aristotle, be felt. Maintaining those distinctions, on the other hand, is essential to the success of Churchyard's spectacle.

Puck pretends to fear that the "gentles" of his audience will take offense at the blurring of distinctions in the play, and so he proposes an even farther-reaching distinction. They can simply deny the play any right to exist, enforce a distinction between dream and reality to the point of dismissing their own common experience. Like Churchyard's Platonist Philosopher, Puck distances himself and his company from the "sillie Shew" (E1r) and endorses Platonist contempt for actors as shades without substance. Blind Cupid, fairy, and actor merge in both Churchyard's and Shakespeare's language of shadow. Thus Puck urges that the offenses of shadows—like the imaginings of lunatics, lovers, and poets—have no reality of their own. Like "noble respect," offense too "takes it in might, not merit" (V.i.91–92). "How easy is a bush supposed a bear" (22), Theseus jests, but the jest is already undercut by Puck's transformation of himself into a variety of animals to chase the mechanicals, and by a stage bush's transformation into hawthorn brake, tiring house, and bower of the fairy queen. Puck's epilogue suggests that any notion that the play contains offensive substance is itself a hallucination, a slumbering audience's paranoid dream. By agreeing that theatrical transformations have no reality and deserve no belief, Puck suggests that those who assent to them, playing their proper role as audiences, are insane.

The boy playing Churchyard's fairy must bid farewell to the queen, knit up all with a dance, and return to apprenticeship to a weaver (in all probability). Shakespeare's Puck is an actor, a craftsmen whose farewells to audiences must attract audiences back the next day. "If you pardon, we will mend," he promises: tinkering, joining, weaving, the actors will put together a better show tomorrow, "Else the Puck a liar call" (419–24). Of course, that is the problem: Puck is a liar, and, in the play's "worst case" presentation of dramatic art, the play itself is a lie, an airy nothing, a baseless fabric. Only the audience confers reality to it, but in so doing, the audience also admits to the possibility that the play might give offense—but with the play's understanding that offense, like its own dubious reality, is a bush supposed a bear. By giving the play its hands, the audience shows itself to be "friends" (426), willing to accept whatever "amends" Robin can restore at a later date. That is, it pronounces itself to be a regular and faithful audience to a regularly performing professional theater, willing to take the good with the bad. Its might is thus highly circumscribed. Not so the might of Thomas Churchyard's audience: his inept performances, like those of Peter Quince and his colleagues, are a one-time-only affair. And the queen, like Theseus, will take it as she pleases. Luckily for Churchyard, as equally luckily for Quince, the prince sees the occasion as an occasion for royal performance as well. By enduring the bad play, by smiling at the strangely attired water-nymphs-turned-fairies, the monarch performs before the national audience the role of gracious prince.

2

"I love the people, but . . ."

Royal Performance and Royal Audience in the Court of James I

~

I

Speaking before Parliament about her reluctance to assent to their demands in the case of Mary Queen of Scots, Elizabeth used a traditional theatrical image to characterize her caution. Special care was necessary, "for we Princes, I tell you, are set on stages, in the sight and view of the world duly observed. The eyes of many behold our actions," she continued; "a spot is soon spied in our garments, a blemish quickly noted in our doings. It behoveth us, therefore, to be careful that our proceedings be just and honourable."[1] The stage as the queen envisions it is like a microscope: spots can be spied out, blemishes noted. The concern with flaws of costume attributes to the speaker a properly feminine modesty. But something more than conventional modesty has been invoked: in stressing the honor and innocence of her conduct in this language, Queen Elizabeth reminds her audience of her spotlessness compared to the less chaste conduct of her rival. Elizabeth treads a fine line here. Scandal and faultfinding are part of the price a prince pays for living in the public eye, but the judging of queens by subjects is in both cases indelicate and inappropriate. "A proper course, forsooth, to deal in that manner with one of her estate!" was the queen's response to requests that Mary be put to trial in "strictness and exact following of common form."[2] She and Mary belong to an estate excluded from "common form" but nonetheless especially vulnerable to common scandal. Elizabeth is able both to declare a princely community with Mary and to suggest, in her language of spotlessness, her difference from Mary. In the process, Parliament becomes a rude, gawking audience, failing to recognize important distinctions in their avid pursuit of scandal.

"I love the people / But do not like to stage me to their eyes," the duke confesses in *Measure for Measure:*

Though it do well, I do not relish well
Their loud applause and aves vehement,
Nor do I think the man of safe discretion
That does affect it.

(I.i.67–72)

With this sentiment he links himself to the same tradition of royal modesty and discomfort under the public eye. Again the audience is seen as an unruly crowd. But where their eyes unsettled Queen Elizabeth, seeking out spots on her clean garments, their voices disturb the duke. The antitheatrical energy here is directed against applause. The bad monarch—or bad actor in the language of the image—is not the one whose costume or makeup is flawed, but the one who plays to the crowd, whose discretion is therefore unsafe. The breath of scandal is infectious.

James I used the image, too, in *Basilikon Doron:* "For Kings being publike persons, by reason of their office and authority, are as it were set (as it was said of old) upon a publike stage, in the sight of all the people; where all the beholders eyes are attentively bent to looke and pry in the least circumstance of their secretest drifts."[3] Elizabeth's concern, and the duke's, was for the ruler's reputation. Vulnerability to scandal-mongering and intoxication with public adulation are pitfalls the wise monarch avoids. The metaphor of prince as actor is sustained, for spotted garments and playing to the audience are both theatrical pitfalls as well. For James, the image, which he ostentatiously points out to be dated, is developed in a different direction. What the beholders pry into is "the least circumstance of their secretest drifts." Their interest is not in the monarch as actor, but in the monarch as playwright. Audiences attentively scrutinize the king's plots. The duke, here like James, worries about the "safe discretion" of a ruler who relishes the applause of crowds. Keeping secrets, in theatrical terms, refers to the actor's discretion in not revealing all of the twists and turns of the plot yet to come; the mystery of the trade that the actor and playwright conceal from the audience is their knowledge of how, when, and why what happens will happen. While for Elizabeth the monarch's role is split into assertion of common cause with other monarchs and assertion of distinction from Mary, James asserts a disharmony between the king's necessary availability to the public eye and the mysterious secret drifts of his profession.

When we look at Elizabeth, James, and Duke Vincentio together, however, we must also be aware of the difference between the way the actual monarchs use the hoary theatrical image and the way the character in *Measure for Measure* uses it. Elizabeth worries about the audience spying out spots; James worries about it prying into secrets. Both real monarchs do not enjoy being seen. Duke Vincentio speaks of the hazard to a ruler's discretion involved in the excessive relishing of public applause. That is, Elizabeth and James see the image of the public stage as demeaning and humiliating; a king is most like an actor when most exposed to public scrutiny. *Measure for Measure*'s duke, however, speaks with the voice of an actor, and his concern is for the morality of the craft he practices. Playing to the audience mars royal performance. The "safe discretion" the duke speaks of is not the discretion recommended by James; instead it is the professional discretion of the actor who does not overplay his royal role.

The rude mechanicals' worries in *A Midsummer Night's Dream* and Churchyard's parallel eagerness not to give offense are typical of Elizabethan court drama, but as we move into the Jacobean period, these worries become particularly acute. The monarchical presence in the Elizabethan drama and progress functions as an audience whose power is to "take or mistake": the ruler's might, not the play's merit, conditions the response. In *Measure for Measure,* and in the plays of Beaumont and Fletcher to be discussed in this chapter, we can see emerging a vision of royal performance that emphasizes secrecy and concealment. The monarch's discomfort, in the passage from *Basilikon Doron,* comes from the threat of being misinterpreted; James assures his readers that the "secretest drifts" are all for the best. This is the most positive way of looking at James's and the duke's distaste for display. But there lurks a sense, expressed in *Measure for Measure* most vocally by Lucio, and expressed in James's time by hostile witnesses like Arthur Wilson and Sir Anthony Weldon, that secrecy and concealment hide sordid truths.

James's conduct as a royal audience on the kinds of state or civic occasions that Elizabeth enjoyed stressed his alienation from the audience and emphasized his difference and isolation. Where Elizabeth played to the crowd and skillfully performed her designated role in the allegorical entertainments that greeted her in her coronation procession and on her royal progresses, James was glumly silent in his first procession. Wilson delineated James's aversion to the "aves vehement" of crowds in his memorable description of the king's procession to his first Parliament, "the City and Suburbs being one great Pageant, wherein he must give his Ears leave to suck in their gilded Oratory, though never so nauceous to the Stomach."[4] Public appearances are an odious and humiliating kind of display.

As audience, too, to the spectacles he himself most favors, the court masques, the monarch responds privately and uniquely. Court masque, as D. J. Gordon, Stephen Orgel, and Roy Strong have argued, is an art form that fully takes shape only in the consciousness of the king. Likewise, the isolated consciousness of the king dominates the daily life of the court. As dramatized by Beaumont and Fletcher, court life is itself highly theatricalized and designed for the king's eyes only. The marriage masque with which *The Maid's Tragedy* begins reads like a parody of Jonson's great Jacobean masques, and, like them, it means one thing to the court and another thing to its all-knowing royal audience, the king. Where Jonson's Platonism and obtrusive classical allusiveness address the king's special wisdom, Beaumont and Fletcher portray the masque as a glamorous façade that hides the king's ugly scheme to marry off his mistress.

Vividly dramatizing the jockeying for place among the court audience in *The Maid's Tragedy,* Beaumont and Fletcher bring to the foreground the dynamic of "who loses and who wins; who's in, who's out" that Lear hopes he and Cordelia can witness from the outside as "God's spies." (*King Lear,* V.iii.15–17). Seating arrangements in court performances testified spatially to one's closeness to the king, one's degree of proximity to "the mystery of things," yet, as in Lear, the rule is constant flux among the "packs and sects of great ones / That ebb and flow by th' moon." The spies, in Jacobean plays, are less likely to be God's spies than to be, like Bosola in Webster's *Duchess of Malfi,* court-galls (malcontents) turned intelligencers in hope of advancement.

The emphasis on the sham and hollowness of court life in the drama, like the masque's glorification of the king's Platonic intelligence, portrays the ruler as the source of theatrical industry. Acting, plotting, spectacle, and intrigue are all in his service. As audience, the monarch's comprehension validates the masque, and his misprisions propel the drama of court life. Contemporary descriptions of court masques and satiric attacks upon the glittering surface of court decorums in the drama share a desire to penetrate the surface of regal indifference (or difference) and read the royal response. The real, as opposed to the sham, meaning of events can only be found in the consciousness of the king, secret and sealed off.

The author of the masque, like the court intelligencer in the drama, presumes upon an intimacy with the monarch and an understanding of his "deep plots" that experience may or may not confirm. Both take their hopes to court. There the hopeful courtier must discover that no one can know the king's "innermost thoughts": "these were mysteries of state," Michael Walzer reminds us, "which only the head of state had the capacity to understand."[5] Just as Ben Jonson's career as author of court masques ended in bitterness and disappointment, disillusionment is pivotal to the plays of Beaumont and Fletcher. The cynical voices of this drama take relish in debunking presumption, in revealing court life itself to be artifice and illusion. And it is this irreverent penetration of the surface that James identified as the ignominious aspect of the traditional image of the king on the public stage.

II

If there is an analogy between the actor's craft and the monarch's, it stands to reason that the monarch might find the comparison demeaning where the actor will find it ennobling. One of a series of absolute dukes in Shakespeare—a series that includes Theseus in *A Midsummer Night's Dream*—Duke Vincentio draws our attention through the play to the theatricality not only of his disguise but also of the process by which Angelo, his deputy, is put to the test of playing a role that is beyond his powers. The duke's claim, and the play's, at the beginning, not to be concerned with unfolding the "properties" of "government" (I.i.1) can be taken seriously in this way: the play's problems and their resolutions are not political except insofar as Vienna's politics is theatrical. The duke's retirement is prompted by his failure to sustain an active role in punishing offenses against the law and by his desire to put Angelo to the test; what is at issue in both cases is the consistency with which the ruler plays his part. This play's successful conclusion relies upon the duke's ability, as actor and playwright, to manage the *coup-de-théâtre* of the final scene to his advantage.

Measure for Measure digs very deep into the conventional analogy between ruler and actor that gives Elizabeth and James momentary discomfort. And it does so in terms that privilege the theatrical, rewarding successful performance with a comic and politically stabilizing conclusion. Thus it inverts what we can assume to be the normal order of court drama, like the masque, with its privileging of the monarch's Platonic truth over the impostures and illusions of antimasque. What Elizabeth and James find disturbing about the theatrical image, its revelation of royal costume and secret drifts to public scrutiny, *Measure for Measure* explores in the duke's disguise and in his discomfort with Lucio's banter. In Lucio's claims to be an "inward of his" (III.ii.123), we can see embodied that presumptuous prying and judging that England's monarchs found intolerable. The tension Lucio generates in the play is the tension the play generates in a royal audience from the moment it disclaims any interest in state secrets in its first line. It is a tension between two worlds—the public world of the playhouse, with its gaping, prying audiences and presumptuous actors in royal garb, and the world of the court to which the players have been invited, at royal command, to appear with their play.

It is vital to bear these two worlds in mind as we look at the drama of the Jacobean court. The controversy about *Measure for Measure* as royal entertainment revolves around whether the play was designed to be seen by King James or was not. But for the playwright the situation could not have been this cut-and-dried. Any play written for performance by Shakespeare's company, the King's Men, could be requested for performance at court; no play could justify its existence, however, as a purely occasional piece. Nor could any play, as far as we can discern, be guaranteed performance before the king. The King's Men served two masters—the public who paid for their regularly scheduled entertainments in the Globe and later at the Blackfriars, and the monarch, their titular patron, who occasionally requested that they bring their plays into the court. There was no reciprocity here: while we hear of professional actors taking part in antimasques at court, we hear no reports of court masques being exposed upon the public stage. The players in the antimasques did not mingle with the courtiers who would dance in the masques: "Like the Puritans," Jean-Christophe Agnew puts it, "the Stuart courtiers were at pains to dissociate themselves from the common player, sealing themselves off via the antimasque from the contagion of the latter's theatricality and the taint of his commerciality."[6] The institutional circumstances make it highly unlikely that a play like *Measure for Measure* could be written with a particular performance at court in mind. Generically, then, *Measure for Measure,* like the Beaumont and Fletcher plays discussed later in this chapter, is best understood as a public playhouse play that was selected to go to court. It was performed before King James on December 26, 1604. As with other Jacobean plays, who chose it for that occasion, and how it was chosen, will never be known.

What we can examine is the play's striking awareness of the complexities of its status. *Measure for Measure,* like the theater that produced it, is both insider and outsider, privy to the "properties of government" and a gawker at the feast. Drama designed exclusively for court performance is necessarily panegyric, and the masque is its dominant form in the Stuart period. *Measure for Measure* is popular drama; the popular theater's presumptions to inwardness, like Lucio's, can be repellent to its royal sponsor. As Elizabeth and James pointed out, theater embarrasses royalty through its process of demystification; court masque, on the other hand, is a transparent attempt at mystification through impenetrable allegory. The duke's disguise is hardly impenetrable, nor does it protect him from Lucio's scurrilous attacks. *Measure for Measure*'s presence at court is like Lucio's presence in *Measure for Measure:* intrusive and presumptuous. Beaumont and Fletcher's popular plays, also performed at court, are similarly intrusive.

James's anxiety about exposure, expressed in *Basilikon Doron,* is, as we have suggested, paralleled in the duke's conduct in the play. As unreadable author, unpredictable actor, and disguised audience in *Measure for Measure,* the duke shares the king's obsession with secrecy and control. Lucio's coarse badinage about the duke of dark corners responds to an audience's doubts about the integrity of the duke's experiment and the invulnerability of his "complete bosom" that are generated at the play's very beginning. The duke's first speech is a nest of intertwined negations and evasions. From the outset, the play's subject seems to be and not to be a matter of state: "Of government the properties to unfold," the duke riddlingly informs Escalus, "Would seem in me t'affect speech and discourse" (I.i.1–2).

Josephine Waters Bennett was willing to see in these opening lines a direct compliment from Shakespeare to King James; the actor-playwright modestly disclaims his presumption in trifling with the monarch's proper secrets. Bennett also interpreted the allusion to distaste for crowds as a flattering reference to James's own shyness.[7] The implausibility of both of her points—that Shakespeare played the duke, that the duke's apparent familiarity with *Basilikon Doron* is meant as a compliment to James—has not undercut her basic awareness that there is something very Jacobean about the confusion of theatrical and political realms in the play. "No exact replay of James at all," as Jonathan Goldberg puts it, "the play yet manages to catch at central concerns: in the disguised Duke, the King's divided self; in the relations between privacy and the public, the play between internal and external theaters of conscience; in the duke's actions, the combination of absence and presence through which James claimed authority."[8] *Measure for Measure* forms the culmination of Goldberg's argument about what is Jacobean in the literature of James's time.

Unfortunately, the play is too early to carry the full weight that Goldberg places on it. There is, as Richard Levin has pointed out most stringently, no need for *Measure for Measure* to have been written with James in mind at all.[9] The coincidence between James's assertion of royal mystique and the duke's mysterious behavior does not reveal topicality in Bennett's sense or awareness of James's discourse in Goldberg's sense. Rather, it may arise out of Shakespeare's recognition in James of a new kind of royal performance. The gracious reconciliation of discords that *A Midsummer Night's Dream* represents as Elizabethan relies upon a royal audience's forgiveness of clumsy dramatic craftsmanship; the opposite of this is James's publicly witnessed "nauceous" response to his people's loving displays. From the idea of a truculent monarch, impatient to get past the display and into the Parliament, a poor sport who refuses to play his gracious part, emerges the corollary: the idea of the monarch as alternative playwright, scripting his response, or lack of it, by his own hidden agendas. The duke functions as just such a monarch and playwright, and his jealous guardianship of his "secretest drifts" of policy and plot making is directly related to the play's most notorious problem, "why," as Robert S. Knapp puts it, the duke's conduct in this play remains "so puzzling, so troubling, so unfunny."[10]

The question of the duke's motives does indeed seem central to any interpretation of the play. "Let him be but testimonied in his own bringings-forth," the duke assures Lucio, "and he shall appear to the envious a scholar, a statesman, and a soldier" (III.ii.135–37). But the duke refuses to appear in these roles. He disclaims scholarship and statesmanship when he defers to Escalus in "the lists of all advice / My strength can give you" (I.i.6–7). Lucio and the two Gentlemen in the second scene discuss the possibilities of joining the duke as soldiers against the king of Hungary, yet by the third scene Lucio at least has decided that the duke is on a secret, diplomatic mission. "The Duke is very strangely gone from hence," he explains to Isabella,

Bore many gentlemen — myself being one —
In hand and hope of action; but we do learn
By those that know the very nerves of state,
His givings-out were of an infinite distance
From his true-meant design.

(I.iv.50–55)

The echo of Lucio's reference here to his "givings-out" when the duke later invokes "his own bringings-forth" is disturbing. It suggests an equation between the rumors he has "strewed . . . in the common ear" (I.iii.15) and his reputation as a soldier and statesman. Lucio earlier suggests a political reason for his departure: "If the Duke, with the other dukes, come not to composition with the king of Hungary, why then all the dukes fall upon the king" (I.ii.1–3). Having delivered "my part" (I.i.41) as ruler to Angelo, the duke abdicates his roles of soldier, statesman, and scholar for that of friar and, beneath that, of beneficent ruler visiting his people in disguise. Instead of preparing for war or negotiating for peace, the duke remains at home, a "looker-on here in Vienna" (V.i.315), or less kindly, a spy.

In an extreme instance of finding the duke's withdrawal from his public responsibilities praiseworthy, Darryl J. Gless has argued that the duke's withdrawal from the public eye endows him "with an attitude toward personal honor that the New Testament, Boethius, the medieval fame literature, Spenser, Montaigne, Calvin, Erasmus, and the early Shakespeare himself had urged men to admire."[11] For Gless, the friar's hood reflects without irony this long tradition. Yet other critics have found the duke's behavior as a friar at least irresponsible: he volunteers secrets of the confessional, arranges a bed trick whose propriety if not legality seems dubious, and counsels Claudio to face death with a speech that is unimpeachably Epicurean rather than Christian. The worldly ruler lurks close beneath the surface of the ghostly father.

Anne Barton and more recently Leonard Tennenhouse have pointed to the popularity of "disguised ruler plays" in the last years of Elizabeth's and the first years of James's reign.[12] If the duke's disguise as a friar is incongruous, the incongruity may point to his assumption of a more complicated but still positive role as the disguised king of romance. The duke's difficulties in sustaining the role of the friar can be seen as comic and still benign; after all, the disguised ruler works, as the duke claims to, for the good of his people, and, as Gless argues, "By definition, such labor is charity."[13] Dressed as an ordinary soldier on the eve of Agincourt, Shakespeare's Henry V finds himself discomfited by the questions of Bates and Williams; embarrassment of a serious nature may often be the fate of a ruler in disguise.

But in *Measure for Measure* the duke asserts the power and authority of his disguise with claims that, in the mouth of a genuine friar, would have disturbing resonance to English Protestants. "The Duke / Dare no more stretch this finger of mine than he / Dare rack his own," he proclaims; "his subject am I not, / Nor here provincial" (V.i. 311–14). "The Duke represents James's divine right claims," Goldberg declares of this moment; "as a divine—a friar—he claims the right not to be subject to the Duke."[14] Such claims are proper only from the ruler, however; divines claiming their own right not to be treated as subjects, or claiming freedom to worship as they pleased, would be treated as traitors to James's or Elizabeth's rule.

"Equally reprehensible to Protestants and Catholics alike," is Harriett Hawkins's judgment upon the duke's conduct as a friar. His choice of garb, however, may add a metatheatrical rather than religious edge to our understanding of his conduct as a duke. Friars on the English stage are often double presences, figures less of divinity than of comic duplicity.[15] The duke's choice of disguise may testify less to his fondness for the "life removèd," (I.iii.8) than it may remind us of Friar Laurence in *Romeo and Juliet,* whose elaborate comic schemes of substitution and mock death end disastrously. A more hopeful Shakespearean precedent for the stratagem could be Friar Francis in *Much Ado About Nothing,* whose proposal to substitute for the disgraced Hero a rumor of her death marks the beginning of that play's resolution into comedy. But neither of these friars claims the right to criticize the secular state.

"Slander to th' state," is the response of the learned Escalus to the friar's assertions about the rampant corruption of Vienna (V.i.321), but the friar's treasonable claims are the very observations made by the duke at the beginning of the play. Making this point, Jonathan Dollimore wonders of the kindly Escalus, "Is his violent reaction to slander paranoid, or rather a strategy of *realpolitik*?"[16] Criticism of the sordid state of affairs in Vienna is appropriate only when expressed by the ruler himself, the duke or his deputy Angelo. Friars who expose iniquities, on the other hand, are dangerous creatures. Lucio attacks, with a series of anti-Catholic taunts, the friar's cowl: "Foh, sir, why, you bald-pated, lying rascal, you must be hooded, must you? Show your knave's visage, with a pox to you; show your sheep-biting face, and be hanged an hour. Will't not off?" (348–52).[17] The play's chief slanderer, paradoxically, unveiling the slanderer beneath the friar's hood, inadvertently reveals the duke.

Under the mask of otherworldly intrigue is discovered the face of temporal power, and under the guise of slander Lucio discovers truth. Yet the question of whether the duke's comic enterprise has been to reform his people (in which case he must be said to have failed) or, in a more limited scheme, to topple and humiliate Angelo (in which case he has spectacularly succeeded) becomes acute. The play offers no support to the contention that Vienna has become a better place to live in as a result of the duke's adventure, nor to the argument that the duke has become a better ruler by studying his people in addition to himself.[18] He remains as convinced of his own impregnability at the end as at the beginning, when he boasted to Friar Thomas of his "complete bosom" and its invulnerability to love. The abruptness of the proposal to Isabella, like the brisk arrangement of weddings between Angelo and Mariana and between Lucio and his "punk," testifies to the perfunctory nature of the duke's participation in the comic agenda of love and marriage. Both marriages are presented as punishments rather than rewards. Angelo begs only for "immediate sentence, then, and sequent death" (V.i.369), and is instead hustled off to marry Mariana "instantly" (373). Lucio is more blunt: "Marrying a punk, my lord, is pressing to death, whipping, and hanging," he protests (517–18).

"Slandering a prince deserves it," responds the duke (519). Lucio's remarks have come home to roost. As Escalus's cry of "Slander to th' state" had revealed, only rulers can make certain kinds of observations with impunity. No "business in this state" can legitimately make a friar "a looker-on here in Vienna," as the duke asserts while still disguised (314–15); he can only be seen as a traitor and a spy. The double nature of slander, its highly negotiable status, is also central in Angelo's case, as he has boasted of his power to transform Isabella's righteous denunciation into the same crime. "Who will believe thee, Isabel?" he rounds on her in their second duologue, and the situation he envisions in which she must "stifle in [her] own report / And smell of calumny" (II.iv.154, 157–58) materializes at the play's end when the duke departs. "Do with your injuries as seems you best," he urges; "stir not you till you have / Well determined upon these slanderers" (V.i.254, 256–57). The power of the state is the power to determine upon slanderers; it awaits the unhooding of the duke to sort out what is slander and what is truth.

"But that slander, sir, / Is found a truth now," a Gentleman declares in *Henry VIII* (II.i.153–54): in that play, the rumors of a separation between Henry and Katherine become truths as the divorce proceedings are made public. In a similar way, the truth of the slanders against Angelo is found in the moment of the duke's unhooding. As father and duke in *A Midsummer Night's Dream* reserve the power to "leave the figure, or disfigure it," (I.i.51), the duke alone can impress a fixity upon the confusions of the play's end. The truth or falsehood of slander—the poles of which are represented in Angelo's insistence on the power of his spotless reputation and Lucio's scandalous assault upon the duke's unimpeachability—resists determination. Angelo's "act did not o'ertake his bad intent" (V.i.447), as Isabella points out, so, thanks to the bed trick, he remains by this strict definition blameless. Lucio's coarse remarks are coarsely punished—in his own terms, the "dark deeds" are "darkly answered" (III.ii.165–66)—but on their falsehood the verdict remains open, for the audience's rigorous exclusion from the private life and true motives of the duke is sustained through the play's end.

The language of truth and falsehood and the language of delegation and substitution meet in recurrent use of an image of counterfeiting in the play. Angelo, from the beginning, recognizes the risk of being found out a counterfeit: "Let there be some more test made of my mettle / Before so noble and so great a figure / Be stamped upon it," he urges (I.i.48–50). Isabella also alludes to the language of coining in her exclamation upon the nature of women: "We are soft as our complexions are, / And credulous to false prints" (II.iv.129–30). The pun on "false prince" links Angelo's desire to impress his will upon Isabella's body to the ruler's ability to impress his likeness upon coins and wax seals. "They cannot touch me for coining," mad Lear proclaims; "I am the King himself" (IV.vi.83–84). Likewise the duke's casting of Angelo in a role his mettle cannot sustain is not counterfeiting, despite the defectiveness of the coin. Far from being "sealed in approbation," as the duke pretends earlier, Angelo's "worth and credit" are false prints, but, despite having introduced them into circulation, the duke disclaims responsibility for their failure (V.i.243, 242). Inflation, an economic phenomenon emerging in the England of the late sixteenth and early seventeenth centuries, offered the analogous spectacle of legitimate money, imprinted with the image of the sovereign, failing to sustain constant value. The festive generosity of James's first year in office, especially his reaction against Elizabethan parsimony in the granting of knighthoods and titles, seemed to some a debasement of the currency of honor.[19]

Like a coin in a time of inflation, Angelo is marked with the duke's image, "at full ourself" (I.i.43), and at the same time set adrift to prove his own value. As deputy, and the "voice of recorded law" (II.iv.61), Angelo can assert his blamelessness. But once the duke returns, apparently, Angelo's actions are his own alone and he must suffer their consequences. The play's muddying of the waters of private and public realms persists beyond its ending in serious questions about the appropriateness of all of the duke's strategies of substitution and delegation. To what extent does Angelo's misconduct, when he speaks with "the voice of the recorded law", redound to the discredit of the duke who installed him in office?

The answer would have been clear to the King James who promulgated a strict ideal of accountability in his advice to Prince Henry in *Basilikon Doron*. In selecting his companions, the king urges, "first see that they be of good fame and without blemish; otherwise, what can the people thinke, but that yee have chosen a company unto you, according to your own humour, and so have preferred these men, for the love of their vices and crimes, that ye knew them to be guiltie of?

For the people that see you not within, cannot judge of you, but according to the outward appearance of your actions and companie, which onely is subject to their sight."[20] "What can the people thinke" about the duke's choice of Angelo instead of Escalus, his senior and the "first in question" (I.i.46)? The scene in which the duke reveals his reason for the unusual choice begins with a disclaimer, like the play's opening line: "No, holy father, throw away that thought," he protests (I.iii.1). Friar Thomas offers the objection that "it rested in your grace" to enforce the laws (31): a gentle chiding that implies a certain negligence on the duke's part. And the duke proceeds to offer both a public and a private reason for his choice of Angelo. First, Angelo is a kind of stalking-horse, selected to protect the duke from adverse publicity:

> Therefore, indeed, my father,
> I have on Angelo imposed the office,
> Who may, in th'ambush of my name, strike home,
> And yet my nature never in the sight
> To do it slander.

(39–43)

The duke, like James, sees himself as "subject" to the people's "sight," and his concern about the possibility of their misinterpretation of his action is acute. In the process, however, the truth—that the duke has been negligent and now wishes he had not been so—is transformed into a "slander" that Angelo, operating from ambush, his office imposed upon him, can deflect. Rather than noticing the duke's fault ("'twas my fault to give the people scope" [35]), the people will instead turn their sight upon Angelo's severity.

Thus the public reason for the deputization reflects the play's larger confusion of slander and truth, while the private reason, too, focuses on the issue of Angelo's reputation. "Lord Angelo is precise," notes the duke: "Hence we shall see, / If power change purpose, what our seemers be" (50, 53–54). The desire to see inside Angelo, to try his blood and appetite against his reputation, relates closely to the desire to use Angelo as a shield to deflect the "slander" of the people's recognition of the duke's prior fault. The duke hopes to forestall the people from inquiring into his darker purpose while at the same time reserving to himself the right to pry into Angelo's darkness. "Twice treble shame on Angelo," he intones later, "To weed my vice and let his grow" (III.ii.

252–53), yet it is precisely this double office that he has imposed upon him from the first.

Angelo's seeming—his good reputation—is suspect to the duke because it is unblemished. Only the duke can pronounce his own reputation blameless and, with the power of the state behind him, judge all attacks upon it to be slander. The duke's assertions of his own blamelessness, like his extortion of praise of himself from the provost, are immune to his own cynicism. Reserving to himself the right to pry into Angelo's seeming, the duke finds unconscionable the slanderous interpretations of his conduct volunteered by Lucio. This kind of cynical inquiry into ducal secrets is the very slander that the duke had hoped that Angelo, in his severity, would deflect. Lucio thus functions in the plot as an important mediator, not simply as an ambassador from the world of Mistress Overdone to Isabella's convent, but as a deputy for the people, especially that class of people with whom the duke as a ruler should be most concerned—the young gentlemen who stand in hope of action. Excluded from the government of peacetime Vienna, they have, as we see in the second scene, nothing to do but idly speculate upon the secrets and mysteries of state.

Lucio's pretension to inside information, his claim to know "those that know the very nerves of state" (I.iv.53), is no doubt presumptuous. But Lucio traffics in a currency that is everywhere in Vienna, gossip. And gossip muddles slander and truth while asserting that it distinguishes between them. Not the duke alone but the hangman and the bawd lay claim to information unavailable to the public, the special mysteries of their trade. Lucio fills the public space left open by the duke's withdrawal into secrecy with noisy explanations; in the absence of truth, his slanders carry weight. The play's depiction at the first of the duke's refusal to unfold the properties of government before Escalus, another adept in the mystery, links the three trades—government, execution, and prostitution—to the play's key metaphor of substitution. All three operate in the dark.

Lucio's gabby bringing-to-light, like his name, is opposed to the duke's principle of government by mystery. Escalus and Angelo are puzzled by their instructions: Lucio knows that the duke's "givings-out were at an infinite distance / From his true meant design." His attribution of the worst motives to the duke, like his pretended intimacy with the duke, embodies to perfection the presumptuous prying and gawking that Elizabeth and James resented in their subjects and that they linked, significantly, to the stage. If the duke functions in the second half of the play as an improvising playwright, Lucio operates as an impertinent audience, persisting in asking the awkward questions that the play's first half has raised. "Unaware and carelessly," Dollimore asserts, "Lucio strikes at the heart of the ideological legitimation of power."[21] It is uncertain how unaware Lucio may be. Through Lucio, an audience can entertain free speculation about the duke's true nature and secret motives. Lucio's prying is a kind of mediation between play and audience.[22] Like the duke's improvisation, it is a feature of the institution to which *Measure for Measure* belongs.

Lucio represents a constituency of idle young men who have nothing better to do than mingle with prostitutes because they have been excluded from the government of Vienna. As such he resembles in his marginal status the Jacobean theater, located outside the City in the Liberties, hard by the brothels, and the Jacobean actor, awaiting the call to perform at court "in hand and hope of action" (I.iv.52). His dubious status equates strikingly to that of a Renaissance playwright like Robert Greene, in Alfred Harbage's words, "a young man uprooted." Because of his "heightened aspirations," Harbage continues, the playwright is doomed to disappointment; "discontent and disillusion stalk him from the moment he steps out into the world."[23]

Lucio resembles a playwright in his actions as well as his status. Without his agency the play's plot would never get under way. As Claudio's friend, he is delegated to introduce Isabella to the deputy. The young men's strategy, with its faith in Isabella's "prone and speechless dialect, / Such as move men" (I.ii.178–79) anticipates in its language the duke's strategies of comic substitution in the second half of the play. The delegation of the "prone and speechless" Mariana to take Isabella's place in the bed trick and the fortuitous discovery of the corpse of Ragozine (certainly speechless and possibly prone) are the comic tropes that save the play from tragedy. Yet the impulse of the young men in sending Isabella to Angelo is also comic, despite the precise deputy's discovery in it of the "cunning enemy, that, to catch a saint, / With saints dost bait thy hook" (II.ii.180–81). Lucio cheers up Isabella's fainting spirits and coaches her in her approaches: "To him, I say . . . You are too cold . . . Ay, touch him, there's the vein" (46, 56, 70). His coaching is echoed by the duke's later on: "it lies much in your holding up" (III.i.254) he urges as he reveals his scheme. "'Tis well borne up," he responds to her report of her offstage encounter with Angelo (IV.i.46).

As Isabella's first acting coach and director, Lucio not only anticipates the duke's activities as a playwright, but he also threatens the
integrity of the play that the duke is crafting. The head of Ragozine
is a prop that is emblematic of bad playwriting, a comic substitution
that looks incompetent next to the skillful baiting of Angelo's hook initiated by Lucio. Lucio's inquiry into the duke's motives and speculation on his private life questions the duke's competence as a playwright, a competence that the audience has been prepared to accept as
a substitute for competence in government.

Rather than regarding the duke's actions as miraculous (in the
uncritical atmosphere of masque), Lucio encourages us to see them in
the context of a complete personality (rather than a complete bosom):
"He had the feeling of the sport, he knew the service, and that
instructed him to mercy" (III.ii.112–13). The integration of darker private impulses into the conscience of the public servant is precisely
what the play counsels for Angelo, but the duke denies us any right to
look within him. "I never heard the absent Duke much detected for
women; he was not inclined that way," he responds to Lucio's remark
(114–15). The use of the word *detected* is revealing: whatever the inclination, and the suggestion here is that he might incline the other way,
the duke's concern is with what remains on the surface, in public view.
Witnesses to James's public displays of affection to his favorites spied
and detected his inclinations: Francis Osborne, for example, notes
that the king's embraces "prompted many to imagine some things
done in the tyring house that exceed my expressions."[24] The king, like
the duke, sees himself as set up on stage; Osborne and Lucio encourage us to imagine what goes on backstage. The theatrical metaphor
incorporates the whole playhouse.

Whatever we may think of James's secrets, the duke's remain hidden. For Richard Wheeler, Shakespeare refuses to search deep into the
duke's secrets for his own private reasons. He "displaces conflict away
from the central figure and into the world around him"; "Lucio's fana-
ticism for slandering Vincentio . . . fits with this as a kind of residual
protest emerging from Shakespeare against his own dramatic strategies."[25] Wheeler's Shakespeare is a self-hating playwright, rebelling
against his own dubious practices. Lucio's insistence that we try to
imagine a full set of motives for the duke leads Wheeler to seek a full
set of motives for Shakespeare himself. In the process, however, Wheeler seems to see Lucio as the duke does, as some sort of fanatical slan-

derer. But a distaste for participatory theatrics and a fanatical hatred of slander are parts, as we have seen, of James's own performance as a king and as a royal audience.

Lucio and the duke agree in seeing Angelo as a seemer; where Lucio differs is in seeing the duke as a seemer as well. Like Malvolio in *Twelfth Night,* Angelo is an unimaginative actor, easily baited into playing his designated role. Lucio's scheme of exploiting Isabella's attractiveness and the duke's desire to deflect public attention from his own weaknesses both profit from Angelo's readiness to see himself as a saint tempted by a cunning enemy. Angelo, in turn, prompts Isabella to play the part he imagines for her: "be that you are, / That is, a woman; if you be more, you're none" (II.iv.134–35). Isabella's refusal to put on "the destined livery" (138) of her sex—her insistence that she must remain a nun and therefore be more than woman—threatens the duke's test of Angelo's seeming. In light of the Jacobean stage practice that used boy actors to play the female roles, the actor playing Isabella can only be a woman when he puts on the destined livery of female costume; the images of dressing and stripping that animate the second duologue reinforce a system of reference to costuming. In his nun's habit (proclaiming, like the "black masks" of women at the playhouse "an enshield beauty" [79–80]), the actor playing Isabella both displays and hides his feminine identity.

The play's other women do not refuse to take the roles prescribed for them: Julietta and Mariana function as prospective wives, and Mistress Overdone willingly puts on the livery of brothel keeper. Isabella's desire for more restraints in the sisterhood she proposes to join marks her as different from these more pliant women. Her status at the end of the play—speechless in response to the duke's proposal— is open to varying interpretation. We simply do not know what Isabella will do at the end; nor do we know whether to read her doing nothing in response to the duke as a rejection, an acceptance, or a stunned bewilderment.

"If we are to see Isabella as a victim of bad playwriting," Marcia Riefer has argued, "we can compare her bewilderment to our own. She has trusted the Duke, as we've trusted our playwright, to pattern events as he has led her to expect events to be patterned—and the Duke, sharing Shakespeare's affinity for surprises in this play, pulls these expectations out from under her."[26] Lucio's questioning of the duke's private motives reaches beyond mere bewilderment to question the duke's competence. Like Barnardine's refusal to die, it threatens the duke's authority, both as duke and as comic, manipulative friar. The fortuitous head of Ragozine, "*caput ex machina,*" as Riefer puts it, puts a stop to Barnardine's resistance, making engagement of it unnecessary. Lucio's mouth, like Isabella's, is stopped only later, and only with the duke's sweeping recovery of his absolute powers.

The play finishes under the duke's control, with surfaces rearranged and Vienna superficially restored to order. "Like Prospero at the conclusion of *The Tempest,*" Steven Mullaney argues, "the Duke pardons what exceeds his grasp: he licenses what he cannot control in a magnanimous gesture meant to turn the manifest embodiment of his own limits into a display of his power to issue such a license, but the act can at best 'flourish the deceit.' The popular playhouses of Elizabethan and Jacobean England were granted a similar license, and in an equally equivocal gesture."[27] In Mullaney's reading, Barnardine "stands for the place of that stage," representing the intractability of the playhouses in the Liberties. But Shakespeare's players did not remain exclusively across the river in "global unconsciousness and radical inacessibility," like Barnardine. Rather, they visited the court regularly and played in private houses to more privileged audiences. Lucio's pretended intimacies with the duke link up with this aspect of the Jacobean theater: players had to speak the language of gentlemen and rulers, unfold the properties of government as they unfolded the draperies with which they decorated the stage. Excessive fluency in the language of rule and excessive familiarity with the secrets of state was an occupational necessity and an occupational hazard.

Lucio's punishment for slander, marrying a punk, reflects the professional actor's social status as next thing to a prostitute. The emotional depths the play has opened up in Angelo and Isabella force us to see their marriages, too, as punishment. The activity of the play's first half, throwing light into the dark corners of Angelo's and Isabella's suppressed sexuality, is parodied in the second half by Lucio's claim to know all the duke's dirty secrets. But the play's drive to reconcile public and private, to explore the secrets of precise deputies and nuns who wish "a more strict restraint" (I.iv.4), is not that easily forestalled. Substituting for an unruly audience, Lucio also becomes, in the second half of the play, the conscience of the theater itself.

And it is a theater explicitly and frequently cited by its opponents for the "unbelievable magnitude," as Philip Finkelpearl has recently pointed out, of its violations of laws against slander. Rather than ex-cercising monolithic control over the playhouses, as some critics have argued, the Office of Revels seems not to have systematically con-trolled libel onstage. As Finkelpearl reminds us: "modern readers tend to forget that drunken kings and power-and-money-hungry courtiers may not have taken seriously the gibes and japes of rogues, vaga-bonds, sturdy beggars, and young boys."[28] Despite the desire on the part of reformers such as John Melton that "some severe law might be enacted for the punishing of such scandalous libelling as is, or may be at any time coloured under the name of poetising, and playmaking," players seemed to avoid serious punishments, at least of the sort vis-ited upon antitheatrical propagandists like William Prynne.

With its regular commitments to play at court and its ordinary com-mitment to the Globe, Shakespeare's theater occupied not one but two places, each with different audiences and different expectations on the part of both audiences and players. After the King's Men took over the Blackfriars in 1609, the professional players now had obligations to three different places, each with its own specific concerns and de-mands. It is not surprising that the censorship was inefficient, where the institution to be controlled was so diverse. When the King's Men went to court, they brought their diversity with them, whether they wanted to or not. "For the imported play at court and for court the-atricals," Keith Sturgess properly insists, "the King . . . was not only the chief spectator but a rival performance."[29] Lucio's rivalship with the duke, we might venture, suggests turning this paradigm on its head. The imported play is a rival to the monarch's performance, a leering challenger, dropping the tasteless hints that invite prying spec-ulation. Its visit is somehow off-color, bringing with it a breath of the stews. Lucio, as the players so often did, gets off easy: marrying a punk is not necessarily a death sentence, after all. Rather, the duke is forcibly reminding Lucio of where he belongs in the world of the play, where plays belong in the world. In this, as in the self-loathing with which he participates in Vienna's iniquities, the duke seems much like King James.

II

Slander, presumptuousness, arrogant pretension to inwardness: these characteristics of Lucio are, *Measure for Measure* suggests, baggage the public playhouse play carries with it when it leaves its neighborhood in the stews and unfolds its properties before the monarch. When the King's Men took possession of their playhouse at Blackfriars, the company added an indoor, "private" environment to the two stages upon which *Measure for Measure* could be expected to appear. Court, private theater, and public theater now housed the King's Men's plays. The Blackfriars and the other private theaters appealed to a narrower audience of gentry than did the large public houses. Keith Sturgess suggests that a progressive "closing of ranks" occurred in the later years of the private playhouses, the 1630s, as their audiences defined themselves more clearly as a coterie, and the atmosphere became "club-like."[30] The plays of Beaumont and Fletcher began this trend, and where *Measure for Measure* remains conscious of its status as an import from the tainted world of the Globe, their dramas address an audience that both at court and in the private theater thinks of itself as inward.

"Hardly anything about the Beaumont-Fletcher-Massinger pieces is more remarkable," Tucker Brooke wrote long ago, "than the abnormally low quality of the kings who display themselves in this literature written by, and for, cavaliers."[31] The echo here of Rymer's contention that the early Stuart playwrights treated kings like "*Dogs*" is unmistakable. The conflation of the three playwrights under the anachronistic rubric of "cavaliers" reveals a common prejudice in early discussions of Beaumont and Fletcher. Charged with snobbishness, carelessness, immaturity and decadence, these playwrights seem to epitomize a generation of idle monarchists, whose very superficiality can be blamed for the Civil War itself. Yet, as even Brooke recognizes, there is a strong satiric edge in their treatment of court life and monarchy that contradicts any absolute identification of these plays with facile royalism. The fact that Charles I consoled himself in his last days with the writings of Beaumont and Fletcher should not, clearly, redound to their discredit. Concentrating upon the lives of courtiers, the three plays to be discussed here—*The Maid's Tragedy, Philaster,* and *A King and No King*—suggest powerful tensions between the young gentlemen, soldiers, and statesmen who are the protagonists of the dramas and the kings who govern and misgovern their lives. Intimacy characterizes the Jacobean private playhouse, and a mutual familiarity with court life and with court drama animates the exchange between audience, actor, and playwright.

If *Measure for Measure* runs the risk of slander by bringing the world of the public theater into the court, *The Maid's Tragedy* runs even graver risks. It begins with a sustained parody of the court's primary dramatic form, a wedding masque, and exposes the falsehood of a marriage that the king has arranged. The king himself is murdered onstage in "a grotesque travesty of a wedding night," as Michael Neill puts it.[32] This play is recorded as one of those performed during the Christmas season of 1612–13 to celebrate the impending marriage of Princess Elizabeth to Frederick the Elector Palatine. Its relation to this occasion must be seen as complex. *Philaster* and *A King and No King* are also on the list of plays presented that Christmas; *Philaster* was performed twice.[33] We are certainly safe in agreeing with the assumption that all three plays were regularly in repertory at that point; again, none of the twenty plays presented seems to have been written with the specific occasion in mind. Selection was probably governed by popularity. Among this group Shakespeare's *Tempest,* with its masque elements, fits so neatly that it is hard to remember that it had been first performed at court in 1611. But if appropriateness of tone and subject matter had been rigorously enforced, none of the three Beaumont and Fletcher plays would have passed muster.

The Maid's Tragedy* differs from the other two plays in its satirical representation of a court masque. It is a masque that contains allusions, or hints of them, to a number of recently performed masques. Sarah Sutherland has detected echoes of Ben Jonson's *Masque of Beauty* (written in 1606, performed in January 1608) and *Hymenaei,* written to celebrate the first marriage of Lady Frances Howard in 1607.[34] The satire is thus particular as well as generic: the audience of *The Maid's Tragedy,* when it first appeared at the Blackfriars, could apparently be expected to recognize references to specific masques and to the language of marriage masque as a genre in its own right. Beaumont and Fletcher transplant the court masque into the private playhouse, just as Shakespeare, in *A Midsummer Night's Dream,* translates the royal progress onto the public stage. What is presented is not simply an obvious ironic disjunction between the idealism of the masque (as we shall see, the masque in *The Maid's Tragedy* is not particularly idealistic) and the sordid world of the court, but a vision of court life as highly theatricalized. The action of the play comes to imitate the nuptial fantasies aroused by the masque. The metatheatrical device points in two ways, calling attention to the artificiality of theatrical illusion in the masque and at the same time revealing the tyrannical artificiality of the court world in the play.

"What think'st thou of a maske, will it be well?" asks Lysippus at the beginning of the play. "As well as maskes can be," responds the cynical Strato, and, prompted by the king's brother, he elaborates:

> Yes, they must commend their King, and speake in praise
> Of the assembly, blesse the Bride and Bridegroome,
> In person of some god, there tied to rules
> Of flatterie.
>
> (I.i.6–11)[35]

The verbal linkage of "Bride and Bridegroome" to "tied" looks proleptically forward to the end of the play, where Evadne will tie the king to the bed before she murders him. Poets are tied down by rules of flattery when they set out to write masques; such rules, indeed, can be seen to be in force throughout the court of Rhodes. Beaumont and Fletcher make the point by introducing Melantius on just this line. "See good my Lord who is return'd," Cleon interrupts (11). Before the audience sees the masque, the audience sees the soldier, who "with blood abroad [buys] us our peace" (14). As Lysippus continues, we note the inroads the rules of flattery have made into court language: "The breath of Kings is like the breath of gods, / My brother wisht thee here and thou art here" (15–16). The juxtaposition of this exchange to the cynical discussion of the masque highlights the difficulties Melantius, as a man of honor and a man of action, will have in Rhodes.

"The breath of Kings" also reaches out as a reference to Shakespeare's *Richard II*, where Bolingbroke admiringly and ambitiously observes Richard's ability to shorten his sentence of banishment: "Four lagging winters and four wanton springs / End in a word: such is the breath of kings" (*Richard II*, I.iii.214–15). In Shakespeare's play, Richard's apparent power to make his word effective proves illusory; silent Bolingbroke returns from banishment and ascends the throne in the face of Richard's eloquence. Beaumont and Fletcher, alluding to this line, echo Shakespeare to some purpose, for in their play royal utterance, and the efficacy of royal utterance, will come under similar scrutiny. Melantius's return, ushered in as it is by Bolingbroke's words, becomes a return from exile and a challenge to the language of royal authority.

Melantius's greeting to Lysippus summons up his credo, one that will in fact lead to his rebellion against the king later in the play: "where I finde worth / I love the keeper, till he let it goe, / And then I follow it" (I.i.23–25). After expressing some concern that his own brother Diphilus did not join him in the wars, he learns that the king's express order kept him at home, awaiting Amintor's wedding. When Aspatia appears, Melantius further reveals his unsuitability for court life by assuming that she will be Amintor's bride: "Haile Maide and Wife" (58). Lysippus corrects his misreading of the situation, informing him that Amintor has married Evadne, "Your vertuous sister" (75):

> The King my brother did it
> To honour you, and these solemnities
> Are at his charge.
>
> (76–78)

"'Tis royall like himself," Melantius comments, regretting his "infortunate" speech to Aspatia. "She had my promise, but the King forbad it," Amintor admits when Melantius accuses him of having "growne too fickle" (135, 132). Such is the breath of kings. Yet the actions of the king in forbidding Diphilus to go to war and in compelling Amintor to forsake Aspatia are troubling to Melantius, whom an audience of young gentlemen would see as admirable in his loyalty and bluntness.

This bluntness almost leads to blows later on, when Calianax objects to the seating of Melantius's lady. Melantius has seated his friend among "the best of *Rhodes*" (I.ii.30). "Who plac'd the Lady there / So neere the presence of the King?" Calianax demands; "The place is kept for women of more worth" (58–59, 61). "This *Rhodes* I see is nought / But a place priviledg'd to doe men wrong," Melantius explodes (83–84). Place, privilege, preferment, proximity to the king: all conspire against the honest soldier and his lady. The idea of a place reserved for a lady of more worth, too, carries the suggestion of Aspatia's displacement. Order and rank are based upon principles of worth that are unfathomable to Melantius and that emanate from the king. Neither the vengeful and senile Calianax nor the courageous and honest Melantius can fully comprehend the new dislocations.

The marriage masque unfolds against this backdrop of confusion and hostility. It opens as "Night *rises in mists*" (111, s.d.). The conceit of the masque is that it anticipates the wedding night: the masque ends as night vanishes with the coming of day. In Ben Jonson's *Hymenaei,* the dancers are "importun'd . . . to a fit remembrance of the time" (343) lest they waste the whole wedding night in dancing.[36] In the masque-within-the-play, the lords and ladies of the court function as "those easterne streaks / That warne us hence before the morning breaks" (I.ii.124–25). As the masque ends, the sun rises, in terms that follow masque convention by directly referring to the king: "see / A greater light, a greater Majestie," Cinthia counsels Night, "The day breaks here" (272–74). The first night's solemnity in *Hymenaei* ended with an epithalamium. Here, the epithalamium is in the center, and the masque's ending, the break of day, intervenes before the plot is resolved: Boreas has escaped from the cave of winds (blowing trouble) and Neptune has descended to "strike a calme," but whether he succeeds is not known. Cinthia (the goddess of the moon), who has been summoned to illuminate the spectacle, concludes by promising higher tides that ever before: "You shall have many floods fuller and higher / Than you have wisht for" (257–58). Boreas is a baleful influence brought under control at the very beginning of Jonson's *Masque of Beauty*. He remains free at the end of Beaumont and Fletcher's masque, and its whole action takes place under the borrowed light of the moon, limited by the powers of the night.

In alluding to her own "swarthie face" (118) Night also seems to be making reference to the twelve Ethiopian women of Jonson's *Masque of Blackness* (1605), who were set wandering in search of the British realm where they could be bleached white. The moon, surnamed Aethiopia, presides over the dances in *Blackness,* a masque that like the masque-in-the-play anticipates an ending in the full beams of a royal "SUNNE," whose "light scientiall is, and (past mere nature) / Can salue the rude defects of euery creature" (256–57). The masque-within-the-play, however, merely ends as Night melts and Cinthia departs; day breaks without a sense of cure. By foresaking the affirmative resolutions of the Jonsonian masques that it imitates, the masque in *The Maid's Tragedy* anticipates the horrible consequences of the marriage it celebrates.

While the masque-within-the-play follows the "rules of flatterie" in praising the beauties of the audience at the beginning and in deferring to the king's sunlike "Majestie" at the end, its unstable dependence upon the Night, the moon, and Neptune to control the winds inadvertently unleashed with the dancers is disturbing. So, too, is Cinthia's promise of unprecedented high tides to conceal Neptune's "dwellings" from the eyes of day (I.ii.259). Neptune exits to still his storm "Least your proud charge should swell above the wast / And win upon the Iland" (261–62). The language here is a language of appetites out of control. The image of an island inundated with high tides has a range of traditional references that extend beyond the Rhodes of the play to English visions of Atlantan apocalypse. Night's and Cinthia's attempts to structure and organize an appropriate festivity seem (at best) clumsily improvised; taken as an allegory looking forward to the rest of the play, the masque releases destructive energies that are both sexual and political. Unruly winds, nocturnal authorities, paradoxical images of control and inundation, all look toward (as the masque does) the figure of the king, whose "breath" has caused such disruption, whose nighttime activities Amintor will soon learn about, and whose strategies of control will unleash revenge.

Truth and falsehood figure in the masque as they do in the play. Cinthia denies that the moon and Endymion have ever been lovers. When Night suggests that he would be an appropriate celebrant, she replies:

Thou dreamst darke Queene, that faire boy was not mine
Nor went I downe to kisse him, ease and wine,
Have bred these bold tales, poets when they rage
Turne gods to men, and make an hour an age.

(158–61)

Why the goddess of the moon should feel compelled to deny her unequal liaison with a mortal is unclear, until we recall the masque's occasion as an elaborate screen concealing the king's liaison with Evadne. Truth and Opinion, themselves, appear as characters in *Hymenaei,* confronting each other on the second night's Barriers. Opinion introduces herself as Truth, and Truth replies: "I am that TRUTH, thou some illusiue spright; / Whom to my likeness, the black sorceresse *night* / Hath of these drie, and empty fumes created" (701–3). Cinthia's protestations of innocence, in a masque presided over by Night, may be as false as the bold tales of poets. In addition to the general unreliability of Night, Beaumont and Fletcher, by referring their audience to *Hymenaei* in the structure and language of their marriage masque, refer to a precedent in which Night is the mother of false Opinion, the enemy to Truth.

It is in the songs of the masque in *The Maid's Tragedy* that the echoes of *Hymenaei* are most obvious; both Jonson's masque and the masque in the play emphasize the passage of time and the bride-groom's eagerness to enjoy his bride. Lady Frances Howard and the Earl of Essex, whose marriage *Hymenaei* celebrated, were at that time too young to consummate the marriage. Seven years later, they would be divorced on the grounds of the earl's impotence (toward Lady Frances alone) and she would marry King James's favorite, Robert Carr, Earl of Somerset. When Jonson came to publish *Hymenaei* in the 1616 Folio, as David Lindley puts it, his "sense of the uncomfort-able disparity between the idealised vision his work attempted to create and the stubborn intractability of the real world" led him to sup-press mention of the masque's occasion.[37] The masque's celebration of married love must be seen as utterly conventional when the bride was thirteen and the bridegroom fourteen. "By early 1613," according to G. P. V. Akrigg, "it was common talk at court that the young Essexes wanted a divorce. It was also becoming common talk that the royal favourite Carr was in love with the Countess. Some said that she was his mistress. Other scandalous tales were heard in the corridors. Some said that Lady Frances had relieved Prince Henry of his virginity and that jealousy over her had been the real cause of his hostility to Carr."[38] When *The Maid's Tragedy* was written (1610?), these rumors were not current, of course, although the disparity between the lan-guage of married love in *Hymenaei* and the actual situation would have been obvious. Then, the elaborate bringing to bed of the bride in the masque's epithalamium could only be seen as absurd, as both fam-ilies had agreed to postpone such an encounter for two years.

But at court over the Christmas holidays of 1612–13, where rumors of Lady Frances Howard's improprieties and Essex's impotence were circulating, the play's reminders of *Hymenaei* would have been even far more suggestive. At the very least, both the masque-within-the-play and Jonson's masque insist upon a consummation that the "con-trivers" or sponsors of the masques knew (in the case of Jonson) or hoped (in the case of the king in *The Maid's Tragedy*) would not take place. When King James did in fact arrange the divorce of the Essexes and sponsor Lady Frances's marriage to his favorite, Beaumont and Fletcher's masque would take on, in later years, a prophetic air.

Jonson's masque, however, insists upon the chastity of married love. "So, now you may admit him in," runs the epithalamium, "The act he covets is no sin / But chaste and holy love, / Which Hymen doth approve" (501–4). Thus the bridegroom is urged to "keepe the *Brides* fair eyes / Awake, with her own cryes, / Which are but *mayden feares*: / And kisses drie such teares" (521–24). The song in *The Maid's Tragedy,* on the other hand, is susceptible of a double reading, as it calls upon the night:

> *Stay gentle* Night *and with the darkeness cover*
>   *the kisses of her lover.*
> *Stay and confound her teares and her shrill cryings,*
> *Her weake denials, vowes and often dyings,*
>   *Stay and hide all,*
>   *but helpe not though she call.*
>
> (229–34)

This could be a night of licit or illicit love, though Hymen is shortly summoned to lead the bride to bed. But even in that conventional appeal the play adds a double dimension:

> *Bring in the virgins every one,*
> *That grieve to lie alone;*
> *That they may kisse, while they may say a maid,*
> *To morrow t'will be other kist and said*
>
> (243–46)

The first passage, with its suggestion that the bride might have a lover, carries a strong reference to the king's relationship to Evadne; the second, equally, identifies the conventional virgins of an epithalamium with the grieving Aspatia, whose cause for grievance is not merely the conventional one. Furthermore, the song looks to the next day, when it will indeed be "other kist and said" as Amintor and Evadne enact their conventional roles so well that the king becomes suspicious. "Helpe not" becomes, again ironically, the response of the king's bodyguards on his last night in bed with Evadne, as she kills him and no one heeds his cries.

What the masque in *The Maid's Tragedy* dramatizes, then, as the parallels with *Hymenaei* suggest, is the way masque itself fits into court life. The disingenuousness, the susceptibility to double readings, of the king's masque is present in Jonson's masque, too, despite the high ideals of its author. Beaumont and Fletcher use the masque to demonstrate that the circumstances of performance and the underlying motives of the contriver have as much to do with what a masque means as do the mythological figures who appear in it. In both ways they show the instability and confusion of a Rhodes ruled by an absolute and lustful king.

The air of artifice continues in the scene immediately after the court masque, in which the bride is prepared for bed by her ladies. The masque's *doubles entendres* are vividly rendered single by the smutty remarks of Dula, and Aspatia plays the role of grieving virgin just as the songs prescribe. Amintor's eagerness is also utterly conventional, though he hesitates slightly: "I did that Lady wrong," he murmurs as Aspatia takes her leave; "It was the King first mov'd me too't, but he / Has not my will in keeping,—why doe I / Perplex my selfe thus?" (II.i.127, 130–32). "To bed my love," he urges Evadne, having suppressed this shudder of conscience, "*Hymen* will punish us, / For being slack performers of his rights" (143–44). As extension of the king's plan, the masque in its language dominates Amintor's expectations. The breath of kings, in this sense of the language dictated by the conventions of masque, infuses Amintor's speech.

The shattering of Amintor's expectations as Evadne reveals the truth of her relations with the king shatters his faith in the language of masque: "Are these the joyes of mariage? *Hymen* keepe / This story (that will make succeeding youth / Neglect thy ceremonies) from all eares" (214–16). Deprived of his anticipated role as eager bridegroom, Amintor is lost: "What a strange thing am I?" (318). Incapable of taking action against the king—whose "sacred name" fills him with terror (307)—Amintor now consciously elects to enact the scenario of marriage into which he has been unconsciously cast. "Come let us practise, and as wantonly / As ever loving bride and bridegroome met / Lets laugh and enter here" (355–57). Amintor substitutes a witting roleplaying, but he retains the now unwelcome role of bridegroom. From belief in the language of masque he shifts to recognition of its, and the king's, falsity: "why is this night so calme?" (248) he exclaims hopelessly, reminding us of the masque's stormy conclusion.

Aspatia, too, reverts to the language of the masque as she examines the needlework depiction of Ariadne in the next scene: "You have a full winde, and a false heart *Theseus*" she protests, "could the Gods know this / And not of all their number raise a storme?" (II.ii.45, 49–50). Thoroughly intertwined with the language and action of the play, the language of the masque—the breath of the king—dominates, as Michael Neill has pointed out, the "whole work." Evadne's revenge plays out the masque's *doubles entendres;* Aspatia's return as a boy heightens the theatricality of the close. The loose ends of the masque, William Shullenberger points out, are resolved in the "brilliant subterranean dramatic conceit" of "Evadne's binding and murder of the king." The masque's status as theatrical embodiment of the king's breath, and its transformation of the monarch into a kind of natural force or god, defines the whole world of the play. "The deep motive for Melantius's indirection and for Amintor's paralysis is the same," Shullenberger argues. "The king is taboo, a kind of living totem, a sign of cosmic and social coherence, and the incalculable power of the Deity stands behind him."[39] The play goes beyond merely expounding, to questioning the mystique of royalty, by identifying its language so strongly with the lies of the masque and with the constant playacting in the court.

The king is the contriver of the masque, its subject, and its victim. As architect of the scheme whereby Amintor is humiliated and Melantius recalled, he enforces his will upon the young men of the court and at the same time releases chaos—Boreas, as it were, escapes. His credulity in believing Amintor's boasts after the wedding night and in rejecting Calianax's warnings of Melantius's plan to take the fort marks his identity with, rather than difference from, ordinary men. The assertions of total control represented by the masque and by the wedding itself founder in the king's own susceptibility to his appetites. "What prettie new device is this *Evadne?*" he asks as he awakens bound to the bed:

> What, doe you tie me to you? by my love
> This is a queint one: come my deare and kisse me,
> Ile be thy *Mars,* to bed my Queene of love,
> Let us be caught together, that the gods may see,
> And envie our embraces.
>
> (V.i.47–52)

The reversion to masque language here as the king reads Evadne's "device" in mythological rather than political terms, and does so as a royal interpreter recognizing an iconographic allusion, emphatically asserts the king's bondage to a style that now masters him. "Significantly," Lee Bliss notes, "despite Strato's conviction that such entertainment is by its nature mendacious, the masque in its way tells the truth."[40] To put it more bluntly, the truth the masque tells is that it is mendacious. Amintor can only recognize the truth of his love for Aspatia once he has, as he thinks, killed her brother, and Melantius can only demonstrate his faith in monarchy by egging his sister on to regicide and by seizing the fort.

Lysippus's recognition at the end of the play is reductive, and it too takes the shape of paradox:

> May this a faire example be to me,
> To rule with temper, for on lustfull Kings
> Unlookt for suddaine deaths from God are sent,
> But curst is he that is their instrument.
>
> (V.iii.292–95)

Lysippus's famous lines call attention not simply to the paradoxical problem of tyrannicide, but they also reshape the whole play into a kind of masque itself, a "faire example . . . to me." Court masque ideology identifies rule with temper and idealizes moderation and continence in the monarch. The appetitive energies of the antimasque are always transformed into the orderly ranks of dancers at the close. Yet the close here looks toward the beginning. "What think'st thou of a maske," Lysippus wondered there, "will it be well?"

"How now, what maske is this?" demands the king in the final act of *Philaster,* as Philaster, Arathusa, and Bellario enter "*in a Robe and Garland*" (19). Where the duke in *Measure for Measure* functions as a comic manipulator and playwright, and the king in *The Maid's Tragedy* as contriver and victim of the court masque, here the king is a hostile, misprizing audience. Bellario offers to "sing you an Epithelamion of these lovers" (21), to which the king responds by losing his temper. "Call in the Captain of the Citadell," he cries:

> Ther you shall keepe your wedding:
> Ile provide a Masque shall make your *Himen*
> Turne his saffron into a sullen coat,
> And sing sad Requiems to your departing soules;
> Bloud shall put out your Torches, and instead
> Of gaudy flowers about your wanton necks,
> An Axe shall hang, like a prodigeous Meteor,
> Ready to crop your loves sweetes.
>
> (53–61)

This vision of a bloody antimasque is but the latest of this king's attempts to impose his will upon the world of the play. His plan to marry Arathusa to Pharamond, the boastful prince of Spain, has foundered because of Megra's baseless accusations. Trying to chase down his daughter in the forest, the king asserts his power:

> goe, bring her me,
> And set her here before me: tis the King
> Will have it so! whose breath can still the Winds,
> Unclowd the Sunne, charme downe the swelling Sea,
> And stop the flouds of heaven: speake, can it not?
>
> (IV.iv.37–41)

"No," Dion answers bluntly. "No? Cannot the breath of kings doe this?" "No," repeats Dion, "nor smell sweete it selfe, if once the lungs / Be but corrupted" (42–44).

This interchange prompts a recognition on the part of an audience seeing both *Philaster* and *The Maid's Tragedy* (like the audience of the Christmas season of 1612–13) that masque language permeates monarchical self-definition. In *Philaster,* the king's dreams of power are constantly undercut by the realities around them, as he is forced to recognize in the hunting scene. The cosmic powers of monarchs to still storms exist merely in the language of masque, allegorically representing control over the passions. Stymied in the forest, the king of Cicilie rages at the unfairness of the royal condition:

> Alas, what are we Kings?
> Why doe you gods place us above the rest,
> To be serv'd, flatter'd, and ador'd, till we
> Beleeve we hold within our hands your thunder?
> And when we come to try the power we have,
> There's not a leafe shakes at our threatenings.
>
> (46–51)

The king's desire to impose the rule of masque upon the realm of nature finds expression in comic self-pity; Dion's deflating remarks underline the futility of these complaints.

Peter Davison has argued that in *Philaster,* Beaumont and Fletcher pursue a serious political agenda: direct echoes from the writings and speeches of King James underscore a specific critique of Stuart absolutist pretensions. The play reflects the opening stages of the struggle between king and Parliament and functions as an "attempt to reconcile the irreconcilable."[41] Under this reading, the Countrey Fellow who rescues Arathusa in the woods becomes an "idealization of the Country Member of Parliament." Davison's historiography is resolutely Whig, but his conviction that the play has a political dimension and makes references to King James's writings need not be dismissed out of hand. "*Credulitie* and *Ignorance*," James argued in a 1610 speech to Parliament singled out by Davison, make kings "subiect to flatterie." The belief that the language of flattery constitutes real power is shared by the kings in both *The Maid's Tragedy* and *Philaster*. Credulity and ignorance lead the king of Rhodes to believe that the wedding masque's vision of a satisfying night of love has taken place and to dupe himself into believing that Evadne has bound him up in order to enact a masque of Mars and Venus. The king of Cicilie credulously mistakes the words of royal mystique for actual powers, just as he gives his daughter to Pharamond, that "large speaker" of his own commendations (I.i.157).

He is not alone in this problem: even the crusty Dion among his courtiers is capable of egregious errors of perception. Megra's scandalous charge that Arathusa and Bellario are lovers convinces everyone, including Philaster, whose jealousy leads him to wound both innocents (and, since Bellario is a woman in disguise, two women) in the forest. The Countrey Fellow's intervention is less parliamentarian in nature than simple decency: "Hold dastard, strike a woman! Th'art a craven" (IV.v.85). Philaster's bondage to the language of masque is almost as total as the king's as he begs Arathusa to kill him: "Forgive my passion: Not the calmed sea, / When *Eolus* locks up his windy brood, / Is less disturb'd than I" (42–44). Forty lines later, he is ready, Othello-like, to execute his faithful love.[42]

Philaster's jealous delusions are the result of theatrical impositions. Megra's assertion of the princess's faithlessness is also couched in the language of public display: "The Princesse your deare daughter, shall stand by me / On walls, and sung in ballads, any thing" (II.iv.155–56). Her threats allude to King James's anxieties about exposure to the "publike" view in *Basilikon Doron,* and identify the stage with city walls and with scandalous publications. Megra's threats mirror Isabella's threats to expose Angelo in *Measure for Measure,* but, unlike Isabella, she is lying and is believed. "What I have knowne," Megra proclaims,

Shall be as publique as a print: all tongues
Shall speake it as they doe the language they
Are borne in, as free and commonly; I'le set it
Like a prodigious starre for all to gaze at,
And so high and glowing, that other Kingdomes far and
    forraigne,
Shall reade it there; nay travaile with it, till they finde
No tongue to make it more, nor no more people;
And then behold the fall of your faire Princesse.

                      (169–77)

The threat of making the princess into a spectacle cuts deep, for it challenges the idea that there is any difference between the language of royalty and the free and common language that all are born to. What will be set up for all to gaze at is not a prodigious difference between the princess and the people, but a spectacular emblem of identity in shame. Unlike the sun that attracts the Ethiopian princesses to Britain in the *Masque of Blackness,* the foreigners will read in the sky the princess's disgrace. "Has she a boy?" is the only answer the king can make to Megra's accusations (178). He assents to her slander only to avoid its becoming common knowledge.

Yet the princess's shame does become common—at least in the world of the court. Silencing Megra may have the effect of suppressing publication; but the news passes, circulated like a manuscript in private circles. Attempting to conceal his love for the princess, Philaster is only convinced of her infidelity by Dion's eyewitness testimony: "Oh, noble sir, your vertues / Cannot look into the subtle thoughts of woman. / In short, my Lord, I tooke them: I my selfe" (III.i.109–111). But the usually trusty Dion is lying here, hoping to force Philaster into rebellion against the king. Megra's threat to make a spectacle of the princess becomes Dion's tool to "confute" Philaster's love for her (III.i.25). Dion's scheme does not work out as planned; plunged into jealous despair, Philaster wildly abandons all ambitions and takes to the forest.

Both schemes are based upon the central misprision in the play: Bellario, as she reveals at the end, is Dion's daughter Euphrasia in disguise. Thus the boy whom Megra and Philaster dream (in different ways) to be dallying with the princess is no boy at all. *Philaster*'s treatment of this device differs markedly from that in *The Maid's Tragedy.*

There, Aspatia makes it clear to an audience who she is when she enters in *"mans apparell"* (V.iii.1, s.d.). But here Bellario's true identity is kept secret from audience as well as from the man she hopelessly loves and who wounds her while she sleeps. Disgraceful as Philaster's conduct may be toward a man, it becomes more disgraceful in retrospect. Not letting an audience in on the stratagem must divide that audience into two factions — those who have seen or read the play and know the secret, and those who are experiencing it for the first time. The performance at court in 1612–13 was a revival, so both sorts must have been in attendance. In concealing the imposture from a first-time audience member, *Philaster* is not alone. Jonson's *Epicoene* likewise permits Dauphine to dupe not only his uncle Morose, but also his friends Truewit and Clerimont, not to mention the audience as well, with the true sex of the silent woman.

Both plays offer the occasional clue. Here, suspicions might be aroused when Philaster inquires about Dion's daughter at the end of the first scene, "Is she yet alive?" "Most honor'd sir, she is: / And for the penance but of an idle dreame / Has undertooke a tedious pilgrimage" (I.i.320–22). Philaster's description of his first encounter with the boy, too, suggests hidden depths:

> Then tooke he up his Garland, and did shew,
> What every flower, as Countrey people hold,
> Did signifie: and how all, ordered thus,
> Exprest his griefe.

> (I.ii.130–33)

An audience that has recently seen *The Maid's Tragedy* would find here a strong echo of Aspatia's artificial way to grieve: or, if the plays were seen in the other order, Aspatia would remind it of Bellario. Bellario merely begins where Aspatia ended.

Seeing her love for Philaster as an "idle dreame," Euphrasia has taken on male costume before her play begins. Both as a boy and as a woman, she is a threat to the love of Philaster and the princess. "The love of boyes unto their Lords, is strange," Philaster muses, in a speech that must strike an audience in on the secret as full of *double entendre:*

I have read wonders of it, yet this boy,
For my sake (if a man may judge by lookes,
And speech) would out-doe story.

(II.i.57–60)

In Megra's scandalous indictment of Arathusa and in Philaster's admiration of Bellario, both are singled out as prodigies, extraordinary
examples. Both instances are likewise false: Arathusa is not a prodigious sinner, and Bellario is not a wonder among boys.

The utter falsehood of the charges against the two women permits
Beaumont and Fletcher to insist upon the extraordinariness of the two
women in their proper identities. Both are prodigies, but in their true
persons: Arathusa's faithfulness belies the custom of the court, and
Euphrasia is a wonder in her chaste devotion to Philaster, the man she
cannot have. The comic denouement, saving the play from tragedy,
foregrounds the arbitrariness of Beaumont and Fletcher's brand of tragicomedy. The artifice of the disclosure of Bellario's true sex reminds
an audience of the fragility of the play's resolution.

For Dion, Euphrasia's return is cause for grief, rather than joy. The
exposure and shame that the princess has avoided, as Megra's charges
are disproved, rebounds against him. "Now I doe know thee," he
admits;

　　　oh that thou hadst dyed
And I had never seene thee, nor my shame:
How shall I owne thee, shall this tongue of mine
Ere call thee Daughter more?

(V.v.114–17)

The king's disgrace and Arathusa's shame are displaced. In this play,
full (like *Measure for Measure* and *The Maid's Tragedy*) of substitutions and replacements, Euphrasia shoulders the burden. "Would I
had died indeed, I wish it too," she assures her father,

And so must have done by vow, ere publishd
What I have told, but that there was no meanes
To hide it longer: yet I joy in this,
The Princesse is all cleere.

(118–22)

Breaking her vow and publishing her shame (and her father's shame) sets Euphrasia up on the stage before the public eye, ironically fulfilling the king's order "Sirs, strip that boy" (81). Her disclosure deflects the public gaze from Arathusa and Philaster and from Megra's disturbing attacks. "Can shame remaine perpetually in me / And not in others? or have Princes salves / To cure ill names that meaner people want?" Megra asks (30–32). The salve the play offers, Bellario's revelation, reinforces the difference between the princess and Megra, but does so at the cost of Euphrasia's vows "by all the most religious things a Maid / Could call together, never to be knowne" (179–80).

The pathos that attends Euphrasia's plea to be allowed to "serve the Princess, / To see the vertues of her Lord and her" (189–90) is engendered by her sacrifice of her secret, her love for Philaster, and its theatrical manifestation, her boy's costume. In the wonder that attends her exposure, an audience is permitted to forget Philaster's outrages in the forest, his scandalous jealousy, and his violent attacks upon women (or sleeping boys). The clearing of the princess's reputation (falsely impugned) clears his as well. The play's drive, from the first, has been to reveal Philaster as a true prince, to show his priority over the king and over Pharamond as ruler of Cicilie. What its ending shows, however, is less Philaster's desert than the prodigious fidelity and chastity of the women who love him.

The Countrey Fellow may observe Philaster's shameful conduct in the forest, but the fate of exposure before the mob is reserved for Pharamond. Philaster's vindication necessitates the humiliation of his rival. The "pretty Prince of Puppets" is swept up and exposed before the rabble as a coward: "O spare me Gentlemen," he whimpers (V.iv.26, 49). "The man begins to feare and know himselfe," observes the captain (50). Pharamond's exposure is also (like Bellario's) a kind of stripping: "Shalls geld him Captaine?" cries a citizen (62). "Ile have his little gut to string a Kit with, for certainely a royall Gut will sound like silver," adds a fourth as the citizens claim parts of Pharamond's body (71–72). Here the question of difference between royal and common men is reduced to the level of crude jest. Pharamond's "Bugs-words" are contrasted to the "nimble tongs" of the people as they proclaim Philaster and verbally dissect the Spanish prince (28). Pharamond's humiliation is complete when Philaster appears before the crowd, as "free as *Phoebus*" (94) and stills them; "Looke you friends," Philaster announces, "how gently he leads, upon my word / Hee's tame enough" (130–31).

Gelded by the people's voice, Pharamond becomes docile. Proclaimed by the populace, Philaster takes his proper place, "I am my selfe, / Free as my thoughts are," he proclaims (97–98), and later emphasizes, "I am what I was borne to be, your Prince" (107).

The dynamic in this scene is in no way democratic. Rather, what is displayed mimics the relationship of masque and antimasque in a court entertainment. Pharamond is an impostor, a disruptive presence driven by passion, a blowhard Boreas. Philaster's stilling of the crowd is a stilling of the stormy sea by the royal authority of the masque proper. The play's concluding lines, spoken by the king as he blesses the marriage of Philaster and Arathusa, stress the allegorical dimension: "Let Princes learne / By this to rule the passions of their blood, / For what Heaven wils can never be withstood" (V.v.216–18). Like that of *The Maid's Tragedy,* the final moment of *Philaster* proposes a masquelike lesson for the prince to learn. Lysippus's reduction of *The Maid's Tragedy* into an "example to me" is disturbingly paradoxical; in *Philaster* the final lines force us to recall that Philaster's ability to rule his passions has only been demonstrated metaphorically in his calming of the rebellious crowd. His most explicit comparison of himself to Eolus locking up his "windy brood" (IV.v.43) immediately preceded his attempt to murder Arathusa.

The play's treatment of the public further complicates matters. For while the mob's exposure of Pharamond is satisfying and just, the specter of scandalous and unjust exposure revives after that scene as Megra continues to press her charges. Only the wholly arbitrary exposure of Bellario as Euphrasia can still the tongue of scandal in the final scene. If we persist in seeing the popular voice as a voice of truth in the play, then we must give some credit to the Countrey Fellow's charge that Philaster is a craven. The play is royalist in that Philaster becomes what he is born to be without demonstrating any particular fitness for the job: the people love him simply because he is their prince by blood. The grandiose claims of absolute power in the play are voiced by a usurper king and a pretender prince; Philaster's appearance before the crowd like a Phoebus is the real thing. But the artificiality and imposture and theatrical deceit that define the play's whole world permit us to question such simple formulations, just as the apparently simple couplet at the end reminds us of major issues elided by the comic resolution. "Encouraging our detachment" Lee Bliss argues, "suits Beaumont and Fletcher's dramatic method throughout:

this play asks us to participate in its self-conscious, sophisticated, double view of itself."⁴³ A double view would necessarily result from seeing the play twice, and it was performed twice before the court audience. As a revival, and as a play that was repeated before the same audience, *Philaster* would assume an audience to whom Bellario's secret was known.

Like *Philaster, A King and No King,* the third of the Beaumont and Fletcher plays presented during the Christmas season 1612–13, requires for its success as a tragicomedy a bit of theatrical sleight-of-hand, as Arbaces is demonstrated to be no king by birth. Thus his incestuous passion for Panthaea is not incestuous, and he is free to marry her and become a kind of prince consort. The scene in which Arbaces is told the truth by Gobrius and Arane again alludes freely to the language of court masque. "Forbeare these starts," Gobrius urges as Arbaces keeps interrupting the narrative,

> Or I will leave you wedded to despaire,
> As you are now: if you can find a temper,
> My breath shall be a pleasant westerne wind,
> That cooles, and blastes not.
>
> (V.iv.194–98)

The conflict of Boreas and Zephyrus, of winds that blast and that blast not, can be found in this play as well as in Jonson's *Masque of Beautie* and the marriage masque in *The Maid's Tragedy.* The blustering Arbaces introduces himself, like Pharamond in *Philaster,* with a loud string of self-commendations, undercut by the remarks of Tigranes and Mardonius, as he boasts and brags about his victory. Proposing limits to his breath strikes him as undermining his royalty: "While you confine my words," he rages in the first scene, "by Heaven and Earth, / I were much better bee a King of Beasts / Then such a people" (I.i. 230–32). But as Gobrius and Arane begin to reveal his origins, he proclaims himself calm:

> Ile lie, and listen here as reverentlie
> As to an Angell: If I breathe too loude,
> Tell me; for I would be as still as night.
>
> (V.iv.199–201)

But Arbaces, despite listening quietly to the story, must break forth and commend his own exemplary behavior as an audience:

Doe I not heare it well; nay I will make
No noise at all; but pray you to the point,
Quicke as you can.

(220–22)

Like Philaster identifying himself with an Eolus controlling the winds,
Arbaces restrains his royal voice—with which he has dominated the
play and which constitutes a major part of his self-presentation as a
monarch—and pays attention.

The disclosure he receives from Gobrius and Arane is, like the discovery of Bellario, one that calls attention to its own theatricality and
artificiality. The queen, Gobrius tells Arbaces, "fain'd herself with
child" out of the fear that she and the old king would not produce an
heir. This royal performance led to good results:

She fain'd now to grow bigger, and perceiv'd
This hope of issue made her feard, and brought
A farre more large respect from everie man.
And saw her power increase, and was resolv'd,
Since she believ'd she could not have't indeede;
At least she would be thought to have a child.

(214–19)

Delivering his own child to the queen, Gobrius participated in the imposture, staging a funeral in his own house, "and had an emptie coffin
put in earth" (231). The successful substitution foundered when the
queen, much to her surprise, found herself

Truly with child indeed of the faire Princesse
Panthaea: Then shee would have torne her heire,
And did alone to me, yet durst not speake
In publike; for shee knew she should be found
A Traytor, and her talke would have beene thought
Madnesse, or any thing rather then truth.

(240–45)

The pun on *hair* and *heir* stresses the murderous dimension of the
queen's device. Her attempts upon Arbaces' life make sense, for she
must destroy the artificial heir that she herself fabricated. In the
queen's dilemma we again find a character caught in the space between
slander and truth, like Arathusa and Bellario, and incapable of speaking out, like Amintor.

Arane's cryptic remarks in the first scene of act 2 function as clues to an audience unaware of the secret. "Thou know'st the reason why," she says to Gobrius, "Dissembling as thou art, and wilt not speake" (II.i.13–14); "You talke to me as having got a time / Fit for your purpose; but you know I know / You speake not what you thinke" (26–28). Their urgent quarrel takes place before an uncomprehending audience made up of Panthaea, Bacturius, and waiting women. "Nay, should you publish it / Before the world," Gobrius asks, "thinke you 'twill be believ'd?"

> ARANE: I know it would not.
> GOBRIUS: Nay, should I joine with you,
> Should we not both be torne? And yet both die
> Uncredited?
> ARANE: I thinke we should.
>
> (45–49)

This whispered interchange raises questions of truth and slander that relate closely to the language and actions of the play's other plots. Bessus has won his status as a hero through cowardice, and Arbaces boastfully proclaims his modesty.

The play evokes the instability of a world in which a king can be no king by insistent use of a language of paradox. "We inhabit a world of embodied oxymoron," as Michael Neill puts it, paraphrasing Guarini, "for which tragicomedy is the perfect mirror."[44] The tragic alternatives—the tearing of the heir, the tearing of Arane and Gobrius should they speak—are subsumed in the conventional tragic figure of incestuous tyrant that Arbaces finds himself playing. His entrance in act 5, scene 4 *"with his Sword drawne"* marks his determination to enact the tragic villain:

> It is resolv'd, I bore it whilst I could,
> I can no more, Hell open all thy gates,
> And I will thorough them . . .
> . . . .
>   I must beginne
> With murder of my friend, and so goe on
> To an incestuous ravishing, and end

My life and sinnes with a forbidden blow
Upon myself.

(V.iv.1-3, 6-10)

"What Tragedie is nere?" Mardonius asks as he interrupts these dark proceedings (11). But Arbaces' arrogation to himself of the role of monster forces the comic denouement. "There is the King," says Gobrius upon seeing the same desperate spectacle that so disturbed Mardonius, "Now it is ripe" (64-65). Tragedy and comedy, like truth and slander, are fluid terms in this drama. The love of Arbaces for Panthaea, which Arbaces and Mardonius see as horrible, becomes for Gobrius the means by which he can be freed to speak the truth.

The tragicomic climax of *A King and No King,* in which tragic resolve and comic ripeness fuse in one moment, brings to the forefront a metatheatrical question of authorship. Throughout the play, Arbaces has functioned as a playwright, engineering a tragedy. But this script of despair and bottomless crime, his tragedy, is proved to be a delusion. Rather, Arbaces is an unconscious actor in the scheme of Gobrius's comic wisdom; his love for Panthaea, which he thought monstrous, is proved wholesome. Like the king of Cicilie, who thinks his breath to be thunder, or the king of Rhodes, who contrives a masque and is entrapped in its violent energies, Arbaces, the king who is no king, is deluded. But where they are deluded by baseless fictions, he has been a victim of Gobrius's superior skill in manipulation. The royal power to pronounce upon truth and slander, so central to *Measure for Measure,* is here diverted to an underling. A comic manipulator, a contriver of the masque, Gobrius rescues the erring monarch.

Arbaces' desire to plunge into tragic doom is an aspect of a heroic role that he is unfit to play. His joy at discovering his true identity is at least part relief for not having to sustain a role in which he has been miscast. Paradoxically, he becomes a generous hero when he is no longer king. Releasing Tigranes to the Armenian ambassador, he slips easily into the Marlovian style, but this time the boasts are kind:

He shall have Chariots easier then ayre
That I will have invented; and nere think
He shall pay any ransome; and thy selfe
That art the Messenger shall ride before him

On a Horse cut out of an entire Diamond,
That shall be made to goe with golden wheeles,
I know not how yet.

(V.iv.314–20)

"They belied this King with us / And sayd he was unkind," marvels Ligones (321–22). There is a playfulness in Arbaces' wild fancies now that they are comic (and now that he is freed from the royal delusion that he has the power to bring them about). Arbaces' attempts to sound like a Tamburlaine early in the play are comic in that they are undercut by plain speakers like Tigranes and Mardonius. Here, he exuberantly explores the language of artifice for the fun of it: "wele have the kingdome / Sold utterly, and put into a toy, / Which she shall weare about her carelesly / Some where or other," he promises Ligones (323–26). Fantasies of control are entertained as pure fantasies.

The impostures that define the world of *A King and No King* and accord mock-heroic and mock-tragic status to Arbaces are marked as benign. This is less clear in *Philaster,* where Euphrasia/Bellario's vows are sacrificed to the happiness of the princess and Philaster. The consequences of imposture in *The Maid's Tragedy* are wholly tragic. Beaumont and Fletcher repeatedly identify the worlds they dramatize with artifice and illusion. *The Maid's Tragedy* is structured upon the repetition through the kingdom of the impostures of the royal masque. *Philaster* hinges upon a discovery of disguise. The reliance upon a structure of allusion to heroic, Marlovian language in *A King and No King* likewise characterizes the world of that play as alive with metatheatrical confusion. Royal misprision figures the kings' entrapment within the fictions of their worlds. Arbaces concludes his play with what seems to be a call for a masque to celebrate his marriage to Panthaea: "Come every one / That takes delight in goodness, helpe to sing / Loude thankes for me, that I am prov'd no King" (351–53). "Loude thankes": the phrase reminds us of Arbaces' verbal extravagance throughout the play, now transformed, in his speeches of the chariot, the horse, and the toy, into pure decoration.

IV

The three Beaumont and Fletcher plays presented at court in 1612–13 share a skepticism about masque and an ironic self-consciousness about theatrical conventions and genres. The "light-hearted icono-clasm" that Michael Neill detects in *A King and No King* is to a degree common to all the plays, despite *The Maid's Tragedy*'s adherence to the rules of its tragic genre. The audience that saw the plays in antici-pation of the royal wedding was a young audience, and it did not include King James. The royal family was represented by Prince Charles, Princess Elizabeth, and Frederick, her fiancé. These plays might have been selected, then, as plays more likely to appeal to a younger audience. J. F. Danby's notorious identification of Beaumont and Fletcher as "second-generation exploiters of a theatre now no longer, possibly, open to the sky" is tempting. "Brilliantly opportunis-tic," they reflected "the habits of mind of an actual section of histori-cal society," Danby argues. "Beaumont and Fletcher's work indicates the collapse of a culture, an adult scheme is being broken up, and replaced by adolescent intensities."[45]

This particular gathering of young people, however, might have felt, in a way more specific than that imagined by Danby, that their world was dangerously incoherent—might, indeed, have questioned order and authority with something like the frenzy of Beaumont and Fletcher's lost protagonists. The festivities of that Christmas season took place under the shadow of Prince Henry's death in November. The court was not officially in mourning, but the circumstances fused delight and dole to a high degree, and thrift did dictate that the fune-ral baked meats were served at the wedding tables. The uncertainties, paradoxes, "brilliant and gruesome moral puns"[46] of the Beaumont and Fletcher plays suited this occasion's discordant temper. "Pardon thou holy god / Of marriage bed," Amintor exclaims, "and frowne not, I am for'st / In answere of such noble teares as those, / To weep upon my wedding day" (I.i.128–31). In a moment such as this, a play conceived without such an occasion in mind nonetheless takes on particular poignancy before an audience whose situation it seems to reflect.

Prince Charles, at least, was rumored to hold powerful feelings about the death of his brother, possibly to share in gossip about the cause of his death. A report from Girolamo Lando, the Venetian ambas-sador, referring to a performance he attended in January 1620, makes it clear that these feelings could find expression in the court theater:

> The comedians of the prince, in the presence of the king his father, played a drama the other day in which a king with his two sons has one of them put to death, simply upon suspicion that he wished to deprive him of his crown, and the other son actually did deprive him of it afterwards. This moved the king in an extraordinary manner, both inwardly and outwardly. In this country however the comedians have absolute liberty to say whatever they wish against any one soever, so the only demonstration against them will be the words spoken by the king.[47]

Although we do not know what play this was, and in what circumstances it appeared, or what words of anger the king spoke in response to it, the simple fact that the Venetian ambassador would assume that Charles could sponsor a performance that would allude to rumors that James had had Henry murdered is in itself striking. There is no record of Charles's or Elizabeth's inward and outward responses to the Beaumont and Fletcher plays they attended during the Christmas season of 1612–13. But the tormented paradoxes of the plays' treatment of marriage and inheritance must not have been lost on them.

The important point is that these plays were not generated to meet the paradoxes of this occasion. Rather, the occasion arose to meet the plays' skeptical vision of an unstable and incoherent world. Discussion of Beaumont and Fletcher's plays, with their witty paradoxes, moral puns, and ethical conundrums, has long evoked the cynical and relatively more exclusive audience at the Blackfriars, many of whom were involved in legal studies at the Inns of Court. Such an audience does seem to have existed, and the pleasure it took in the plays would be different from the pleasure taken in the plays by the audience at court. But, as William C. Woodson has recently argued, *A King and No King* had also enjoyed considerable success at the Globe. For Woodson, the play's appeal to "the vast majority of Londoners" is to be found in its adoption of a Puritan theology, a strategy that allowed the playwrights to have their cake and eat it too: "By incorporating a twofold treatment of lax casuistry, *A King and No King* was at once a successful exploitation of and a fey triumph over an alien sentimental audience."[48] It does not require such elaborate theological arguments, however (and in many ways the play cannot support them) to make the point that different audiences will see the same plays in different ways. A Blackfriars audience's delight in argument, a Globe audience's sentimentality, are conjectural reconstructions that the plays permit but that can be confirmed only by circular arguments.

The picture of the status of drama in the Jacobean court that emerges from our discussion of *Measure for Measure* and the Beaumont and Fletcher plays is likewise suggestive. What links these plays is a vision of a governing royal intelligence that dominates dramatic action. Duke Vincentio and the Beaumont and Fletcher kings are presented as playwrights, contrivers, actors, and misprizing audiences—more often than not, all at once. Images of display and slander mark these theatrical activities as shameful and degrading. Behind the image of the king as masterful puppeteer lurk the disturbing images of the king as spy and the king as puppet himself. "But however much James prided himself on spying into the secret recesses of his subjects' souls, the theater of apprehension staged in *Measure for Measure* was both unavailable to him and not fully within his own powers of containment or control," Steven Mullaney has argued. Paradoxes of authorship and authority reach beyond the plays themselves into the relationship between the monarch and the theater he sponsored and (nominally) governed. Determining slander from truth is the office of the censor, but this was difficult when, to quote Richard Burt, "licensing under the early Stuarts was more a means of allowing entertainment than a means of censoring it."[49] *Measure for Measure* evokes the tensions between public playhouse and court theater, and the Beaumont and Fletcher plays allude satirically to the language of court masque: the metatheatrical dimension of these entertainments points directly to failures of royal control. Outright slander might not please, but cynical dissections of court life as a debased kind of theater, with the king at its center, apparently could be tolerated.

"There tied rules / Of flatterie," Strato says of court masques. Such events, at least, should be firmly under royal control. For in a masque the royal audience is not a rival performance; it is the focus of the whole performance. Sounding very much like Strato, the world-weary courtier, Sir Francis Bacon discusses his experience of staging masques for King James. "These Things are but Toyes," he begins the essay *Of Masques and Triumphes,* "to come amongst such Serious Observations." Since the essay is preceded by *Of Ambition* and followed by *Of Nature in Man,* Bacon's self-conscious placement suggests that masques have much to do with ambition and with human nature. "But yet, since Princes will have such Things," he proceeds, "it is better, they should be Graced with Elegancy, then Daubed with Cost." Bacon's essay discusses such matters as the "Colours, that shew best by Candlelight" and the appropriate way to release perfumes: "Some *Sweet Odours,* suddenly comming forth, without any drops falling, are, in such a Company, as there is Steame and Heate, Things of great Pleasure; and Refreshment."[50] Bacon clearly writes from experience. One masque for which he served as "contriver" was the *Masque of the Inner Temple and Grays Inn,* written by Francis Beaumont and presented February 20, 1613, before the king and queen and the newly married Princess Elizabeth and her husband. When the royal party arrived for the occasion, however, they found that the room was too crowded. As John Chamberlain reported the incident, the king was tired and Bacon was seriously embarrassed:

> But the worst of all was that the King was so wearied and sleepy with sitting up almost two whole nights before that he had no edge to it. Whereupon Sir Fra. Bacon adventured to entreat his Majesty that by this disgrace he would not, as it were, bury them quick. And I hear the King should answer that then they must bury him quick, for he could last no longer; but withal gave them very good words and appointed them to come again on Saturday. But the grace of their masque is quite gone when their apparel hath been already showed and their devices vented, so that how it will fall out God knows, for they are much discouraged and out of countenance, and the world says it comes to pass after the old proverb: the properer men, the worse luck.[51]

"But all is Nothing," Bacon ruefully concludes his essay, "except the Roome be kept Cleare, and Neate."[52] Like the entertainments sponsored by Churchyard before Elizabeth, the court masque, too, could collapse into fiasco.

For Bacon, as "chief contriver" (Chamberlain's words), and for Chamberlain, smooth operation of the masque is of paramount importance, as is the surprise of the "apparel" and the "devices." There is little concern on the part of either for the substance, or what Ben Jonson called the "soul" of the masque, its writing. This they assume to be as conventional as the rest of the exercise. Overcrowded rooms and the steam and heat of company contributed to the audience's sense of disjunction between the splendor they were viewing and the discomfort in which they were viewing it. The miraculous transformations of masque took place before courtiers and ambassadors who spent most of their time eagerly watching each other and watching the king, rather than watching the show.

Horatio Busino's report of his visit to the court on Twelfth Night 1617–18 is richly detailed in its descriptions of the clothes worn by other members of the audience. "We were so crowded and ill at ease," Busino admits, "that had it not been for our curiosity we must certainly have given in or expired." On this occasion, the dancers drooped:

> being well nigh tired they began to lag; whereupon the king, who is by nature choleric, got impatient and shouted aloud, "Why don't they dance? What did they make me come here for? Devil take you all, dance!" Upon this the Marquis of Buckingham, his Majesty's favourite, immediately sprang forward, cutting a score of lofty and very minute capers, with so much grace and agility that he not only appeased the ire of his angry lord, but rendered himself the admiration and delight of everybody.

Here it is Buckingham, not the splendid spectacle, who earns the "admiration and delight of everybody," a crowd that, including the king, has been fatigued by the whole tedious business. At the end of the masque the courtiers rushed upon the food set out for their entertainment. "At this first assault they upset the table," wrote Busino, "and the crash of glass platters reminded me precisely of a severe hailstorm at Midsummer smashing the window glass."[53]

John Harington's famous report of the drunken collapse of a masque of the Queen of Sheba presented to King James and his brother-in-law, Christian of Denmark, again focuses upon the lack of discipline in the performance. Harington forces the reader's attention to the disparity between the allegory and the reality as Charity joins "Hope and Faith, who were both sick and spewing in the lower hall." His purpose is to contrast the debasement of this occasion to the dignity of similar occasions under Queen Elizabeth, to shame the present with a recollection of the past. "I have much marvalled at these strange pageantries, and they do bring to my remembrance what passed of this sort in our Queens days: of which I was sometime an humble presenter and assistant," Harington continues wistfully: "but I neer did see such a lack of good order, discretion, and sobriety, as I have now done." Harington's dismay at the lack of good order extends beyond court masque to the ladies' practice of wearing masks: "The great ladies do go well-masked, and indeed it be the only show of their modesty, to conceal their countenance; but, alack, they meet with such countenance to uphold their strange doings, that I marvel not at ought that happens."[54] The disordered realm Harington portrays suffers by contrast to his vision of the good order under Queen Elizabeth, but in his disillusionment with masque and in his disgust with disguise and dissembling at court, Harington does not seem so distant from the young protagonists of Beaumont and Fletcher.

Harington's nostalgia for Elizabeth is a nostalgia for the ideal of royal audience and royal performance we have found in *A Midsummer Night's Dream*. There, the monarch graciously pieces out the imperfections of performances that are gifts of love. In Harington's narrative, the Queen of Sheba tripped on the steps and spilled "wine, cream, jelly, beverage, cakes, and other good matters" into the Danish king's lap; "his Majesty then got up and woud dance with the Queen of Sheba; but he fell down and humbled himself before her, and was carried to an inner chamber and laid on a bed of state." By contrast, Churchyard's account of events at Norwich and the mechanicals' play in *A Midsummer Night's Dream* do seem to offer an orderly idyll. Offense, caused only by incompetence, is forgiven. Noble condescension is a far cry from drunken collapse.

Shakespeare's awareness of the professionalism of his own company subjects the ideal of royal performance to some question in *A Midsummer Night's Dream;* in *Measure for Measure* a new dynamic of royal audience and performance comes into view. The later play's interest in slander, its linkage of public theater with shameful and invasive exposure and display, its manipulative and spying duke, all suggest tense similarities between theater and court life. Unpredictable, paranoid, deluding and self-deluded, the monarchs of the Beaumont and Fletcher plays extend the paradigm of their misrule out to the Jacobean court, through the plays' reference to court masque. As they do so, they also enact something very much akin to Michael Goldman's version of the actor's "terrific" freedom, challenging everything that their audience should hold sacred. Discords between an ideal of royal performance and actual conditions could be smoothed over by a Duke Theseus or by Churchyard's Elizabeth. But the Jacobean dramatists, like Harington or Busino, insist upon the discords, forcing the recognition that the transformations of masque are tied to rules of flattery and constrained to technical limits (such as the "Steame and Heate" of a crowded room). The satiric representation of the masque in *The Maid's Tragedy* and the obtrusive artificiality of *Philaster* and *A King and No King* put the court's shame on display. The image of a royal audience that sees and comprehends the mysteries of the masque, celebrated by Jonson's image, in the *Masque of Blackness,* of a British sun radiating a "light scientiall," finds a counterpart in these plays. The manipulative intelligencer, the self-flattering contriver of masques, the misprizing audience, the bombastic impostor: these, too, are necessary parts in the Jacobean role of the monarch in the theater.

3

The King in Love

The Union of the King's Two Bodies in the Court of Charles I

~

I

T he assassination of the Duke of Buckingham, in 1628, was a key event in the life of Charles I. In the *History of the Rebellion,* written some forty years after the event, the Earl of Clarendon described Charles's reception of the news. The king was at prayer. Sir John Epsly "came into the room, with a troubled countenance and without any pause in respect to the exercise they were performing went directly to the King and whispered in his ear what had fallen out. His majesty continued unmoved, and without the least change in his countenance, till prayers were ended," whereupon he retired to a private chamber and collapsed in tears. Clarendon's tale makes this moment an epitome of Charles's admirable self-discipline: the contrast between Epsly's "troubled countenance" and Charles's "unmoved" countenance is pointed by Clarendon's characteristic parallel structure. "Yet the manner of his receiving the news in public when it was first brought to him in the presence of so many (who knew or saw nothing of the passion he expressed upon his retreat) made many men to believe that the accident was not very ungrateful," Clarendon continues.[1] This misinterpretation of blameless royal conduct, even at the moment of insupportable private grief, is central to Clarendon's characterization of Charles. The disjunction between private and public man in the person of the king is epitomized here as performance. The king's skill in dissembling in public his private despair is so persuasive that he is thought to be secretly gratified with Buckingham's death. Clarendon, of course, is looking back with historical hindsight. He recognizes here an anticipation of the larger misunderstandings that will lead to the calamity of regicide.

At the time, the shock of the assassination worked in another, more grateful, direction. It "left Charles free to love another," as John Miller puts it, "and removed the main obstacle to his loving his wife," pretty, eighteen-year-old Henrietta Maria. In 1630 there followed the birth of a son, Charles, and for the next twelve years, "this model couple presided over a model court."[2] The masques of the period of Charles's personal rule, 1631–40, glorified their mutual passion. In addition to promulgating an ideal of neoplatonic love, as Stephen Orgel and others have argued, the masques also interpreted the political problems of the realm in these same terms.[3] The king and queen's perfect love resolves all disputes just as the scenes and machines of Inigo Jones's staging could transform riot into dance and storm into tranquillity. The very bedroom of Jupiter, in Thomas Carew's *Coelum Britannicum,* was engraved with the inscription CARLOMARIA. In the masques, the king's two bodies are united through marriage.

Both Clarendon's account of Charles's grief and Orgel's characterization of the new glorification of married love in the court masques as "Platonic politics" are anachronistic, for both operate in the knowledge of Charles's execution in 1649. Clarendon can write his story as a kind of prologue to tragedy. Even as Charles comes into his own, released from under the thumb of the great favorite, he comes to be misunderstood. His ability to play the royal role will, ironically, never be fully appreciated until the moment of his death. Orgel, too, succumbs to the temptation to indulge in flights of historical irony. "If we can really see the king as the tamer of nature, the queen as the goddess of flowers, there will be no problems about Puritans or Ireland or Ship Money," he puts it. The court's infatuation with theater marks a pathology of displacement and avoidance. "After a decade of ideals, a disenfranchised Parliament at last declared its authority by virtue of the realities of its power, and the absolute rule of the Stuart monarchy was revealed as a royal charade, a theatrical illusion," he concludes.[4] Or-

gel's portrayal of Charles, desperately fending off his inevitable exposure in a courtly theater of flattering illusion, like Clarendon's characterization of Charles as a misunderstood player preparing for a tragic
role, reveals in both a deep mistrust of the Caroline court's participatory and proprietary interest in the theater.

Charles and Henrietta Maria participated in the court theater as
actors and dancers; Charles suggested plots for plays, censored offending passages, rewrote passages he deemed offensive. King and queen
celebrated their mutual love in the masques they presented to each
other, and appeared together, finally, in *Salmacida Spolia,* the last
masque of the reign. It has become traditional for historians of English
drama and of Charles's reign to portray this court's interest in theater
as excessive and as a foreign import, brought in by Henrietta Maria.
She brought with her from France an enthusiasm for theater, certainly,
but the British royal family were already lively sponsors of theatrical
activity. Charles's mother, Queen Anne, had enjoyed dancing in the
masques and had even shown her legs. Dudley Carleton, who noticed
them ("we might see a woman had both feet and legs, which I never
knew before," he wrote), also commented on the queen's heavy stage
makeup in *The Masque of Blackness.* The Spanish ambassador, he
reported, danced with the queen "and forgot not to kiss her Hand,
though there was Danger it would have left a Mark on his Lips."[5]
While King James participated in masques mostly as an observer,
Charles, both as Duke of York and as Prince of Wales, was far more
active, dancing with the coaching and support of Buckingham. His
older brother, the activist and militaristic Prince Henry, made his first
appearance as Prince of Wales in the magnificent *Barriers* written for
him by Jonson. Charles's new level of participation merely continued
the trend.

The degree of involvement was highest in the case of the court
masques. The serious purpose of the masque was to display to the
court and to the nation the union of the king's two bodies. In the age
of James, this union was effected by the creation of an image of the
king as a Solomonic ruler, a "light scientiall," an intelligence beyond
normal understanding. In the Caroline masque, the new image was
derived from the king's happy marriage. The royal couple appeared in
apotheosis as one. This difference is one not simply of style but of substance. James could be united with his realm on a level of abstraction,
but the concreteness of the royal couple's manifestation in Caroline

masque impresses upon the spectator's eye a stubborn vision of doubleness. Transforming the queen in the language of the masque into a representative of the populace was one strategy adopted by the authors of masque. Another was a reliance upon images of doubleness made one drawn from nature: vines entwining trees, oceans blending into skies in distant horizons. For one recent historian, such imagery helped to transform Charles's kingdom into a "cloud-cuckoo-land" of aristocratic fantasy.[6] Others, preeminently Kevin Sharpe, have disagreed with such dismissals, offering instead the possibility that Caroline writers, in their dramas, poetry, and masques, practiced the time-honored humanistic endeavor (most frequently associated with Jonson) of instructing their prince by means of a carefully balanced poetics of criticism and compliment.[7]

The plays of the period engage the problem of doubleness raised by the royal marriage, and employ in doing so the images used in the masques. The purpose, as Sharpe has suggested, can range from the satirical, as in Davenant's *The Platonic Lovers,* to an aspiration on the part of the drama to achieve the theophanic glories of masque, as in Cartwright's *The Royal Slave.* A preoccupation with the idea of the union of the king's two bodies through marriage leads the plays to focus upon marriages, happy and unhappy. Love was the subject of the royal masques, and the idea of the king in love became an image extending beyond the commissioned court masques into the dramas that the royal audiences attended.

The king and queen's mutual devotion and open celebration of that devotion was a determining factor in the dramaturgy of professional as well as amateur playwrights. Therefore this chapter examines both of these aspects of Caroline drama, professional and amateur. Sir William Davenant's plays (rather than his far more familiar court masques) serve as a point of departure, beginning with *The Platonic Lovers* (1635), an apparent satire of court fashion written for the professional stage, and moving on to *The Unfortunate Lovers* (which the queen saw at the Blackfriars in 1638) and *The Fair Favourite* (1638). Despite his complicity in the Platonic politics of masque, Davenant in these plays subjects the self-absorption and self-idealization of couples in love to complex scrutiny. Kevin Sharpe has argued that Davenant here discloses a "politics of love," in which marriage comes to represent an ideal fusion of monarch and kingdom. This is certainly true, but in the process, Sharpe denigrates the extent to which Davenant is interested in the psychological dynamics of love and marriage. The three plays show Davenant to be reworking, with a concern for women's interests and feelings promoted by the queen's special status in the court, situations and even specific scenes from the plays of Beaumont and Fletcher. *The Platonic Lovers* and *The Unfortunate Lovers* allude, the first as comedy and the second as tragedy, to *The Maid's Tragedy,* and *The Fair Favourite* models its tragicomic dilemmas upon *A King and No King.*

Davenant attempts to engage in these plays the feminist ethics of French *préciosité,* closely associated with Henrietta Maria.[8] It should be no surprise that his attitudes are ambivalent; and the uncertainties of genre and tone that result, as the new fashion for feminism encounters the old models that Davenant works from, are characteristic of Davenant's dramas. Such uncertainties are in fact characteristic of the drama of the period in general. The amateur dramatists whom we will examine later in this chapter, William Cartwright and Sir John Suckling, also followed the lead of Davenant's patron, the queen, and scrutinized with a new feminist bent the conduct of monarchs in love.

The preoccupation in the drama with love as a force that can unite or divide a king's two bodies necessitates, as we shall see, one kind of double perspective on the part of audiences, which must perceive union where they also see two bodies before them. A further effect of double vision is created when we recall the extent to which the Caroline repertoire was composed of and dependent upon the plays of the earlier generation. Davenant's plays are specifically allusive to Beaumont and Fletcher. But even plays written without such direct references could find themselves juxtaposed to old, standard members of the repertoire. Cartwright's *The Royal Slave* did not immediately demand comparison with *A King and No King* (despite the similarity of their oxymoronic titles) when it was first performed at Oxford. In the records of Sir Henry Herbert, royal master of the revels, however, we find that the performance of this play at Hampton Court on January 12, 1637, was immediately preceded by a performance of *A King and No King* on January 10.[9] A play that might seem to be about the education of a prince when staged by university students must have been seen differently when staged by professionals who had just appeared in Beaumont and Fletcher's play. Cartwright's fear, expressed in the epilogue for the performance at Hampton Court, that the new venue and new performers might change his play is not merely conventional. "For though the Peece be now mark'd his, and knowne," he worries, "Yet the Repeaters make that Peece their owne" (9–10).[10] Most playwrights would share Cartwright's mistrust of actors; as an amateur, he expresses it more nakedly than most.

Suckling takes amateur playwriting in the other direction. Where Cartwright worried that his play might change in the actors' hands, Suckling paid the actors for his *Aglaura* out of his own pocket, furnished their costumes, and when the play came to be revived on a later occasion, he rewrote it as a tragicomedy rather than a tragedy. The royal audience to the tragicomic version on April 3, 1638, would have seen Chapman's *Bussy d'Ambois* the week before, on March 27. In this instance, however, *Aglaura* demands comparison not with Chapman's play, but with its own prior appearance at court as a tragedy. The playwright assumes that its audience has seen both. *The Maid's Tragedy*, too, serves as a subtext for *Aglaura*. The play breathes, as Harbage complained, "a Fletcherian atmosphere," and it expects its audience, steeped in the plays of Beaumont and Fletcher, to recognize and to appreciate complex allusions to its predecessors.[11]

The abuse of male power, the failure to govern unruly passions, the insane jealousies that cripple the lustful kings of Beaumont and Fletcher's dramas are subjected, in the plays of Davenant, Cartwright, and Suckling, to a critique that identifies good government with decorum, modesty, and gentleness. In the idea of personal rule, the Caroline playwrights found potential for drama that could examine the tension between the public and private man in the person of a king. In a court which featured frequent revivals of older plays, like those of Beaumont and Fletcher, as well as repetitions of successful new plays, like *The Fair Favourite*, *The Royal Slave*, or *Aglaura*, the playwrights found an audience that could be expected to recall previous treatments of the same issues. Just as a king's private and public motives might be at odds with each other, so a play could utterly change under different conditions of performance, as Cartwright recognized. The royal audience, in its expertise as performers, could thus judge plays in terms of their craftsmanship as well as their politics. This chapter concentrates on the way the royal couple (and especially the queen) could reshape, as audience members, the plays they saw.

II

"This Love sets the Wits of the Town on work," James Howell wrote of the fashionable *préciosité* of Charles's court in the 1630s; "and they say there will be a Mask shortly of it, whereof Her Majesty, and her Maids of Honour, will be a part."[12] The masque was Davenant's *The Temple of Love* (1635), featuring the descent of Chaste Love from a flying machine to celebrate the union of Charles with his queen at the end of the dancing. Nonetheless, the masque itself is not without some wry commentary on "strange doctrines, and new sects of love." *The Platonic Lovers* was performed at the Blackfriars by the King's Men late in 1635 and printed in 1636 with a dedication to Henry Jermyn, the queen's favorite, appealing to his judgment against the "severe rulers of the stage." That the play did not succeed on the public stage may be due to its mockery of "a subject cherished by the queen," as some have suggested,[13] but the masque itself twitted the fashion. The genre of masque permitted Davenant to engulf his critical comments in the scenic splendor of the close. The generic rules that govern *The Platonic Lovers* require, on the other hand, the perils to happiness and the sudden, wonderful deliverance associated with Beaumont and Fletcher's variety of tragicomedy.

The complications in Beaumont and Fletcher plays derive from the dominant figure of the lustful king. In *The Maid's Tragedy,* the king's lust perverts his whole kingdom, but in the tragicomedies, such as *Philaster* and *A King and No King,* the problem of royal lust and self-control is no less present. Philaster's wild jealousy is tamed metaphorically, as we see him quell the crowd, and by the revelation of Bellario's disguise; Pharamond embodies and carries away into exile the purely negative aspects of the lustful prince. In *A King and No King* the lustful tyrant seems destined to hurl the play into tragedy until his true origins are disclosed. Yet the ability of either Philaster or Arbaces to control his passions is never demonstrated: in the tragicomedies, the issue of lust is finessed. We are not encouraged to speculate on the happiness of the marriages that will follow.

The influence of *préciosité* can be seen in Davenant's encouragement, in *The Platonic Lovers,* of precisely this sort of speculation about relationships between men and women. For Beaumont and Fletcher, once a marriage has been made possible, tragedy converts to comedy and the beastly appetites that have been aroused by obstacles to marriage are likewise converted into conjugal joys. The emphasis on women as adjudicators of love disputes in the literature of *préciosité* and its glorification of female celibacy challenge Beaumont and Fletcher's easy assumption of male dominance and their complacent application of the rules of genre.[14] Both of the women in *The Platonic Lovers* wonder why the exchange of vows should legitimize male lust. Inflamed with passion by a powerful drug, Theander hastens into marriage with Eurithea. "I thought / The holy priest had a mysterious power / To make these troubles cease," Eurithea says as her new husband still appears to be agitated on their wedding night (IV, p. 82). "The sweetness of thy soul / Is sour'd," she cries, as he presses the demand that they share a bed. "Know all / Our married vows (which certainly were first / Ordained for holy use) I merely took, / As formal helps to my pernicious lust," Theander confesses in despair (p. 84).

Davenant replays the wedding night scene from *The Maid's Tragedy* here with special differences.[15] Where there the innocent Amintor was appalled as he discovered the king's lust and Evadne's corruption at the bottom of his marriage, finding mockery where he expected virgin modesty, here both young lovers are horrified by the power of physical desire. Eurithea cannot understand Theander's change, but then neither can he: he is as frightened of his passion as she is. Even the procedures of platonic love have been reversed: "I dare not," he answers to her plea to stay,

> for thine eyes augment my smart,
> Each small neglected beam they shed
> I gather up in flames, and quite pervert
> Their virtuous influence to a lustful fire.

(p. 85)

"Thou lost remainder of the noblest prince / The active war or wiser courts e'er knew," Eurithea pronounces Theander in Ophelian farewell. Theander at the end of the fourth act has been ruined by lust.

And in the fifth act, manipulated by the villainous Fredeline, he will fall victim to jealous rage, as he is lured to witness the departure of Castraganio "*in a night Gown unready*" (V, p. 86, s.d.) from Eurithea's chamber. He leaps to the conclusion that Fredeline, staging the encounter, intends: "My wife! / That title's new, and will grow horrid now! / Her chamber was their sphere of revelling: / They came from thence" (p. 87). This instance of royal misprision marks a decline from the beginning of the play, where Theander and Eurithea have been portrayed as less troubled in their wooing than Phylomont and Ariola, the more conventional lovers.

One index of their difference is Theander's free access to Eurithea's chamber, another their friendly greeting on their first appearance together. *"Eurithea runs cheerfully to embrace Theander. Ariola seems to retreat a little at Phylomont's salute,"* reads the stage direction as the ladies enter (I, p. 16), and Castraganio comments on the contrast. "The first are lovers of a pure / Coelestial kind, such as some style Platonical," Fredeline explains,

> A new court epithet scarce understood;
> But all they woo, sir, is the spirit, face,
> And heart: therefore their conversation is
> More safe to fame. The other still affect
> For natural ends.

> (p. 17)

There is an apparent contradiction here, leading an audience to wonder at the "natural" pair, for the unaffected lovers are linked to the strange new court fashion. Castraganio is likewise surprised: "As how, I pray?" Fredeline obliges by defining the "natural ends" of love:

> Why such a way as libertines call lust,
> But peaceful politicks and cold divines
> Name matrimony, Sir; therefore although
> Their wise intent be good and lawful, yet
> Since it infers much game and pleasure i'th'event,
> In subtle bashfulness she would not seem
> To entertain with too much forwardness,
> What she perhaps doth willingly expect.

The platonic affectation, the new court fashion, seems simple and refreshing in contrast to the "subtle bashfulness" that Ariola must put on. The natural lovers conceal their affection, where the platonic lovers are able to keep each other's company without fear or shame. Theander can visit Eurithea at all hours, even, in the second act, drawing the canopy in her bedchamber to reveal her *"sleeping on a couch, a veil on, with her lute"* (II, p. 33, s.d.).

Fredeline's cynical account of the difference between platonic and natural love, however, takes on a further dimension in light of the play's prologue. The courtier's speech directly echoes the mocking tone with which the prologue introduced the play. The prologue, spoken by a veteran member of the company, presumably John Lowin, teases the play's dependence upon the new court fashion. The author, according to the prologue, is attempting to boost his play by capitalizing on the vogue for platonic love:

> Ours now believes the Title needs must cause,
> From the indulgent Court, a kind applause,
> Since there he learnt it first, and had command
> T'interpret what he scarce doth understand.
>
> (p. 6)

Fredeline calls platonic love a "new court epithet scarce understood"; both the character and the prologue echo the poet's claim that ideal love defies ordinary comprehension. The prologue's putative author is counting upon the "indulgent Court" to help him out, despite his failure to make sense of the new fashion, and because, he further claims, he "had command" to write about platonic love without understanding it once before, in *The Temple of Love*.[16] The prologue is not convinced that the success of the masque will make the play a success, for the title is "so hard / 'Bove half our city audience would be lost, / That knew not how to spell it on the post." The court fashion is too arcane for the theatrical public, and, perhaps, meaningless outside the court itself: "some critics lately spent / Their learning to find out, it nothing meant."

The court poet who bluffed his way through a masque devoted to platonic love cannot expect the same response in the public theater, so in the prologue Davenant creates a persona who counts upon recognition of the fashion from his audience without expecting any understanding. Even more cynically, the prologue suggests to the audience that platonic love is "that which nought or little signifies"—a purely empty fashion. The poet cowers backstage, the prologue continues, expecting "scorns and censures." His reliance upon such "shifts," does not impress John Lowin, "your servant, who have labour'd here / In Buskins and in Socks this thirty year." The professionals of the stage can see through the playwright's tricks, while apparently the devoted apostles of platonic love in the court cannot. The prologue announces that Davenant's attempt to link the two worlds of court and professional theater is doomed from the start. Neither court poet nor theater audience understands platonic love, and Lowin, in his persona as theater professional, sees no value in importing court fashions into his territory.

Fredeline's echo of the prologue as he introduces the motif of platonic love in the play is therefore multidimensional. The first appearance of the new fashion shows it to be pleasantly different from ordinary courtship. Fredeline, the play's villain, is baffled by the mutual trust of the platonic lovers. Fredeline strikes the same cynical pose of man of the world struck by the prologue's actor, who has seen thirty years of fashions come and go and playwrights struggle to exploit them. Fredeline is also a theatrical entrepreneur. His Machiavellian schemes are designed to alter the behavior of the platonic lovers, as he slips Buonateste's drug to Theander. His lust awakened, Theander can no longer visit Eurithea's chamber untroubled. As audience witnessing Castraganio's departure from the chamber, he succumbs to Fredeline's Iago-like promptings.

Through Fredeline's intrigue and Buonateste's drug, the play comes to focus upon the difficulty of determining what kinds of behavior in love are natural. Buonateste's drug functions as a natural force, bringing to the surface appetitive drives that we know must be part of love, yet it also functions as an artificial, arbitrary device. A similar confusion arises out of the use of the love-juice in *A Midsummer Night's Dream:* it appears to be both a natural substance, distilled from flowers, and also artificial, in its ability to rearrange the lovers according to Oberon's fairy plan.

Like *A Midsummer Night's Dream,* too, *The Platonic Lovers* contains a subplot that extends the play's range out from the two ducal couples to a lower social scale, by introducing the soldier Gridonell, son to the old courtier Sciolto, who has been raised in army camps and who has never seen a woman. (Davenant would use this motif again in his adaptation, with John Dryden, of Shakespeare's *Tempest, The Enchanted Island*). Gridonell, too, is exposed to Buonateste's drug, and in him it inspires a random and insatiable lust. "O, Arnoldo," he assures a friend when the drug's effect has passed, "thou may'st be glad thy sister / Was dead: I had so maul'd her else" (V, p. 97). Gridonell's desire for any woman alive contrasts with Theander's desire for Eurithea, but both are provoked by Buonateste's drug and Fredeline's help.

Buonateste's motives are, as his name implies, wise and good; but it is part of the play's strategy that he appear to be a conventional comic figure, a kind of *commedia dell'arte* doctor who claims personal knowledge of Plato's amorous habits. "I beseech you not to wrong / My good old friend Plato," he begs Sciolto, "with this Court calumny;

> They father on him a fantastic love
> He never knew, poor gentleman. Upon
> My knowledge, sir, about two thousand years
> Ago, in the high street yonder,
> At Athens, just by the corner as you pass
> To Diana's conduit—a haberdasher's house,
> It was, I think,—he kept a wench!

> (II, p. 38)

Comedy traditionally brings down high-flown idealism by reminding it of the imperatives of the flesh, and in this joke Buonateste fulfills that function. But his role in this play is double. Seeming to be Fredeline's dupe and accomplice in the main plot and to be a foolish doctor in the subplot, he becomes the agent of Fredeline's exposure at the end, with the aid of a second drug.

The wit of Davenant's prologue is analogous to the wit of the play's larger design. Both operate on the premise that platonic love is a fashion that cannot be understood. Both insist—the prologue through the actor's contempt of the poet's attempt to capitalize on court fashion and the play through Buonateste's administration not only of drugs but of good counsel to the lovers—that its mysteries are inaccessible to ordinary people. This includes the author of *The Temple of Love*. The symmetrically paired lovers and the echoing low-comic subplot add to the play's witty game.

One important effect of the matching plots is that the attractive innocence of the platonic lovers reduces Phylomont's insistence upon a traditional marriage to the level of Gridonell. "Your sister I would marry, sir," he tells Theander, "and then / As lord and princes use, that love their wives: / Lye with her." "You are too masculine!" exclaims the revolted Theander (III, p. 48). When Gridonell refuses to attend Theander's wedding, his father demands "Speak! What's the cause you dare not go?" "Sir," he answers, "I should ravish the bride" (IV, p. 75). In the early stages of her courtship by Phylomont, Ariola recognizes the danger of his passion: "Alas, we must / Be married, Sir, which may perhaps enforce / Your inclination to a dangerous hope." "Where is thy safety then, Ariola?" Phylomont responds,

> This is the dismal silent time when ravishers
> Reach forth their trembling hands to draw
> The curtains where unpractis'd virgins sleep;
> False Tarquin's hour, when he did hide his torch
> From Lucrece eyes, and would not suffer her
> Wak'd beauty to eclipse that sickly flame,
> Till she had quenched a greater in his blood.
> How would thy courage faint, if I should make
> Thee subject to my eager youth and strength?
>
> (II, p. 31)

Marriage, his speech suggests, furnishes the opportunity to rape.

This scene is immediately followed by the matching scene in which Theander, in all innocence, "*draws a canopy*" and gazes at the sleeping Eurithea (p. 33, s.d.). Even under the influence of the lust-inducing drug, Theander refrains from threats of rape and flees Eurithea's company. Phylomont, who appears to be a spokesman of common sense and custom, as against the idealism and novelty of platonic love, also appears, disturbingly, to anticipate the behavior of Gridonell and Theander when they have taken the drug. Where Theander fears his lusts and recoils from them, Phylomont relishes imagining the triumph of his "eager youth and strength." When the natural lover cannot keep from imagining himself a Tarquin, the restraint of the platonic lover appears more attractive. *The Platonic Lovers* scrutinizes the fashionable insistence on female celibacy from perspectives that are both skeptical and sympathetic.

With similar complexity, the play alludes not just to court platonism in general, but to a specific instance of court theatrical activity. In 1633, Queen Henrietta Maria appeared on the court stage with her ladies-in-waiting in a production of *The Shepherd's Paradise* by Walter Montague. Joseph Taylor, the successor to Richard Burbage as first actor in the King's Men, went to court "every day to teach them the action."[17] This appearance by the queen as a shepherdess led, probably coincidentally, to the trial and punishment of William Prynne for his reference to "Women actors, notorious Whores" in the index to

Histriomastix. Davenant reminds his audience of this famous episode
of court pastoral in *The Platonic Lovers,* when Theander, dressed
"like a noble shepherd" and Eurithea *"like a shepherdess"* meet in a
shady glade. The pastoral scene in the play works comically, however,
for Theander is beginning to feel the effects of Buonateste's drug. As
he beckons Eurithea to sit beside him, we recognize the drug's corruption of his language:

> Here sit, where nature made the sharper scented briar,
> And luscious jes'mine meet to qualify
> And reconcile their diff'ring smells within
> The honey woodbine's weak and slender arms.
> Sit nearer! we are too remote.
>
> (III, p. 58)

What cost Prynne his ears apparently costs Davenant nothing: where
Prynne probably could not have anticipated Montague's pastoral
while compiling his index, Davenant seems deliberately to poke fun at
the very idea of a chaste pastoral interlude.

In so doing, he addresses his satire not just to the language of a silly
court fashion but to the language of pastoral by which the court of
Charles defined its relation to the kingdom as a whole. This appears
not only in court masques, but also most explicitly in Thomas
Carew's "Answer to Aurelian Townshend," a poem that responds to
Townshend's request that Carew write an elegy for the death of Gustav Adolph of Sweden and defends Charles's refusal to join with the
Protestant armies in the Thirty Years' War. The first years of the personal rule, Carew insists (and some modern historians would tend to
agree) were marked by peace and prosperity:

> Then let the Germans fear if *Caesar* shall,
> Or the United Princes, rise and fall,
> But let us, that in myrtle bowers sit
> Under secure shades, use the benefit
> Of peace and plenty, which the blessed hand
> Of our good King gives this obdurate Land,
> Let us of Revels sing, and let thy breath,
> (Which filled Fame's trumpet with *Gustavus'* death,
> Blowing his name to heaven), gently inspire

Thy Pastoral Pipe, till all our swains admire
Thy song and subject, whilst thou dost comprise
The beauties of the SHEPHERD'S PARADISE.[18]

Pastoralism becomes in Carew's poem a matter of public policy; the king's refusal to involve himself in European wars offers "secure shades" for poetic shepherds. The reference to Montague's play makes clear the implication that the poet's duty is to participate in the entertainments of the court. The pastoral scene in *The Platonic Lovers,* though, is full of foreboding: at the outset, Theander suggests that "we a while / Grow pensive in this gloomy shade" (III, p. 58). He imagines scenarios of defeat and captivity, and as the drug takes hold *"rises and starts"* (p. 60, s.d.) with "sudden terror" (p. 61). Davenant's play does not share Carew's complacency about the pastoral any more than it shares his own masque's triumphant platonism.

For apotheosis and transformation, the play substitutes a conventional comic ending. Buonateste has converted Ariola to Phylomont's view of marriage: "Well, sir," she quips, "y'had best to take me whilst / My new religion is i'th'fit. He has / A mighty reason, and a fluent tongue" (V, p. 103). Theander agrees to "hear this brisk philosopher one hour" but also thinks back fondly on the mutual platonism under which he and Eurithea "rul'd each other with nice fears" (p. 104). The play's epilogue, addressing separately the men and the ladies in the audience, conveys "scarce one courteous word" from the author to the men and offers "obsequious homage" to the ladies (p. 105). The world of comedy must be peopled, and *The Platonic Lovers* achieves this end, as the two couples are appropriately taken to the altar. The doctrine that will "recreate the mind, and not the blood" is antipathetic to that comic drive. Yet it is an ideal that is presented throughout the play as more admirable than the conventional attitude, and indeed less inhibited and treacherous, although admittedly fragile. Theander's struggles against his appetites are more attractive than Phylomont's blunt insistence on his rights. While not endorsing platonic love, the play suggests that a platonic lover might be more sensitive to a woman's rights and fears than a "natural" one.

Theander's court is distinguished from Phylomont's by its futile cultivation of "nice fears." Charles I attempted to distinguish his court from his father's by an insistence upon order and decorum. His program of reform extended to the manners of his courtiers, and he espe-

cially sought to curb their sexual license. The masques offered a platonic model that showed the king and queen to be an embodiment of
a perfect marriage, both chaste and fruitful. "An incidental difficulty
of the Platonic sexless vision which Charles and Henrietta Maria
came to prefer in their masques was that the royal couple nevertheless
had to be praised for prolifically producing heirs to the English
throne," Suzanne Gossett writes. The masques resolve the difficulty
through magical transformations; for *The Platonic Lovers,* such magic
is impossible. In the court itself, practical difficulties accompanied
enforcing the desired decorums. "The day [Charles] published new
rules regulating access to the court," John Miller points out, "two of
his body servants quarrelled and spat in each other's faces; a sermon
extolling virginity prompted the comment that it was not appropriate
to the court." John Selden, looking upon the court with the jaundiced
eye of an older generation, saw not reform but decline: "In Queen
Elizabeth's time, Gravity and State were kept up. In King James's time
things were pretty well. But in King Charles's time there has been
nothing but Trenchmore and the Cushion-Dance, omnium-gatherum,
tolly-polly, hoite come toite."[19] By portraying Theander's court as a
court of comic inversion, and his rule as a type of misrule, Davenant's
play points to the need for a higher standard in love relationships but
also comically points to its impossibility. The symmetrical pairings
that constitute the structure of the play are symptomatic of an attitude
that is not so much ambiguous as it is double. But in the professional
theater, the rules of comedy prevail.

It is possible to read the play in a way that makes Davenant's wit
appear less disloyal to his royal sponsor (in 1635 the queen "did graciously take him into her family," making him a member of the household.[20]) The disappointment of Theander and Eurithea as they fail to
sustain their platonic relationship and the rough wooing of Phylomont may be due to their social standing: the young protagonists of
the play are, after all, only dukes and their sisters. The platonic love
of a king and queen, on the other hand, is of a different order, and
requires its own special genre, the court masque. This play, then, has
to be a failure in the professional theater, because the only audience
that could appreciate this nice distinction and validate the ideals of
higher love through their mere presence, the king and queen, are not
known to have seen it.

The primary conceit of *The Platonic Lovers* in fact requires the queen's absence, so that an audience can entertain the possibility that the playwright has somehow betrayed her trust, making the whole endeavor slightly risky. The dedication to Jermyn, about whose familiarity with the queen rumors had begun to spring up, implies a degree of inside knowledge of court affairs that just borders on the scandalous. For Kevin Sharpe, the irony of the dedication is central to Davenant's meaning, for "Jermyn had recently seduced and impregnated one of the queen's maids." For this misconduct he had been dismissed from the court, but by the time the play had been printed, Jermyn was restored to the queen's favor. Like the play, the dedication can be read as satirical, or as a testimony to the platonic affection of the queen for her favorite: her love, like that of the queen in *The Fair Favourite,* is above jealousy. "Eurithea is plainly the Queen," J. B. Fletcher speculated of *The Platonic Lovers* in 1903; "Can D'Avenant be intending an apology?"[21] Such thoughts about the dedication and about Jermyn's connection to the play can occur only to the reader, however, or to an audience that could have seen the play after its publication. But the insistence in the play that what appears to uninitiated eyes to be dubious intimacy is platonic propriety encourages rather than stifles cynical speculation. The queen's absence from *The Platonic Lovers* is a presence in both the audience's and the reader's mind.

Davenant had far better luck, a few years later, with *The Unfortunate Lovers.* In 1638 the play was performed three times for royal audiences: the queen visited the Blackfriars and saw it on April 23; on May 31 *The Unfortunate Lovers* was staged at the Cockpit in the court, and it was again performed for the queen on September 30, this time at Hampton Court. The visit to the Blackfriars is one of four by the queen, and the players were paid for their performance of *The Unfortunate Lovers* the regular fee for a court appearance. According to G. E. Bentley, these payments indicate that the queen did not attend regular afternoon performances, but that the playhouse was probably taken over for an evening performance before an invited court audience. Such visits to professional theaters by members of the royal family, while previously unheard of in England, were not unusual in Henrietta Maria's native France. In February 1609, for example, the Dauphin attended three performances at the Hôtel de Bourgogne.[22]

For a special occasion of this sort, the Blackfriars theater would be artificially illuminated. *The Unfortunate Lovers* is structured around a series of powerful scenes that would show to advantage under candlelight, and its scenic richness reflects Davenant's collaboration on court masques for the past four years with Inigo Jones.[23] Like *The Maid's Tragedy,* however, *The Unfortunate Lovers* uses these spectacular scenes as critiques of masque aesthetics. Viewers in the play repeatedly misunderstand the spectacles set before them, spectacles engineered and presented by their enemies. Through the whole play runs a motif of marriage procession and marriage masque perverted, interrupted, and misprized.

The visual center of the first act is a procession that, like the wedding masque in *The Maid's Tragedy,* conceals a cruel miscarriage of justice and itself represents the opposite of its own apparent meaning. The situation again involves the return of a soldier to a corrupt court. While the general Altophil has been away, holding the enemy king Heildebrand at bay, the prince's crafty favorite, Galeotto, has suborned witnesses to swear that Altophil's chaste mistress is a prostitute. When Altophil learns the news, he rages and threatens to raise his troops against the city. Barely restrained by his loyal captains, he must then endure the sight of Arthiopa's humiliation: "*Enter a* CARTHUSIAN, ARTHIOPA, *who is held by him, clothed in white, a taper in her hand, people and boys following her*" (I, p. 24, s.d.). "What means this sad and bashful spectacle, / My friends?" Altophil wonders, approaching the Carthusian monk, "Pray, Sir, instruct me in this lady's name! / And what's the cause her penance is expos'd / Thus to the public view?" (p. 24). Because of his vows of silence, the monk cannot answer, and Altophil's recognition of Arthiopa is drawn out to greater length. At the end of the scene he persuades himself to transform the spectacle of humiliation into a marriage procession:

> My fair white mourner, rise!
> You with your priestly office lead the way,
> 'Tis to the church, she shall obey the law.
> Hold high the taper, and move boldly on!
> Know, injur'd Hymen, 'tis thy torch, and this
> My wedding day.
>
> (p. 28)

The act concludes with shouts of joy from within; but the conversion of disgrace to triumph is forestalled, as we learn in the second act that Prince Ascoli, himself inflamed with love for Arthiopa, has forbidden the banns.

Galeotto's revenge, in the third act, takes the form of a mock wedding between Altophil and Arthiopa, as this motif continues to dominate the play. "Rich hangings of the antick Persian loom," Altophil marvels as he and Arthiopa enter what they think is to be their wedding chamber,

> Venetian tapers gilt, and bedding
> Of Italian Nuns' embroidery, purl'd and imboss'd.
> Galeotto shows his bounty great to deck
> Our bridal chamber with such foreign pomp;
> But where's the priest, that with his holy words
> Should make us fit to enter here?
>
> (III, p. 54)

He shortly learns that Galeotto has promised Arthiopa and the bed to Heildebrand, his enemy. The ornate bed, with its lush hangings, looks back to the king's bed of death in *The Maid's Tragedy* even as it represents, in its Caroline context, a grotesque inversion of Carew's bed of Jupiter bedecked with CARLOMARIA. As in *The Maid's Tragedy,* the specter of royal lust mars the comfortable shows of the wedding night, but with a perverse difference. "How divers are the changes of his tyranny," Altophil wonders of the witty Galeotto, "Erewhile he flattered us with pleasant shows / Of comfortable hope, then suddenly / Presents us with more horrid forms than death" (p. 55).

"Know, thou art hither come, to lay thy white / Attractive hand upon my sceptre," Heildebrand coarsely woos (IV, p. 63), but Arthiopa turns this language back against him:

> If you
> Subvert the furious danger of your will,
> Be still a King; and may your sceptre grow
> Within your hand, as heaven had given it
> A root; may it bud forth, increase in boughs,
> Till't spread to the Platan tree, and yield
> A comfortable shade, where other kings
> May sit delighted and secure from all
> The storms of war and tyranny.
>
> (p. 65)

The language of fruitful platonism subdues Heildebrand; and the image is a conventional one in Davenant's masques. "Corn fields and pleasant trees," for example, provide a backdrop to the descent of the "good Genius of Great Britain" in *Salmacida Spolia*.[24] As in Carew's poem, sitting in the shade in a pastoral setting epitomizes the peace and plenty of Charles's personal rule. Such a pastoral vision tempts Heildebrand, briefly, away from his vile designs.

The image of Arthiopa in disgrace from the first act is fulfilled in the fifth act with her entrance "*her hair hanging loose about her*" (V, p. 72, s.d.). Despite her effective marshaling of masque language in the fourth act, Heildebrand could not long sustain his "piety":

> In a short moment he was quite
> Declined from good, ev'n to the extacy of vice:
> For in the blackest and most guilty hour
> Of night, he came and found my curtains drawn;
> But so uncomely rude were his intents,
> That though I there had slept as in a shrine,—
> A place which death or holiness did privilege
> With reverend esteem,—yet he would force
> His way. You sacred powers! conceive how fit
> It is the rest should make me dumb.
>
> (p. 73)

The literary precedent for this is Tarquin's rape of Lucrece, and so Heildebrand recognizes it when, later on, he is lured by Rangone, now an ally of Altophil, to meet a willing Arthiopa. She "wonders why the Roman Lucrece did complain," Rangone explains, "because enforc'd, since boldly she / Concludes it now the only subtle way / To compass pleasure without sin." "Wise Aretine's philosophy," concurs Heildebrand, "he'd read / It to his niece" (p. 76).

Suitably, and with yet another direct echo of *The Maid's Tragedy*, Heildebrand's final scene is constructed as a kind of antimasque. "*Strange music is heard above*" as he waits, he thinks, for Arthiopa; a song, "*to a horrid Tune*" greets his ear. "This sure is some preparative," he murmurs, "although / The sound's not very amorous" (p. 78). His surprise is like that of the king who awakens to Evadne's pretty new device. Altophil appears and confronts him with a series of ghastly shows. Drawing the hangings, he displays the corpse of Galeotto, then drawing them "*further*" (p. 80, s.d.) he reveals the body of Amaranta. "I'll see no more," exclaims Heildebrand, but there remains the "living spectacle" of Arthiopa, "*her hair dishevelled as before.*"

Unmanned by his guilt, he can make only token resistance to Altophil's attack, and dies. Wounded "just here / About the heart" (p. 82), Altophil dies, too, and Arthiopa expires in his arms, as shouts of victory proclaim Ascoli's restoration to power.

The play's powerful sights heighten the turns of plot and insist upon its moral vision. In place of the wry awareness of the power of desire in *The Platonic Lovers,* Davenant supplies here a grim view of men circumscribed and driven by love's influence. Heildebrand, as the conventional lustful king, is the extreme case. But more troublesome is the way in which love transforms Prince Ascoli. He declares himself less a rival to Altophil than a fellow sufferer:

> How hardly then hath nature dealt with us:
> For we are prisoners all; all circumscrib'd
> And to our limits tied: the fortunate,
> And luckless, are alike; for thou art with
> As strict necessity unto thy happiness
> Confin'd as others to their evil fate.
>
> (II, p. 33)

The prince's fatalism is the tragic obverse to the comic sense of human limitation in *The Platonic Lovers,* and it leads him to kidnap Arthiopa and imprison Altophil with Amaranta. "In this, Sir, you perceive the intricate / Though pow'rful influence of love," observes Rangone as he enforces the separation,

>   that doth
> Pervert most righteous natures to attempt
> Unjust designs. His God-head's not full known
> And's miseries have been but dully taught
> To men: for I am charg'd to say this new
> Constraint is but a sad experiment
> To try if you to Amaranta can
> Pay equal love for hers, and nice Arthiopa
> Return unto the prince what's passions now
> May challenge as a debt?
>
> (p. 41)

Where the first act concluded in a procession toward marriage, the second ends in this "sad experiment" of divorce. Rangone's speech here has been singled out as "strong criticism" of the prince by Martin

Butler.[25] Rather, it conveys a resigned awareness of the love's ability to pervert even righteous natures.

Against the vision of the limitations of men in love, Davenant sets up a contrasting picture of women calumniated and misunderstood. Arthiopa, victim of her beauty, begins the play disgraced and humiliated and ends it violated. Amaranta generously sacrifices her love and helps Altophil, only to find disappointment and grief. When the men are incapable of resisting the temptation to plunge into rage and lust, the women who attempt to restrain them become their victims. The masque vision of peaceful groves is a pastoral dream in the play. Altophil, Arthiopa, and Ascoli entertain the dream as they discuss the vanity of ambition in the third act: "A rural residence, / Near woods and meads, though it be humble is / The place where we may love, and be secure" (III, p. 47). Where the pastoral dream is undercut in *The Platonic Lovers* by the drug in Theander's system, in the tragic world of *The Unfortunate Lovers* it is utter impossibility.

If the play can be said in any way to defer to Henrietta Maria's vision of her own special centrality in politics, it does so not by endorsing her policies, but, instead, by dramatizing her sense of being right and of being misunderstood. By 1638, Davenant had become poet laureate, and the queen had come under the influence of George Con, the papal agent. The victimization of the two women in the play, by the politicians they abhor and by the men they love, could easily speak to the queen's sense of righteous isolation. While the lurid plot, with its reminiscences of *The Maid's Tragedy,* offers little to please the *précieuse,* the play's presentation of only women as faithful and constant in love is some consolation. In *The Temple of Love,* "the queen was saluted as the leader of all men's true affection," giving her a sovereignty over them that was absolute in contrast to the king's. In the dances at the end of the masque, the male dancers were guided by the female dancers, and Chaste Love recommended the submission of masculine reason to feminine will.[26] Beauty's power in *The Unfortunate Lovers* is less comfortable; the way in which men, from Prince Ascoli to King Heildebrand, instantly find themselves overwhelmed by Arthiopa's beauty leads not to self-mastering sovereignty but to perversion of goodness (on Ascoli's part) and to rape (on Heildebrand's). The triumph of Arthiopa's virtue over Heildebrand is short-lived, for the world of tragedy is not the world of masque.

Where the kings of Beaumont and Fletcher's world disrupt their own courts, Ascoli is lost in his, deceived by Galeotto, pushed aside by the monstrous Heildebrand. Too trusting, too "gentle" (I, p. 16), too self-absorbed, the young prince is no match for his evil adviser or for the first onslaught of love. His tyrannies arise out of weakness. The play's "hostility to kings"[27] is confined to its representation of Heildebrand, and that is wholly conventional. Ascoli's passion is seen from the first as tragic. Yet the ease with which Ascoli trusts in Galeotto at the play's beginning causes some misgivings. Ascoli is no more a clear representative of Charles than is Arthiopa of Henrietta Maria. The play's acquiescence in Henrietta Maria's ethos of chaste love does not imply an acquiescence in Charles's emerging policies. Rather, the uncertain portrayal of Ascoli might reflect similar uncertainty about that royal audience member himself.

April 1638, the month when Henrietta Maria first saw *The Unfortunate Lovers* at the Blackfriars, was also the month that Charles decided to impose a new prayer book upon Scotland. This decisive confrontation developed over the year (Charles set off on his ill-fated expedition to Scotland in the spring of 1639). On November 20 and again on December 11, 1638, Davenant's *The Fair Favourite* was presented at the Cockpit in the court at Whitehall.[28] Full of surprises, a tragicomedy in the Fletcherian mode, *The Fair Favourite* is an elaborate reworking of *A King and No King*. It resolves its riddles by uniting the king's two bodies, divorced through a cruel imposture, through the wonder of married love.

Duped by a false funeral (like the court in *A King and No King*), the king in *The Fair Favourite* has married a neighboring princess, despite his true love for Eumena. As the play begins, he greets the queen coldly and reserves his warmest greetings for Eumena: actions that, as in *The Platonic Lovers*' scene of greeting, provoke comment. Thorello, "a travell'd gentleman," cannot understand the king's apparent fickleness, but Saladine explains:

> I soon shall vindicate the King, for, sir,
> These subtle managers of his affairs, before
> They treated with him for the Queen, surprized
> Eumena from his sight; proclaim'd her dead.
> And, more to cozen his belief, did celebrate
> Her funerals with much solemnity.
>
> (I, pp. 214–15)

In *A King and No King,* the king loves where he must not and does so because of a deceptive court intrigue in the past. The reversal here is that the king's love for Eumena is chaste and admirable. Not only that, but it is also platonic by definition, for he is able to visit Eumena at all hours without threatening her virtue. In this, as in Thorello's first response to the novel situation, he is misunderstood. Eumena herself complains about his visits:

> Why will
> You force your visits on me in the night's
> Suspicious hours? making your Kingly pow'r
> Shew tyrannous, where you would seem most kind,
> Discolouring the beauty of my fame
> Till she turn black, and all the strictly chaste
> Gaze on her now with pity, and with fear?
>
> (II, p. 230)

She is worried that the king might appear to be a lustful tyrant. Both lovers know that this is not the case, but ordinary watchers might interpret his night visits otherwise.

As in Beaumont and Fletcher's play, the plot turns on mistakes of perception. When Arbaces is revealed to be no king, the threat of incest is removed; the king in *The Fair Favourite* yearns for just such a deliverance. "Had you but any share / Of love for me," he complains to his courtiers, "you would un-King me strait / And teach me a sudden way to be no monster" (I, p. 211). "A monster, sir! We understand you not," exclaims Phylenio. "What am I else," replies the king,

> that still beneath
> Two bodies groan; the natural and the politic?
> By force compounded of most diff'rent things.
> How wearisome, and how unlucky is
> The essence of a King, gentle, yet by
> Constraint severe; just in our nature, yet
> We must dissemble; our very virtues are
> Taken from us, only t'augment our sway!

The monster that the king sees in himself is an actor. The doctrine of the king's two bodies forces him into a life of role-playing, in which he must dissemble the cruelty, injustice, and severity that his position demands of him. "In what's our pity, or our kindness more / Ex-

press'd, than when we father other's crimes?" he demands, "As if it
were a great prerogative / To make the guilty safe" (pp. 211–12). Yet
this complaint reveals him to confuse being an actor with being a
hypocrite. By persisting in his love of Eumena, by accepting the scandal that his visits arouse, by permitting himself to appear to be a lustful tyrant, the king serves his "gentle" nature to the detriment of his
body politic. Instead of wholly sacrificing his love to the public interest, he slights the queen.

The resolution the play pushes toward is an inversion of this theatricalized state of affairs: yet the inversion will itself prove "monstrous"
if the king is forced to foresake Eumena out of duty and constraint.
Therefore the king must fall in love with his queen, and Eumena must
be provided with a husband of her own. Davenant works to this end
by characterizing the queen as an embodiment of virtue. She does not
resent the king's fidelity to Eumena:

> If it were low, and sinful love, I should
> Not think it worth my envy or my fear;
> If pure and noble, as my strictest faith
> Believes, it is too great a treasure to
> Be made particular and own'd by me
> Alone, since what is good doth still encrease
> In merit of that name, by being most
> Communative.
>
> (IV, p. 264)

This is the platonism of *préciosité* at its most extreme, in its rejection
of the particular for the universal. "This doctrine, madam, will / Be
new, and much unwelcome to your sex," responds the king; "True
love admits no jealousy," she assures him (p. 265). With a sudden
announcement in the final act, the queen's "constant virtue" finally pre-
vails (V, p. 278). The change is nothing short of miraculous.

> Who is it, that will doubt
> The care of Heaven? Or think th'immortal
> Pow'rs are slow, because they take the
> Priviledge to chuse their own time when they
> Will send their blessings down?

exclaims the queen. The court is summoned to "Celebrate this miracle
of love," and the king discovers that Eumena, too, has found an acceptable love in Amadore, seemingly risen from the dead.

This king resembles Arbaces in *A King and No King* not simply in his miraculous deliverance from tyranny and tragedy. Like Arbaces, he also loudly voices his blamelessness and repines at the unnatural condition of monarchy. "Who is he so rash, that can / Desire to be a King," he protests to Eumena,

> since all the justice that
> We do is father'd on the makers of
> Our laws, and all their cruelty on us?
> Make much, you greedy Monarchs, of that
> Dignity, which with such toil in war
> You labor to attain: I'm weary of't!
> For, like the castle-bearing elephant,
> We groan beneath that load, which we support
> To guard and strengthen others, not ourselves.
> And what a useless glory 'tis, to be the chief
> Of men, wanting the charter to command
> A tender lady's love.
>
> (IV, p. 260)

"Strange remedies you bring unto / The sick!" Eumena chides, "You deaf'n those complaints, you / Came to hear, with louder of your own." In his vocal self-pity, this king threatens to become another Arbaces. In Beaumont and Fletcher's play, the crudeness of the king is explained when he is exposed as no king, but here the king must come to master his resentment by other means.

The imposture by which his marriage was engineered leads him to see kingship as hollow performance, empty prerogative, useless glory. "He was more a Statesman than / A Priest, and married provinces, not us," he remarks of his wedding day (I, p. 209), and he continues through the play to portray his reign as empty playacting. "Ay, but the people understand not this," he protests against the queen, when she intercedes on Oramont's behalf,

> For that dull crowd, whom Kings through cursed fate
> Must please, will have all laws observ'd, and
> They must stand, not 'cause th'are wise, but
> 'Cause th'are old.
>
> (IV, p. 262)

Enforcing the law is like acting before a public playhouse audience, whose dull, old-fashioned tastes reject innovation of any kind, and must be pleased with bad acting. His counselors, too, are bad actors. They

> Pretend great wisdom till y'attain to dignity
> And place, then strait supply't with empty
> Forms, austere and rigid looks; by which
> Your age—made dreadful, with that power
> High office brings—begets you an unjust
> Esteem.
>
>   (V, p. 268)

This king's struggle to express his natural, gentle self in a context of imposture and faction appears doomed to failure. He cannot integrate his two bodies; he cannot successfully play his royal role. Indeed, he sees himself as a rival in performance to his statesmen, who take credit for the "justice" of the law, while leaving him alone to shoulder the burden of its "cruelty."

It is the queen who resolves the riddle and transforms the king from self-obsessed monster into a "delighted" husband. Above jealousy, her love ignores narrow distinctions of station and person. "There is no harm in love," she says, freeing him to love Eumena,

>   your nicety
> Hath wrong'd us both. Peculiar and distinct
> Affections are but small derived parts
> Of what we call the universal love;
> And universal love, undoubtedly,
> Must be the best, since 'tis ascrib'd to heaven.
> Take, sir, the freedom you desire!
>
>   (IV, p. 255)

The queen's paradigmatic self-abasement in virtuous love is the direct opposite to the king's selfish demand that his two bodies conform to his private will. Her patience and constancy are finally rewarded by a miraculous change, paralleled in the plot by Amadore's quasi-miraculous return from the dead.

Butler reads into this play a hint "that Davenant was already moving towards an idea of the queen as a channel of communication between king and people, and supplying Charles's need for more moderate counsel, as early as 1638." In 1641, Davenant referred to Henrietta Maria as "the Peoples Advocate" in a letter to Parliament, and

Butler sees Eumena as performing this function in the play.[29] But the king's change is not engineered through Eumena's mediation between king and people; rather, the disintegration of his two bodies is only halted by the queen's constant and virtuous love. The "perfect will" by means of which "Monarchal sway would be beloved" (II, p. 232) is achieved not by negotiation but by miracle. The change happens off-stage and is prepared for only by the queen's unending prayers. The play may look, not forward to 1641, but back to the beginning of the personal rule, when the ideal of CARLOMARIA emerged out of what at first had been a marriage of neighboring provinces.

This play comes the closest of Davenant's plays to the transformative dynamic of court masque: it simply shows forth the king's new attitude. It applies with a certain literalness the platonic code enunciated by the queen, agreeing that love's objects are interchangeable because true love is universal. "The action of *The Fair Favourite,*" Erica Veevers argues, "thus confirms a moral principle of *honnête* writers, that good women save men from men's own worst impulses by somewhat passive, but correctly virtuous, behavior."[30] The king's "gentle nature" can now express itelf as gentle, rather than as selfish, because it is no longer at war with his body politic.

All three of these Davenant plays—a comedy, a tragedy, and a tragicomedy—place a celibate female constancy at the center of their different dramatic actions, to be comically tamed, to be tragically violated, to be tragicomically misunderstood and at length rewarded. By contrast, the male will in these plays always tends, through weakness, to lust and the risk of tyranny. The young dukes in *The Platonic Lovers* cannot rule themselves; Prince Ascoli in *The Unfortunate Lovers* is displaced by Heildebrand. When the king in *The Fair Favourite* comes to his senses, it is through no act of his own. In *L'Astrée,* the pastoral novel that so influenced Henrietta Maria's cult of love, true lovers must learn to submit themselves to their ladies' rule.[31] Like his masques, Davenant's dramas invite the ladies to lead the dance and the men to follow.

In order to become full dramatic experiences, in other words, Davenant's dramas require in their audiences an extraordinary sensitivity to the queen's presence. As we have seen in the case of *The Platonic Lovers,* this principle applies as well to plays she did not attend as to those she did. The plays she did attend draw energy from her presence, even as, like the comedy, they obey the rules of genre. The tragedy of *The Unfortunate Lovers* requires a platonic counterexample, an ideal marriage in which royal self-mastery beneath the spreading "Platan tree" bears chaste fruit and shelters neighboring kings. Less conspicuously than in a masque, but still readily available to the audience's eye, the royal couple viewing the play fill this necessary role. The tragicomic drive of *The Fair Favourite,* finally, seems fully to evoke the miraculous royal marriage itself: from excessive, self-destructive devotion to an unpopular favorite, the king comes to find true love with a devoted wife who has faithfully endured slander, isolation, and neglect. By 1638 this situation was part of the myth of Charles and Henrietta Maria's romance. With Charles preoccupied by disobedience in Scotland, the queen could find in the professional theater a replaying of her victory over Buckingham. The transformation of the haughty favorite into a chaste platonic lady heightens the poignancy of the drama. With the dimension of political infighting eliminated, the story of neighboring provinces awakening into love becomes one of constancy rewarded, a vindication of platonic truth.

The discords between the king's two bodies—which lead the king in *The Fair Favourite* to complain that he is a kind of "monster . . . by force compounded of most diff'rent things" (I, p. 211)—are resolved by a structural substitution that also glorifies platonic unity. The play splits the figure of the queen into two, the chaste Eumena and the wronged, and nameless, queen. The king's natural and his political love fuse through the ladies' mutual platonism. Manifest in the design of this play, the king's two bodies figure in Davenant's other dramas as well. In *The Unfortunate Lovers,* the monarchy splits between the gentle, misled Ascoli and the lustful Heildebrand: in both, the natural susceptibility to desire overcomes political responsibility. The exploration, through the ducal pairs in *The Platonic Lovers,* of natural and affected love leads to a recognition of union and division as love's mutually contradictory goals. Equally paradoxical is the politics of masque, with its glorification of platonic fruitfulness and its suggestion that the happiness of the king's natural body can be translated to his political body through the metaphor of marriage.

In an essay on the dramas of Philip Massinger and John Ford, Philip Edwards noticed a fashion for plays featuring royal pretenders in the 1630s. While none of the Davenant plays discussed here features a royal impostor like Ford's Perkin Warbeck, their interest in the notion of the king's two bodies permits us to see them, too, as engaging the major issues of Charles's reign in similar terms. Edwards characterizes the political situation as one "of national humiliation coupled with fear of the encroachment of a new kind of absolutism" in which "many of Charles's subjects looked on the occupant of the throne as the dried husk of a king." "Pretender plays" in this context became a phenomenon "exploring the meaning of the terms 'counterfeit' and 'natural' in the period of perturbed relationships between monarch and people about the year 1630."[32] Massinger and Ford are dramatists who looked at the court from the outside; neither enjoyed royal sponsorship and patronage. Massinger's patrons, the Herberts, were powerful courtiers who, as "renowned opposition leaders in the House of Lords, sponsored an opposition ideology in the arts," Albert H. Tricomi has argued.[33] By expressing the proper relationship of monarch and people in terms of idealized love and marriage, Davenant is not retreating into vapid fantasy but is using against the opposition drama a traditional vocabulary of great force. Counterfeit and natural love, true and false marriage, public and private selves are issues that animate both court and opposition drama. The desire for a mythic, legitimate king, a kind of Arthur "appearing from the mists," as Edwards puts it, "to bring succor to an ailing nation" is not, despite Edwards's clear bias, merely an opposition desire. Yearning for a true union of king and people is not in itself subversive.

Throughout Davenant's plays and masques, audiences are forced to question the public and private dimensions of the marriages that the characters make. Seeing the plays more than once, watching the royal audiences watch the plays, Davenant's audiences find themselves in the actual presence of the metaphor. The marriages in the plays — tragically violated or comically achieved — are animated with political ideas. The union of the king's two bodies in *The Fair Favourite* is effected, for the court audience, by Queen Henrietta Maria herself. Identifying the queen in the audience with the queen in the play is one part of the experience, and identifying her, too, with the suffering Eumena is another. An audience's sympathies with these two characters becomes focused into a sympathy with Henrietta Maria: her body in the audience unites the two bodies onstage.

III

No less than kings and queens, plays have more than one body: a play exists in the form of a text that fully comes to life in performance. Efforts to reconstruct the first night of *Measure for Measure* or Henrietta Maria's second viewing of *The Fair Favourite* must be only speculative. But for two of the most famous amateur plays of the Caroline period there exist printed texts that make direct reference to the conditions of performance. Because these printed versions refer indeed to different occasions of performance, the plays take shape as, in a sense, twins. William Cartwright's *The Royal Slave* was published in 1639 in Oxford; by that time it had been performed three times, in two different contexts. As a play presented by Oxford University to the king and queen on the occasion of their visit to Christ Church in 1636, under the personal sponsorship and supervision of Archbishop Laud, the play carries one kind of meaning. Its repeat performance at Oxford, three days later, offered an opportunity for town and gown to witness the spectacle that the court had witnessed before. But performed at Hampton Court by the King's Men at the special request of the queen, the play became part of a regular postholiday sequence of performances: following *A King and No King* with a repertory cast, the play changes shape and meaning, much as Cartwright had feared, worrying that "the Repeaters" would make his play "their owne" (p. 253, l. 10). Suckling's *Aglaura* takes the testing of generic limits that we have seen in Davenant to an extreme; its printed version has two endings, one tragic and one tragicomic. Both plays defer in their printed texts to the royal audiences that had graced their performances. Both plays demonstrate the extraordinary interest which Charles and Henrietta Maria took in dramatizations of the phenomenon of royal role-playing.

Davenant, as a professional playwright and as commissioned author of the court masques, never finally crosses the line that separates play from masque. Cartwright, in *The Royal Slave,* attempts to conflate tragicomedy and masque. The performance at Oxford is especially notable for the invitations to Inigo Jones and Henry Lawes to furnish the scenes and the music for the play. The visit of the king and queen, then, can be seen as both the "last of the great royal progresses" (p. 174) and a court masque transported to the university environment.

The local, amateur playwright defers to the monarch in the audience as "both th'Entertainer and the Guest" (Prologue to the King and Queen at Oxford, p. 195, l. 12). The play takes on some of the character of Churchyard's entertainments for Queen Elizabeth. But insofar as the court's architect and musician are imported to add their contributions to the amateur script, the professionalism of the play's scenes, machines, and songs rises far above Churchyard's clumsy efforts. Cartwright's awareness of the occasional nature of his play, unlike the professional playwright's awareness that a play must please more than just the courtly audience to survive commercially, pushes it further in the direction of both progress entertainment and masque. Like a progress entertainment, it does so in the terms that are commonly associated with the monarch: Churchyard couches his conflicts in terms of chastity's victory over lust, and Cartwright, no less sensitive to fashion, couches his in terms of platonic love's victory over jealousy.

Unlike Norfolk, however, Oxford asserts a particular superiority to the court's normal habitat. As an offering by the university to the visiting monarch, who is also the university's chancellor, the play addresses "the central importance of education for the business of government," as Sharpe contends.[34] Churchyard's Norfolk may put London to shame with the loyalty and affection its citizens spontaneously display to the queen, but Oxford is portrayed as performing its traditional educational mission. The role of Archbishop Laud in the whole entertainment of Charles and Henrietta Maria (several days and evenings of plays) was both to display the loyalty of the university, its desire to follow the king in his personal rule and in his religious reforms, and also to display the university's desire and fitness to lead the way in those reforms. Laud, as producer of the spectacle of which Cartwright's play is the capstone, offers to the king an example of a reformed drama (just as Madame de Maintenon would offer *Esther* to Louis XIV in 1689). *The Royal Slave* functions at Oxford as a model of what plays could be like when uncorrupted by the vulgar breath of players and crowds. University drama is free of dependence upon popular favor, and it is also free of the fear of being misunderstood. The enlightened monarch and the academic performers share a mutual sense of the university's mission of intellectual leadership.

On one level, this sense of the special status of the university's production comes through in the story of the queen's request for a performance at Hampton Court. The archbishop consented reluctantly to send the sets and costumes for this use. G. Blakemore Evans quotes Anthony à Wood's account:

> In November following, the Queen sent to the Chancellor that he would procure of Christ Church the Persian attire of the Royall Slave and the other apparel wherein it was acted, to the end that she might see her own Players act it over again, and whether they could do it as well as 'twas done by the University. Whereupon the Chancellor caused the Cloaths and Perspectives of the Stage to be sent to Hampton Court in a Waggon, for which the University received from her a letter of thanks. So that all of it being fitted for use (the author therof being present) 'twas acted soon after, but by all mens confession, the Players came short of the University Actors. At the same time the Chancellor desired of the King and Queen that neither the Play, or Cloaths, nor Stage, might come into the hands and use of the common Players abroad, which was graciously granted. (p. 180)

This proviso was sufficiently unusual to be noticed: Evans describes two letters, from Lord Pembroke, the lord chamberlain, and from the Earl of Dorset, "assuring the university that their 'commands' respecting the scenes and costumes will be most faithfully carried out." The queen herself, in her response to this request, is conciliatory and reassuring: "In the Meane time you may be confident that no Part of these things that are come to our hands shall be suffered to bee prostituted vpon any Mercenary Stage, but shall bee carefully Reserv'd for our owne Occasions and particular Entertainements att Court," she wrote to the University (pp. 180–81). What is interesting here is the queen's willingness to use a language as hostile to the "common Players" as that implied by the university's request. The queen shows a disdain for the "Mercenary Stage" that does not accord with her status as patroness of the company that should offer the play, as a regular visitor to the Blackfriars, and as an actress herself. Nor does Laud's fixing of conditions to the loan of the properties seem a fitting obedience to the royal request.

We glimpse here the hint of a struggle to define and control the play. The university's insistence upon retaining possession of the expensive costumes and scenes is understandable in economic terms, but the language of the exchange reshapes the usual antitheatrical language of the day into a particular reference to professional players. The queen, or whoever wrote the letter for the queen, assents to this denigration of her servants. She makes a distinction between those plays "prostituted vpon the Mercenary Stage" and those "carefully Reserv'd for our owne Occasions and particular Entertainements att Court." That is, she redefines *The Royal Slave* as a masque.

This redefinition was expensive. When the play was performed at court, the records show that a sum of 154 pounds was spent on "additions and alterations made in the scene, apparel, and properties" and that the players, in addition to their regular ten pounds for a court performance, received "Thirtye pounds more for their paynes in studying and acting the new Play sent from Oxford" (pp. 181–82). Borrowing the materials from Oxford led to the inconvenience of remodeling the Hampton Court stage and to the inconvenience of the actors as well. The university's desire to insist upon the special status of *The Royal Slave* seems to have been satisfied. Herbert refers to it in his records as the "Oxford play."[35]

"The Players came short of the University Actors," Wood reported. The rivalry between the university and the professional stage goes beyond the issue of ownership of sets and costumes: the university wanted its actors to be perceived as superior to the common players. At Oxford, the part of Cratander was played by "Master Busby, to whom Roscius should yield the palm in acting," again according to Wood (p. 176). Such remarks, coming from Wood, are of course partisan, but they reveal a desire to insist upon the play's special status and to distance it from the ordinary repertory. Common players simply lack the skills to enact drama that is in tune with the highest values and aspirations of the court.

"The Sentence was universally given by all the Spectators in favour of the *Gown*," Langbaine wrote many years later, "tho' nothing was wanting on Mr. *Cartwright's* side, to inform the Players as well as the Scholars, in what belong'd to the Action and Delivery of each part." Langbaine derives his account from Wood, and he develops Wood's hint ("the author thereof being present") into a scenario in which Cartwright functions as an interpreter, directing the "Players as well as the Scholars." This would augment the tension, of course, for the players would certainly resist an outsider's interference with their expertise in "Action and Delivery." The struggle for control over the play broadens, as the university seeks to possess it entirely, as the court attempts to transform it into masque, as Cartwright attempts to direct it, and as the players demand extra money for their "paynes." One final hint of conflict: the request originally came from the queen, who intended that the performance should be done by "her own Players." This refers to the queen's company, led by Christopher Beeston, but the court performance was undertaken by the King's Men, as part of their regular holiday season of performances. Bentley speculates that Beeston's company had broken up between the time of the queen's invitation and the Hampton Court performance.[36] Thus the King's Men found themselves confronted with a challenge that they had never sought. As the preeminent company of the day, with experience in the fashionable court drama (they performed Davenant's plays), they could hardly have been out of their depth in Cartwright's platonic play. Joseph Taylor, after all, had instructed the queen and her ladies for *The Shepherd's Paradise:* as leading actor of the company, he would play Cratander in *The Royal Slave* after, two nights before, acting Arbaces in *A King and No King.*

The selection of *A King and No King* for Tuesday, January 10, could have been random. Or it could equally easily be that the presentation of these two plays in sequence was deliberate, that the players or the master of revels, or whoever was in charge of the repertory for the season, recognized the symbiotic potential in the juxtaposition. The rivalry between university and professional players remarked upon by all the commentators on *The Royal Slave* could shape the selection. In contrast to the novelty, the "Oxford play," the King's Men offered one of their most dependable tragicomedies, a play that never failed to please. And it was a play on the same theme. The royal audience saw on Tuesday and on Thursday, in effect back to back, claimants to kingship challenging traditional definitions. With Taylor in both roles, Arbaces becomes Cratander: that is, the casting itself can become a turn of wit. The tyrannical bombast that marks the low birth of Arbaces contrasts with the modest platonic wisdom of Cratander, although both are slaves miscast in the role of king. The movement from the earlier play to the new play, then, marks an ethical progress. Cratander, made a king for three days before he must be executed, implements a series of reforms in the Persian court; Cartwright's play, following upon Beaumont and Fletcher's, is itself a specimen of reform, a kind of drama that offers positive rather than negative models of kingship. Criminal behavior is limited to the crim-

inal classes, Cratander's fellow prisoners. The performance itself enacts the contrast between Charles's reformed court and his father's
debauched one.

"Things twice seene loose; but when a King or Queene / Commands a second sight, they're then first seene," runs the final couplet
of Cartwright's prologue to the Hampton Court performance (p. 198).
Cartwright's concern is not with the Beaumont and Fletcher play, but
with the way *The Royal Slave* may suffer by contrast to its first performance at Oxford. The paradox of single and double seeing here is
witty compliment, but at the same time it erases the Oxford performance. There the Persian magus speaking the prologue directly addressed the monarchs: "Whiles by such Majesty our Scene is drest, /
You come both th'Entertainer and the Guest" (p. 195, ll. 11–12). This
conventional modesty recognizes the inherent paradox of royal performance. The effort in the first prologue is to transform the monarchs
into "sacred Lights," splendid decorations, illuminating the special
scene. The second prologue, on the other hand, treats the revival as a
re-creation:

> Things of this nature scarce survive that night
> That gives them Birth; they perish in the sight;
> Cast by so far from after-life, that there
> Is scarce ought can be said, but that they were.
> Some influence yet may crosse this fate; what You
> Please to awaken must still come forth new.
>
> (p. 198, ll. 7–12)

The theatrical fact of revival is transformed by these lines into a be-
stowing of life by the monarchs. Cartwright does not engage whether
any play, resuscitated at royal command, "must still come forth new,"
nor does he wonder how an audience, most of whom have seen the
play before, will recover their first sight of the play. In fact, the costly
transportation of sets and costumes from Oxford for the occasion suggests that what is requested is not novelty at all, but a repetition of the
previous experience.

Novelty, however, was a key feature of that experience: so Cartwright is correct in noticing that his play's success at Oxford was due
in large part to its occasional nature. He hopes to forestall disappointment at Hampton Court by making this performance an occasion as
well. The royal command for a second performance makes his play

unique. But *A King and No King* is again a counterexample. If both recorded performances of Cartwright's play can be seen as unique, and the play thus a novelty on both occasions, *A King and No King* is a theatrical workhorse, in no way special even when performed at royal command. The only way that it can "come forth new" time after time is by means of the actors' professionalism.

Cartwright's epilogue for the Hampton Court performance takes the language of new life introduced in the prologue and alters it into a language of death. The anxiety that the actors may have made "*that Peece their owne*" leads to a fear that the author has been eliminated: "*Being then a new Reciter some way is / Another Author, we are thus made his*" (p. 253, ll. 11–12). This fear in turn leads to another, darker fear that the king and queen may themselves have changed:

> *Wee therefore hope nothing shall here be seene*
> *To make the Slave appeale from King or Queene:*
> *From your selves here, t'your selves at* Oxford; *grace*
> *And favour altring with the time and Place,*
> *So that some thence may deeme it happy fell*
> *There only, where you meant to take all well.*
>
> (13–18)

This epilogue, like the epilogue to the Oxford performance, is spoken by Cratander. The complaints of the author against the players' rival authorship, in other words, are put in the mouth of the player. The primary change from Oxford, of course, is in personnel, so that Joseph Taylor, as Cratander, can hardly remember "*your selves at* Oxford" the way the poet can. Yet he reminds the king and queen of their complicity in the play's previous success: "*He feares ill fate the less, in that if you / Now kill him, you kill your owne favour too*" (21–22). If they dislike the revival, their own judgment is called into question. Seeming to flatter the monarchs with their life-and-death power over his art, the poet, by subscribing to the normal practice in the epilogue, must put his words into the mouth of a player. And the player's suggestion that the monarchs reject the play they so enjoyed at Oxford only at the peril of rejecting their own integrity takes on an edge all its own.

Cartwright transmits the circumstances of the play's presentation by publishing all the prologues and epilogues, including those to the audience of dons and scholars at the second university performance, in the 1639 edition of the play. As a result, he conveys his extraordinary awareness of the complexities of royal performance. The Hampton Court prologue and epilogue project an urgency that goes beyond the masque language at Oxford; the whole event is a struggle for control among playwright, players, university, and crown. At stake is the question of to whom the play belongs — or who should bear responsibility for its failure. The concern about who makes the play, in the play's supporting apparatus, is connected with the play's "inquiry," in Martin Butler's words, into "what makes a king?"[37] The two are linked by the fact of royal performance, in which the monarch commands a second view of a play which itself presents two putative monarchs to his view.

Criticism of the play has tended to disregard Cartwright's sensitivity to the problem of multiple audiences and to the doubleness inherent in the royal performance, where the royal audience is "both th' Entertainer and the Guest." The play's earliest commentators — G. Blakemore Evans, who edited Cartwright's works, and Allardyce Nicoll — dismiss the play itself as an example of the court fashion of effete platonism, and Nicoll focuses on the masque elements in Inigo Jones's design.[38] Yet Cartwright knows the play is not a masque: if it had been seen as such, the question of moving it to Hampton Court, and trying it out with professional actors in friendly rivalry to the university actors, would never have arisen. Nor, of course, do the monarchs in the audience join in a final dance. Anne Barton has noticed the main problem involved in seeing the play as a specimen of abject sycophancy: as she notes, "the implied association of Cratander, as paragon of kingship, with Charles himself becomes all the more remarkable in view of Cartwright's refusal ever to make the orthodox discovery that, really, this man possesses royal blood." For Barton, the play's ending points subversively at a flaw in the divine right theory of kingship. Butler goes further, postulating that "if any figure was meant for Charles, it was the Persian king, Arsamnes, himself, who continually finds himself outdone by the superior kingliness of the common slave." The play becomes the queen's play in Butler's reading, directed to Charles as a kind of admonition. "It is difficult not to conclude that Cratander, whose strenuous discipline contrasts so favourably with Charles's rather dreary and inglorious policy of 'Thorough,' resembles the strong and serious leader who would have been much more acceptable to Charles's puritanical subjects." Kevin Sharpe has transferred possession of the play from the queen's circle to the university: "The university might teach the rulers of the commonweal the virtues of self-regulation which equipped them for government, but it was the king who gave authority to the university and places of power to its students."[39] These readings all treat the play as single, however, and disregard the significance of Cartwright's multiple prologues and epilogues: a play can mean different things to different audiences on different occasions.

The self-consciousness of the published text of the play is an aspect of a larger self-consciousness in the body of the play. The basic situation cries out to be seen as metatheatrical: Persian custom dictates that a prisoner be made king for three days and then executed. What ensues is a scrutiny not of kingship in all its ramifications but of the ways in which being a king and acting the part of a king intersect, sometimes contradictorily. Cratander's fellow prisoners see the custom as an opportunity to indulge their appetites freely: "If I have the fortune of't, I'le Revell it all night," says Leocrates; "Kings, they say, ought not to sleep for the good of the people" (I.i.90–91). The Persians, too, anticipate a similarly coarse enactment of liberation from the "Three-dayes King" (I.iii.231). Atossa, the queen, wonders "How doe you thinke hee'le beare his State?" "As Schoole-boyes / In time of Misrule," replies Masistes, "looke big awhile, and then / Returne dejected to the Rod" (234–37). Masistes has failed to perceive what Arsamnes has as he interviewed Cratander for the post. Cratander, according to the king, looks the part, not of a monarch, but of a wise advisor to a monarch: "See, there comes one / Arm'd with a serious and Majestique looke / As if hee'd read Philosophy to a King" (I.ii. 105–7). Arsamnes, in choosing him, shows a willingness to learn philosophy: Cratander's reign, for him, becomes an educational theatrical experience, in which watching the philosopher play the role of the king instructs the king in the philosophy of rule.

The play sets into opposition two views of the Persian custom. One, expressed by the ordinary Persians of the court and by Cratander's fellow Ephesians, is that the interim performance is, as Praxaspes fears, a particularly dangerous kind of festive inversion. "Be my feares / No Omen to the Kingdome, ô ye Gods," he worries, "But I suspect this Comicke folly will / Sport our free Monarchy into a Nation / Of cheated slaves" (224–28). This view is analogous to a view of theater as comic folly at its best and destructive of public morals at its worst, a view of course current in the first half of the seventeenth century in England. Cratander's wholly serious enactment of his role, however, points in the direction of a view of theater as a valuable public institution, capable of offering, in its personifications of royal performance, visions of monarchical behavior worthy of emulation by kings.

Cratander's test in the play is a test of acting. He plays the part of the king before an audience that contains the real king, Arsamnes, and his queen, Atossa. Cratander's position, in other words, is precisely analogous to that of Master Busby, playing the role at Oxford before Charles and Henrietta Maria, or Joseph Taylor, as he faces the same royal pair in the audience at Hampton Court. What is at risk is that the enactment of royal virtue could be a travesty. The question of whether a man of common (or slave) blood can rightly undertake the role of king is a theatrical as much as a political one. The answer reached by the Oxford partisans, that Busby carried away the palm, is, conversely, as much a political as a theatrical one.

As befits a play participating in the platonic language of the court, and, indeed, as befits a play following hard upon a performance of *A King and No King,* royal behavior is understood in terms of continence. The first surprise about Cratander's rule, to the Persians, is his failure to select a concubine. "I wonder / No woman's chosen Queene for company," says Mandane, one of Atossa's ladies (I.iii.238). The Persians' bafflement at Cratander's behavior amounts to a confusion at a switch of genres. "Why then hee'le turne the Scene," exclaims Ariene (another of the queen's ladies) at a description of Cratander's model behavior; "we did expect / Something that would have saved us the labour / Of reading Play-bookes, and Love-stories." (I.iv.281–83). "Away, let's go and view again; he promiseth / Something that is not sport," Atossa concludes at these reports (298–99). Her viewing prompts Arsamnes' suspicions: "Doth she then / Seeme to compassionate his fortune? we / Must watch his actions narrowly" (I.v.319–21).

Arsamnes' jealousy consists in misinterpreting the gracious regard bestowed upon Cratander by Atossa. He disregards Hydarnes' recognition that Atossa's

> pure Affections
> Are as sacred as her Person, and her thoughts
> Soaring above the reach of common Eyes,
> Are like those better Spirits, that have nothing

Of Earth admixt, but yet looke downe upon
Those numbers of Inhabitants, and where
They see a worthy minde oppress'd, vouchsafe
At least to helpe with pitty.

(311–18)

This is precisely the position in which we see Atossa in the second act, as she and her ladies *"appeare above"* (II.iii.1, s.d.) to watch Cratander tried "to the utmost" (368). First he is exposed to the temptation of tables loaded with food and wine; then he is tempted by a lascivious song and a pair of women. His rejection calls our attention to the doctrine of the king's two bodies in a new way: "If you will / Needes put yourself to th' trouble of Procurers," he scolds the Persian lords,

Bring me a Kingdome in one face, or shew me
A People in one body; then you might
Happily worke on my Affections.
There I durst powre my selfe into Embracements,
Loosing my selfe in a Labyrinth of joy.
As 'tis, you only make me colder, by
Surrounding me with these your hostile flames.

(407–15)

Atossa's admiring presence above the stage ("What doe you thinke Mandane? is he mortall?" [446]) offers a chaste counterpoint to the two impudent women. She figures just such a union of the two bodies as Cratander craves and as the Caroline masque offered in the image of CARLOMARIA.

An equation is made between Cratander and Atossa here in the second act, as the other Ephesian prisoners enter, now dressed in Persian robes, and Cratander becomes an onstage audience: "I'le step aside, and watch their actions" (445). Atossa sends her two ladies down to "try their Courtship" (455). Both the royal slave and the platonic queen take up positions as viewers. What they watch is the grotesque masquerade that the Persians expected Cratander's rule to be. "A little Love-sport only," Leocrates says in response to Cratander's challenge as *"they carrye out the Ladyes"* (II.v.509 s.d.): "We were arguing / *Pro,* and *Con* out of *Plato,* and are now / Going to practise his Philosophy." "What they stile Love-sport only, and misname / An arguing out of Plato," Ariene angrily replies, "would have prov'd / A true and downe-right Rape, if that your presence / Had not become our Rescue" (511–17). The comic scene that Persians and Ephesians have expected runs its course from folly to crime in less than fifty lines. The jest about Plato demonstrates the Ephesians' willingness to "transpose all crimes upon / Him that should moderate them," as Cratander recognizes: "so perhaps / Their faults might be accounted mine" (536–37). As in *The Fair Favourite,* the monarch is acutely aware of the misreadings and misrepresentations that his conduct can undergo.

"When all eyes see't, a blemish is a Monster," Cratander continues, left alone onstage as he drives the Ephesians out and rescues the ladies. Unknown to him, he stands beneath Atossa, who continues to function as a onstage audience. And more, for she tests him, by throwing on the stage a golden chain. "Why this / Is but an Exprobation of my late / Distressed fortune," Cratander muses in the first of several attempts throughout the play to make sense of this item. "'Tis rich yet, / And Royall; It cannot be the wealth of any, / But the Throne" (548–50). The language makes it clear that the chain is paradoxical, like the royal slave, a sign of bondage and of royalty. Cratander accuses the Ephesian agents who enter next of trying to bribe him with it: "Why you threw it in before you, to make way / Unto your Suit." "Is't not lawfull to / Salute the Persian Mock-King, think y', unlesse / We bring a Guift?" Hippias angrily replies (II.vi.593–96).

Resolving the meaning of the chain implies resolving the paradox of royal slavery. Cratander and Atossa, in their first duologue in the play, treat the chain not as just a courtly favor, but as a token of the highest kind of love. "Where honour is transmitted in a true / Mysterious Gage of an Immaculate minde," Cratander vows,

I will defend it as some sacred Relique,
Or some more secret pledge, drop'd downe from Heav'n
To guard me from the dangers of the Earth.

"But in that / You make it common," Atossa protests, "you bereave it of / All that you call Divinity" (III.iv.883–88.) The dispute about its meaning becomes an enlistment of Cratander on Atossa's side as her knight and Atossa's enlistment on Cratander's side as he resists the Persian lords' attempt to seize his power before the three days are up. They share a mysterious faith, an ability to "distinguish betwixt Love, and Love" as Cratander puts it (939), passing this final test.

"If James had ruled as a royal Solomon, praised for his wisdom, pru-

dence, and magnanimity," R. Malcolm Smuts argues of the distinction
between the Jacobean and the Caroline court, "Charles preferred the
more romantic role of a royal knight, inspired by the beauty of his
wife to purge the realm of vice and discord."[40] Cratander's platonic
debate with Atossa constitutes an investiture as virtue's champion in
the Persian court. The chain ties him to her and to the kingdom in
"one eternall simplenesse" (954) of service to virtue.

"Was't not enough that you perus'd his Actions," rages Arsamnes in
the next scene,

> And surfetted your Eyes upon his follies,
> Seeing, and seene againe, but you must cast him
> A Chayne, an Emblematicke Chayne?
>
> (III.v.991–94)

This scene and the one that precedes it mark the center of the play:
Cratander's instruction of Atossa in platonic love gives way here to
Atossa's instruction of Arsamnes. His jealous complaints ("But what
should make you / Present him with a guift?" [1024–25]) yield to her
superior wisdom. Put to the test for two and a half acts, Cratander
proves to be master of himself.

The Persian king attempts platonic language, too:

> Thou art still vertuous, my *Atossa,* still
> Transparent as thy Crystall, but more spotlesse.
> Fooles that we are, to thinke the Eye of Love
> Must alwayes looke on us. The Vine that climbes
> By conjugall Embracements 'bout the Elme,
> May with a ring or two perhaps encircle
> Some neighbouring bough, and yet this twining prove.
> Not the Offence, but Charity of Love.
>
> (1045–52)

Despite this attempt on his part to participate in the language of Caroline masque, the tranquillity he wins here is short-lived. For when he
sees Cratander seated with the queen and her ladies on the castle walls
in the fifth act, Arsamnes again succumbs to jealousy. "Can you con-
taine Sir?" asks Praxaspes,

> looke how proudly hee
> Sits in the midst, hemm'd in on every side

With Beauties, which his wheeling eye runs o're
All in a minute.

(V.ii.1287–90)

The freedom of Cratander's gaze goads Arsamnes. Dressed "*in war-like habits,*" he and his courtiers face the spectacle, above them, of a king in a female court. Masistes continues the process of inflaming Arsamnes that Praxaspes has begun:

> Here's a delicacy
> That ne're was practis'd by a Captive yet,
> Nor heard of since the Custome first began,
> That Conquer'd Slaves should personate their King.

(1290–93)

Cratander has violated the Persian custom by personating, rather than merely playing, the king. Personation suggests substitution or replacement: Cratander is showing Arsamnes himself. "What I've condescended / To ayde thus farre, is only a faire likenesse / Of something that I love in you," Atossa ventures in clarification (1313–14). Arsamnes' victory in battle leads to celebrations, as he spares Cratander, that further complicate the language of personation and likeness. "Descend then," he invites the court ladies and Cratander,

> And when wee've joyn'd our hands, as Pledges of
> Our hearts combining so, let us returne
> To th'Celebration of an equall Triumph
> In an united marriage of our joyes.

"There I confesse a Conquest," Cratander concurs, "where I finde / He that subdu'd my body, gaines my mind" (1436–42). The final scenes of the play take the shape of a marriage masque, but one in which the true marriage takes place between Cratander and Arsamnes, joined in mind by the platonic love of Atossa.

The masque follows convention, as it is introduced by an antimasque in which the Ephesian slaves appear with the two prostitutes who had earlier tested Cratander. The Ephesians dance "*in their Cripple postures,*" wearing the disguises they had put on in order to ambush Cratander in the fourth act. Next the younger court ladies perform an Amazon dance. The masque concludes with the entrance of the priest, demanding that Cratander be delivered up to sacrifice.

Arsamnes proposes substituting oxen and perfumed fires for the human captive, and when this is rejected by the priest, he promises to immortalize Cratander with statues: "I'le people all my Kingdome with thy Images" (V.vi.1525). The gods reject this substitution as they refuse the sacrifice itself. A spectacular eclipse interrupts the rites of death.

Scenic transformation effects the delivery of Cratander; Cartwright's play incorporates the dynamic of masque in a way that Davenant's tragicomedies do not. The transformation of the king's love in *The Fair Favourite* takes place mysteriously, offstage. Here the gods directly intervene to preserve the union of the king's two bodies that has been celebrated by the masques of marriage in the Persian court. Cratander recognizes that he himself has become a spectacle, as he acknowledges the gods' gift of a new life:

> I'le thus divide
> That life they lend me, one halfe shall be yours,
> The other Ephesus's, that mine Actions
> Wearing both Gratitude and Piety,
> Like to some well wrought Picture, may at once
> Behold both you, and that.
>
> (V.vii. 1588–93)

The apparent paradox of union and division are confounded in the vision of the "well wrought Picture." Arsamnes will himself install Cratander as king of Ephesus, "that what was meant / For sport and mirth, may prove a serious honour" (1599–1600), and the play, at Oxford and at Hampton Court, throws itself on the mercy of the royal couple in its epilogue.

The image of Cratander as a picture that can both behold and be beheld encapsulates the whole strategy of the play, itself a model of royal performance staged before a royal audience. In its incorporation of the dynamics of Caroline masque, *The Royal Slave* provides not just dazzling spectacle, but an enactment of the marriage of the king's two bodies through the platonic mediation of the queen. Davenant's more troubling attempts to separate the genres of masque, comedy, tragedy, and tragicomedy point out the uniqueness of Cartwright's play. The interest stirred up in court circles by *The Royal Slave,* like the anxieties expressed in Cartwright's multiple prologues and epilogues, testifies to the novelty of this fusion of masque and tragicomedy, of amateur and professional theater, of university and court. Successful in effecting a union of the king's two bodies in its plot, the play struggles to perpetuate that union beyond its close. The etiquette of epilogues to royalty demands that the play pronounce its closure to be tentative until *"seal'd by you,"* requesting at Oxford forgiveness for the *"madnesse"* of the enterprise (p. 251, l. 4, 9). At Hampton Court, such conventional solicitations give way to a tone of desperation: *"'Tis then your Countenance that is the price / Must redeeme this, and free the Captive twice,"* Taylor as Cratander sues (p. 253, ll. 19–20). Favoring the play once is generosity enough; for the play to demand a repeat of that generosity borders on temerity. The assent royalty gives to the fictions of masque is a one-time phenomenon, circumscribed by the dynamics of the occasion; the assent given to plays that are regularly repeated before royalty, like *A King and No King,* is of a different sort. Cartwright is afraid *The Royal Slave* does not deserve it.

Like Cartwright, Sir John Suckling throws the second version of his play upon the mercy of the court. *Aglaura* was performed in its tragic version at the Blackfriars and at court in late 1637 and in its tragicomic version at the Cockpit in the court on April 3, 1638. Court comment noticed the extravagance of Suckling's exercise, for he staged the play's performances at his own expense: *"Sutlin's* play cost three or four hundred Pounds setting out," remarked George Garrard, "eight on the Suits of new Cloaths he gave the Players; an unheard of Prodigality."[41] Thus, again like *The Royal Slave, Aglaura* is set apart from the ordinary repertory by its author's amateur status. But where Cartwright had university sponsorship, Suckling sponsors (and promotes) himself in his enterprise. And where Cartwright offers his play as a model of reformed drama, platonic and inspirational, Suckling offers *Aglaura* as an entertainment that can take either tragic or tragicomic form as the author's (or the audience's) whim demands.

"'Tis strange perchance (you'll thinke)," runs the prologue to the tragicomic version at court,

> that shee that di'de
> At Christmas, should at Easter be a Bride;
> But 'tis a privilege the Poets have,
> To take the long-since dead out of the grave.
>
> (p. 96, ll. 1–4)

The sentiment expressed here runs counter to the prologue for the Blackfriars, in which "the Ladies . . . who never lik'd a plot / But where the Servant had his Mistress got," (11–12) bear at least some of the responsibility. The poet's "privilege," in fact, is disclaimed later in the court prologue as a vain claim "to doe all those things / That can be done onely by Gods and Kings" (21–22). Suckling toys with the idea that a playwright's power over life and death rivals a king's; indeed, the allusion to Christmas and Easter suggests that his power is divine. But then the playwright disclaims this power: "Of this wild guilt, hee faine would bee thought free, / That writ this play," the actor speaking the prologue begs. The matter of Aglaura's survival (both the character and the play fuse here, as in Cartwright's *Royal Slave* epilogues) is left up to the king himself: "Shee's not to live, unless you say shee shall" (23–24, 27). This is not, as Harbage put it, the "cool" gesture of a "dauntless resurrectionist."[42] Rather, like Cartwright, Suckling as amateur playwright is aware of the unique nature of his project and fears that it might be received as madness.

But there is less at stake. Without university backing and without didactic purpose, *Aglaura* has no ax to grind. Harbage is certainly correct when he describes the play as "Fletcherian tragedy of court intrigue, with greater excesses and complications and a more fetid and unwholesome atmosphere." In fact, Suckling has not only resurrected his heroine, but like Davenant, he has reanimated *The Maid's Tragedy* and *A King and No King* in his play, replaying one and then the other in the tragic and the tragicomic versions. The extraordinary persistence with which Caroline dramatists returned again and again to these models points not so much to a poverty of imagination on their parts as to an intense interest in the issues raised by these dramas of court intrigue.

Davenant and the amateur playwrights all find themselves forced to set their plays in a context determined by Beaumont and Fletcher. It is *this* theatrical fashion, rather than the court fashion of platonic love, that determines the shapes of their plays. Even Cartwright's university play must compete directly with *A King and No King* for the royal favor, stressing its difference from the regular repertory but encased in it, at Hampton Court, just the same. Suckling works in the opposite direction, outdoing Beaumont and Fletcher at their own game.

Where *The Royal Slave* unites the king's two bodies in marriage, playing out the dynamic of Caroline masque, *Aglaura* violently commingles them through the dynamic of incest. The play's king, "Lust-full and cruell," as the *dramatis personae* announces, loves his son's betrothed, Aglaura. The two young lovers are secretly married in the first act, but this does not deflect his rage. Orbella, the queen, mean-while, has given her favors to the king's ambitious brother, Ariaspes; but her former lover, Zorannes, haunts the court disguised as Ziriff, craving revenge for his father's murder by the king and a restoration to the queen's love. In a comic subplot, courtiers find themselves rebuffed by platonic ladies. The poisonous ambiance pollutes all who inhabit it.

This is particularly true of the tragic version, which is identical with the tragicomic version through the first four acts. Thersames, the prince, and Aglaura never consummate their marriage, forestalled throughout the play, as in Davenant's *Unfortunate Lovers,* by interrup-tions and misunderstandings. "You now my Lord, must raise his Jeal-ousie," urges the villainous Jolas after he and Ariaspes have, con-cealed, witnessed the secret wedding: "Teach it to looke through the false opticke feare, / And make it see all double" (I.iv.76–77). The double vision of jealousy provokes the king to see the marriage as trea-son and to take revenge by summoning Aglaura to him on the wed-ding night: "The King must have her —— " Zorannes announces. "How?" cries Thersames; "The King must have her (Sir)" (I.vi.42–43). Like the disappointed bridegrooms of *The Maid's Tragedy* and *The Unfortunate Lovers,* Thersames comes to rail against the royal prerog-ative: "Is there no way for Kings to shew their power, / But in their Subjects wrong? no subject neither / But his owne sonne?" "Right Sir," concurs the duplicitous Jolas, "No quarrie for his lust to gorge on, but / On what you fairely had flowne at, and taken" (II.i.8–12).

The darkness of the cave to which the chase leads permits the sub-stitutions and fatal mistakes that complicate the catastrophe in both versions. Entering with "*a torch in one hand, and a dagger in the other,*" Aglaura awaits her rendezvous with the king, for she has been warned by Zorannes of the lustful tyrant's plan to supply his son's place. "How ill this does become this hand," she comments, "much worse / This suits with this, one of the two should goe" (V.i.100–101). The torch that would show the way to the predatory king and the dagger that would put an end to his oppression become symbolic representations of an internal debate:

The shee within me sayes, it must be this —
Honour sayes this — and honour is *Thersames* friend.
What is that shee then? is it not a thing
That sets a Price, not upon mee, but on
Life in my name, leading me into doubt,
Which when 'tas done, it cannot light mee out?

(102–7)

The distinction between the "shee" that would preserve Aglaura's life
and "*Thersames* friend," honor, strains the normal terms of a love
and honor debate by substituting for love in the opposition a more natural desire for survival. What can live on if Aglaura lights the king the
way to her bed is not "mee," however, but "life in my name": a hollow
existence. She "*puts out the light,*" and immediately wavers:

Ha! — would 'twere in agen.
Antiques and strange mishapes,
Such as the Porter to my Soule, mine Eye,
Was ne're acquainted with, Fancie lets in,
Like a disrouted multitude, by some strange accident
Piec'd together; feare now afresh comes on,
And charges love to home.

(110–17)

The image of a "disrouted multitude" introduces into Aglaura's uncertain meditation the language of antimasque, where confused passions
also figure political disruptions. The masque's resolution is transformation, the magical appearance of the king or queen in state to still
the rout. What happens in *Aglaura* is an appearance as well: Thersames enters "*rising from the vault, shee stabs him two or three times,
hee falls, shee goes back to her chamber*" (120, s.d.). Unknown to her,
Zorannes and his men have already killed the king. What she takes to
be Thersames' substitute is Thersames himself. "Woman, / If thou
would'st be subject of mans wonder, / Not his scorne hereafter," she
cries just before striking the fatal blows, "now shew thy selfe" (118–
120). The play's tragic climax takes the climax of masque — the showing in wonder of the union of the royal selves of king and queen in
marriage — and converts it to a confusion of "strange mishapes" in the
dark.

All that remains for the consummation of the tragedy is Zorannes' revelation of Aglaura's mistake, his discovery of the queen's faithlessness, and a riot of deaths at the end. The tragicomic version, however, follows another pattern. Where the tragedy alludes, in Aglaura's putative stabbing of her oppressor in the royal trysting place, to *The Maid's Tragedy,* the tragicomedy alludes in its dynamic of concealment and sudden conversion to *A King and No King.* Merely wounded in this version, Thersames resolves not to die, and Zorannes has spirited away, not killed, the king. "*A bed put out,*" reads the stage direction for act 5, scene: "THERSAMES *and* AGLAURA *on it.*" The scene changes as the two awake, and the bed is drawn in. Thersames ascends the throne that has taken its place: "This place is yours," Zorannes declares, having brought in the king, the queen, Ariaspes, and Jolas as prisoners (V.iii.40). The substitution of the state for the bed is a scenic change that identifies the prince's union with Aglaura to his rightful throne.

"Have I not pitcht my nets like a good Huntsman?" Zorannes asks as he presents his prisoners, "Looke, Sir, the noblest of the Herd are here" (37–38). Thersames has been changed from prey to hunter. But the substitutions do not end here. Thersames steps down from the state and forces Zorannes, at sword point, to take the throne. The king himself then volunteers to take Zorannes' place: "Come downe, come downe, I will be King agen" (134). With the situation now wholly reversed, courtiers loyal to the king burst in: Thersames and Zorannes are seized as traitors.

But the king's transformation is complete. Becoming "king agen" not merely in appearance and power but in justice and mercy, he restores Zorannes to his property, passes sentence upon his brother, his wife, and the faithless Jolas, and vows to perform "three whole yeares penitence" for his own misdeeds (155). This union of the king's two bodies is as miraculous as any in masque, and like masque it involves an act of viewing. "What a strange glasse th'have shew'd me now my selfe in," the king comments earlier, as Zorannes and Thersames document his wrongdoings (92). His education in kingship takes place as he watches Thersames and Zorannes. Each in turn sits on the throne and each in turn functions as an advocate, respectively representing justice and mercy. Zorannes vigorously prosecutes the king as Thersames sits in state as judge; then Thersames pleads for clemency as Zorannes reluctantly sits in state. The king's gesture of taking the throne resolves into one person these complementary aspects of rule.

The movement of the tragicomic *Aglaura* toward marriage and union, toward the king's full acknowledgement of his responsibilities and incorporation of two bodies, is a scenic movement. From the dark chaotic vault, through the queen's bedchamber to the soft bed of Thersames and Aglaura, the shifting scene comes to itself in the throne room. The opening décor, Diana's grove, anticipates the nuptial bed and royal throne of the close: a chaste marriage supplants the fetid atmosphere as the king, newly united with his virtuous subjects, proposes a special feast. "Plays are like Feasts," the epilogue announces, "and everie Act should bee / Another course, and still varietie" (p. 114, ll. 1–2). With its elaborate sets and its transformations at the close, *Aglaura,* like *The Royal Slave,* seeks the special status of masque.

But less pretentiously it also aspires toward "varietie." It is worth remembering that the audience for the tragicomic *Aglaura* would not differ significantly from the audience for the tragic *Aglaura.* A considerable part of the pleasure in viewing the play on the second occasion, then, would be the suspense of waiting for Suckling to pull off his daring trick, and transform Aglaura, dead at Christmas, into an Easter bride. The play's previous identity as a tragedy functions as an ironic counterpoint to the play's new comic close. When we see Aglaura show herself as a wonder of women, stabbing Thersames, we may recall the dire effect of this gesture in the earlier play. When the king announces that he will become himself again and takes the throne, we may recall the unitary, lustful and cruel, identity he enjoyed in the tragedy. The multiple riddles of identity proposed in the tragedy are not so much resolved as finessed in the tragicomedy. The unions figured at the end of the second play remind the playgoer of the horrors at the end of the first. And perhaps those seem, in retrospect, more authentic, more convincing.

The court's regular practice of second viewings of plays complicates their meanings. The deference in the epilogues to both *The Royal Slave* and *Aglaura* to the royal power of life and death over the play's title characters, and by extension over the plays themselves, reveals a recognition that the plays' relationships to their royal audiences are dynamic, contingent, negotiable. Kevin Sharpe's terms, criticism and compliment, and Martin Butler's contention that "romantic courtier-plays of these years derived a certain heady excitement from trespassing dangerously into sensitive and otherwise forbidden areas, and increasingly they seem to be doing this with deliberateness and purpose" are both attempts to evoke the double-edged nature of these dramas.[43] But Butler fails to distinguish between the tragic and the tragicomic *Aglaura* in his discussion of that play, and Sharpe concentrates only on the Oxford production of *The Royal Slave*. Neither of these plays received a single viewing, however, and the playwrights themselves were quick to note the extent to which a second viewing could qualify or alter the equilibrium achieved in the first.

The reliance in the plays of Davenant upon earlier models, the plays of Beaumont and Fletcher, presupposes that for Caroline audiences even new plays were in a sense revivals. Certainly Suckling's frequent allusions to Shakespeare and to the Beaumont and Fletcher plays require an audience familiar with the originals. The original plays, as we have seen in the case of *The Royal Slave* at Hampton Court, could indeed demand comparison with their reformed revisions. "What wretch is this that thus usurps / Upon the priviledge of Ghosts," Aglaura cries when Thersames secretly enters her chamber in the third act, "and walks / At mid-night?" (III.ii.1–3). The reference is clear enough for an audience to recognize Hamlet in Thersames, frustrated in claiming his rights from the lustful tyrant. The old plays themselves usurp the privilege of ghosts, stalking such new offerings as Davenant's and affording their audiences, like Aglaura, a pleasurable recognition.

Repetition was a fact of Caroline court theater. New plays did not supplant old plays in court performance, and, given their persistent evocations of the old plays, the new plays achieve the status of revisions. Likewise the Caroline masque's model of the king's two bodies united in married love infuses the plays. Davenant's plays resist the temptation to adopt the dynamic of masque, insisting instead upon the integrity of their genres of comedy, tragedy, and tragicomedy. The amateur plays, however, aspire toward the ceremonial dignity of masque. But *The Royal Slave,* as performed by professional actors at Hampton Court, is absorbed into the repertory, and *Aglaura,* revived as tragicomedy, nonetheless reminds its audience of its tragic origins.

What we can learn from this is that the dramas of this period should not be, as so often happens in both traditional and recent criticism, confused with the masques. The playwrights were conscious, certainly, that their endeavors were in some ways analogous, but they also remained aware of the differences. Davenant especially, as author of many of the masques, jokes with the masque's ideals in *The Platonic Lovers* and offers a panoply of hideous distortions of masque in

The Unfortunate Lovers. What the masques effect magically, the union of king and people through marriage, forms the heart of the plays' riddling conflicts. Only the tragicomic model, with its sudden changes of heart and wondrous substitutions, permits successful resolution of this conflict on the common stage. But masque has no room for the ambiguities of a tragicomic close.

Rather than see these ambiguities as either flattery or subversion, it might be more useful to see them as evidence of confusion. The Caroline court drama, characterized by repetitions of standards, by revisions and requests for repeat performances of new plays, necessarily generates double meanings. "What a strange glasse th'have shew'd me now my selfe in," says the king in the tragicomic *Aglaura* (V.iii.92). What Atossa loves in the royal slave, she tells her royal husband, "is only a faire likenesse / Of something that I love in you" (V.ii.1314–15). Throughout these plays, kings are confronted with mirrors or images of themselves, alternative selves that they accept or reject. In performance before the king and queen, the effect is complicated, for what the royal audience witnesses are actions of royal witnessing. While dramatists may wittily chide a court fashion like the language of platonic love, they hold up a mirror to the royal couple's mutual love that challenges the simplicity of masque. "In this, Sir, you perceive the intricate / Though pow'rful influence of love," Altophil is told of his imprisonment in *The Unfortunate Lovers* (II, p. 41). The plays offer a glimpse of love's intricacy as well as its power, where the masque celebrates its power alone.

"Wee did not very well like the men," testified Captain Hugh Pollard about his role in the ill-fated Army Plot of 1641, "for *Suckling,* Jermaine and Davenant were in it."[44] The author of *The Platonic Lovers,* its dedicatee, Jermyn, and the author of *Aglaura* were finally to find themselves miscast on the political stage. Davenant defended himself (the other two escaped to the Continent) with a "Humble Remonstrance," in which he reminded Parliament of his advice to the queen to be "the Peoples advocate." What he had urged then was a vision of the union of the king's two bodies through love: "To cure this high obnoxious singleness / (Yet not to make their power but danger less) / Were Queens ordain'd."[45] "So much peculiar and alone," Davenant describes the king's situation in the poem to Henrietta Maria, "so uncompanion'd in a Throne." The double kings, the confrontations with alternate selves, that the plays present to the royal view counter "high obnoxious singleness" with images of union. In *The Fair Favourite, The Royal Slave,* and the tragicomic *Aglaura,* the king comes to his senses. But the marriages in the plays fall short of that union of king with people that the masques extoll as the fruit of chaste love. "High obnoxious singleness," the abuse of love, translates into jealous rage, kidnapping, rape, and tyranny on the stage. The double visions of the king's two bodies offered in these plays complicate the royal audience's vision of a polity shaped by "the intricate / Though pow'rful influence of love."

4

"Je suis maître de moi comme de l'univers . . ."

In Search of Absolutism
in the Court of Louis XIV

~

I

When Beaumont and Fletcher's lustful tyrants cry out for the forces of nature to rise up and defend them, they bluster. It is the special work of the Stuart court masque to enact royal theophany; scenic transformation is its method. The transformative power of masque eludes the Caroline dramatists, professional and amateur. Their response to the language of masque ranges, as we have seen, from the satirical to the emulative, but even in Cartwright's *The Royal Slave* the difference between masque and play is maintained. But when Thésée, in Racine's *Phèdre* (1677), calls upon Neptune to hear him and destroy his son Hippolyte, the god's response is prompt. Théramène reports with horror what he has seen:

> Cependant sur le dos de la plaine liquide
> S'élève à gros bouillons une montagne humide;
> L'onde approche, se brise, et vomit à nos yeux
> Parmi les flots d'écume, un monstre furieux.

> (Meanwhile on the horizon of the liquid plain there rises up with great bubbles a wet mountain; the wave approaches, breaks

open, and vomits up before our eyes, amid floods of spume, a raging monster.)[1]

Sea monsters are not uncommon in Stuart masque, and Elizabeth herself had seen, at Elvetham in 1591, a mermaid on a dolphin's back sur-
facing in an artifical lake. Learning their craft, as Inigo Jones had,
from the Italians, French scene designers and theatrical architects were
themselves skilled in aquatic entertainments. What Théramène describes is, then, both a loathsome answer to Thésée's prayer and a
machine from the world of court spectacle.

Emerging from the sea like Venus, or like the daughters of Niger discovered in a shell in the *Masque of Blackness,* this monster embodies
all that is horrible in the pagan, doomed world of *Phèdre.*[2] In the allegorical convention of masque and in the language of Racine's play, it
is appetite out of control, sensuality run amok. Its ready response to
the monster-slaying Thésée reminds us of his other history as a rapist:
for his son Hippolyte, in this play (and perhaps for Hippolyta, who
marries him in *A Midsummer Night's Dream*), Thésée's heroism
against monsters almost outweighs his abuse of women. Hippolyte
emulates his father and kills the beast, but his horses, panicking at its
loud death throes, drag him to his death entangled in the reins. Thus
ends the fruit of the happy marriage that is the main event of *A Midsummer Night's Dream.*

Conflating the English Theseus and the French Thésée in this way
yields one distinction: Shakespeare's Theseus is a duke, Racine's Thésée
a king. The powers of fairies and monsters, dismissed by Theseus as
"toys," encircle and contain his world at the end of his play; Thésée
receives the divine aid he invokes, but he invokes it in error, and his play
ends as he grieves for the death of his only son. Both Shakespeare and
Racine write with an awareness of the rich, untidy mythic background
of this figure. And both portray in Theseus/Thésée a royal audience.
Proud of his gracious forbearance, Shakespeare's Theseus fails to notice
his own rudeness at the rude mechanicals' play or his own embroilment
in the world of fairies and monsters. Racine's Thésée, too, is a monarch
who mistakes what he thinks he takes, and he dooms his own line. Calling upon Neptune for revenge, he becomes through his curse a monster
himself. Tricked and blinded, the cyclops Polyphemus calls upon Neptune for revenge against Odysseus in the *Odyssey;* in Racine's play,
Thésée is cyclopean in his blind, jealous rage.

He is a model of absolute monarchy gone wrong, the royal eye erring, royal power unrestrained. The beast ceremoniously slain in court aquatic spectacle here drags death in its wake. *Phèdre* is unique in Racine's production and in French classic tragedy in the extravagant horror of its close. Néron in *Brittanicus* is a monster, Racine confesses in his preface to that play, but he will be merely a "monstre naissant" (p. 385: "monster in the making.") His great crimes remain outside the scope of the play. This chapter is devoted to seeking not the monsters in French classic drama, but their converse. The plays under examination here—Corneille's *Cinna,* Molière's *Tartuffe,* and Racine's *Esther*— all enjoy particularly close ties to the ideology of absolutism. They represent a quest for a positive absolutist model: a monarch whose grasp of his world is not cyclopean, whose power is tempered by wisdom and love. The risk is there: Corneille's Auguste is fresh from a homicidal past as Octave; Orgon's household is at the mercy of his one indiscretion, which only the king can forgive; Racine's Esther fears that Assuérus will kill her before she can perform her divine mission. But such grim possibilities are forestalled in all three plays.

In Beaumont and Fletcher and in *Phèdre,* royal misprision is the mainspring of tragedy. The kings misread the spectacle and leap to wrong conclusions. An antitheatrical skepticism is not far to seek in these plays, and the French plays, too, note the danger of illusion. The Puritan critique of theater in England had its counterpart in assaults upon the theater by French divines. Despite lavish royal sponsorship, French theater was likewise hammered as vain, sinful, and blasphemous. *Tartuffe* is the most famous case in which to see the complex embroilment of the monarchy in both the theater and its opposition; *Esther* is an experiment in reformed theater, a pious play on a scriptural subject, acted not by professionals, but by innocent young girls.

Theater is damnable because it interferes with the audience's power to see things as they are. In fact, it requires the abdication of that power. A double danger ensues when the king attends the theater, for his real political power depends precisely on that ability to see things as they are. Hence the urgency of antitheatrical critique in England and France in the seventeenth century: the monarchy's active sponsorship of theater is self-destructive. The whole theater event thrives on misrepresentation. Monarchy itself, when the monarch on stage is a mere actor, is susceptible of misinterpretation as imposture. The project of the three plays in this chapter is thus not only to erect a positive image of the absolute monarch, but also to elude the charge of falsifying that image by portraying it onstage at all.

Charles I's status after his death as a royal martyr renewed for English royalists in exile a sense of the sacredness of the monarch's image. The presence in the French court of his widow, Henrietta Maria, before and after the restoration of the British monarchy, was a reminder of the tenuous nature of the royal role and of the painful doubleness of the king's two bodies. Having survived the Fronde, Louis XIV was careful, as he secured his power in the 1660s, to insist upon the sacred nature of the royal role. The ceremonies of his court were highly theatricalized, structured around subtle gradations of rank and focused always upon the king's person. Even at church, as Nathan Gross has pointed out, the king took center stage: "The significant exception to the normal direction of worship is worth noting: while the king faced the altar, courtiers turned toward him, as though the king, in the act of communicating with God in prayer on behalf of the entire kingdom, reflected the divinity and were himself an object of adoration."[3] In the frontispiece of *Eikon Basilike,* Charles was portrayed at prayer, Nancy Klein Maguire reminds us, "holding a crown of thorns while looking at a heavenly crown; his earthly kingly crown is at his feet, and there is a garden beyond his prie-dieu."[4] The fusion of theatrical and religious energy that can be seen in both these instances of monarchs at prayer, as in Clarendon's tale of Charles's private martyrdom as he received the news of Buckingham's death, pushes in the opposite direction from antitheatrical critique. Here the king is an actor in the sense that an actor is an incarnation, an embodiment, playing the sacrificial role.

In the court of Louis XIV, the king's physical body dictated the progress of the day. Courtiers attended upon the king's rising, his dressing, his hunting, his dining, his retiring. For each phase of this attendance, elaborate rituals were devised. Even more than the Stuart court, the Bourbon court was animated by the doctrine of the king's two bodies. The absolutist ideology promulgated by the court identified the king as the source of the nation's being.[5] Where Charles and Henrietta Maria had appeared only fleetingly in royal apotheosis in the masques, Louis was watched, venerated, and adored whether he was dancing the role of Apollo or being dressed for the day's business. Because Louis is in this sense never offstage, the disjunction between private self and royal role that Charles came to epitomize is, or should be, an irrelevancy to Louis' royal performance. His apotheosis is a never-ending process, a constant project.

II

Voltaire reports in *Le Siècle de Louis XIV (The Age of Louis XIV)*:

J'ai connu un ancien domestique de la maison de *Condé,* qui disait, que le grand Condé, à l'âge de vingt ans, étant à la première représentation de *Cinna,* versa des larmes à ces paroles d'Auguste:

Je suis maître de moi comme de l'univers;
Je le suis, je veux l'être. O siècles, ô mémoire!
Conservez à jamais ma nouvelle victoire.
Je triomphe aujourd'hui du plus juste courroux,
De qui le souvenir puisse aller jusqu'à vous!
Soyons amis, *Cinna,* c'est moi qui t'en convie.

C'étaient là des larmes de héros. Le grand Corneille faisant pleurer le grand Condé d'admiration, est une époque bien célèbre dans l'histoire de l'esprit humain.

(I knew an old servant from the house of Condé, who used to say that the Great Condé, at twenty years of age, watching the first performance of *Cinna,* burst into tears at these words of Auguste: "I am master of myself as of the universe; I am, I wish to be. Oh centuries, oh memory! Preserve forever my latest victory. I triumph today over a most just anger, the memory of which might extend even to you. Let us be friends, Cinna; it is I who invite you." These were the tears of a hero. The great Corneille reducing the great Condé to tears of admiration constitutes a famous moment in the history of the human spirit.)[6]

The old servant's testimony, if reliable, would fix the premiere of *Cinna* in 1641, for this particular prince de Condé was born in 1621.[7] There is no contemporary account of this great moment, or indeed of the first night of *Cinna.* The young prince's attendance at a similar event is recorded, however. On February 22, 1637, according to the *Gazette,* a comedy entitled *L'Aveugle de Smyrne* was presented at the Hôtel de Richelieu, to the king, Louis XIII, the queen, Anne of Austria, Monsieur, the king's brother, Mademoiselle, his daughter, the prince de Condé, along with the duc d'Enghien (his son, who would succeed to the title and later become known as the "Grand Condé") and a host of other dignitaries.[8] The appearance of so grand a company at what was a private showing in the cardinal's palace was not uncommon, and it testifies to Richelieu's status as "the most important patron of drama," in the years leading up to his death in 1642.[9] While visits to the professional theaters at the Hôtel de Bourgogne and the Marais were not uncommon for members of the royal family, Richelieu himself avoided visiting the playhouses. Instead he brought the actors before him on special occasions. Married to Richelieu's niece, the duc d'Enghien was a regular part of audiences to such performances. What the old servant in Voltaire's account seems to be describing, then, is a performance at the Palais Cardinal.

Such a performance would not have been a premiere, however. Richelieu's practice was to bring to his theater plays that had already made their débuts at the Marais theater, of which he was a leading sponsor. In January 1641, Richelieu opened a second theater at the Palais Cardinal, the specially designed Salle de la Comédie. Where the other playhouse seated six hundred invited guests, the large Salle de la Comédie had room for three to four thousand. With the latest scenic machines, this hall was inaugurated with the performance of *Mirame,* a spectacular tragicomedy written by five poets in Richelieu's employ. On this occasion, Timothy Murray has argued, the Cardinal himself, seated on the dais with the king and queen, was the focal point of attention, showing himself a prince.[10] More ordinary occasions would see a similarly select audience in the smaller hall. These performances did not receive special comment. Corneille, during the quarrel of *Le Cid,* had to remind his opponent Scudéry that the play had been performed three times at the Louvre and twice at the Hôtel de Richelieu; none of these performances was officially recorded.[11] Voltaire's anecdote of the duc d'Enghien's tears is the only corroborative evidence that *Cinna,* like the major portion of Corneille's dramatic production in the years before Richelieu's death, would have had its premiere at the Marais theater and then moved on to the Palais Cardinal and to performances at court.

Whatever the circumstances of its original production, *Cinna* became the play most often performed in the court of Louis XIV. From 1680, when the Comédie Française was formed of the two remaining professional companies under royal sponsorship (and began to keep

records), twenty-seven performances of *Cinna* are listed, fifteen between 1680 and 1700, twelve from 1700 to 1715.[12] Molière's company,
after a year of tenancy at the Petit-Bourbon, premiered *Les Précieuses
ridicules* (*The Ridiculous Précieuses*), the play that would become the
sensation of the town for the next four months, as an afterpiece to
Cinna, on November 18, 1659.[13] In 1674 a court performance of *Cinna*
so moved Louis XIV that he was tempted to pardon the chevalier de
Rohan, in emulation of the gesture of Auguste.[14] For Voltaire, the
tears of the duc d'Enghien epitomize the greatness of an age that could
produce both a "grand Corneille" and a "grand Condé." The title of
Voltaire's history places Louis XIV at the center of this age of greatness. *Cinna*'s subtitle, *La Clémence d'Auguste* (*The Clemency of
Auguste*), similarly suggests that the center of the drama lies not in the
soul of Cinna, but rather in the self-conquest of Auguste. Young Condé's tears, if we are to believe Voltaire, began to flow at the very
moment in which the absolute ruler chooses to sacrifice his sense of
self, his just anger with the conspirators, to a higher sense of responsibility to the future.

The emperor's victory is described in the play as a victory over one
kind of memory, "le souvenir" (V.iii.1700) — that recalls the disloyalty
of Cinna, in favor of another kind, "ô mémoire!" (1697), that is the
imagined memory of future generations. Auguste achieves his status
as hero of the play by transcending the conflicting family loyalties, the
complex of mutual revenge, that has characterized Rome up until this
moment. Voltaire thus in his anecdote places Condé at what the play
itself represents as a famous moment in the history of the human
spirit: Rome's movement from fratricidal republic to the stability of
empire. By calling the young duc d'Enghien by the name that he will
only later earn through his heroic deeds, Voltaire recapitulates the
complex historical irony enacted by *Cinna* itself. The index of greatness, for both Condé and Auguste, lies in the remembered future of
history. At the Palais Cardinal in 1640 or 1641, however, the audience
members would have found themselves implicated in another kind of
historical irony. The sort of self-mastery and absolute rule that the
play shows emerging in Auguste is available to the audience's eye only
in the person of Richelieu. When the king was present, as Murray has
pointed out, on these occasions "Richelieu's performance tended to
upstage the king" as they shared the dais.[15] If he were not present, the
cardinal, sponsor of the troupe presenting the play and host to his

invited audience, would as sole impresario of the event immediately suggest analogies between his position and Auguste's. Richelieu took most of the credit for the extirpation of civil war in the recent French past, just as Auguste proposes his victory as an end to civil war in the play's Rome.

Fully fledged absolutism, couched in the body of the king, would not emerge until Louis XIV consolidated his power over foreign and domestic faction in the late 1660s. Only in that context, at Louis XIV's court, as Jacques Sherer has pointed out, is it possible to see *Cinna* as "un hymne à la monarchie." At Richelieu's palace, however, the battle had not yet been won. Thus *Cinna,* presenting Rome on the verge of empire to an audience on the verge of absolutism, only dimly projects a possible future greatness against a vivid backdrop of past violence. Uncertainty about the characters' motives further darkens the action, nine-tenths of which, again in Scherer's words, is "sordide." The play is, as Mitchell Greenberg has suggested, itself a hall of mirrors, "reflecting its own contradictory readings."[16]

Greenberg makes this remark with reference to another famous anecdote about the play's reception by a royal audience. Napoleon declared himself unable to understand the ending of *Cinna* until he saw Monvel play the role of Auguste. Then what he saw was not only the consummate acting of Monvel in the role, but Auguste's own proficiency as an actor: "Mais une fois, Monvel, jouant devant moi, m'a dévoilé le mystère de cette grand conception. Il prononça le *Soyons amis, Cinna* d'un ton si habile et si rusé que je compris que cette action n'était que la feinte d'un tyran et j'ai approuvé comme calcul ce qui me semblait puéril comme sentiment" ("But one time Monvel, acting before me, revealed to me the secret of this great mystery: he spoke the line 'Let us be friends, Cinna' in so skillful and tricky a tone that I understood that this action was only the stratagem of a tyrant, and I approved as calculation what always seemed puerile to me as a sentiment").[17] By crediting Monvel with the revelation, Napoleon recognizes the degree to which the play can change its meaning according to an almost infinite number of variables over its life, through successive different performances, by different actors before different audiences.

Critics of the play, too, have created their own *Cinna*s. Machiavellian or Hobbesian readings, accepting Auguste's absolute rule as the only alternative to a self-perpetuating culture of familial vendetta, rebut readings that see the heart of the drama in Auguste's own struggle with his emotions, and in the art of self-control that he teaches to his dependents.[18] Placed as it is, at a famous turning point in history, the play is structured to throw up contradictory responses. It bears witness to the struggle to control memory, the effort to write history, as it occurs. No vision of a stable future consoles any of the characters, including Auguste, who begins the play toying with the idea of pastoral retirement. Contemplating withdrawal from the political sphere, the period's master politician contemplates the historically impossible. For many of the play's audiences, such a retreat would conjure up the specter of a leaderless Rome, pursuing the spiral of internecine violence into the beginning of the Christian era.

Just as Auguste must be urged by his confidants (in the scene in which he turns to the conspirators Cinna and Maxime for help) to give up dreams of retirement and recognize his responsibility, so Emilie must be brought to give up her obsession with the past, her dream of revenge, and awaken to the future. But making a proper use of the memories of the past is difficult, as Auguste points out, examining his own situation in light of his predecessors: "Sylla m'a précédé dans ce pouvoir suprême; / Le grand César mon père en a joui de même" (II.i.377–78: "Sylla preceded me in this supreme power; great Caesar, my father, also enjoyed it.") Neither of these models offers the guidance he needs:

> Ces exemples récents suffiraient pour m'instruire,
> Si par l'exemple seul on se devait conduire;
> L'un m'invite à le suivre, et l'autre me fait peur,
> Mais l'exemple souvent n'est qu'un miroir trompeur;
> Et l'ordre du destin qui gêne nos pensées
> N'est pas toujours écrits dans les choses passées.

(385–90: These recent examples would be sufficient to instruct me, if one could learn how to behave by example alone. The one invites me to follow, the other frightens me. But example is often a deceptive mirror, and the order of the destiny that troubles our thoughts is not always written in the events of the past.)

Auguste's situation is unprecedented; the decisions he must make must be made without the help of historical memory.

Emilie's problem, at the very outset of the play, is analogous to Auguste's in that she is troubled by an excessively vivid historical mem-

ory. Unlike Auguste, she surrenders totally to its power. Her monologue that opens the play pictures her vengeful desires as incestuous
children:

> Impatients désirs d'une illustre vengeance,
> A qui la mort d'un père a formé la naissance,
> Enfants impétueux de mon ressentiment,
> Que ma douleur séduite embrasse aveuglément,
> Vous régnez sur mon âme avecque trop d'empire.

> (I.i.1–5: Impatient desires for a glorious vengeance, brought to
> life by the death of a father, my grief, seduced, blindly embraces
> you: you reign over my soul with tyrannical power.)

Political and sexual language fuse here, as in the English dramas and
court masques. Forbidden sexual energies, from *A Midsummer Night's
Dream* through the plays of Davenant and Cartwright, express the
horrors of misgovernment. Emilie's monologue is as explicit as a Stuart antimasque in making this connection. Her possession by bad
memories is a kind of lurid ecstasy: at the memory of her dead father's
"sanglante image" (13: "bleeding image"),

> Je m'abandonne toute à vos ardents transports,
> Et crois, pour une mort, lui devoir mille morts.

> (15–16: I abandon myself totally to your ardent transports, and
> think that for one death I owe him a thousand.)

Extravagant sexual appetite transfers its political meaning intact from
the Caroline dramas to this most classical of Corneille's plays. William Davenant's *Salmacida Spolia* was presented to Charles I and Henrietta Maria in 1639, not long before Corneille offered *Cinna* to
Richelieu, Louis XIII, and Anne of Austria. For the miraculous purga-
tion of excessive desire through royal marriage that was Davenant's
resolution to the conundrum of the king's two bodies, Corneille substitutes Auguste's gesture of self-mastery.

   The art of the English court displayed the royal couple in epiphany,
mastering nature in their chaste and fruitful love. Corneille's play begins instead with Emilie's frenzied imagination of Auguste in his
"trône de gloire" (9: "throne of glory"). Here he shows himself as her
tyrannical enemy, a vile substitute for her dead father. The play must
trace his movement from monster to "maître de moi comme de

l'univers" (V.iii.1696: "master of myself as of the universe"). Auguste must assume, by the end of the play, for Emilie as for Cinna, a paternal role: alone he replaces all the assassinated and slaughtered fathers with whom the play's language is littered. He cannot arrive at the moment of clemency by himself, however; he requires prompting from Livie. Her "conseils de femme" (IV.iv.1245: "womanly counsels") are bluntly rejected in the fourth act. Yet it is precisely her strategy of forgiveness that Auguste adopts at the end.[19] Livie is given the play's final prophetic vision: "Vous avez trouvé l'art d'être maître des coeurs" (V.iii.1764: "You have discovered the art of being master over their hearts"), she declares of Auguste's new authority. What is glorified here, however, is not a royal couple, but rather Auguste's own "royales vertus" (1767).

But before he accepts (endures?) apotheosis, Auguste has been tempted to succumb to the past's repetitious tyranny and die:

Octave, n'attends plus le coup d'un nouveau Brute;
Meurs, et dérobe-lui la gloire de ta chute,
Meurs; tu ferais pour vivre un lâche et vaine effort,
Si tant de gens de coeur font des voeux pour ta mort.

(IV.ii.1169–72: Octave, wait no more for the blow of a new Brutus; die, and deprive him of the glory of your fall. Die; your attempt to continue living would be feeble and vain, with so many courageous people swearing oaths for your death.)

The desire for death, like the desire for retirement, is a desire to opt out of history. As Emilie is haunted by the specter of her father's death, Auguste is haunted by the assassination of his father. The past in this play is bloody bondage, doomed to repeat itself, unless Auguste has the courage to break the cycle.

Paradoxically, the only way to break out of the cycle of repeating the past, and thereby permit Rome to fulfill its historical destiny, is to forget the past. Oblivion must replace the obsessively imagined spectacles of past wrongs, just though the grievance may be. "Et que vos conjurés entendent publier / Qu'Auguste a tout appris, et veut tout oublier" (V.iii.1779–80: "And let your fellow conspirators hear it announced that Auguste has learned all, and will forget all"), Auguste orders in the final lines of the play. Such oblivion is an almost divine forgiveness, as Jean-Marie Apostolidès has suggested: imitating God, "le monarque voit tout et oublie tout en un seul regard" ("the monarch sees all and forgets all in one single gaze").[20] Auguste's line uncannily repeats Emilie's panicky cry at the end of the first act, when Cinna and Maxime are ordered to attend upon Auguste: "Vous êtes découverts. . . . Il n'en faut point douter, Auguste a tout appris" (I.iv.286, 291: "You are discovered! . . . There can be no doubt, Auguste has learned all.") The conspirators' greatest fear, of discovery, of apprehension, becomes their greatest boon, for Auguste's act of apprehension is also an act of oblivion.

"I do arrest your words," Angelo, the duke's deputy in *Measure for Measure,* says, rounding on Isabella (II.iv.134). His act of tyrannical apprehension is countered by the disguised duke's vigilance. Theseus, in *A Midsummer Night's Dream,* defines himself as an ideal monarch in his confident assertion of mastery of both apprehension and comprehension, in his ability to take what others mistake. Auguste in *Cinna,* too, is a ruler whose ability to apprehend, to take others in their mistakes, fills his courtiers with fear. *Apprendre* is close kin to *appréhender* and to *prendre.* As in Shakespeare's vocabulary, so too in Corneille's: royal understanding is a more problematic *taking* in other senses of the word. Just as Theseus's power may make the rude mechanicals apprehensive, Auguste's discovery of the conspirators' plot, his learning about it, is a kind of arrest. As with Theseus, so with Auguste: noble respect takes it in might, not merit. What Auguste chooses to overlook, as he takes Emilie and Cinna, is the merit of his own complaint against them, as well as the merit of their claim against him.

History in this play is thus paradoxically a learning to forget the past. Enslavement to the past is figured as a kind of repetitious oblivion, in which individuals are condemned to revert to generic type. Auguste's fear that he is another Caesar and Cinna another Brutus reminds us that in Corneille's Roman world these types are familial types. Cinna's strange first speech—a set piece of oratory in which he assures Emilie of his success as an orator before an audience of conspirators—evokes the chaos of this reversion:[21]

Vous dirai-je les noms de ces grands personnages
Dont j'ai dépeint les morts pour aigrir les courages,
Ces illustres proscrits, ces demi-dieux mortels,
Qu'on a sacrifiés jusque sur les autels?

Mais pourrais-je vous dire à quelle impatience,
A quels frémissements, à quelle violence,
Ces indignes trépas, quoique mal figurés,
Ont porté les esprits de nos conjurés?

(I.iii.205–12: Shall I tell you the names of those great men whose deaths I painted to sharpen their courage? Those famous men condemned, those mortal demigods, literally sacrificed upon the altars? But could I tell you to what impatience, to what shudders, to what violence, these unworthy deaths, however poorly described, aroused the spirits of our fellows?)

The famous men blur into a pattern of interchangeable fathers: each conspirator is entitled to figure a personal revenge of his own, because Cinna's oration is generic in its application. Worse yet, each conspirator becomes a shuddering reflection of Emilie: the acts of revenge they dream of are acts of love.

The play's dialectics of love and honor, revenge and law, are not precisely, as Greenberg would have it, "ruses." Rather, Emilie and Cinna are as characters entrapped within that illusion of symmetry, of matching demands that must be weighed against each other. That is because their loyalties remain personal, despite the evidence in Cinna's speech that the personal is in fact typical, de-individualized. Emilie's recognition that Cinna's success in avenging her father's death would mean his death as well does not deter her, but it signals to an audience the futility of such vengeful self-assertion (as does her assertion that any murder of Auguste except by Cinna on her account would be a failure). "Qui méprise sa vie est maître de la sienne" (I.i.130: "He who scorns his life is master of his life"), she declares in her first speech; ironically, Auguste, "maître de moi-même," echoes this line as he masters his life by pardoning his would-be murderers.

The ambiguities of *Cinna*'s conflicts are reflected in the play's definition of space. The abbé d'Aubignac questioned the mixture of public and private space in this play's transition from the first to the second act:

Je n'ai jamais bien pu concevoir comment Monsieur Corneille peut faire qu'en un même lieu Cinna conte à Emilie tout l'ordre et toutes les circonstances d'une grande conspiration contre Auguste, et qu'Auguste y tienne un Conseil de confidence avec ses deux

favoris: car si c'est un lieu public, comme il le semble puisqu'
Auguste en fait retirer les autres courtisans, quelle apparence que
Cinna vienne y faire visite à Emilie avec un entretien de cent
trente vers et un récit de choses si périlleuses, qui pouvaient être
entendues de ceux de la cour qui passaient en ce lieu? Et si c'est
un lieu particulier, par exemple le cabinet de l'Empereur, qui en
fait retirer ceux qu'il ne veut pas rendre participants de son secret,
comment est-il vraisemblable que Cinna y soit venu faire ce discours à Emilie? et moins encore qu'Emilie y fasse des plaintes
enragées contre l'Empereur? Voici ma difficulté que Monsieur
Corneille résoudra quand il lui plaira.

(I have never been able clearly to conceive how M. Corneille can
manage it that in one and the same place Cinna relates to Emilie
the whole organization and all the circumstances of a great conspiracy against Auguste, and that Auguste then holds a confiden-
tial council with his two favorites. Because if it is a public place,
as it seems to be, since Auguste makes the other courtiers leave,
what probability is there that Cinna would come there to visit
Emilie with a conversation of one hundred thirty lines and a nar-
ration of such dangerous business, when they could be overheard
by any members of the court who passed through this space? And
if it is a private place, for example the closet of the emperor, who
makes the courtiers leave because he does not want them to be
sharers in his secret, how could Cinna realistically have come
there to make his speech to Emilie? And it is even less realistic
that Emilie should make enraged complaints against the emperor
there! This is my problem, which M. Corneille will resolve when
he pleases.)

"Il est vrai qu'il s'y rencontre une duplicité de lieu particulière," Corneille responded in his *Examen* of *Cinna:*

La moitié de la pièce se passe chez Emilie, et l'autre dans le cabinet d'Auguste. J'aurais été ridicule si j'avais prétendu que cet
empereur délibérât avec Maxime et Cinna s'il quitterai l'empire
ou non, précisément dans la même place où ce dernier vient de
rendre compte à Emilie de la conspiration qu'il a formée contre
lui. . . . Emilie ne parle donc pas où parle Auguste, à la réserve
du cinquième acte, mais cela n'empêche pas qu'à considérer tout

le poème ensemble, il n'ait son unité de lieu, puisque tout s'y peut passer, non seulement dans Rome ou dans un quartier du Rome, mais dans le seul palais d'Auguste, pourvu que vous y vouliez donner un appartement à Emilie qui soit eloigné du sien.

(It is true that a certain duplicity of place can be found here. Half of the play takes place in Emilie's room, half in Auguste's closet. I would have been foolish if I had maintained that this emperor consulted with Maxime and Cinna in precisely the same place where the latter had just informed Emilie about the conspiracy he had formed against him. . . . Emilie does not speak where Auguste speaks, with the exception of the fifth act. But this does not hinder considering that the poem as a whole does indeed observe unity of place, in that everything that happens there takes place not merely in Rome or in a part of Rome, but in the very palace of Auguste, as long as you are willing to imagine there an apartment for Emilie at some distance from his own.)[22]

This is not an idle squabble about the "rules." The confusion that D'Aubignac recognizes, and that Corneille attempts to explain away by invoking the good will of the spectator, is an essential aspect of the struggle in the play to define the range and limits of the authority of Auguste. By the fifth act, when Emilie and the emperor do share the same space, a transformation has been effected that mirrors the transformative drive of the plot. "Chez Emilie" has vanished, subsumed into "chez Auguste." The spatial absurdity of conspirators conspiring against an emperor within his own private closet speaks to the horrid instability of Rome at large. That Corneille urges his spectator to envision the whole play as taking place within the confines of Auguste's palace reinforces the overwhelming sense of claustrophobia induced by Emilie's first monologue. Trapped within the space of Auguste's palace, Emilie and Cinna are later trapped within the confines of Auguste's clemency. His mercy embraces them. There is no escape.

The paradox of the play's space is mirrored in its politics. Cinna's rigorously argued defense of absolute monarchy in the second act, when Auguste asks his advice about retirement, is a notorious example. Cinna's speech must be disingenuous in one way or another. Either the argument represents his true political leanings—in which case his adoption of Emilie's position is wholly motivated by amorous passion—or he is merely flattering Auguste, telling the emperor what he wants to hear. "Quel est votre dessein après ce beau discours?" (II.ii.647: "What is your plan after this fine speech?") Maxime queries in disbelief. For Maxime, who has actually spoken in favor of republican principles before Auguste, Cinna's apology for monarchical rule is grotesque: "Un chef de conjurés flatte la tyrannie!" (649: "A leader of a conspiracy flatters tyranny!"). As Cinna argues for Auguste to remain in power, he seems himself to have become carried away by his own eloquence. "Le pire des Etats est l'Etat populaire" (II.i.521: "The worst of states is the popular state"), he concludes one oration. As in his speech before the conspirators, described for Emilie's benefit in the first act, Cinna evokes the massacres of great men in times past. "Ainsi la liberté ne peut plus être utile / Qu'à former les fureurs d'une guerre civile" (585–86: "Therefore liberty can have no other use than creating the furies of civil war"), Cinna argues. Both his narrated oratory before the conspirators and his defense of authoritarianism before Auguste rely upon the same horror of the anarchy of the previous age. Either Auguste's triumph or his death can be substituted for the vital missing element: what matters is that the spiral of ambition and revenge be brought to an end.

It appears that Cinna the orator has persuaded himself.[23] Both the oration he reports and the oration the audience sees him perform take fire from the visualization of the massacres of the past generation. But the resolution of the first, the planned assassination of Auguste, is opposite to the resolution of the second. In effect, the speech we see and the speech we hear about are the same: only the perorations differ. Cinna returns to Emilie, questioning her determination upon revenge, reminding her of Auguste's many benefits. Maxime's republicanism, on the other hand, is revealed by the play to be another aspect of his enslavement to passion. His faked suicide, his reliance upon the freedman Euphorbe to betray the conspiracy, his odious proposal that he and Emilie flee Rome together, all reveal his inadequacy. Caught between the imperatives of love and a nascent sense of principle, Cinna demands if not an audience's admiration (this is reserved in the play for Auguste) at least a modicum of sympathy. The disturbing sense of failure, of weakness, of vanity, that Cinna evokes in the first two acts dissipates as Corneille loads Maxime with his bad qualities.

Thus as Cinna makes his speeches before Auguste he discovers the monarchist within himself. His gifts as a persuasive performer (shared, with all due false modesty, with Emilie in the first act) set the

seed for his conversion. Emilie's is more abrupt, and, like the king's
sudden change of heart at the end of *The Fair Favourite,* the work of
divinity:

> Le ciel a résolu votre grandeur suprême;
> Et pour preuve, seigneur, je ne veux que moi-même.
> J'ose avec vanité me donner cet éclat,
> Puisqu'il change mon coeur, qu'il veut changer l'Etat.
> Ma haine va mourir, que j'ai crue immortelle;
> Elle est morte, et ce coeur devient sujet fidèle;
> Et prenant désormais cette haine en horreur,
> L'ardeur de vous servir succède à sa fureur.

(V.iii.1721–28: Heaven has decided upon your supreme greatness,
and for proof, my lord, I need only myself. I dare the vanity of
making this claim: since Heaven has changed my heart, heaven
favors changing the state. My hatred is dying, although I believed
it immortal; it is dead, and my heart becomes a faithful subject;
henceforth, feeling horror at such hatred, the ardor of serving
you takes the place of its fury.)

Emilie's passions consent to an orderly succession, from furious
hatred to the ardor of servitude. Livie seconds this extravagant picture
of passionate devotion to the emperor in her vision of a state utterly
submissive to Auguste, now "maître des coeurs." Cinna, kneeling before Auguste in the second act, now kneels before him in earnest in the
fifth. "Votre Rome à genoux vous parle par ma bouche" (II.i.606:
"Your Rome on its knees speaks to you through my mouth") he
declared then; here the image is literalized in his and Emilie's submission. Livie proclaims over the spared conspirators:

> Après cette action vous n'avez rien à craindre,
> On portera le joug désormais sans se plaindre;
> Et les plus indomptés, renversant leur projets,
> Mettront toute leur gloire à mourir vos sujets.

(V.iii.1757–60: After this action you have nothing to fear; henceforth the yoke will be carried without complaints; and the most
stubborn, forsaking their plans, will find all their glory in dying
your subjects.)

Perhaps the language here is a bit excessive. Carrying the yoke without complaint does not sound particularly glorious; and what glorious deaths are those that await the conspirators? As long as Auguste's royal will is accepted as congruent with the will of the heavens, his oblivion remains in effect. Auguste "veut tout oublier" just as, earlier, his position as "maître de l'univers" was one he sustained by will: "je veux l'être." He wills his forgetting just as he wills his mastery. And for the moment, his royal will and the divine will are one.

The insistence of Corneille's play upon the historical particularity of this moment warns us to distinguish between the *Cinna* of 1641 and the *Cinna* that the Comédie Française would perform twenty-seven times at court. The latter play celebrates absolutism achieved: "The entire Cornelian endeavour," Mitchell Greenberg pronounces, "has traced the 'incorporation' of the monarchy as an Absolutist imperative. . . . The 'King' subsumes in his person all the historical contradictions of society and transcends them." The *Cinna* that was reprised time and again from 1680 to 1715 is in this sense—a sense that Greenberg borrows from Louis Marin—a portrait of the king. Drawing the analogy between the doctrine of transubstantiation and the political strategy of royal portraiture, Marin proposes that "the king is only truly king, that is, monarch, in images. They are his *real* presence."[24] Like Voltaire reading the greatness of Condé back into the duc d'Enghien's response to *Cinna,* Greenberg reshapes Corneille's project with the help of hindsight. But *Cinna,* in 1641, offers a royal portrait that is only ideal. In its audience, there is no one monarchical body to redirect the disordered ardors of a conspiratorial world.[25]

Rather, there is a triumvirate. The archbishop on the dais with the king and queen offers both an image of victory and stability (for the moment the wars are over; the Fronde has yet to begin) and a visual counterpart to the play's problem with the Roman past. The whole sphere of reference within the play is to the two triumvirates, and to Auguste's transformation from Octave the triumvir into Auguste the emperor. Any desire to see the cardinal as a kind of Auguste is challenged not only by a decent sense of loyalty to the king, but also by the position he takes as one of three. The play is not prophetic; rather, it expresses a monarchical hope. The deaths of Richelieu and Louis XIII in quick succession, the regency of Anne of Austria and Cardinal Mazarin: these and other events that succeeded *Cinna* remind us of the extent to which *Cinna*'s Auguste is a fictive projection.

Perhaps Condé wept, as Voltaire would no doubt have it, because Auguste's vision of an imperial self spoke to an inchoate yearning that he would later see fulfilled in Louis XIV. But if he indeed wept, it is equally possible that he wept because that sense of autonomy was something he could not share. Forced into a loveless marriage with Richelieu's hunchbacked niece by the king's intervention, Condé might instead have seen himself in Cinna, hopelessly embroiled in contradictory demands over which he has no control. Master of himself as of the universe, Corneille's Auguste may figure not just a particular impossibility for Condé but also a more universally impossible coherence.

III

During the week of May 7, 1664, Louis XIV entertained his courtiers and a number of distinguished visitors at the Palace of Versailles. *Les Plaisirs de l'île enchantée* (*The Pleasures of the Enchanted Island*) was the name given to the first three days of festivities, which included, according to the published program, "Collation ornée de Machines, Comedie meslée de Danse et de Musique, Ballet de Palais d'Alcine, Feu d'Artifice: et d'autres Festes galantes et magnifiques" ("Banquet with machines, comedy mixed with dance and music, the Ballet of the Palace of Alcina, fireworks, and other elegant and magnificent festivities").[26] The gathering drew its theme from Ariosto's *Orlando Furioso*. The enchanted island of Alcina, the Circe-like sorceress who holds Ruggiero (played by the king on this occasion) and "plusieurs autres bons chevaliers" prisoner in sensual bondage, was built in an artificial lake (*Plaisirs*, p. 110). The first day was devoted to processions in which the courtiers assumed their Ariostan roles; it concluded with a dinner served by the Seasons, each presenting an appropriate course with appropriate verses. On the second day, Ruggiero and his knights amazed the company with feats of horsemanship, and the group retired that evening to view a new play by Molière, *La Princesse d'Elide*. The third day offered the ballet of the palace of Alcina: specially constructed small islands in the lake disgorged monsters, which the courtiers vanquished in combat. This brought to an end the activities centered on the main theme of the *Plaisirs;* but the party continued for four more days.

On May 12, "le soir, Sa Majesté fit jouer une comédie nommée *Tartuffe*," runs the *Relation* published with *La Princesse d'Elide,*

> que le sieur de Molière avoit faite contre les hypocrites; mais quoiqu'elle eût été trouvée fort divertissante, le Roi connut tant de conformité entre ceux qu'une véritable dévotion met dans le chemin du Ciel et ceux qu'une vaine ostentation des bonnes oeuvres n'empêche pas d'en commettre de mauvaises, que son extrême délicatesse pour les choses de la religion ne peut souffrir cette ressemblance du vice avec la vertu, qui pouvoient ètre prise[s] l'une pour l'autre, et, quoiqu'on ne doutât point de bonnes intentions de l'auteur, il la défendit pourtant en public et il se priva soi-même de ce plaisir pour n'en pas laisser abuser à d'autres, moins capable d'en faire un juste discernement.

> (In the evening, his majesty had them play a comedy named *Tartuffe,* which Molière had written against hypocrites. But although it was found to be extremely entertaining, the king noticed so much similarity between those who are set in the way of heaven by a true devotion and those whose empty display of good deeds does not restrain them from doing bad ones, that his extreme sensitivity to matters of religion could not tolerate this similitude between vice and virtue, the one of which could be taken for the other, and, although one should not at all suspect the good intentions of the author, he nonetheless forbade it in public and he even denied himself this pleasure in order not to allow others, less capable than he of just discernment, to be abused.)[27]

This is a cautious account, the words carefully weighed; although the *Relation* is the work of André Félibien, Molière's nineteenth-century editors suspect the presence here of his own hand (*Plaisirs*, p. 92). As it delicately works out the king's reasoning on this occasion, the *Relation* also hints at the problem at the core of the play. It is the theatricality of hypocrisy that is in question here. Where Louis XIV is capable of distinguishing between the true appearance of piety and the false enactment of piety, his less discerning subjects are not. Despite the good intentions of the playwright, this piece is so susceptible of mistaking by ordinary audiences that even the king must deny himself the pleasure of viewing it.

A different report of the king's response to the play was published in the *Gazette* that appeared on May 17. Praising the king's piety, the report mentions a recent example of it in action: "comme il le fit encore voir naguère par ses défenses de représenter une pièce de théâtre intitulée *l'Hypocrite,* que Sa Majesté pleinement éclairée en toutes choses, jugea absolument injurieuse à la religion et capable de produire de très dangereux effets" ("as he recently showed it again in his prohibitions of performances of a play entitled *The Hypocrite,* which His Majesty, fully enlightened in all things, judged to be utterly harmful to religion and capable of producing very dangerous consequences"). Later in the summer of the same year, in a narrative account of the activities of Louis XIV entitled *L'Homme glorieux ou la dernière perfection de l'homme achevée par la gloire éternelle* (*Glorious Man, or, the Perfection of Man Achieved by Eternal Glory*), an even less temperate account appeared:

> Sa Majesté est maintenant en son château royal de Fontainebleau, qu'elle a pris très grand soin elle-même qu'il fût fait beau, délicieux, agréable, parfait et accompli de toutes parts sans que rien n'y manque pour sa gloire, mais il n'y est allé qu'après une action héroïque et royale, véritablement digne de la grandeur de son coeur et de sa piété et du respect qu'il a pour Dieu et pour L'Eglise et qu'il rend volontiers aux ministres employés de leur part pour conférer les grâces nécessaires au salut. Un homme, ou plutôt un Démon vêtu de chair et habillé en homme et le plus signalé impie et libertin qui fût jamais dans les siècles passés, avait eu assez d'impiété et d'abomination pour faire sortir de son esprit diabolique une pièce tout prête d'être rendue publique en la faisant monter sur le théâtre à la dérision de toute l'Eglise et au mépris du caractère le plus sacré et de la fonction la plus divine, et au mépris de ce qu'il y a de plus saint dans l'Eglise, ordonné du Sauveur pour la sanctification des âmes, à dessein d'en rendre l'usage ridicule, contemptible, odieux. Il méritait par cet attentat sacrilège et impie un dernier supplice exemplaire et public et le feu même avant-coureur de celui de l'Enfer, pour expier un crime si grief de lèse-Majesté divine, qui va à ruiner la Religion catholique en blâmant et jouant sa plus religieuse et sainte pratique, qui est la conduite et la direction des âmes et des familles par de sages guides et conducteurs pieux. Mais Sa Majesté, après lui avoir fait

un sévère reproche, animé d'une juste colère par un trait de sa clémence ordinare, en laquelle il imite la douceur essentielle à Dieu, lui a par abolition remis son insolence et pardonné sa hardiesse démoniaque, pour lui donner le temps d'en faire pénitence publique et solennelle toute sa vie.

(His majesty is currently at his royal palace at Fontainebleau, which he has taken great pains himself to make beautiful, delightful, agreeable, perfect, and adorned in all aspects so that nothing is lacking for his glory, but he did not go there until after a heroic and royal action, truly worthy of the greatness of his heart and of his piety and the respect he bears for God and for the Church and which he offers freely to those ministers employed on their part in conferring those sacraments necessary for salvation. A man, or rather a Demon clothed in flesh and costumed as a man, and the most notorious unbeliever and libertine there has ever been in all past ages, had had sufficient impiety and abomination to allow to emerge from his diabolic spirit a play, fully ready to be performed in public, making a mockery on the stage of the whole Church, exposing to contempt its most sacred character and most divine function, all that is most holy in the Church, commanded by the Savior for the sanctification of souls, with a view to making its practice ridiculous, vile, odious. For this impious and sacrilegious assault, he deserved the final, exemplary public sacrifice of the fire itself, precursor to that of Hell, to expiate so grave a crime of divine *lèse-Majesté,* which tends to the ruin of the Catholic religion, by criticizing and making a game of its most holy and sacred practice, which is the guidance and counsel of souls and families by pious guides and advisors. But His Majesty, after having severely reproached him, moved from a just anger by an effect of his characteristic clemency, in which he imitates the gentleness of God himself, has by suppression forgiven his insolence and pardoned his devilish boldness, in order to give him time to make a public and solemn penance for the rest of his life.)[28]

These last two accounts recognize no good intentions on the part of the author. All three accounts share a vision of the king as quasi-divine, however. The *Relation* in Molière's works confers upon the king the power to discern hypocrisy, to read the secrets of others' hearts. The hostile accounts portray in the king a divine wrath, suppressing the play, and a divine love and mercy, sparing the life of its loathsome author.

These documents, the sources of the riddles about *Tartuffe,* revolve around a blank center. The king's personal response is unknown. Perhaps he enjoyed the play but suppressed it out of concern for others less wise. Perhaps he loathed the play, and just barely restrained himself from committing Molière, with it, to the devouring flames. Molière's supporters and his opponents jockey for territory in a mysterious place, the king's very conscience. Another riddle, equally impossible of solution, is what the king actually saw. By strenuously denying that clerical garb of any kind figured in the original costume of Tartuffe, Molière has convinced recent scholars that he protested too much. Tartuffe must have worn at least a cassock: "L'iruption de l'homme noir en ce milieu bariolé fit scandale," writes Jean-Marie Apostolidès: "Le choc apporté par *Tartuffe* est d'abord visuel" ("The irruption of the man in black into this multicolored environment created a scandal. The shock delivered by *Tartuffe* was primarily visual").[29] What Tartuffe wore, however, like what the king thought, remains a matter of speculation and conjecture.

More difficulties await if we attempt to reconstruct the text of the play performed on May 12, 1664. The entry in the account books of Molière's company, scrupulously kept by La Grange, his fellow actor and business manager, specifies "trois actes du *Tartuffe* qui étaient les trois premiers" ("three acts of *Tartuffe* which were the first three").[30] These three would indeed make a bitter comedy, with the hypocrite triumphant after his first public exposure, as Orgon repudiates his family and embraces Tartuffe. As a result, La Grange's words have been tortured to constitute alternative *Tartuffe*s: a three-act version of the play which condenses the current five acts (thus attaching the *rex ex machina* ending to the first play), or a three-act play made up of acts 1, 3, and 4. This latter alternative would be as bitter as the first three acts alone. La Grange's words are clear: the play Louis saw must not have ended as does the version of the play finally permitted to be performed and published in February 1669. Instead, in violation of all the rules of comedy, it left the young lovers separate and deprived the young hero of his inheritance. It would have closed on Tartuffe's triumph.

Under the pressure of time, by direct "commandement du Roi" ("command of the king"), Molière was forced to finish *La Princesse d'Elide* in prose after setting only the first act and a half in verse (*Plaisirs,* p. 166). There is a possibility that *Tartuffe* was itself the victim of such undue haste, and that it was simply not finished when first performed.[31] Lost, virtually unreported by the invited audience to the *Plaisirs,* the three-act *Tartuffe* can exist only in the imagination. Yet the evidence of the *Princesse* suggests that Molière would sketch out a plot to its comic conclusion rather than stop after three acts. Nor is the plot of the *Princesse* without interest. This play (with dances and musical interludes) dramatizes the wooing of a princess who is a second Diana, who will marry none of the three princes her father has invited to Elide as suitors. Euryale, prince of Ithaca, discerns her vulnerability and wins her love by pretending to ignore her and falsely declaring his plans to marry another. The strategy works. Thus, the two new plays that Molière wrote for the *Plaisirs* focus upon hypocrisy as wooing (two others, *Les Fâcheux* and *Le Mariage forcé* were also performed, but these were already part of the repertoire). Euryale wins his princess by feigning indifference; Tartuffe wins control of Orgon's family and property, wins Orgon's love, by feigning piety.

This putative *Tartuffe,* then, would violate the basic rules of comedy which the *Princesse d'Elide* so clearly observes. By concluding with the man in black totally in charge, the play also appears to violate principles of its own comic structure set forth in the second act. Long considered a separable "*hors d'oeuvre,*" a self-contained *dépit amoureux* unnecessary to the whole play, the second act projects a comic structure that anticipates the comic structure of the five-act 1669 version of the play. W. G. Moore, applying the principles of the New Criticism to *Tartuffe,* insisted upon the unity of the play by noticing this structural coherence.[32]

Only the 1669 version of *Tartuffe* supports this reading, however. What preceded it, whatever combination of three acts it comprised, would fall short of being a true comedy: the rules of the form demand the triumph of the young lovers over parental opposition. The coherence and unity that Moore argued for, in opposition to the prevailing critical attitudes of his time, is thus in some way the direct result of the play's suppression. The completeness, the coherent structure, of the later play is due to the incompleteness, the failure, of the play's first version. The lovers' quarrel in the second act follows a structure of mutual misunderstanding that reflects the play's serious concerns with misprision and misplaced trust. Michael Spingler, more recently, has argued that Dorine's conduct in the scene, while thoroughly conventional, structurally mimics the play's *rex ex machina* ending. Dorine watches the spat, waiting until the lovers' quarrel reaches a critical peak of mutual hostility, and then, as the lovers decide to break it off, the maid breaks in and forces them to concede their true feelings. This "model of interrupted performance," Spingler argues, is repeated through the rest of the play in the form of "a theater piece which can end only if a spectator chooses to intervene and stop it." Just so does the presence of the king make itself felt only when events at the end of the play threaten to veer out of control.[33]

Both Moore's New Criticism and Spingler's metatheatrical criticism have in common an insistence that the play's discordant elements—its incorporation of farcical routines, its difficult ending—are only apparently discordant. Thematic unity or a metatheatrical revenge for the banning of *Tartuffe* both become ways of imputing absolute control over the play's text to the playwright. Despite the historical record of repeated suppressions and a five-year campaign to put the play into a shape in which it would be permitted to take the stage, Molière remains for these critics firmly in control, even to the point, as Spingler says, of entrapping Louis XIV himself in a "final nullifying mirror" at the end. In contrast to these arguments there is another tradition in the criticism of the play that sees Molière as desperately rewriting, reacting improvisatorily to Louis XIV's self-contradictory behavior through the years of *Tartuffe*'s difficulties. The king enjoyed the play but forbade its performance; he supported Molière's enemies but stood godfather to his son. By these lights, the play's discords come about inadvertently, and the praise of the monarch at the end is flattery, an expression of gratitude that the play was allowed its existence at all.[34]

"The hidden joke in *Tartuffe*," Spingler argues on the other hand, "is that for the play to end properly, it must once again be banned by the King."[35] Spingler is right in noticing a metatheatrical dimension to the play; its constant interest in social performance is represented as an interest in acting. But rather than offer a "hidden joke" against the king, the play instead presents, like the *Relation*, an ideal of royal performance and royal audience. As a performance for the king, the play can only be understood by the king. The play's mixing up of theatrical worlds, as in the combination of high-toned Cornelian resolve and *commedia dell'arte* farce in the *dépit amoureux*, requires a royal audience's imaginative piecing together to permit it to make sense. As *Tartuffe* totters on the verge of collapse into generic incoherence (although it could be argued that the humiliation of Orgon and of his younger relations at the end is an appropriate comic punishment for his blindness and their complacency), a royal gesture alone can save it. The play imitates its own history, for only the king saved it, and simultaneously, as Jacques Guicharnaud has pointed out, it imitates the king's version of his own history, for he himself was miraculously saved to fulfill his destined function as the most Christian king.[36] The restoration of order, the play's comic agenda, coincides with the suppression of disorder, the king's political agenda, and the two fuse in the play's vision of the monarch as perfect audience.

Throughout *Tartuffe,* Molière strives to achieve an identity of these comic and political agendas. From the first, Orgon's house is presented as a kingdom in disorder, presided over by a lord of misrule. "On n'y respecte rien," complains Mme Pernelle, "chacun y parle haut, / Et c'est tout justement la cour du roi Pétaut" (I.i.11–12: "Everyone speaks right out on everything: / It's like a court in which Misrule is king").[37] Despite Mme Pernelle's stupidity, her observation here is correct, although misapplied. While she accuses the younger members of the family of functioning like a court of misrule, she asserts that Tartuffe's guidance is a necessary corrective. In so doing, she inadvertently points out the vacancy at the top in the organization of the household. Orgon's abdication of his authority to Tartuffe is characterized as a kind of festive inversion. Mme Pernelle's refusal to remain in this "tour de Babylone" (161: "tower of Babylon"), where visits, balls, and conversations are the main activities, emphasizes not only her rigidity and prudishness but also the holiday atmosphere of Orgon's house. Tartuffe's presence should be salutary, but Mme Pernelle's angry departure suggests that he is not in control when Orgon is not around. Since Mme Pernelle is wrong about Tartuffe, an audience is certainly within its rights to expect her description of the house as a court of misrule to be ironically fulfilled with Tartuffe as the comic inverter of order.

Falstaff, in Shakespeare's *Henry IV* plays, similarly functions as a fat and disruptive liar who threatens to invert the social order. He insists throughout on remaining faithful to his own genre of festive comedy despite his presence in a history play. The background of *Tartuffe* is also historical. While it is certainly not a history play, it relies upon an audience's awareness of the Fronde and of Orgon's role in those recent troubles. "Nos troubles l'avaient mis sur le pied d'homme sage," Dorine explains, offering to Cléante and more appropriately to the audience some biographical information about Orgon, "Et pour servir son Prince il montra du courage" (181–82: "During our civil wars he showed good sense / And served with courage in his king's defense"). Dorine's remarks have the effect of suggesting that Orgon's "good sense" during the Fronde was a kind of aberration, or at least that she was pleasantly surprised by his courage. There is a multiplication of comic inversions here. Just as Orgon's house seems to Mme Pernelle and to the audience to be a court of misrule in opposite ways, the Fronde, chaotic and traumatic though it may have been, brought out hidden virtues in Orgon. With the restoration of order and the defeat of the Frondeurs, however, Orgon has disintegrated into "un homme hébété" (183: "his sanity has been reduced to zero"). Orgon is perfectly out of step with the rest of the world; his house mirrors the kingdom in reverse. The realm's new stability, which permits to Elmire and Cléante the elegant life of visits and balls, and permits Valère and Mariane to make marriage plans, permits Orgon to embark upon a foolish, holiday infatuation with Tartuffe.

By identifying instability and misrule with repression, Molière toys with an audience's traditional comic expectations. Tartuffe, as he is described throughout the first two acts, apparently functions according to comic rules. He fools no one but the play's gross dupes, Orgon and Mme Pernelle, the "tasteless few," as Judd Hubert puts it, "who applaud Tartuffe's fraudulent performance."[38] Insisting upon Tartuffe's corpulence and physicality both in the "pauvre homme" scene and in her negotiations with Mariane, Dorine makes it clear that Tartuffe is an obvious fraud, blatantly greedy. Orgon's description of the displays of piety that moved him to shelter Tartuffe is a report of overacting so grandiose that Cléante can only respond with amazement: "Parbleu! vous êtes fou, mon frère, que je crois. / Avec de tels discours vous moquez-vous de moi?" (311–312: "Good lord, brother, you're mad, I do believe. / Are you sure you're not laughing up your sleeve?")

The idea that Orgon and Tartuffe are involved in some sort of preposterous performance, with a view toward ridiculing and humiliating the smart set, reinforces the identification of Tartuffe's repressive regime with comic misrule. The expectations built up in the first and second acts (that his piety is a fraud and that his intentions are amorous) seem to be confirmed by his utterly conventional attempt to seduce Elmire in the third act. As disguised lover, invading Orgon's house in pursuit of his much younger wife, Tartuffe would be at home in the world of the *commedia*. Equally a *commedia* type and likewise at home, Orgon, under the table in the fourth act, continues the perverse inversion. As Susan Tiefenbrunn suggests, Orgon, in this demeaning position, "assumes the function of an all-seeing but far from omniscient audience. . . . capable of stopping the show at his will."[39] In this position, as in his position as head of a headless household, Orgon functions as a parody of the central monarchical authority that the play praises at its end. Unlike Orgon, however, the king in the audience is omniscient as well: as the *Relation* notes, he is fully aware of the playwright's good intentions.

Tartuffe's assumption of a stance of exaggerated piety when he is unmasked the first time, at the end of the third act, is in keeping with his playing of the stock role of comic would-be adulterer. Likewise Orgon, as he foolishly accepts this repentance at face value, plays his predestined role. But the fourth act reveals to us that the lover's part is only one of many roles that can be assumed by the chameleonlike Tartuffe. Jonas Barish's exploration of the revulsion from Protean virtuosity that constitutes the "antitheatrical prejudice" becomes useful here, for what makes Tartuffe both theatrically and politically dangerous is his refusal to be fixed to a particular role.[40] Orgon's assumption of his proper authoritative role as he emerges from under the table is made irrelevant by Tartuffe's refusal to be discomfited by exposure. Nor has Tartuffe, in the wooing scene with Elmire, revealed himself as he truly is. Upon this latest exposure, he becomes instead the wronged householder, defamed and libeled by Orgon, the scandalous Frondeur. Conscious of his worth, Tartuffe, now playing the good man, claims his own.

The contemporary campaign against the play, which formed part of a larger campaign against theater, insisted upon the difficulty of distinguishing hypocrites from good men and upon the value of the good deeds that hypocrites may perform despite their impure motives. Bourdaloue's sermon against hypocrisy, which attacks Molière's play savagely, insists upon the impossibility of knowing for certain the difference between pious behavior that is false and pious behavior that is true. "L'hypocrisie, dit ingénieusement St. Augustin, est cette ivraie de l'Evangile, que l'on ne peut arracher sans déraciner en même temps le bon grain" ("Hypocrisy, St. Augustine ingeniously says, is the weed in the parable, which cannot be pulled up without uprooting at the same time the good wheat"), Bourdaloue maintained; given the problems of perception that beset all of fallen humanity, detecting and punishing hypocrisy lie outside our capacity.[41] "The hypocrite and the *dévot*," wrote "Rochemont" in his *Observations sur le Festin de Pierre*, "have the same appearance and are one thing to the public; it is only the inner life which distinguishes them; and in order 'to avoid equivocation and remove anything that might confound good with evil,' it is necessary to show what the *dévot* does secretly, as well as the hypocrite."[42] "Sous prétexte de ruiner la fausse dévotion," Coustel charged of Moliére in 1694, "il représente les brutalitez de son Tartuffe avec des couleurs si noires, et il lui fait avancer des maximes si détestables, que la corruption du coeur humain ne manquera pas de les faire appliquer, non à un Tartuffe de Theatre: mais à un véritable homme de bien" ("Under the pretext of destroying false devotion, he represents the brutalities of his Tartuffe in such dark colors and makes him utter such detestable maxims that the human heart, in its corruption, cannot avoid applying them not to a Tartuffe of the theater, but to a truly decent man").[43] To the antitheatrical divines, hypocrisy is a theatricalization of everyday life that brings into focus the human heart's inability to know what is good and what is evil without divine guidance. The play's spoofing of the language of that guidance, by portraying Tartuffe as a lay director of conscience (involved, as *L'Homme glorieux* would have it, in the most sacred and religious of Christian activities) is blasphemous because it suggests that the unaided human eye can indeed read the hypocrite's secret.

Cléante argues as much explicitly in the first act, and Tartuffe's exaggerated performance upon his entrance permits an audience, too, to see immediately that he is a fake. "Mais, en un mot, je sais, pour toute ma science, / Du faux avec le vrai faire la différence," Cléante assures Orgon (I.v.353–54: "My only knowledge and my only art / Is this: to tell the true and false apart"). The basic good sense of Cléante's attitude towards events in the play should not blind us to the glaring complacency of this remark. Not only does the action of the play leave us wondering what good Cléante's "science" can do once Tartuffe has seized Orgon's property, the speech that follows relies upon exterior performance as much as Orgon's infatuation with Tartuffe does. The performance of the good men whom Cléante praises is simply more subtle than that of Tartuffe in the Church. As Guicharnaud has pointed out, Cléante can only praise the truly pious for what they do not do: they are not members of cabals (like the secret society that banned *Tartuffe*); they do not flaunt their virtue, do not censure or criticize.[44] Cléante proposes a series of alternative models for Orgon: "Voilà mes gens, voilà comme il en faut user," he concludes:

Voilà l'exemple enfin qu'il se faut proposer.
Votre homme, à dire vrai, n'est pas de ce modèle.

(403–05: These are the men that win my admiration.
These are the models for our emulation.
You know your man is not at all like these.)

In a sense, Cléante is pointing out to Orgon Tartuffe's failure to be an effective hypocrite. The virtuoso dissimulator of virtue would not fail to exercise an appropriate moderation.

The family's aim of stripping Tartuffe of his pious role and exposing him to Orgon's view backfires because Tartuffe has so little invested in it.[45] He is not a successful pious fraud, nor does he need to be. Nor does an audience that is not royal need the king's just discernment to notice this. Tartuffe readily switches into the part of disguised lover when encouraged to do so by Elmire. Dorine's nauseous vision of what it must be like to be "tartuffiée" almost materializes before the audience's eyes in the fourth act's table scene. A failure to sustain the role of hypocrite (in his first entrance, the stage direction suggests that Tartuffe only takes on the pious part after he perceives Dorine watching him) is followed by a failure to triumph as the discreet and skillful lover, but at the end of the fourth act Tartuffe's ineptitude as a performer does not seem to matter. He becomes an actor without a role, an appetitive and assimilative force without face or name. A horror at the pure greed of the actor for others' property and selves animates the play's climactic moment. "I am not what I am," Iago declares as the definition of his virtuosity and his villainy, and Tartuffe is similarly an actor and a villain. As Orgon reclaims his rightful role as master of the house, Tartuffe reveals himself in the new role of Orgon. He has replaced his master and, in possession of the black box with its secret papers, owns him. Heaven alone can expose and punish imposture, and at the end of act 4 Tartuffe lays claim to even that role: "On n'est pas ou l'on pense en me faisant injure," Tartuffe thunders, "j'ai de quoi confondre et punir l'imposture" (IV.viii.1561–62: "You are not where you think you are if you wrong me; I have the power to confound and punish imposture" [my translation]). We are not where we think we are; Tartuffe has moved from possessing Orgon's property and his secret to possession of his role. It is now Tartuffe, not Orgon, who restores order and promises justice. He arrogates the power to tell right from wrong that Cléante blithely assumed was his and that the antitheatrical divines asserted was only God's. He lays claim to a wisdom and power that the Exempt will shortly reveal to be the king's. In Molière's play the king must curtail Tartuffe's dizzying seizure of roles and fit him back into his social role by unveiling him as a notorious confidence man with a long criminal record.

While the comic structures of *Tartuffe* stand in for larger political realities, the comic resolutions of exposure and expulsion cannot meet the threat of an actor who plays comedy with such bad faith. Tartuffe pursues his own private ends while simultaneously appearing to satisfy the generic demands of the comic world. He is a dangerous actor, for he refuses to limit himself to one role. Playing the role of Orgon in the first and subsequent performances of *Tartuffe,* Molière confronted himself with an adversary who is an actor, and nothing but an actor; in a way, his confrontation with the hypocrite reenacts the origin of the word in the ancient Greek sense. On the Athenian tragic stage, the playwright was the first actor; the second, or *hypokrites,* was a professional actor, and only an actor. In social terms, Tartuffe's acquisition of Orgon's house, money, and black box figures the destablizing energies that theater (again, traditionally) ought to control. Actors may put on the clothes of monarchs and exercise regal power, but they do so in the circumscribed world of the stage. Tartuffe's desire to use his acting skills to get ahead in the world, like his refusal to remain fixed in any of the traditional comic roles that the play proposes for him, defies this circumscription.

Dorine's intervention in the lovers' quarrel figures the way theater should work: everyone plays an assigned role; misunderstandings, duly manufactured, are cleared up. Dorine recognizes Tartuffe's greed from the beginning, but caught in her role as clever maid, she is effectively powerless to resist it. A voice of traditional comedy in the play, she offers the wisdom of the soubrette. Dorine's freedom and her limitations are played out in act 2, scene 2, as she interrupts Orgon's advice to Mariane, but stills herself each time he raises his hand. Comically speaking what may not be spoken, reining in her words with each gesture of Orgon's raised arm, Dorine functions in *Tartuffe* as Lucio does in *Measure for Measure*. But where Lucio's intrusion into the duke's secrets of power is embarrassing and severely punished, Dorine's challenges to authority are appropriately circumscribed within her traditional role. If Lucio figures theater's ability to shed light where none is wanted, Dorine figures theater's futility. She cannot save Mariane.

In Molière's France, theater is powerless to effect or resist social changes. What powers the institution has derive from the pleasure and permission of the king. Only the king can transform a confidence trickster and vagabond into an actor by means of royal license. And the king, the play suggests, can return an actor to the condition of confidence trickster if he threatens to escape his prescribed confinement within the theater. *Tartuffe* enacts both the actor's freedom (in Michael Goldman's phrase) to engage in forbidden, blasphemous activities, and society's restrictions of that freedom through traditional genres, and, failing that, through legal restraints and direct royal interventions.[46] The story of Tartuffe is the story of *Tartuffe,* but with a twist. Louis XIV finally freed the play from the restraints of censorship and permitted its performance, but in the play, Tartuffe's free play concludes in imprisonment by royal command.

The reason that Louis himself must become part of the play is that Tartuffe, in his triumph, assumes that he can continue to play out his freedom to select his own parts before the royal audience. This is a serious miscalculation. His audiences in the play have been of two sorts: the dupes, Mme Pernelle and Orgon, who take him at face value and accept coarse performance as truth, and the more sophisticated of his victims, Elmire and Dorine, who assume that behind the mask of piety lurks a conventional comic figure, and hope to expel the disgraced lover with ridicule. But, as the Exempt, the king's representative, who comes to deliver the family from Tartuffe at the end of the play, points out, the king is an audience of a far different sort:

Nous vivons sous un Prince ennemi de la fraude
Un Prince dont les yeux se font jour dans les coeurs,

Et que ne peut tromper tout l'art des impostures.
D'un fin discernement sa grande âme pourvue
Sur les choses toujours jette une droite vue.

(V.vii.1906–10: We live under a king who hates deceit,
A king whose eyes see into every heart
And can't be fooled by an impostor's art.
The keen discernment that his greatness brings
Gives him a piercing insight into things.)

This perspicacious royal audience sees behind Tartuffe's improvisa-
tional impostures a historical reality. "D'abord il a percé, par ses vives
clartés / Des replis de son coeur toutes les lâchetés" (1919–20: "His
insight penetrated from the start/The twisted treason of that scoun-
drel's heart"). But more importantly, the king also recognizes Tartuffe
as a criminal with a dossier, "un longue détail d'actions toutes noires"
(1925: "His record is a long and ugly one"). As Ralph Albanese has
pointed out, at this moment Tartuffe's groveling self-portrait at the
end of the third act becomes reality: for Albanese, the whole play resembles a juridical proceeding.[47]

The ultimate exposure of Tartuffe by means of his criminal record
is a surprise both for the rest of the characters in the play and for the
audience. Throughout the play, Tartuffe has functioned without history, without social rank, without definition: hence his skill in switch-
ing among his many roles. Dorine's saucy vision of his origins in rural
life is conventional, and we have no basis for believing it or not. In
staging the family's deliverance from Tartuffe's clutches as an act of
royal intervention, Molière celebrates the monarch's solitary ability to
recognize Tartuffe for what he is. Yet the monarch's memory here is
institutional. Tartuffe's previous crimes, committed under a previous
alias, are the property of the king's investigative authorities. The
world of the play is a "règne policier," as Albanese puts it:[48] a police
state.

The author of the *Relation* takes us into the king's mind as he
watches the play. But the "juste discernement" to which both the *Relation* and the Exempt's speech in the play allude are of different orders.
In the *Relation* the king's response to the play is internalized; his
thought process is shared with the reader, who is assured of Molière's
good intentions and the king's perspicacity. The theological complexities of hypocrisy, so thorny for the antitheatrical divines, are invoked

as part of the royal response to the first version of the play. The king knows that the play might raise issues that less sophisticated audiences would find troublesome. Audiences that would see the play as a libertine satire upon true piety could be made up of either worldly cynics or angry clerics.[49] But the king in the play is not presented as thinking through the issues in this way. He recognizes Tartuffe, recalls his history of crime, and swiftly crafts the just punishments of both Tartuffe and Orgon. He does so by staging his own play of imposture, permitting Tartuffe to believe himself in power and empowering the Exempt to delay his exposure until the best possible moment. The king in the *Relation* is a wise and all-knowing audience; the king in *Tartuffe* is a playwright more skilled than Molière. Molière, unable to control the Protean energy of Tartuffe, is embroiled in a play that will end, if it ends with the third or the fourth act, unsatisfactorily. Not only did the playwright act the part of Orgon, he shares the plight of Orgon. Only the king's assistance can rewrite the ending, and transform the renegade actor back into the vagabond.

The *Relation* proposes—as do the hostile reports, with their news of a total suppression of the play—an alternative ending. According to it, the king has suppressed the play, so that misunderstandings will not proliferate in public (or in private). But just as it is impossible to imagine the ending of the first version of the play, so it was impossible to curtail debate about it. In the five years that followed, Molière persisted in announcing his good intentions in a series of *Placets,* petitions to the king. These, like the *Relation,* insisted upon the monarch's private enjoyment of and perfect understanding of the play. The secret society of Saint-Sacrament de l'Autel, on the other hand, continued to impugn Molière's name and his play. Instead of putting a stop to confusion, suppressing the play compounded it. In just the same way, Tartuffe's repressive regime is represented in the play as a reign of misrule. The play's censorship led to the proverbial result: slanders that would be published unnoticed take on new life when suppressed. The king's enmity toward fraud, in the Exempt's speech in the final act of the play, is also a hostility toward slanderers. His exposure of Tartuffe is an act of both publication and suppression.

Tartuffe's appearance before the king is replayed as a humiliating exposure: "Venant vous accuser, il s'est trahi lui-même" (V. vii. 1921: "Coming forward to accuse you, he betrayed himself" [my translation]). Comic inversion again comes into play. For Tartuffe's attempt to publish Orgon's secret and reveal the treasonable contents of the box, the king substitutes his own publication of Tartuffe's "volumes d'histoires" (1926). Orgon's papers, on the other hand, are not only returned to him but plucked (1934) from Tartuffe, and the deed of gift is rendered void. The interplay between repression and license, suggested by Mme Pernelle at the beginning of the first act, furnishes the dynamic of the ending. The king suppresses Orgon's treasonous secret and voids his foolish contract at the same moment that he publishes Tartuffe's black past and strips him in public. The rationale for both actions is political and historical: Orgon's good deeds in the past (seen by Dorine as aberrant) earn his deliverance now, and Tartuffe's history of black deeds earns his disgrace.[50] The play alludes to the praise of the king's discernment in the *Relation* in order to hint that censorship can often defeat itself, and its comic strategy suggests that repression can be misrule in another guise.

The king's final act of exposure and publication, at the end of the play, figures Louis XIV's act of finally permitting *Tartuffe* to be performed. And it also incorporates in it the complementary elements of Auguste's clemency in *Cinna:* as the Exempt reports, the king both knows all and forgets all.[51] His recognition of Tartuffe arises from his knowledge; Orgon's black box is forgotten in his royal oblivion. This ending, unlike the ending of *Cinna,* is not within the playwright's power, however. Molière needs the royal audience not merely to understand the play, but to publish the king's understanding of it. Further, he needs this understanding to be published with all the force of a criminal prosecution. In the dossier of Tartuffe and in the black box of Orgon are figured the tools of an absolutist government. Louis destroyed the records of those who had participated in the Fronde, and he published the fact of this destruction. The king's forgiveness of Orgon in the play recalls this act of clemency and publication. His exposure of Tartuffe suggests that the records of common criminals (unlike those of Frondeurs) are still part of the state's knowledge of the conduct, loyal or disloyal, of all subjects.

For *Tartuffe* as a play to receive a clean bill, the criminal record of Tartuffe as a character must be exposed. This knowledge is special royal knowledge: but once the king shares his files with the public, Tartuffe can be truly exposed and known. An ordinary citizen, like Cléante, may think himself as capable as the king of knowing truth from falsehood; but Cléante, like Molière and unlike Louis XIV, can do nothing about it. Like Orgon, Molière the playwright has become the victim of his creature. His *Tartuffe,* which he thought he knew and could control, took on a life of its own. Instead of a traditional comedy about hypocrisy, Molière began a play in which the stakes had become the legitimacy and institutional status of theater itself. It remained to the king alone to finish it.

IV

On January 7, 1689, James II of Britain arrived at Saint-Germain; his exile, after his expulsion from his kingdom by Parliament, had just begun. Louis XIV met him with a hundred six-horse carriages, and introduced him to the palace of Saint-Germain as his new home. "Voici votre maison; quand j'y viendrai, vous m'en ferez des honneurs," Madame de Sévigné reports Louis as saying to James; "et je vous les ferai quand vous viendrez à Versailles" ("This is your home; when I come to visit, you will be my host; and I will be your host when you come to Versailles").[52] Madame de Sévigné marveled at William's restraint (the gossip at the French court had been that he would have James executed), but even more she admired Louis's generosity on this occasion:

> Cependant le Roi fait pour ces Majestés angloises de choses toutes divines; car n'est-ce point être l'image du Tout-Puissant que de soutenir un roi chassé, trahi, abandonné comme il est? La belle âme du Roi se plaît à jouer ce grand rôle.
>
> (p. 310: However, the king does things for their English majesties that are totally divine; because is it not precisely to be the image of the Almighty to succor a king who is hunted, betrayed, abandoned as he is? The beauteous soul of the king is pleased to play this great role.)

Madame de Sévigné makes the same identification of divine wisdom and clemency with the royal role that is made in *Cinna* and *Tartuffe.* The king is an actor, in her use of the image, not insofar as he resembles players like Tartuffe, but rather insofar as he strives to play the only role that can challenge him, the role of God. The professional actor playing Auguste on one of twenty-seven court occasions set before the king's eye not a model to be emulated but a type: as the Old

Testament kings are imperfect anticipations of Christ, Corneille's Auguste is an imperfect anticipation of Louis. Louis himself, the most Christian king, is a type of the Almighty, playing the "great role" as he welcomes his pursued fellow. Madame de Sévigné's conventional language points up the difficulties the convention entails. For although playing God is admirable to her and other courtiers, such role-playing is antipathetic to the antitheatrical *dévots* who savaged *Tartuffe.*

Her concern about the royal role extended at this time to a specific theatrical occasion. *Esther,* Racine's new play, written at the command of Madame de Maintenon for the girls of her new academy at Saint-Cyr, was in rehearsal at the time of the British king's arrival with his queen and the Prince of Wales. On January 28, Madame de Sévigné wrote to her daughter with some relief that the premiere (on the 26th) had been a great success: "J'étois en peine qu'une petite demoiselle représentât le roi," she confesses; "on dit que cela est fort bien" (p. 332: "I was worried that a young girl would be representing the king; they say that it went very well"). While the king's approximation of the divine role is admirable, Madame de Sévigné worries about the girl's ability to play Assuérus: the child might fall short of the dignity (or succumb to the violence) needed for the role. The project of *Esther* was risky in more ways than this. Certainly there was concern that the girls might find themselves overmatched by the great biblical roles; there was also the more mundane concern that the performance would be amateurish and embarrassing.

More importantly, though, *Esther* was risky as an experiment in addressing the charges laid against the theater by the clergy. It was to be, Madame de Maintenon informed Racine, a model of pious drama, and one that would be limited exclusively to Saint-Cyr, in no way open to the public.[53] As such it would function as a sort of vindication of the theater itself and, in addition, as a vindication of Madame de Maintenon's special status in Louis XIV's court. Madame de Maintenon's influence over Louis (along with the fear of death that came with bouts of illness) was widely given the credit for the court's new atmosphere of reform. Secretly married to Louis since 1684, Madame de Maintenon had to play the part of his mistress in the court. And she had to show her difference, as a virtuous and pious woman, from her predecessors: her difficult task, as she told her confessor, was that of creating a personality ("composer son personnage").[54] She sought to save the soul of the king (and with it her own) by functioning as a model of piety. *Esther* emerges out of her larger project of saving the king's soul and of reforming his kingdom. It would be a new kind of play, appropriate to a court, but pious, virtuous, educational.

"Madame de Maintenon avoit un goût et un talent particulier pour l'éducation de la jeunesse," recalled her niece, Madame de Caylus ("Madame de Maintenon had a particular relish and talent for the education of young people").[55] She had first caught the king's eye as tutor to his children by Madame de Montespan. She continued to show her interest in youth by supporting institutions devoted to raising poor girls of noble rank at Rueil and Noisy, and in 1686 she persuaded the king to purchase the Abbey of Saint-Cyr, adjacent to Versailles, for a foundation exclusively committed to this goal. Called the Institut de Saint-Louis, this was not to be an ordinary convent. "Nous voulions une piété solide," she wrote of the rules of the foundation, "éloignée de toutes les petitesses de couvent, de l'esprit, de l'élévation, un grand choix dans nos maximes, une grande éloquence dans nos instructions, une liberté entière dans nos conversations, un tour de raillerie agréable dans la société, de l'élévation dans notre piété, et un grand mépris pour les pratiques des autres maisons" (Lavallée, p. 79: "We wanted a firm piety, removed from the pettinesses of the convent, witty, elevated, with great variety in our maxims, lofty eloquence in our instruction, total freedom in our conversations, a touch of pleasant mockery in society, greatness of spirit in our piety, and a great contempt for the practices of other houses"). To this end, she encouraged the performances of plays, written at first by Madame Brinon, the first director of the institute. Finding these, despite their pious subjects, "détestables, à la vérité" (Madame de Caylus, p. 95: "truly odious"), Madame de Maintenon carefully selected some plays from the regular repertoire with a view to their lack of amorous intrigue. Corneille's *Cinna* and Racine's *Iphigénie* and *Andromaque* were performed for the purpose of polishing the diction and encouraging the grace of the students. "Nos petites filles ont joué *Andromaque*," she wrote to Racine, "et l'ont joué si bien qu'elles ne la joueront plus, ni aucune de vos pièces" (Lavallée, p. 83: "Our young girls played *Andromaque,* and they played it so well that they will never play it again, nor any other of your plays"). Out of this letter came the command to Racine to write something pious and improving.

Racine's career at this moment demonstrates that both poles of the contemporary debate about theater could indeed exist within one person. Madame de Maintenon's desire to resolve the two in a special play for Saint-Cyr required his return from a highly publicized retirement from professional theater. After *Phèdre* in 1677, Racine had renounced the theater, sought forgiveness from his former teachers, the Jansenists of Port-Royal, married a good bourgeoise, and won employment, with his friend Boileau, as historiographer royal in the court of Louis XIV. The sincerity of this conversion has been the subject of much debate. For Raymond Picard, it was an opportunistic maneuver, a matter of noticing which way the wind was blowing: the king's renunciation of his dissolute ways extended to the theater and made Racine's renunciation a precondition of his royal appointment.[56] For Jean Pommier, however, the career of dramatist naturally evolved into the career of court poet and historian; it was a logical promotion to a world more stable and less controversial than that of the professional theater. Despite Racine's confession, reported by his son, that playwrights were no better than "empoisonneurs publics" ("public poisoners"), he had participated in preparations for an opera, *L'Idylle de la paix,* presented by the marquis de Seignelay before the king at Sceaux in 1685.[57] For others, such as Jean Orcibal and René Jasinski, the religious motive was indeed paramount, the conversion motivated by guilt not simply at the time wasted in the theatrical profession but at the gulf that had opened between Racine and his religious upbringing, and between Racine and his God. For them, Racine, far from being an unprincipled and successful courtier, risked his career by maintaining connections with the Jansenists (under attack throughout this period by Jesuits, led by Louis' confessor, père de la Chaise, and Harlay de Champvallon, the archibishop of Paris). Moving closer to the king, becoming his personal historian, accompanying him on his campaigns, Racine was not advancing his career, but advancing his salvation.[58]

For Racine as for Madame de Sévigné, then, the king becomes a special, paradoxical image of God, inimical to the exaggerations of theater but incapable of description in any but theatrical terms. The project of *Esther,* rooted in Madame de Maintenon's attempt to reconcile the court's new drive toward piety with a recognition of theater's humanistic justifications, is likewise fraught with contradictions. So, too, are the rules of witty, worldly piety that she inscribed for the order of Saint-Louis (and would later renounce after the experience of

Esther). For the play's audience was not exclusively confined to Saint-Cyr. Rather, the performances of *Esther,* through late January and February of 1689, became a court event of major proportions. The music for the choruses was composed by Jean-Baptiste Moreau, who had replaced Lully, after his death, as the king's primary composer; the sets were decorated by Bérain, the king's designer for court festivals. The costumes were especially spectacular, in Persian style, ornamented with pearls and diamonds from earlier royal ballets. The cost was 14,000 *livres* (Lavallée, p. 88). In many ways, *Esther* was a continuation of the prior magnificence of Louis XIV's court: as Jean Pommier puts it, "A Mme de Montespan—Lulli—Quinault ont succédé Mme de Maintenon—Racine—J.-B. Moreau, pour dispenser à Louis XIV sa nouvelle nourriture spirituelle" ("Madame de Maintenon—Racine—J.-B. Moreau succeeded Madame de Montespan—Lulli—Quinault in serving to Louis XIV his new spiritual nourishment").[59] The king's operas are now being provided by new team of collaborators. For the courtiers in the audience, though, this shift of emphasis might well have been enjoyable merely as part of the novelty and splendor of the occasion.

Madame de Sévigné, recording the court's frenzy of interest, was herself delighted to receive one of the coveted invitations. It was for the final performance, on February 19, and she was almost the only member of the audience who had not already seen the play at least once. The king, who came over to speak to her afterward, was present at all the performances. So proprietary was his interest in the play that he performed the unusual role of doorkeeper, checking the invitations: "il se mettait à la porte en dedans, et, tenant sa canne haute, pour servir de barrière, il demeurait ainsi jusqu'à ce que toutes les personnes conviées fussent entrées; alors il faisait fermer la porte," reported the official memoirs of Saint-Cyr (Lavallée, p. 93: "he placed himself at the inner door, and, holding his walking-stick high, to serve as a barrier, he remained thus until all the people invited had entered; then he had the doors closed"). From the Almighty to the ticket taker: the king can play all roles. To Madame de Sévigné he played the gracious host:

Le Roi vint vers nos places, et après avoir tourné, il s'adressa à moi, et me dit: «Madame, je suis assuré que vous avez été contente.» Moi, sans m'étonner, je répondis: «Sire, je suis charmée: ce que je sens est au-dessus des paroles.» Le Roi me dit: «Racine a bien de l'esprit.» Je lui dis: «Sire, il en a beaucoup; mais en vérité ces jeunes personnes en ont beaucoup aussi: elles entrent dans le sujet comme si elles n'avoient jamais faite autre chose.» Il me dit: «Ah! pour cela, il est vrai.» Et puis Sa Majesté s'en alla, et me laissa l'objet de l'envie: comme il n'y avoit quasi que moi de nouvelle venue, il eut quelque plaisir de voir mes sincères admirations sans bruit et sans éclat.

(p. 351: The king came toward our seats, and, after turning around, he addressed himself to me, and said, "Madame, I am told you were pleased." Without getting too excited, I answered, "Sire, I was delighted: what I am feeling is beyond words." The king said to me, "Racine is very witty." I said to him, "Sire, he is; but so, truly, are these young people: they enter into the story as though they had never done anything else." And then His Majesty left, leaving me the object of envy: since hardly any one else was there for the first time, he got some pleasure from seeing my sincere admiration without noise or fanfare.)

The king's proprietary interest in *Esther* extends to his making sure that even so relatively minor a courtier as Madame de Sévigné has enjoyed herself. By praising Racine's wit, of course, he praises himself as Racine's patron. Madame de Sévigné turns the praise from the playwright to the young performers, extending the range of the king's patronage. She lightly makes fun of her own awe in the royal presence, and revels in the "envy" the king's attention has aroused in those nearby.

Madame de Sévigné continued to wax enthusiastic over the event in her correspondence. When her daughter complained that the printed text of *Esther,* when she finally received a copy, was a disappointment, she responded: "L'impression a fait son effet ordinaire. . . . Pour moi, je ne réponds que de l'agrément du spectacle, qui ne peut pas être contesté" (p. 380: "Printing has had its usual effect. . . . As for myself, I only answer for the pleasure of the performance, which cannot be denied"). Later she went further:

Pour *Esther,* je ne vous reprends point du tout les louanges que je lui ai donnés: je serai toute ma vie charmée de l'agrément et de la nouveauté du spectacle; j'en suis ravie: j'y trouve mille choses si justes, si bien placées, si importantes à dire à un roi, que j'entrois, avec un sentiment extraordinaire, dans le plaisir de pouvoir dire, en se divertissant et en chantant, des vérités solides: j'étois touchée de toutes ces différentes beautés; ainsi je suis bien loin de change de sentiment.

(March 23, 1689, p. 394: As for *Esther,* I will not take back any of the praises I gave it; I will be delighted for my whole life by the charm and novelty of the performance; I'm ravished by it; I find in it a thousand things that are so right, so well placed, so important to say to a king, that I joined, with extraordinary feeling, in the pleasure of being able to say, while entertaining oneself and singing, such solid truths; I was moved by all these beauties; therefore I am far from a change of heart.)

A month after seeing the play, and after her daughter's skeptical response, Madame de Sévigné introduces into her discussion a new dimension to the experience. Now what she enjoyed, in addition to the performance itself, includes the "solid truths" the play contained, "so important to say to a king." The experience is legitimized as an educational one, not just for the girls of Saint-Cyr, but now for the king himself, with the lesser lights of the audience joining in the "pleasure" of this instruction.

Thus she, too, like Madame de Maintenon and Racine, must defend the play against traditional antitheatrical assumptions, and she does so by suggesting that it has a deeper agenda. The play's occasion is so well documented that it can stand as a model for the discontents that arise from "local" readings.[60] Madame de Caylus reported that from the first her aunt found Racine's choice of subject flattering: "Madame de Maintenon en fut charmée, et sa modestie ne put l'empêcher de trouver, dans le caractère d'Esther, et dans quelques circonstances de ce sujet, des choses flatteuses pour elle" (Madame de Caylus, p. 97: "Madame de Maintenon was delighted with it, and her modesty did not prevent her from finding, in the character of Esther and in some circumstances of this story, some flattering things about herself"). French Protestants, in exile after the Revocation of the Edict of Nantes, happily interpreted the text of *Esther* to reflect their own situation. The embarrassing reminder that Madame de Maintenon had been raised a Protestant led to their identification of the Jews in the play with the persecuted Huguenots.[61] Certainly this could not have been one of those flattering details.

Like all plays, then, *Esther* meant different things to different audiences. To Madame de Maintenon, apparently, it legitimized her position with the king by analogizing it to a biblical precedent, in which a royal mistress could be seen to function as an agent of divine providence and guide her royal master toward salvation. The occasion cements her special relationships to the king and to Saint-Cyr, and the king's constant and eager attendance at the performances makes them visible to all. To exiled Protestants, the play seemed rich with applications of another sort. Modern critics have found in the play other agendas: a plea to the king for clemency on behalf of an order of nuns cruelly disbanded in Toulouse in 1686 (Orcibal); an appeal on behalf of the Jansenists at Port-Royal, under threat of disbandment in the later 1680s (Jasinski); or a more generalized Jansenist propaganda (Pommier). Probable or improbable as these topicalities might be, there is no question that the play opened with an aggressively topical prologue, delivered by Madame de Caylus.

Madame de Caylus's own participation in the project was anomalous, and a sense of the magnitude of this anomaly is necessary before the full impact of her delivery of the prologue can be judged. According to her own account, the prologue was written for Madame de Caylus when Racine urged Madame de Maintenon to let her take a part in the play:

> Jusque là il n'avoit point été question de moi, et on n'imaginoit pas que je dusse y représenter un rôle; mais, me trouvant présente aux récits que M. Racine venoit de faire à Madame de Maintenon de chaque scène à mesure qu'il les composoit, j'en retenois les vers; et comme j'en récitai un jour à M. Racine, il en fut si content, qu'il demanda en grâce à madame de Maintenon de m'ordonner de faire un personnage; ce qu'elle fit: mais je n'en voulus point de ceux qu'on avoit déjà destinés; ce qui l'obligea de faire pour moi le prologue de la Piété.

> (Madame de Caylus, p. 97: Up until then there was no question of me, and no one imagined that I should play a part; but, since I was present at the readings of each scene that M. Racine did for Madame de Maintenon as soon as he finished it, I learned the lines; and when I recited some of them one day to M. Racine he was so delighted that he asked the favor of Madame de Maintenon that she order me to take a character; which she did; but I

did not want any of the parts that had already been assigned; which made it necessary for him to write the prologue of Piety for me.)

This is stage-door romance. Madame de Caylus's narrative permits, as actors' memoirs so often do, another way of looking at the story, one in which the innocent proficiency of the understudy who knows all the lines masks a voracious ambition.

After the opening performance, the prologue was dropped, and Madame de Caylus took on the role of Esther, which she performed at least twice, on January 29 and February 5. On the first occasion, Madame de Maintenon had invited eight prominent Jesuits ("Aujourd' hui, nous jouons pour les saints," she told the girls [Lavallée, p. 91: "Today we are playing before saints"]). On the second, Madame de Caylus played Esther before the most brilliant audience of them all: James II and his queen attended the performance.[62] If *Esther* had a single performer who stood out from the rest, it was Madame de Caylus. "Toutes les Champmeslés du monde," enthused the abbé de Choisy after the January 29 performance, "n'avaient pas les tons ravissants qu'elle laissait échapper en déclamant" (Lavallée, p. 91: "All the Champmeslés of the world did not have the ravishing tones that she produced in her declamations"). Madame de Sévigné assumed, incorrectly, in reporting the premiere to her daughter, that Madame de Caylus had played the title role: "Mme de Caylus fait Esther, qui fait mieux que la Champmeslé" (January 28, 1689, p. 332: "Madame de Caylus played Esther, and played better than Champmeslé").

At fifteen years old, although she had been married for almost three years, she was the right age for the production. Racine and Boileau had decided against casting any older girls (Saint-Cyr housed sixty students between the ages of sixteen and twenty); the girls cast, as Lavallée put it, "avaient ainsi les grâces de l'enfance sans les séductions de la jeunesse" (Lavallée p. 85: "thus possessed the graces of childhood without the seductiveness of youth"). Such a qualification could not apply to a married woman, however young, as Saint-Simon makes clear in his portrait of Madame de Caylus: "Jamais un visage si spirituelle, si touchant, si parlant; jamais tant de grâce ni plus d'esprit; jamais tant de gaieté, et d'agréments; jamais créature plus séduisante. Elle surpassait les plus fameuses actrices à jouer les comédies; elle s'y surpassa à celle d'Esther devant le roi" ("Never a face so spirited, so touching, so moving; never so much grace nor more wit; never so much gaiety and such pleasantness; never a more seductive creature. She surpassed the most famous actresses in playing in comedies; she surpassed herself in the role of Esther before the king").[63] She played, by her own account, all the other parts as one girl or another fell sick, all winter long (Madame de Caylus, p. 97.) Madame de Sévigné, however, tells a different story of pride and a fall: "Madame de Caylus, qui en étoit la Champmeslé," she wrote on February 11, "ne joue plus; elle faisoit trop bien, elle était trop touchante: on ne veut que la simplicité toute pure de ces petites âmes innocentes" (p. 344: "Madame de Caylus, who was its Champmeslé, does not act in it any more. She was doing too well; she was too affecting; what is wanted is only the wholly pure simplicity of those innocent little souls").

The case of Madame de Caylus makes clear the confusions that abounded in the audience's responses to Esther. A certain degree of passion and enthusiasm was expected of the actresses, but not too much. A certain amount of sexual attractiveness was appropriate, but, again, not too much. Nonetheless, some of the girls were fortunate enough to catch the eye of prospective husbands: Madame de Caylus's father, the marquis de Villette, recently widowed, found a wife in the person of Mademoiselle de Marsilly, who played Zarès in the premiere (Lavallée, p. 86.) The repeated allusions to the famous actress La Champmeslé in accounts of the play were doubtless fueled by the scandalous tale of Racine's relations with her in his days as a theater professional. "Il aime Dieu comme il aimoit ses maîtresses," Madame de Sévigné put it cruelly in a letter of February 7, 1689 (p. 341: "He loves God as he used to love his mistresses"). Far safer, of course, to make fun of Racine for a sudden conversion to piety and to impute to Madame de Caylus a lack of innocence and simplicity: the alternative would be to question the king's conversion (for now he, too, loved God as he had loved his mistresses) and Madame de Maintenon's motives in presenting him with Esther. The decking out of the girls in Persian costumes did not, as Madame de Maintenon later acknowledged, enhance the moral content of the play. Later, when Racine's Athalie was performed by the girls of Saint-Cyr, they acted without costume, in their regular uniforms, without scenery, in their regular classroom.[64] The idea of an antitheatrical theater experience, a reformed and pure spectacle, foundered from the very beginning. It foundered when the lively, attractive Madame de Caylus spoke Piety's first words in the prologue and took over the part of Esther for the two most important performances.

The experiment was tainted by the playwright's professional past, by the composer's usually worldly function, by the scene designer's past and future employment in profane court entertainments, by Madame de Maintenon's own desire to showcase her niece, by the desire of some of the girls to find husbands among the audience, and by the two self-contradictory notions it was meant to embody: a purified (but still pleasurable) theater and a convent without pettiness or restrictive rules. Although *Esther* was performed again in the winter of 1690, with *Athalie* in 1691 reform became more stringent. And after *Athalie,* performances at Saint-Cyr were suspended. Madame de Maintenon confessed her error: "Il faut encore défaire nos filles de ce tour d'esprit railleur que je leur ai donné et que je connais présentement très-opposé à la simplicité; c'est un raffinement de l'orgueil qui dit par ce tour de raillerie ce qu'il n'oserait dire sérieusement. Nos filles ont été trop considérées, trop caressés, trop ménagées; il faut les oublier dans leurs classes, leur faire garder les règlements de la journée, et leur peu parler d'autre chose" (Lavallée, p. 116: "It is still necessary to rid our girls of that spirit of mockery which I gave them and which I now know to be utterly opposed to simplicity; it is a subtle kind of pride to say in a mocking way that which one dares not say seriously. Our girls have been too much on view, too flattered, too spoiled; it is necessary to leave them to their classes, make them observe the rules of the day, and speak to them of little else"). Thus began the transformation of Saint-Cyr from noble experiment to ordinary convent.

That took place in February 1691, with the replacement of Innocent XI by Alexander VIII as pope, and Louis XIV's consequent rapprochement with the papacy. Just before the staging of *Esther,* however, a small *coup d'état* of a different sort had taken place at Saint-Cyr. Madame de Brinon, the head of the institute, had unceremoniously left after a series of disagreements with Madame de Maintenon. Madame de Sévigné's first mention of *Esther,* on December 31, 1688, suggests a connection between the two events: "On ne parle non plus de Madame de Brinon que si elle n'étoit pas au monde. On parle d'une comédie d'*Esther,* qui sera représentée à Saint-Cyr" (p. 297: "Now they only talk about Madame de Brinon as though she were no longer of this world. They are talking about a play of *Esther,* to be performed at Saint-Cyr"). The balanced sentences reflect Madame de Sévigné's delicate awareness of the ins and outs of court life: with Madame de Brinon expelled and humiliated, Madame de Maintenon reigned supreme at Saint-Cyr. In Madame de Sévigné's letter, this news carries equal weight with the breaking story of the English revolution.

The prologue that Racine wrote for Madame de Caylus takes its impetus from this background of small and large upheavals. It presents Louis as an embattled king: "De ta gloire animé, lui seul de tant de rois / S'arme pour ta querelle, et combat pour tes droits" (Prologue, p. 815: "Inspired by your glory, he alone of so many kings takes arms in your defense and fights for your rights"). Even the pope has foresaken him: "Et l'enfer, couvrant tout de ses vapeurs funèbres, / Sur les yeux les plus saint a jeté ses ténèbres" ("And hell, covering all in its deadly fumes, has hurled its darkness over the holiest of eyes"). Piety, played by Madame de Caylus, intercedes on his behalf, urging God to shatter the League of Augsburg. The prologue draws some comfort from the dauphin's recent victory at Philipsburg, and draws also an analogy between the king's and divine power:

> Pareil à ces esprits que ta Justice envoie,
> Quand son roi lui dit: «Pars», il s'élance avec joie,
> Du tonneur vengeur s'en va tout embraser,
> Et tranquille à ses pieds revient le déposer.

> (Prologue, p. 816: Like those spirits sent out by your Justice, when his king says "Go," he rushes out joyfully, departing to immolate all with vengeful thunder, returns to lay it in peace at his feet.)

The image of the king as a kind of Jupiter, hurling vengeful lightning, and of the dauphin as an angel of death, is grandiose in the tradition of court entertainments.

It also sharply qualifies the earlier image of a king who uniquely abases himself before his God:

> Tu m'écoutes. Ma voix ne t'est pas étrangère:
> Je suis la Piété, cette fille si chère,
> Qui t'offre de ce roi les plus tendres soupirs.
> Du feu de ton amour j'allume ses désirs.
> Du zèle qui pour toi l'enflamme et le dévore
> La chaleur se répand du couchant à l'aurore.

Tu le vois tous les jours, devant toi prosterné,
Humilier ce front de splendeur couronné,
Et confondant l'orgueil par d'augustes exemples,
Baiser avec respect le pavé de vos temples.

(p. 815: You hear me. My voice is no stranger to you. I am Piety,
so dear a daughter, who offer to you the most tender sighs of this
king. I ignite his desires with the fire of your love. The heat of the
zeal for you that inflames and devours him extends from sunset to
dawn. Every day you see him, prostrate before you, abase that
forehead crowned with splendor, confounding pride by august
examples, respectfully kiss the pavement of your temples.)

Here the king is a lover, full of desire, groveling before his beloved.
The eroticism of the language is in no way defused by the speaker, for
however Madame de Caylus recited the lines (and even the churchmen
were moved by her "ravishing tones" as Esther), here her character,
Piety, is presented as a flirtatious go-between. Piety may well be, icon-
ographically, the deity's dearest daughter; but here the terms of intimacy are drawn from the amorous vocabulary of the professional
stage.

The agenda of Madame de Maintenon propels this jarring effect.
She used her considerable sexual power over the king to deflect him
from other mistresses, even to force him to reconcile with his wife
before her death. The key notion that Racine found in the story of
Esther (and that Madame de Caylus pronounced "flattering" to
Madame de Maintenon) is here embodied in the figure of Piety, who
arouses the king's desires for the greater glory of God. Not lost on the
original audience would be the implications of Madame de Caylus's
special relationship to Madame de Maintenon. The royal mistress's
inseparable niece becomes her deputy on the stage; and the two
women fuse in the greater role of Piety, God's favorite daughter. Later,
when Madame de Caylus moved into the body of the play itself to
undertake the role of Esther, the identification shifts. Madame de
Maintenon, the second Esther, appears both as sponsor of the event,
sitting discreetly (for their marriage was secret) behind the king and,
through Madame de Caylus, as Esther herself.

"L'Innocence s'y plaît" (p. 815: "Innocence takes its pleasure there"):
so the prologue describes the activity about to begin at Saint-Cyr.
Innocence is the key word that resonates through all the contemporary

discussion of the play. The whole event is put in service of Madame de Maintenon's innocence, her virtuous goals, her difference from royal mistresses like Madame de Montespan. Yet the selection of fifteen-year old girls to enact this innocence, like the language of the prologue, suggests how much eroticism lies just below the pious surface of the project. "Colombes timides . . . sans secours et sans guides" ("timid doves . . . without help or guides"), the girls have been assembled here by Louis, but the place does not sound very much like a school: "Pour elles à sa port élevant ce palais, / Il leur fit trouver l'abondance et la paix" ("Building for them this palace at his gates, he lets them find abundance and peace"). Expunging from his play the fact that Esther was one of a number of concubines in the seraglio of Assuérus, Racine uses in the prologue images that come perilously close to identifying Saint-Cyr as some sort of harem. Madame de Sévigné's remark that Racine loves God as much as he used to love his mistresses appears less quirky (and Racine less debased) when we realize that she is merely adopting the language that the prologue applies, flatteringly, to Louis and that describes, most clearly, Madame de Maintenon's worthy aim.

The foundation of Saint-Cyr, the prologue maintains, is an achievement worthy of scriptural record:

> Grand Dieu, que cet ouvrage ait place en ta mémoire.
> Que tous les soins qu'il prend pour soutenir ta gloire
> Soient gravés de ta main au livre où sont écrits
> Les noms prédestinés des rois que tu chéris.

> (Great God, let this work have a place in your memory. Let all the cares he takes to sustain your glory be written by your hand in the book where the predestined names of the kings you cherish are written.)

Founding Saint-Cyr has earned Louis XIV a place in the book of kings, both on a metaphoric level (as the book of those kings whom God loves) but also on a scriptural level: Louis belongs rightly in the Book of Kings itself. The line continues unbroken down to him. Racine, as the king's historiographer royal, recognizes here a problem of authorship, much as Molière does in *Tartuffe*. The comic dramatist needs the king's aid to finish and authorize the play; here the royal historian, like the writer of scripture, is divinely inspired by the monarch's achievements. God's hand propels the hand that records the deeds of Louis.

Repudiating "profanes amateurs de spectacles frivoles" ("profane enjoyers of frivolous spectacles"), the prologue makes throughout claims for the uniqueness of *Esther*. The special place of its performance and the scriptural appropriateness of its subject matter (both to the place and to the audience) are linked to the specialness of Louis himself. Alone among the world's kings he fights on God's behalf (and, like God, he can depute a son on his behalf). The playwright, taking a subject from scripture for his play, writes reformed drama based on sacred history: but since the playwright is also the king's historian, the very history he writes is sacred. For at this moment in history, Louis is a kind of Christ, persecuted on all sides, even by the pope (in this analogy a Caiaphas).

As Madame de Sévigné's letters and the journal of the marquis de Dangeau make clear, however, there was another persecuted prince in the picture. The coincidence between the performance of *Esther* and the arrival of the deposed British king leads to an alternation of concern with these two topics in the works of both of these chroniclers. The presence of the British court at Saint-Germain, with its different rules of precedence, intrigued Madame de Sévigné. She found the British queen utterly delightful, but the king less so: "Tout ce qu'elle dit est juste et de bon sens; son mari n'est pas de même: il a bien du courage, mais un esprit commun, qui conte tout ce que s'est passé en Angleterre avec une insensibilité qui en donne pour lui" (January 14, 1689, p. 318: "Everything she says is right and sensible; her husband is not the same; he is very courageous, but of a common wit, and relates everything that happened in England with a lack of feeling that makes for lack of feeling in response"). "Il y a même le Roy et la Reyne d'Angleterre," reported the *Mercure historique et politique* of the performances of *Esther;* "mais l'on doute fort que cela ait été capable de leur faire oublier la perte de leur royaume" ("Even the king and queen of England were there; but one strongly doubts whether [the play] was capable of making them forget the loss of their kingdom").[65] When the instructors at Saint-Cyr gave James a tour of the facility before the performance, they found him preoccupied: the king "paraissait insensible à tout" (Lavallée, p. 94: "seemed indifferent to everything").

Dangeau's journal shows events developing in tandem. Louis attended a rehearsal of *Esther* and then went to greet James on January

7; Parliament extended its invitation to William of Orange on January 20. The play opened on January 26; the king and queen of Britain attended the performance on the fifth of February. On February 6, Dangeau reports, "Le prince d'Orange fait venir en Angleterre la princesse sa femme, qu'il y croit nécessaire à ses intérêts" ("The prince of Orange has had his wife the princess come to England, as he believes her necessary to his interests there"). On February 13, Dangeau learned of the vote in the Commons to accept James's flight as an abdication; on the fifteenth, he went to see *Esther* again. On the eighteenth, he reports a three-and-a-half-hour private walk taken by the two kings; on the nineteenth both Dangeau and Madame de Sévigné saw *Esther*. Performances were suspended when the court went into mourning for the death of the queen of Spain (Madame de Sévigné suspected poison); on February 26, William and Mary were pronounced king and queen of Britain.[66]

Thus there take shape, before the different audiences to *Esther,* two plays: a French *Esther* and a British *Esther*. The insiders who had been invited to Saint-Cyr confidently identified a substratum of allusion to French court affairs. "La comédie représentoit en quelque sort la chute de Mme de Montespan et l'élévation de Mme de Maintenon," wrote Madame de Lafayette; "Tout le monde crut toujours que cette comédie étoit allégorique, qu'Assuérus étoit le Roi, que Vasthi, qui étoit la femme concubine détrônée, paroissoit pour Mme de Montespan. Esther tomboit sur Mme de Maintenon, Aman représentoit M. de Louvois, mais il n'y étoit bien peint, et apparemment Racine n'avoit pas voulu le marquer" ("The play represented in some way the fall of Madame de Montespan and the rise of Madame de Maintenon. Everybody always thought that the whole play was allegorical, that Assuérus was the king, that Vasthi, who was the dethroned concubine, stood for Madame de Montespan. Esther fell to Madame de Maintenon, Aman figured M. de Louvois, but he was not portrayed very well, and apparently Racine did not want to single him out").[67] Perhaps all of these identifications that "tout le monde" agreed upon were fortuitous and unintended. Vasthi appears only in one passing reference, but for the insiders she was the key to the whole allegory. The play does not dramatize either her fall or Esther's rise: when it begins, Esther is already installed as the king's wife. The idea that Louvois appeared in the person of Aman, the evil counselor, strikes even Madame de Lafayette as excessive, and is out of keeping with the prologue's strong endorsement of Louis's and Louvois's policies.

More fortuitous yet is the emergence of a British *Esther,* called into being by the presence of James II at Saint-Germain and in the audience at Saint-Cyr on February 5. When Racine selected the story of Esther, and offered it to the ladies in charge of Saint-Cyr, they approved, "cette histoire leur paraissant pleine de grandes leçons de l'amour de Dieu, et de détachement du monde au milieu du monde même" (812: "this story appearing to them to be full of great lessons of the love of God, and of detachment from the world in the very middle of the world itself"). Racine saw in the chorus of exiled daughters of Zion a reflection of the paradoxical community at Saint-Cyr, a school separated from the social world but located at the very gates of Versailles. By incorporating within the story of Esther choruses based upon the Psalms, Racine went beyond fleshing out the bare narrative and providing lessons for the girls to sing. As Barbara Woshinsky has pointed out, he conflates in the character of Assuérus two Persian monarchs, Darius and Cyrus, with important consequences: "This telescoping of Biblical history places the theme of exile at the center of the Esther story."[68] Esther's request that the chorus sing for her at the play's very beginning "quelqu'un de ces cantiques . . . de la triste Sion" (I.ii, p. 820–21: "one of those songs . . . of unhappy Zion") establishes a context of exile. "Compagnes autrefois de ma captivité" (I.i, p. 820: "Erstwhile companions of my captivity"), the girls sing of a lost kingdom:

O rives du Jourdain! ô champs aimés des cieux!
Sacrés monts, fertiles vallées,
Par cent miracles signalées!
Du doux pays de nos aïeux
Serons-nous toujours exilés?

(I.ii, p. 821: Oh banks of the Jordan! Oh fields beloved by the heavens! Sacred mountains, fertile valleys, revealed by countless miracles! From the sweet land of our ancestors shall we forever be exiled?)

Sung before the British king and queen, this psalm of exile would take on a poignancy undreamt of by Racine when he selected the story (just as, no doubt, he had not considered the possibility of Huguenots reading the story of Esther as they did, or of the French courtiers discovering Louvois in Aman). The Babylonian captivity and deliverance into Persian exile become for James (and this might explain his glumness) figures of his own isolation in England and his safe—but apparently open-ended—exile in France. For while he and Louis spent hours together discussing how he might recover his kingdom, the substantial French financial and military aid that he would need was never fully offered.

"Rompez vos fers / Tribus captives," the chorus sings at the end of the play; "Troupes fugitives, / Repassez les monts et les mers. / Rassemblez-vous des bouts de l'univers" (III.ix, p. 860: "Break your chains, captive tribes; fugitive bands, cross again the mountains and the seas; reunite from the ends of the universe"). Then two soloists: "Je reverrai ces campagnes si chères . . . Je'irai pleurer au tombeau de mes pères" (p. 861: "I shall see again those lands so dear . . . I shall go weep at the tomb of my fathers"). This exalted vision of an end to exile again speaks to the British king in the audience. James had grown to adulthood in exile, like Esther and her companions. Now he found himself exiled again, and by what to his perspective must have appeared to be the same radical Protestant faction that had killed his father. The play speaks to his isolation, and promises (as the prologue speaks to Louis's isolation and likewise promises) a providential intervention.

"Voilà de si grands évènements, qu'il n'est pas aisé d'en comprendre le dénouement, surtout quand on jette les yeux sur l'état et sur les dispositions de toute l'Europe," Madame de Sévigné wrote on January 6, 1689 (noting coincidentally that it was the Feast of the Epiphany, the day of kings), as she anticipated the arrival of James and his queen at Saint-Germain. "Cette même Providence qui règle tout, démêlera tout; nous sommes ici les spectateurs très aveugles et très ignorants" (p. 305: "Here are such great events that it is not easy to understand how they will work out, especially when one casts an eye upon the state and upon the alignments of all of Europe. That same Providence that rules over all, resolves all; we here are very blind and very ignorant spectators"). The play's demonstration of the workings of Providence links up with this attitude of pious resignation. Composed without reference to these great European events, the play becomes topical in spite of itself. Neither the French *Esther* nor the British *Esther* need have figured in the playwright's or the sponsor's designs in order to take shape before their audience. The play spins out meanings for its audiences in ways unforeseen: meanings that could be particularly em-

barrassing for Madame de Maintenon or particularly moving to
James II.

The play's relationship to Louis XIV also bristles with potential
meanings. As royal stage doorkeeper, builder of Saint-Cyr, and patron
of its order, Louis functions in the audience as host and impresario.
But as Madame de Lafayette points out, he is also susceptible of identification with the king in the play. Nor is such an identification
"flattering," as that with Esther could be for Madame de Maintenon.
Assuérus is autocratic, gullible, and easily led, both by Aman, the evil
counselor, and by Esther, "l'innocence et la sagesse même" (III.iv, p.
853: "innocence and wisdom herself"). He has bad dreams (provoked
by his guilty conscience) but is unaware of the wrong he has done to
Mardochée until his historians consult the archives. Hydaspe tells
Aman of the restless night:

Enfin, las d'appeler un sommeil qui le fuit,
Pour écarter de lui ces images funèbres,
Il s'est fait apporter ces annales célèbres
Où les faits de son règne, avec soin amassés,
Par de fidèles mains chaque jour sont tracés.
On y conserve écrits le service et l'offense,
Monuments éternels d'amour et de vengeance.
Le Roi, que j'ai laissé plus calme dans son lit,
D'une oreille attentive écoute ce récit.

(II.i, p. 829–30: Finally, tired of calling for sleep, which eluded
him, to chase away from him those deadly images, he had
brought to him the famous annals, in which the deeds of his
reign, collected with care, are sketched out each day by faithful
hands. There are preserved in writing service and offense, eternal
monuments of love and vengeance. The king, whom I left more
peaceful in his bed, listens to this narrative with an attentive ear.)

Here Racine brings himself and Boileau, the two poets turned royal
historians, into the play. It is through the annalists' meticulous concern with compiling the record of his reign that Assuérus is able to recognize the fact of his ingratitude to Mardochée. Prompted by the reading of this history, the king recalls his deliverance from an attempted
assassination:

Je veux bien l'avouer; de ce couple perfide
J'avais presque oublié l'attentat parricide;
Et j'ai pâli deux fois au terrible récit
Qui vient d'en retracer l'image à mon esprit.

(II.iii, p. 834: I am willing to confess it; I had almost forgotten the
murderous attempt of that traitorous pair; and I blanched twice
at the horrid narrative that has just retraced its image in my spirit.)

"O d'un si grand service oubli trop condamnable!" he exclaims against
himself a few lines later ("Oh how damnable is this negligence of such
great service!"). Without his faithful historians, the king would never
have remembered his debt to Mardochée.

This tale of the annalists directly echoes the prologue's assertion that
Louis deserves to be written in the Book of Kings. What the historians
have written is the way to salvation for Assuérus: the chronicle recalls
him to himself and makes him royal again. As Judd Hubert has suggested, the book being read to Assuérus is further evocative of the great
book of judgment, in which God will distribute his vengeance and
love.[69] Like Orgon's black box, it contains his conscience. But where
the contents of the box are only safe in the possession of the king (and
where, conversely, Tartuffe's past is contained in the king's intelligence), here the king's deeds are in the possession of his recorders. The
annalists function thus as "directeurs de conscience," becoming guides
of the sort that Tartuffe pretended to be. The fretful dreams that make
him summon them to his bedside are sent directly from God.

Assuérus's willingness to be led is the key to the play's lack of dramatic tension, but it is also the key to its vision. This monarch is not
capable, like Thésée in *Phèdre,* of calling upon the gods to unleash the
monsters of misprision. In Thésée's pagan world, error is inevitable,
and the delusions of sensuality hold the king in their grasp as firmly
as they hold Phèdre. But in the sacred history to which Assuérus belongs, the will of Providence rules, and the wise king submits. Providence works indirectly, through virtuous guides: after the historians
have revealed to Assuérus his momentary lapse of gratitude to Mardochée, Esther can turn him away from Aman's plan to massacre the
Jews.

Assuérus only sounds godlike in his power. When Mardochée urges
Esther to confront him, she explains that the death penalty threatens
anyone who interrupts him unannounced in his private chambers.

Even his wife puts herself at risk: "Rien ne met à l'abri de cet ordre fatal / Ni le rang, ni le sexe; et le crime est égal," (I.iii, p. 823: "Nothing can exempt one from this fatal order, neither rank nor sex; the crime is the same"). Only if Assuérus makes the gesture of extending the royal ring to be kissed can the guilty offender be saved ("sauver le coupable"). The irrationality of this order is reminiscent of Thésée's sudden vengeance. Reminiscent, too, of Thésée's mysterious imprisonment in the caverns of Epire is the custom by which Persian monarchs conceal themselves from their people: "Au fond du palais leur majesté terrible / Affecte à leurs sujets de se rendre invisible" ("In the depths of the palace their terrible majesty works to make them invisible to their subjects"), Esther tells Mardochée. But when Esther finally does burst in upon Assuérus in the second act, he merely cries out, upon recognizing her, "C'est vous, Esther? Quoi? Sans être attendue?" (II.vii, p. 838: "Is that you, Esther? What? Without being expected?") Whereupon she faints, and his irritation is replaced by solicitude.

"Tout respire en Esther l'innocence et la paix," (p. 839: "Everything about Esther breathes innocence and peace") he confides in her once she has fully revived. "Je ne trouve qu'en vous je ne sais quelle grâce / Qui me charme toujours et jamais ne me lasse" ("I find only in you an indefinable grace that always charms me and never tires me"): unwittingly, Assuérus names that divine grace that Esther embodies. When Esther declares to him the perfidy of Aman, Assuérus exits, confused: "Ciel, daigne m'éclairer. / Un moment sans témoins cherchons à respirer" (III.iv, p. 856: "Heaven, deign to enlighten me. Let me seek a moment to breathe without witnesses"). "Vérité que j'implore, achève de descendre" ("Truth that I pray for, finish your descent"), pleads a member of the chorus as he leaves. This isolation differs from the willed invisibility inscribed in Persian law: withdrawing to be alone, he is alone with God. When he reenters, Assuérus is now a king like the king in *Tartuffe*: "Ah! dans ses yeux confus je lis ses perfidies" (p. 857: "Ha! I read his treasons in his confused eyes"), he declares as Aman begs for mercy. Like Hippolyte in *Phèdre*, Aman is driven out to be torn to pieces; but the prayers of Esther and the chorus, together with the king's plea for enlightenment, have insured that this judgment is free of mortal error.

The clemency of Auguste and the withdrawal of Assuérus to breathe awhile are both instances of restraint. In Corneille's play, this is represented as self-conquest, and in Racine's as the working of Providence. Although Auguste rejects a policy of mercy when Livie suggests it, he does carry out his wife's recommendation; Assuérus finds himself incapable of resisting Esther's appeal. Thus power is tempered by love in these plays; and in *Tartuffe,* the king's wisdom penetrates the impostor's disguise. Power, love, and wisdom are the three attributes of the trinity's three persons. The English theater left to the machinery of masque this transformation of king into god. There is no need for theophanic machinery when Louis XIV plays the divine role himself in real life, succoring a banished king and facing the enemies of Christendom alone. The tragic alternative, the crazed misprision of Thésée, is confined by Racine to an ancient world of myth and menace. In the little world of Saint-Cyr, we are in the royal presence, a presence that Louis Marin insists is not merely analogous to but identical to the "real presence" of the Eucharist.[70] But at Saint-Cyr, as we have seen, the language of divinity is almost constantly being undercut by the conditions of the performance itself. The power the king displays as he holds his walking-stick in front of the door and checks the invitations can be only tenuously analogized to the divine. The "innocence" that the project proclaimed from its inception and that the play's language iteratively celebrates is similarly mundane. Dramatizing the absolutist ideal of a monarch whose love must be great because his power knows no limits, whose intelligence penetrates all cabals, is possible for Corneille in 1640, before Louis XIV assumed the throne and, indeed, the role of Auguste.[71] Molière's *Tartuffe* gratefully owes its whole being to this offstage monarch. Conceived as court theater's crowning glory, a sacred entertainment, *Esther* points not only to the paradoxes of reformed theater but also to the circumscriptions of the absolutist ideal.

Esther's emphasis on negative capabilities—on innocence, on submission, on restraint—fits with *Cinna*'s and *Tartuffe*'s portrayals of royal apprehension as complementary to royal oblivion. The deification of the monarch posits that he do nothing. As Auguste, he spares the conspirators; as offstage king in *Tartuffe,* he does not suppress the play, forgetting, with Orgon's, its disreputable past; as Assuérus, he bows to the divine will and refrains from the massacre. These models of royal performance are passive, and they draw their force from the model of Christ. But for a king fully to model himself upon Christ would entail his undergoing misunderstanding, betrayal, and sacrifice, as Hippolyte does in *Phèdre.* While the prologue to *Esther* portrays the king as alone, sacrificing himself for his people and his God, the play itself portrays the king's isolation as a place of absolute power which he must be persuaded by intermediaries to forsake. By fluidly identifying the monarch with different attributes of the trinity, playwrights could achieve a partial apotheosis that avoids the Scylla and Charybdis of blasphemy and *lèse majesté*. The reliance upon pagan figures in court entertainments (Apollo was Louis's favorite role before he gave up dancing in the *ballets du cour*) works to similar effect, familiar from the Stuart court masque. As sacred drama, *Esther* points towards *Athalie* and a dead end. But as opera, with its sung choruses and painted sets, *Esther* points beyond tragedy and comedy to the dominant genre of the last twenty-five years of Louis XIV's reign.

"Par l'utilization qu'il fait des machines," Apostolidès argues, "l'opéra présente un monde totalement maîtrisé, dans lequel la technique engendre à la fois le réel et le merveilleux" ("Through the use it makes of machines, opera presents a world that has been totally mastered, in which technology begets at once the real and the marvelous").[72] The emergence of opera coincides with the disappearance of the religious dimension of drama and with the emergence of the theatrical aesthetic of realism, he concludes. In the long view, this argument is compelling, and it coincides with earlier narratives of the decline of tragedy and its absorption into opera like that of H. C. Lancaster. But while it may explain the persistence in the French court of revivals of classic plays, it does not explain the continuing efforts of court poets to write new tragedies and tragicomedies at the same time as they wrote opera librettos and scripts for entertainments. Playwrights continued to write, for the royal audiences they courted, plays which set before kings images of monarchy that derived from familiar models: Roman emperors and Persian autocrats. As the dominant dramatist of the eighteenth century, Voltaire took part enthusiastically in the project of creating royal roles, hopefully seeking employment in the courts of Louis XV and Frederick the Great of Prussia, and playing royal parts himself in his own theaters. The notion that plays are the appropriate vehicle for representing royal performance to a royal audience persists beyond *Esther,* just as the form of drama called tragedy persisted long beyond the generally agreed-upon date of its death.

5

Le Roi Voltaire

The Monarch of Wit in the Courts of Louis XV and Frederick the Great

~

I

"Q ue veut donc Voltaire?" Louis XV is recorded as demanding, in some vexation. "Je l'ai aussi bien traité que Louis XIV a traité Racine et Boileau, je lui ai donné, comme Louis XIV à Racine, une charge de gentilhomme ordinaire et des pensions: ce n'est pas ma faute s'il fait des sottises et s'il a la prétention d'être chambellan, d'avoir un croix et de souper avec un roi: ce n'est pas la mode en France" ("What does Voltaire want? I have treated him as well as Louis XIV treated Racine and Boileau; I have given him, as Louis XIV gave Racine, the place of Gentleman of the Chamber and revenues; it is not my fault if he does stupid things and pretends to the rank of chamberlain, to wear a cross and dine with a king: that is not the way we do things in France").[1] The king's irritation with Voltaire's attempt to insinuate himself into the court draws its energy from the ignominious parallel with the glories of the past. A desire to revive the splendor of Louis XIV's court, along with a sense of falling short of that splendor, animates both parties in Louis XV's complaint. Neither the king nor the courtier feels comfortable in the role assigned to him by his great predecessor. Louis XV complains that he has fulfilled his part of the bargain, and done as much for Voltaire, intolerably rude though he is, as Louis XIV ever did for a poet. Voltaire, despite assuming the positions Racine held as historiographer royal and gentleman of the chamber, cannot play the part as well as Racine played it for Louis XIV. His public gaffes stem from his sense of the violation of personal dignity that assuming the role of court poet entails.

The association of a glorious past with Louis XIV lies behind Voltaire's subsequent adventures when he attempted, against the advice of many of his friends, to fulfill the same role of court poet with Frederick the Great at Potsdam. Dismayed by Louis XV's attitude, Voltaire saw in Frederick not merely a revived Louis XIV, but also a Marcus Aurelius, a philosopher king. Frederick, too, idealized Voltaire: where Frederick, to Voltaire, was *my* king, different from all others, Voltaire, to Frederick, was his own private poet, brought to Prussia to revise the king's verses. Both parties to the relationship were doomed to disillusionment.

Voltaire's dealings with the court of Louis XV will be discussed in this chapter through concentration on the circumstances of the production of his tragedy *Alzire* in the theater at the Petits Cabinets in Versailles, in February and March 1750. This was Madame de Pompadour's theater, and the king's mistress took the title role. In the first months of his stay with Frederick, Voltaire himself took the leading role of Cicéron in his play *Rome sauvée (Rome Preserved)* in repeated performances at Frederick's retreat, Sans Souci, in the summer of 1750: these performances will serve as a key to Voltaire's relationship with Frederick. In the case of *Alzire*, Voltaire functions as a playwright, on the margins of an exclusive social event to which he has been invited but at which he is not welcome. In the case of *Rome sauvée*, Voltaire functions not only as playwright, but also as director, instructing his German cast in the correct readings of lines, and as leading actor. Finally, we move to a discussion of Voltaire as impresario, staging his own elaborate theatrical entertainments at his theaters in the chateaux of Tournay and Ferney, just on the French side of the Swiss border. Here he was an undisputed master of the revels, and his household at Ferney became a court in itself, to which distinguished visitors repaired to be dazzled by plays in which the playwright and his niece would take the leading roles.

For Voltaire, the freedom to act in his own plays and to direct their production betokened a larger freedom of action. As a substantially wealthy man, he was not, like his predecessors Racine and Boileau, utterly dependent upon the king for his livelihood. When he settled at Ferney for the final years of his career, he not only rebuilt the chateau but also refurbished the church and the town. In the 1770s, Voltaire became a virtual monarch to the people of the district: "He built houses and supported industries for them: watches, silk stockings, and other luxury goods streamed from the new industrial center," as Peter Gay puts it. The new idea of "the union of free trade with free religion,"[2] championed by Voltaire at Ferney, found its expression through social arrangements that also seem feudal, paternalistic. Surrounded by a court of friends, in regular correspondence with Frederick and Catherine the Great and other European royalty, Voltaire presided over a peculiar monarchy. "En ce temps-là," Arsène Houssaye began his biography of King Voltaire, *Le Roi Voltaire,* "il était un roi qui s'appelait Voltaire. Son royaume n'avait ni commencement ni fin. Il succéda à Louis XIV et transmit son sceptre à Napoléon" ("Once upon a time there was a king named Voltaire. His kingdom had neither beginning nor end. He succeeded Louis XIV and passed his scepter on to Napoleon").[3] As a monarch of wit on equal terms with other monarchs, Voltaire achieved a stature that eluded professional playwrights like Shakespeare, Beaumont and Fletcher, and Davenant in England, and Corneille, Molière, and Racine in France. As an amateur actor he could, like the amateur playwrights of Charles I's court, assert his superiority to professionals by pointing out that what they do for a living he does as recreation. But unlike Cartwright and Suckling, he need not worry about the king's response to his efforts.

Voltaire's career thus marks a transformation in the relationships among players, playwrights, and kings. He was able, in the 1760s and 1770s, to fulfill all three roles. Yet he did so, not by redefining those roles, but rather by finally achieving the financial and political freedom to play them without fear. The court at Ferney revolved around Voltaire just as the court at Versailles revolved around Louis XIV. And if Louis could find himself in the curious position of taking tickets at Saint-Cyr for performances of *Esther,* Voltaire's theatrical career is composed of embarrassing moments as well. His performance as King Voltaire can be seen as in itself an incongruous combination of old and new. His plays themselves, whose failure to endure as literature is legendary, have also been characterized as self-contradictory attempts to "siphon the new wine of *philosophie* into old poetic bottles," as

Clifton Cherpack has put it.[4] Voltaire's quest for individual freedoms fits as oddly with his patriarchal regime at Ferney as his Louis XIV style of costume, complete with full wig, fitted with the intellectual content of the plays in which he wore it. Voltaire's problems as a court playwright, and his resolution of those problems by forming his own court, have their roots in the Renaissance dynamic of royal performance and royal audience, in which actor, playwright, and king exist together in a shifting mutual self-awareness.

II

Upon his promotion to the rank of gentleman of the chamber, in November 1746, Voltaire expressed his ambivalence about the new role he had to play in a notorious epigram:

> Mon *Henri IV* et ma *Zaïre*
> Et mon Américaine *Alzire*
> Ne m'ont valu jamais un regard du roi;
> J'eus beaucoup d'ennemis et très peu de gloire.
> Les honneurs et les biens pleuvent enfin sur moi
>   Pour une farce de la Foire.

(My *Henry IV* and my *Zaïre* and my American *Alzire* never earned me a glance from the king; I had many enemies and very little fame. Honors and benefits rained at last upon me for a marketplace farce.)[5]

Where Racine was content to allow Madame de Maintenon to command him to write *Esther,* without himself invidiously comparing it to his other works, here Voltaire both insists on the high merit of his *Henriade, Zaïre,* and *Alzire* and impugns the monarch's taste. Or he at least suggests that a cabal of hostile courtiers has kept the king's glance from falling on worthier productions than the opera-ballet, *La Princesse de Navarre,* that provided the occasion for the epigram. Indicting the system of court patronage that rewards mediocre works lavishly, Voltaire stakes out a position of superiority to the king, the source of the "rain" of honors that bless bad farce.

This epigram never fell into the king's hands. To his friends, however, Voltaire continued to make light of his paying court and of his efforts on the tedious play. "Je ne suis mêlé que de plaire au roy," he wrote on April 1, 1745, to the comte d'Argental. "Le reste m'est très indifférent et on peut faire à l'opéra touttes les sottises qu'on voudra sans que je m'en mêle. Mon ouvrage est décent, il a plu sans être flatteur. Le roy m'en sait gré, les Mirepoix ne peuvent me nuire. Que me faut il de plus?" ("I only got involved in order to please the king. The rest doesn't matter to me, and they can do all the foolish things they want at the opera without my getting involved. My work is decent; it pleased without being obsequious. The king is grateful to me; the Mirepoix cannot harm me. What more do I need?").⁶ Although the opera was performed on February 23, Voltaire needed to remain at Versailles until such time as the king would confer upon him the honors he so desired (and so ridiculed in his epigram). To his niece, Madame Denis, Voltaire complained of the delay, writing also on April 1:

> Je comptois bien ma chère enfant vous revoir après le spectacle à Versailles. La lutinerie de la cour en ordonna tout autrement. On me dit qu'il falloit courir après le Roy à bride abatue, et se trouver à un certain coin, pour le remercier, je ne sçai pas trop bien encor de quoy, car j'avois demandé plusieurs choses, et on me disoit qu'il me les avoit toutes acordées. On me présenta donc à sa très gracieuse Majesté, qui me reçut très gracieusement et que je remerciay très humblement. Mais faire signer des brevets est chose baucoup plus difficile, que de faire des remercimens.

> (D3091: I was counting, my dear child, on seeing you after the performance at Versailles. The devilishness of the court ordained otherwise. I was told that one had to run after the king at a gallop and be there at a certain corner to thank him, I don't know very well any more for what, because I had asked for many things and I had been told that they had all been granted. Then I was presented to his very gracious Majesty, who received me very graciously and whom I thanked very humbly. But getting the commissions signed is a much more difficult business than giving thanks.)

Delighting in the pose of reluctant courtier, Voltaire tries to have it both ways. He decries the malice and foolishness of the court, but at the same time he dare not leave the court unless his letters of office have been "cimenté, scellé, et consommé" (D3091: "signed, sealed, and delivered"). Yet the pose of reluctant courtier, pressed into unnecessary rushing around, is one unlikely to please a king whose favorite recreation is the hunt.

What makes Voltaire's rush to encounter the king different from the chance meetings staged by Thomas Churchyard (and missed by Queen Elizabeth in Norfolk) is the contempt for the whole enterprise that he conveys as he mocks the graciousness of his gracious majesty. Just after his arrival at Versailles, he wrote to Cideville on Janaury 31, describing himself as "un pauvre diable qui est boufon du roi à cinquante ans" (D3073: "a poor devil who is the king's buffoon at fifty"). His position, he continued, was virtually impossible: "Il faut louer le roy hautement, madame la dauphine finement, la famille royale tout doucement, contenter la cour, ne pas déplaire à la ville" ("I have to praise the king loftily, madame the dauphine delicately, the royal family discreetly, please the court, not displease the town"). Where Churchyard excuses the lameness of his offerings and invokes the love and service they represent, Voltaire wryly portrays his business as one of measuring out differing varieties and quantities of praise. He is acutely aware of his need to negotiate his way through the demands of various constituencies. It is not merely enough to please the king; the paying audiences of the town must not be neglected either.

As a professional playwright in the King's Men, Shakespeare also had to please both court and town. But where Voltaire expresses his distress best in letters to his friends, Shakespeare was able fully to dramatize the tension among his various constituencies, as he does in *Measure for Measure.* Despite challenging the masque's language of praise and the monarch's patronage of masque in their plays, Beaumont and Fletcher, too, operated without arousing royal wrath. *The Maid's Tragedy* was deemed appropriate to perform at a royal wedding. Like Shakespeare, these playwrights hide the tension between their responsibilities as theater professionals and as court entertainers by incorporating it into their plays. Nervously invoking the king's life-and-death authority over their plays, the amateur playwrights in the time of Charles I risked all on pleasing the court. William Davenant succeeded in continuing the Jacobean tradition of pleasing both court and town, but Cartwright and Suckling disdained the professional help that mounting their plays required.

Despite a different institutional structure, the French theater masks but does not hide a similar tension. Molière dramatizes in *Tartuffe* the impasse in its starkest form: only the king's direct intervention into the play itself can create a comedy that will both please and be legal. *Esther* moves in the same direction as the amateur theater of Charles I's court, toward private performances under direct royal control. Yet even at Saint-Cyr, crowds were drawn, and the play, in spite of itself, became the talk of the town. Voltaire, angered that his preferment at court depended upon trifles while he continued to encounter difficulties in getting his *Henriade* legally published, invokes instead the authority of his successes in the professional theaters. He perceives his court offices as his by desert, and chafes at the court's demand for light comedy and operatic entertainments. Voltaire's dissatisfaction with his treatment at court points not simply to a parallel with the court of Charles I, in so far as the court had developed its own particular tastes in theater, different from those of the town. It points also to a strong new sense of the dignity of authorship. Voltaire plays the indignity of waiting on the king against the dignity of his literary calling and theatrical successes, as he wonders why a poet of epic and an author of tragedies must write a farce or dash madly about to earn the titles he already deserves.

"Obedient to the court in every other particular," John Moore observed in his travels through France in 1774, "the French disregard the decisions pronounced at Versailles in matters of taste. It often happens that a dramatic piece, which has been acted before the royal family and the court with the highest applause, is afterwards damned with every circumstance of ignominy in Paris. In all works of genius the Parisians lead the judgement of the courtiers and dictate to their monarch."[7] The reversal in the balance of power is perhaps not so absolute as Moore would have it, but, by insisting so fiercely upon his desert, Voltaire likewise invokes against the court the authority of his previous literary and theatrical career. Shakespeare delicately balances the demands of the public stage and the expectations of the court through allusions to the dynamics of royal performance within the structures of his plays themselves. Voltaire, on the other hand, contemptuously insists upon the inferiority of the works he has written to royal command.

His second work for the court, commissioned to celebrate Louis XV's recent victories, was the libretto of the *Temple de la gloire*, an opera with music by Rameau, performed November 27, 1745. "La musique est de Rameau, on a trouvé plusieurs morceaux qui ont plu;

et le roi même, à son grand couvert le soir, en parla devant Rameau comme ayant été content. Les paroles sont de Voltaire, elles sont fort critiquées. Voltaire était le soir aussi au souper du roi, et le roi ne lui dit mot" ("The music is by Rameau; many bits of it were found pleasing, and the king himself, at his great banquet in the evening, spoke of it before Rameau as though he had enjoyed it. The words are by Voltaire, and they were harshly criticized. Voltaire was also at the king's supper that evening, and the king did not say a word to him").[8] This frosty response was apparently provoked. Voltaire is reported to have asked, either directly of the king or within the range of his hearing, "Trajan est-il content?" ("Is Trajan content?"). The opera praised the figure of Trajan, who in his bravery and clemency to the defeated was indeed intended to figure Louis XV. But to expose the allegory in this way, to treat the parallel with casual familiarity, is a breach of contract between court poet and king. Part of the monarch's satisfaction with his appearance under the guise of a famous Roman emperor comes from the pretense that the parallel is discovered, not created. In addition to committing the "incredible liberty of addressing the king,"[9] Voltaire went further, suggesting that both king and poet recognize the arbitrariness of the fictive parallel through which the king has been praised. The protocols of the French court under the *ancien régime* were far stricter than those of the English court at any time: the enormity of Voltaire's act can almost be grasped by imagining Ben Jonson asking James I how he liked the analogy of a "light scientiall" in *The Masque of Blackness,* or Thomas Carew asking Charles I and Henrietta Maria if they were satisfied with their apotheosis as Carlomaria.

Voltaire's inability or unwillingness to play by the rules of court etiquette did not prevent his election to the Académie Française in April 1746. But neither did his assiduous dedication to the task of royal historiographer earn him the full honors granted to Racine and Boileau: when he received his charge as gentleman of the chamber, it was with the proviso that he be denied access to the king's private chambers. The title was an empty one. By February 1750, when Madame de Pompadour staged *Alzire* in her theater of the Petits Cabinets at Versailles, Voltaire had withdrawn from actively seeking favor as a court poet. However frosty his relations with Louis had become, Voltaire remained friendly with Madame de Pompadour through the late 1740s. Later he would exaggerate the extent of her aid to him at court. "Je conclus que, pour faire la plus petite fortune, il valait mieux dire quatre mots à la maîtresse d'un roi que d'écrire cent volumes," he wrote in his memoirs in 1759 ("I concluded that, in order to make the smallest fortune, it was more worthwhile to say four words to a king's mistress than to write a hundred volumes").[10] The suggestion here, that court poets and royal mistresses are of the same calling, and that the calling is an ignominious one, reflects Voltaire's considerable bitterness about the treatment he received at the court. Nonetheless, it is true that Voltaire and Madame de Pompadour had a friendship of long standing, and that she sought to palliate the king's distaste for Voltaire (and to keep Voltaire from offending the king). Madame de Pompadour's performance as Alzire at the Petits Cabinets, then, set a play which Voltaire considered one of his best before a royal audience whose attitude toward Voltaire had hardened into contempt. Voltaire was invited to join the select audience at the second performance of the play, on March 6, 1750.

The theater in which the play was to be performed had been especially built for Madame de Pompadour in the wing of the palace at Versailles that housed Louis XV's own private apartments. While popular plays continued to be performed at court by the Comédie Française on their regular visits, the new vogue among the nobility was for private theaters, *théâtres de société,* in which small, select audiences could entertain one another.[11] Madame de Pompadour's theater, which was adjacent to the king's personal dining room, brought this form of entertainment right to the king's doorstep. Having risen to prominence through her performances at private salons when she was merely Mademoiselle Poisson and later Madame d'Etioles, she continued to polish her considerable skills as an actor, singer, and dancer before the king. Less charitably, her project in the Petits Cabinets has been seen as an attempt to "réveiller l'amour allangui" ("reawaken the fading love") of the king.[12] "En haussant les divertissements de la Cour au niveau des spectacles de Paris," writes a recent biographer, "Jeanne-Antoinette avait gagné beaucoup d'amis, l'aura d'un star, une excellente mémoire et la maîtrise infaillible de ses émotions, si utile dans la jungle de la grande politique" ("By bringing court entertainments up to the level of the spectacles of Paris, . . . Jeanne-Antoinette [Madame de Pompadour] had gained many friends, the aura of a star, an excellent memory, and infallible control over her emotions, so useful in the jungle of serious politics").[13] Madame de Pompadour used her theater as a means of securing power and reinforcing her ascendancy over any other possible rivals for the king's favor.

The play that opened the theater on January 17, 1747, was Molière's *Tartuffe,* in which Madame de Pompadour took the role of Dorine. The audience was indeed small and select. The duc de Luynes reports that only fourteen were in attendance; among those not admitted, he recalls with malicious pleasure, were the maréchal de Noailles and the prince de Conty (de Luynes, 8:87). While it was difficult to be part of the audience for the performances at the Petits Cabinets, it was even more difficult to become a member of the cast. Madame de Pompadour and the king drew up a series of statutes for membership in the society. Among the conditions were that only actors with substantial experience on other private stages could be admitted to the society; that each actor was assigned a certain type of role and could not refuse to play roles appropriate to his type; and, finally, there was a series of regulations that declared the theater to be under the rule of women:

7. Les *actrices* seules jouiront du droit de choisir les ouvrages que la *troupe* devra représenter.
8. Elles auront pareillement le droit d'indiquer le jour de la représentation, de fixer le nombre des répétitions, et d'en désigner le jour et l'heure.
9. Chaque *acteur* sera tenu de se trouver à l'heure *très précise* désignée pour la répétition, sous peine d'une *amende* que les *actrices* seules fixeront entre elles.
10. On accorde aux *actrices seules* la *demi-heure* de grâce, passé laquelle l'amende qu'elles auront encourue sera décidées par elles seules.

(7. Only the *actresses* will enjoy the right of choosing the works that the *troupe* will perform.
8. They will likewise have the right to specify the day of performance, to fix the number of rehearsals, and to specify their date and time.
9. Each *actor* will be required to be present at the *precise* hour designated for the rehearsal, under penalty of a *fine* that the *actresses* alone will set among themselves.
10. To the *actresses alone* will be accorded the favor of a *half hour,* after which the fine that they have incurred shall be decided by the actresses themselves.)[14]

The coy deference to the privileges of the ladies marks this project as particularly special to Madame de Pompadour.

The rigorously exclusive quality of the group had its political ramifications as well. Madame de Hausset, lady-in-waiting to Madame de Pompadour, reports that she had sought a military command for one of her relatives from the comte d'Argenson. Disappointed, she ran into the marquis de Voyer, his son, who suggested that in exchange for this command she could secure him the position of "exempt de police":

> Je lui dis que je ne concevais pas la plaisanterie qu'il faisait. «Voici ce que c'est, dit-il, on va jouer *Tartufe* dans les cabinets, il y a un rôle d'exempt qui consiste en très peu de vers. Obtenez de Mme la marquise de me faire donner ce rôle, et le commandement est à vous.» . . . La chose fut faite; j'obtins mon commandement, et M. de V*** remercia Madame comme si elle l'eût fait faire duc.

> (I told him I had no idea what kind of joke he was making. "Here's the way it is," he said. "They are going to play *Tartuffe* in the *cabinets,* there is a role of Exempt that doesn't have very many lines. Get Madame the marquise to have me cast in that part, and the command is yours." . . . It was done; I got my command, and M. de V*** thanked Madame as though she had had him made duke.)[15]

This exchange of a part in a play for a position in the army reveals much about the way business was done in the court of Louis XV. The financial status of Madame de Pompadour's theater became a matter of some dispute in its third season (1748–49), when the duc de Richelieu, who was in charge of *Menus Plaisirs* (the royal entertainments), attempted to take control of the budget. As the duc de Luynes noted with some surprise at the first performance, the theater was funded from the account for buildings (an account under the control of Madame de Pompadour's uncle). Richelieu was defeated, and the theater remained separate from the normal court budget, paid for out of accounts originally designated for construction and repairs to the royal palaces.

Financially independent (or at least not subject to ordinary accounting procedures), ruled over by Madame de Pompadour and her fellow actresses, the theater at the Petits Cabinets was a separate realm with its own laws, a secret world within the larger world of the court. Here Madame could weave her spell over the king, "amuser le roi, le retenir, et s'amuser elle-même," as the duc de Croÿ put it ("amuse the king, keep him, and amuse herself").[16] As Dorine in *Tartuffe,* she plays the king's own soubrette. The duc de Vallière, as Tartuffe, may bid her to conceal her bosom, but the joke becomes more complicated as he parodies the censoriousness of prudish outsiders, those *dévots* who would criticize Madame de Pompadour's relationship to the king. The play becomes less about Orgon's loss of control over his household than about the witty inner circle's expulsion of Tartuffe. As enacted by a group of witty insiders at the Petits Cabinets, the play signals Madame de Pompadour's victory over the hypocrites who have sought to block her rise to power. Within the play, Dorine must endure with the others the wait for deliverance before the king's "exempt de police" arrives. But at the Petits Cabinets, where the audience can never forget that Madame de Pompadour is Dorine, the Exempt himself is Dorine's creature. Indebted to Madame de Pompadour for his role, the marquis de Voyer delivers the family from Tartuffe's clutches, as the play's script insists he should. But here, in addition, the marquis de Voyer enacts his gratitude to Madame de Pompadour for allowing him to appear with her on her own stage.

Molière writes the king's deliverance of his play from the clutches of hostile censors into the *rex ex machina* device of the Exempt. He does so because there is no other way for the play to finish as a comedy; without the king's direct, personal intervention, *Tartuffe* will never see the stage. Such anxious concerns disappear on this occasion. By taking Dorine's role, Madame de Pompadour aligns her considerable power with the pert servant's irreverence. The selection of *Tartuffe* as the first play makes it clear that Madame de Pompadour was no Madame de Maintenon: her theater was in no way envisioned as a reformed theater. Far from being sharply limited in her powers by the generic limits of her role, here Dorine is the key to the whole play and indeed the focal point of the whole event. The king's adoring presence in the audience makes the sending of the Exempt by the king in the play a special gesture of love. Freed from her soubrette costume and role, Madame de Pompadour can move at the play's end upstairs into the king's private apartments, where she will play host to an even more select gathering of the nobility. Finally, after the ceremonials of the king's bedchamber are concluded, she will be joined, alone in her own apartment, by the king himself.

The plays and the scenes from opera and the ballets offered at the theater of the Petits Cabinets are thus all in a sense *hors d'oeuvres,* appetizing allusions to the union of the king and the actress that will take place later in the evening. As Danielle Gallet-Guerne puts it: "Elle chantait chaque fois le triomphe de l'amour" ("Each time she sang the triumph of love"). Whatever part she took, Louis metamorphosed into that nypmh's, that goddess's, that queen's lover, regardless of who stood in for him on the stage. Even in breeches parts, Gallet-Guerne continues, "elle frôlait l'équivoque de la travesti. Ainsi étaient proposés à l'inconscient du roi autant d'obscurs chemins conduisant à l'objet du désir" ("she lightly touched on the equivocal nature of transvestism. Thus were proposed to the king's unconscious various obscure roads leading to the object of desire").[17] Where Madame de Maintenon, providing Louis XIV with the chaste entertainment of Saint-Cyr, hopes to channel the king's desire toward the greater glory of God, Madame de Pompadour, acting out herself an infinite variety of romantic possibilities, stages before the court her own erotic dominion over the king.

Voltaire noticed this perhaps too clearly. On December 30, 1747, Madame de Pompadour sought to win back for Voltaire some of his lost favor. Her company performed his *comédie larmoyante, L'Enfant prodigue* (*The Prodigal Son*) on the stage of the Petits Cabinets. The playwright was not invited to attend the performance of this sentimental comedy, but he heard of its success several days later, and responded with a verse epigram:

> Ainsi donc vous réunissez
> Tous les arts, tous les dons de plaire;
> Pompadour! Vous embellisez
> La Cour, le Parnasse, et Cythère.
> Charme de tous les yeux, trésor d'un seul mortel!
> Que votre amour soit éternel!
> Que tous vos jours soient marqués par des fêtes!
> Que de nouveaux succès marquent ceux de Louis!
> Vivez tous deux sans ennemis!
> Et gardez tous deux vos conquêtes!

(Thus you reunite all the arts, all the gifts of pleasing; Pompadour! you adorn the court, Parnassus, and Cytherea! Enchantment of all eyes, treasure of one mortal alone! Let your love be

eternal! Let all your days be marked with festivals! Let new successes mark those of Louis! Live, both of you, free of enemies!
And preserve, both of you, your conquests!)[18]

Witty though it may be, this poem, with its suggestion that the
achievements of Madame de Pompadour and those of Louis are of
equal merit, scandalized the court and mobilized opposition to both
Madame de Pompadour and Voltaire. As with the remark about Trajan, Voltaire had again violated appropriate behavior. Glorifying Madame de Pompadour's "success"—which can be understood both as
her success as an actress and her success in maintaining her hold over
Louis—he comes too close to declaring the real state of affairs in the
court. The queen and the princesses of the court were offended to be
so pointedly ignored. Much of their anger is attributable less to
Voltaire's gall in penning such a trifle than to the poem's presentation
of Madame de Pompadour and Louis as a royal couple. While flattery
of the royal mistress might be acceptable, celebration of the union of
mistress and king as a victory over unspecified enemies goes too far.
The linkage of the king's military victories with Madame de Pompadour's amorous victory over him suggests that both are equally re-
spectable and equally desirable for the state.

On January 10, 1748, after the performance of *L'Enfant prodigue*,
Madame de Pompadour reprised her performance as Dorine in *Tartuffe;* Voltaire's difficulties negotiating the hypocrisies of the court do
not seem to have interfered with the popularity of her version of
Molière's play. Nor did they interfere with the prosperity of her theater. In the next season, the theater was greatly expanded. The great
marble staircase was fitted with a removable stage and with machines
and décor that could be disassembled in fourteen hours and reassem-
bled in twenty-four.[19] It was in this space that the amateur actors
attemped their first tragedy, Voltaire's *Alzire,* on February 28, 1750.
"Le pièce est difficile à jouer," wrote the duc de Luynes, "et les acteurs
craignoient de ne pas réussir, de sort qu'il y eut beaucoup moins de
gens admis qu'à l'ordinaire" ("The play is difficult to act and the actors
were afraid of failing, so that there were many fewer people admitted
than usual"). They need not have been so timid; as Madame de Pompadour wrote to her brother, "Nous avons joué hier pour la première
fois, la tragédie, c'étoit *Alzire*. On prétend que j'ai été étonnante"
("Yesterday we played tragedy for the first time, it was *Alzire*. They

say that I was amazing"). The duc de Luynes praised both Madame de Pompadour and the duc de Duras, who played Zamore opposite her; she was less kind, writing later that "M. de Duras n'a ni la voix, ni la figure, ni le jeu assez nobles pour la tragédie" ("has neither voice, face, nor acting ability sufficiently noble for tragedy").[20]

If the result when Madame de Pompadour appears as Dorine in *Tartuffe* is to upset the balance of power within that play, this is not the result with *Alzire*. In Voltaire's tragedy, the Peruvian princess is indeed the focal point of the action. Around her revolve all the men of the play: her father, Montèze, the Peruvian king who has converted to Christianity and promised his daughter in marriage to the Spanish governor, Gusman; Alvarez, Gusman's father; Zamore, Alzire's first love and promised husband, whom she believes to be dead at the beginning of the play. When the play was first performed, by the Comédie Française in 1736, it was a great success, with twenty successive performances and two visits to the court, February 21 and March 15. The play was a star vehicle for Mademoiselle Gaussin, a professional actress known for her youthful energy and grace, who created the roles of many of Voltaire's sentimental heroines. Madame de Pompadour thus selected for herself a play that was a standard item in the professional repertoire, a play that was well known, and a play that depended on its principal actress to win the expected emotional effects. Anything short of *étonnante* would not do.

The script of the play, too, insists that an audience keep its eyes fixed upon Alzire herself. "De tout ce nouveau monde Alzire est le modèle," Alvarez declares, before Alzire's first appearance in the play, sketching out for Gusman both the political and the religious consequences attendant upon her consent to their marriage:

> Les peuples incertains fixent les yeux sur elle:
> Son coeur aux Castillans va donner tous les coeurs;
> L'Amérique à genoux adoptera nos moeurs;
> La foi doit y jeter ses racines profondes;
> Votre hymen est le noeud qui joindra les deux mondes;
> Ces féroces humains, qui détestent nos lois,
> Voyant entre vos bras la fille de leurs rois,
> Vont, d'un esprit moins fier et d'un coeur plus facile,
> Sous votre joug heureux baisser un front docile;

Et je verrai, mon fils, grâce à ces doux liens,
Tous les coeurs désormais espagnols et chrétiens.

(I.i, p. 390: Of all this new world Alzire is the model; the unsteady people fix their eyes upon her. Her heart will give all hearts to the Castilians; America will adopt our customs on its knees. Faith must here strike its deep roots; your nuptial is the knot that will tie the two worlds. These fierce humans, who hate our laws, when they see the daughter of their kings in your arms, will, with a spirit less proud and a gentler heart, abase their docile foreheads under your happy yoke. And I will see, my son, thanks to these sweet bonds, all hearts at that moment Spanish and Christian.)

Alvarez's vision is highly theatricalized. When the unsteady people see the wedding performed, their response will be an instantaneous obedience, a miraculous humbling. What the kind old Spaniard dreams of is analogous to Stuart court masque, a transformative show that overwhelms political (and here also racial) difference with love. The Peruvians function here as an audience that awaits a spectacular vindication of imperial rule. The question before the audience of the play is whether this vision of harmonious marriage of old and new world can be realized. As stand-in for the whole new world, Alzire becomes not just a romantic prize but also a validation of the Spaniards' imperial dream.

With the zeal of a recent convert, Montèze goes further, urging his daughter on to the marriage by invoking the divine will: "Dieu t'ordonne par moi de former ces liens; / Il t'appelle aux autels, il règle ta conduite; / Entends sa voix" (I.iv, p. 392: "Through me God orders you to form these bonds; He calls you to the altars, He rules your conduct; hear His voice"). For both of the fathers in this play, the marriage is divinely ordained, and at the play's beginning it represents a vision of colonial harmony that is purely utopian. The play's full title, *Alzire, ou les Américains,* insists that the conflict between old and new worlds is central. "Vous sentez bien, messieurs," Voltaire wrote to the actors of the Comédie Française, "tout le mérite de ce sujet consiste dans la peinture des moeurs américaines, opposée au portrait des moeurs européens" (D965: "You certainly realize, gentlemen, the whole merit of this subject consists in the painting of American customs opposed to the portrait of European customs"). Most critics of the play have found this anthropological explanation unconvincing, except insofar as the actors could use exotic scene decorations and sport native American costume.[21]

The play appears to juxtapose an American, natural religion to an oppressive Spanish Christianity. Voltaire claimed in his prefatory discourse to the play that *Alzire* demonstrates "combien le véritable esprit de religion l'emporte sur les vertus de la nature" (p. 379: "by how much the true spirit of religion transcends the natural virtues"). This claim is only borne out in the play if the "true spirit of religion" is seen to be toleration of diverse faiths rather than the Spaniards' particular version of Christianity. In fact, the Spaniards differ in their creed, with Alvarez advocating toleration and conversion by pious example and Gusman advocating conversion of the Indians by force. Montèze, by forcing his daughter to marry Gusman, appears to subscribe to the latter version of Christianity, and Zamore, Alzire's lover and by religion apparently a noble savage, disgraces himself (and his heroic creed) with his dishonorable attack upon Gusman between the fourth and fifth acts. Thus only a particular understanding of Christianity is vindicated in the play: "Stated bluntly, [Voltaire's] aim is to teach Christians the real significance of Christianity," R. S. Ridgway puts it.[22] As Alvarez's speech in the first scene makes clear, the play offers a "modèle," not simply to the eyes of an imagined audience of uncertain Peruvians, but also to the eyes of its European audience. Alzire, who struggles to obey the commands of her father and to follow the dictates of her heart, functions as a model of virtue assailed by mutually exclusive and tyrannically imposed demands.

From the very first versions of the Pocahontas story early in the seventeenth century, the representation of America as a virtuous Indian maiden electing European dominion out of love became standard in procolonial literature. Like Pocahontas, Alzire represents an entire population; but unlike Pocahontas, she does not defy her tyrannical father. Voltaire has turned the fable in upon itself, by presenting Montèze as a Christian. Thus, where Pocahontas interposes herself between the warlike savage and the helpless Christian, Alzire is at risk of being forced by a tyrannical Christian father to wed a tyrannical Christian husband. The marriage altar to which her father wants to lead her is a Christian one, but it is also the altar of barbarous sacrifice.

Despite his political adherence to the doctrine of force, however, throughout the play Gusman refrains from forcing himself upon Alzire as a husband. "Plus que vous ne pensez, je porte un coeur sensible," he tells Alzire, "Et ce n'est pas à vous à me croire inflexible" (IV.ii, p. 421: "More than you think, I bear a heart capable of sentiment; and it is not for you to believe me inflexible"). It is this capacity for sentiment that motivates Gusman's change of heart at the end of the play when, dying, he forgives Zamore for striking the fatal blow. Zamore's conversion to Christianity at this moment is a response to Gusman's astounding generosity.

While Gusman is revealed at the end to be Christian in the way Voltaire prefers to understand the term, Alzire is presented as such throughout. Her honesty is antitheatrical as well. Alvarez describes his scheme of marriage in theatrical terms, as a grand masque of union between the two worlds, but for Alzire, such a spectacle would be dishonest feigning. "Faut-il apprendre à feindre?" she demands of Montèze when he urges her to dissemble her remembered passion for Zamore; "Quelle science, hélas!" (I.iv, p. 393: "Must I learn to feign? Alas, what a skill!"). "Tel est mon caractère," she continues:

> et jamais mon visage
> N'a de mon coeur encor démenti le langage.
> Qui peut se déguiser pourait trahir sa foi;
> C'est un art de l'Europe: il n'est pas fait pour moi.

> (p. 394: Such is my character, and my face has never yet given the lie to the language of my heart. She who can disguise herself could betray her faith. That is a European art: it is not for me.)

"Je n'ai rien déguisé," she reminds Gusman when he reproaches her for her continued love for Zamore in spite of their marriage (IV.ii, p. 420: "I have disguised nothing"). "Peut-être une Espagnole eût promis davantage," she urges. "Elle eût prodiguer les charmes de ses pleurs/Je n'ai point leurs attraits, et je n'ai point leurs moeurs" ("Maybe a Spanish girl would have promised more; she would have been prodigal with the charms of her tears. I have none of their allure, and I have none of their morals"). What is Indian about Alzire is her distaste for European arts and Spanish charms. She despises hypocrisy and proposes herself as a model of honesty, incapable of dissembling. Even at the end, begging for death at the hand of Alvarez, she rejects applause: "Que je sois de ton peuple applaudie ou blâmée / Ta seule opinion fera ma renommée" (V.v, p. 431: "Let me be applauded or blamed by your people, your opinion alone will create my renown").

Such an insistence upon frankness, upon the incapacity to dissemble, cannot survive without qualification in the atmosphere of the Petits Cabinets. Madame de Pompadour's astonishing skills are the occasion for the whole, select gathering. While this is to a certain degree true also of the skills of Mademoiselle Gaussin on the stage of the Théâtre Français, the disclaimer of the ability to act is more clearly read by an audience there as a feature of the character, not of the performer. But at the Petits Cabinets, the ordinary conventions of enactment do not apply. Alzire's disdain for Spanish hypocrisy, enacted by Madame de Pompadour, becomes, like her selection of the role of Dorine, part of a frontal attack upon what she sees as a hypocritical faction at court. Alzire's antitheatricality, paradoxically, becomes enlisted in Madame de Pompadour's campaign against the antitheatricality of the *dévots*. As Alzire, Madame de Pompadour celebrates her own spontaneity, her own disingenuousness, her own lack of ulterior goals. The play's movement toward a spectacular resolution, in which the scaffold of execution becomes transformed into the altar of marriage for Alzire and Zamore, becomes a movement of vindication. Alzire's virtues are rewarded, and Madame de Pompadour's acting skills are vindicated in the process, as they are proved to be sufficient to the task of playing tragedy.

The representational problem that Voltaire invokes in Alzire's honesty is not a simple one, either in the play considered as a play text or in the professional performance for which it was originally designed. Like *Tartuffe,* the play raises the idea of acting as itself an issue. The complicated metatheatrical dimension of *Alzire* consists in a repudiation of acting that is a vindication of acting. When Hamlet informs his mother that the signs of grief he displays (his inky cloak, his sighs, his tears) are mere seeming, "actions that a man might play," the actor playing Hamlet is accepting a challenge from the playwright and relaying it to the audience. He will play "that which passeth show," and enact Hamlet's *being* rather than his *seeming*.[23] Alzire's sentimental repudiation of display is of this order. Mademoiselle Gaussin, accepting the challenge, must play Alzire's modesty, honesty, and chastity without seeming to do so. This is the essential paradox of acting, and Madame de Pompadour must accept this challenge as well. But where the private reputation of Richard Burbage or Mademoiselle Gaussin is subsumed within the professional identity of actor (institutionally stable, however disreputable), for Madame de Pompadour the case is reversed. That Madame de Pompadour can act, sing, and dance is well known in the court; but the professionalism of her acting, singing, and dancing is always worthy of note (as Mademoiselle Gaussin's professionalism would not be). The vehemence with which amateur actors proclaim their professionalism shows through in the rules of Madame de Pompadour's company, to which only properly experienced performers need apply.

If Madame de Pompadour and her fellow amateur performers want to enjoy all the trappings of professional theater—moveable scenery, lavish costumes, regular performances—they do so with the understanding that at any point their difference from professional actors can also be invoked. Thus they can hand-pick their audience for their experiment in tragedy, and their achievements must be celebrated as "*étonnants*," as triumphs far surpassing those of mere professionals. But if the kind of performance that took place in the Petits Cabinets thus permits actors and audiences to eat the cake of professionalism and have it too, *Alzire* is the perfect play for this environment.

For *Alzire* itself tries to have it both ways. Voltaire's vindication of the principles of Christianity, as we have seen, is paradoxical, especially insofar as the spirit of tolerance the play teaches seems to be identical to the "natural virtues" whose inferiority to true religion the play sets out to demonstrate. The preface's description of the play may be a slippery deist's way of misleading a gullible reader, but the play's contradictions run deeper. As Clifton Cherpack has noted, going beyond earlier critics' recognition that Spanish and Indian cultures do not seem all that different in the play, the play treats "not the contrasts between two widely differing cultures but the results of the sudden and brutal mingling of these cultures."[24] The playwright's announced anthropological purpose is undermined by ambivalence about the historical phenomenon of colonialism. Voltaire neither represents the Indians as noble savages (Zamore's savagery outweighs his nobility until the final moments of the play), nor does he represent the Spaniards as tyrannically (Gusman retains a decent heart) or benevolently imperialistic (Alvarez participates, as does Montèze, in preparations for the forced marriage). The play holds up Alzire as a model, while she repudiates the idea of models. The situation at the play's end is ambiguous to an extraordinary degree. Gusman's sudden clemency and Zamore's sudden conversion (which Voltaire declares not to be a conversion in a note to the 1736 edition) are perceived by Alvarez to reveal "le doigt de Dieu" (V.vii, p. 436: "the hand of God"), but an audience can be forgiven if it does not share his perception.

   Alzire is typical of Voltaire's tragedy in raising large philosophical and historical questions—about the nature of religion, about the relations of cultures and customs, about the imperial ventures of Europe—in a framework of mutually contradictory amorous and familial imperatives. But the religion it professes offers no consolations for the deaths it exacts; and the humans engaged in the tragic action find no knowledge at the end of their suffering. The flaw of Voltaire's tragedy, Eva Jacobs has recently argued, is not that it is optimistic and didactic in spirit; the situations are presented as irreparable and horrible, but the characters seem merely to exemplify ideas.[25] Thus it is difficult, extending the terms of Jacobs's argument to *Alzire,* for audiences to care about Alzire, Gusman, or Zamore except as they represent, almost allegorically, what is at stake in the Spaniards' conquest of Peru.

   Alain Niderst is more positive about the value and power of Voltaire's tragedy: "Ce tragique presque athée est celui de notre temps," he declares. The contempt for psychological complexity, the violence, the rich and luxurious spectacle in Voltaire's tragedy anticipate not Victor Hugo's *drames romantiques,* but the plays of Sartre and Genet. "Ils suscitent le rêve d'un théâtre à la fois primitif et somptueux, une sorte de sacrifice solennel et sanglante offert à un ciel toujours voilé, à des dieux peut-être cruels, en tout cas muets" ("This almost atheistic tragic vision is that of our times. . . . They inspire the dream of a theater at once primitive and sumptuous, a kind of solemn and bloody sacrifice offered up to a heaven that is always veiled, to gods who are perhaps cruel, but in any case mute").[26]

   But did the audiences who wept so freely at Alzire's sufferings in the Théâtre Français do so because they were moved by the ideas in conflict in the play? Were they touched by the nihilistic power of an early version of Artaud's theater of cruelty? And if it is impossible to describe their responses in ways that are not hopelessly anachronistic, is there any chance that the response of the audience at the Petits Cabinets can be recovered or understood? To what extent did Madame de Pompadour see herself in Alzire, and did the audience make any attempt at all to puzzle out the play's religious and theatrical riddles? As these questions proliferate, it becomes clear that the problem is not simply one of Voltaire's drama in its context, remote and irrecoverable as that may seem, but of any drama in its context, no matter how familiar and recoverable it may seem (as Shakespeare in the Globe sometimes seems).

We know that Madame de Pompadour wanted to play the role of Alzire, for she did so, and in a theater in which she made the rules. She did it with a sense of peril, for she did not want to make a fool of herself. If she succeeded, she would win further praise as an actress, having proved herself equal to (and therefore superior to, because an amateur) a professional actress like Mademoiselle Gaussin. Succeeding as Alzire would mean presenting herself as an Indian princess, an exotic beauty embodying all that is good and noble, in the language of the play, in the true religion. In the play Alzire's beauty is essential to her virtue; so, too, the audience would see, there is no contradiction between Madame de Pompadour's beauty and her virtue. Her acting reveals something true about her: if Madame de Pompadour is something of a soubrette outside the role of Dorine, then she is also something of an Alzire outside that role as well. Her ability to play such virtue — again, because she is not a professional — implies that she possesses such virtue: that, in short, she is, as Alzire is, incapable of feigning, utterly honest, true. That Alzire is an Indian, a savage, and that Madame de Pompadour was humble in her origins, struggling against the snobbery of many powerful members of the court, can only heighten the pathos of her performance.

The king, the only member of the audience whose response mattered to her, was sufficiently pleased that the play was offered again, on March 6. Voltaire was invited to attend, as a special courtesy. And once again Voltaire suffered the fate of those who hang on the words of kings: "A la fin du spectacle," the duc de Luynes reported, "le Roi dit tout haut qu'il était étonnant que l'auteur d'*Alzire* pût être le même que celui qui avoit fait *Oreste*" (de Luynes, 10:227, "At the end of the performance, the King said out loud that it was astonishing that the author of *Alzire* could be the same as the one who wrote *Oreste*"). This remark was especially insulting, for it showed that the king was aware of, and contemptuous of, Voltaire's campaign to rewrite the tragedies of his most successful rival, Prosper Jolyot de Crébillon. *Oreste* was written as a counterplay (as Brecht would call it, a *Gegenstück*) to Crébillon's *Electre;* the king indicates here his preference for the older man's play and is able to suggest, in passing, that

Voltaire is an upstart, offering presumptuous and offensive plays like *Oreste* when he could clearly do better. To add injury to this insult, Crébillon was the royal censor, to whom Voltaire had to submit all of his plays before they could be licensed. At times, Voltaire took a kind of sardonic pleasure in this state of affairs. But he was equally sensitive to the fact that, like himself, Crébillon enjoyed the favor and protection of Madame de Pompadour, and that Madame de Pompadour had urged him not to persist in attacking Crébillon with plays on the same subjects.

This advice came as a response to Voltaire's suggestion that the rivalry between the two playwrights could be analogized to that between Corneille and Racine in the time of Louis XIV. Despite being warned off, Voltaire permitted the performance of *Oreste* by the Comédie Française in January 1750, and it is a sign, as Conlon puts it, of "an unusal degree of forbearance"[27] on the part of Madame de Pompadour that this gesture went unpunished and that plans for the performance of *Alzire* continued. Louis XV's remark, however, makes it clear that such a rivalry of poets would not be tolerated in his court. In fact, royal protection had earlier been extended to Voltaire. Voltaire's *Sémiramis* (1748), a *Gegenstück* to the *Sémiramis* (1717) of Crébillon, was in rehearsal when he learned of plans to stage a parody at Fontainebleau and at the Comédie Italienne in Paris. He unleashed a volley of letters protesting this indignity, and the parody was not staged.[28] While Voltaire saw his versions of tragic subjects touched by Crébillon as vindications of the ancients, not as parodies, there is little doubt that this distinction was lost at the highest social levels.

Voltaire celebrated the royal performances of *Alzire* with an epigram to Madame de Pompadour:

> Cette Américaine parfaite
> Trop de larmes a fait couler.
> Ne pourrai-je me consoler
> Et voir Vénus à sa toilette?

(This perfect American has caused too many tears to flow. Couldn't I console myself by seeing Venus at her *toilette*?)[29]

The verses are lame, and again, Voltaire succeeds in somehow being rude. Only a few special friends were admitted to the favorite's *toilette*, and Voltaire had never been among them. The idea of Venus as a curative sight for eyes sore from weeping is witty, but the invitation, as far as we can tell, was never extended. To his niece, after seeing this production, Voltaire also wrote of his tears: "Je vous en rendray un fort bon d'Alzire; vous auriez été étonnée. Je l'ay été, et j'ay pleuré. Les larmes ne se commandent point. Un courtisan peut battre les mains, s'exstasier, exagérer. Mais il n'y a que le coeur qui pleure. Je vous aurois bien voulu lâ. . . . Vous êtes ma famille entière, ma cour, mon Versailles, mon Parnasse, et la seule ressource de mon coeur" (D4119: "I will give you a very good [account] of *Alzire;* you would have been amazed. I was, and I wept. Tears do not appear on command. A court-ier can clap his hands, be transported, exaggerate. But it is the heart alone that weeps. I really wished you could have been there. . . . You are my whole family, my court, my Versailles, my Parnassus, and the sole support of my heart"). This letter sets in relief the exaggeration and false ecstasy of Voltaire's epigram to Madame de Pompadour. His contempt for the hypocrisy of the courtier taints his attempts at courtly performance.

It is surprising how often the word *étonner* shows up in the accounts of these performances of *Alzire.* Madame de Pompadour tells her brother she was acclaimed as *"étonnante"*; the king was *"étonné"* that the author of *Oreste* could write so moving a play; Voltaire assures Madame Denis that she would have been *"étonnée"* had she been able to attend. Amazement, astonishment, seems the only appropriate re-sponse to the event. It is likewise the appropriate response demanded by the play itself: readers as well as audiences are forced to admire, to be amazed by the astonishing virtues of Alzire. "Quel changement, grand Dieu! quel étonnant langage!" exclaims Alzire in response to Gusman's change of heart (V.vii, p. 435: "What a transformation, great God! What amazing language!"). The peculiar context of the Petits Cabinets becomes thus a reinforcement of the play's resolution of the contradictions of religion, race, and rank through wonder. Designed for and successful on the professional stage, *Alzire* achieves a special fulfillment in amateur court performance.

Voltaire did not remain long after this at Versailles. During the spring of 1750 he decided at last to accept Frederick the Great's repeated invita-tions to join him in Berlin, and, after some tough negotiations with Fred-erick over money for traveling expenses, received permission from Louis to depart from France that summer. The year 1750 was also the last season for the theater at the Petits Cabinets; with the construction of a new palace (including a custom-built, smaller theater) at Belle-vue, Louis XV suspended theatrical performances at Versailles.

III

"Je vais me faire pour mon instruction un petit dictionnaire à l'usage des rois," Voltaire wrote to Madame Denis from Berlin December 18, 1752:

> *Mon ami* signifie *mon esclave. Mon cher* veut dire, *vous m'êtes plus qu'indifférent.* Entendez par *je vous rendra heureux, je vous souffrirai tant que j'aurai besoin de vous. Soupez avec moi ce soir,* signifie, *je me moquerai de vous ce soir.* Le dictionnaire peut être long. C'est un article à mettre dans l'Encyclopédie.

> (D5114: I am going to make, for my own instruction, a little dictionary of royal usage. *My friend* signifies *my slave. My dear friend* means *you are utterly unimportant to me.* Understand by *I will make you happy: I will put up with you as long as I have need of you. Dine with me this evening* signifies *I will ridicule you this evening.* The dictionary could be long. It's an article for the *Encyclopédie.*)

For his part, Frederick reported that he too had learned a lesson from Voltaire's stay in Prussia. "Je ne m'étonne pas qu'on parle chez vous de la querelle de nos beaux-esprits," he wrote in April 1753 to his former secretary Darget, now in Paris; "Voltaire est le plus méchant fou que j'aie connu de ma vie; il n'est bon qu'à lire. Vous ne sauriez imaginer toutes les duplicités, les fourberies et les infamies qu'il a faites ici; je suis indigné que tant d'esprit et tant de connaissances ne rendent pas les hommes meilleurs" ("I am not surprised that they are all talking in Paris about the quarrel between our great wits [Voltaire and Mauper-tuis]. Voltaire is the most wicked madman I have ever known in my life; he is good for nothing except to be read. You cannot imagine all the double-dealing, confidence tricks, and infamies that he has done here. I am outraged that so much wit and so much erudition cannot make men better").[30] This mutual disillusionment testifies to dashed high hopes. The correspondence between Frederick and Voltaire had begun with an admiring letter from the young crown prince in 1736, moving on to a process of idealization, with the prince idealizing the philosopher and the philosopher seeing in Frederick an enlightened alternative to the sullen Louis XV. Voltaire represents his difficulties with the court of Louis XV as those of a court playwright who finds his works misunderstood, who sees the works of inferior rivals praised, and who cannot bend to flattery. He deals with Frederick in a wholly different tone: "J'aime vos vers, votre prose, votre esprit, votre philosophie hardie et ferme," he wrote in 1759. "Je n'ai pu vivre sans vous, ni avec vous. Je ne parle point au roi, au héros, c'est l'affaire des souverains; je parle à celui qui m'a enchantée, que j'ai aimé, et contre qui je suis toujours fâché" (D8218: "I love your verse, your prose, your wit, your tough, solid philosophy. I couldn't live without you, or with you. I am not talking to the king, the hero; that's the business of rulers. I'm talking to the person who charmed me, whom I loved, and with whom I am always angry"). His betrayal by Frederick he portrays as that of one friend by another, who happens to be a king.[31]

Upon his arrival at Frederick's court in the summer of 1750, Voltaire was immediately admitted into Frederick's most intimate circles. Frederick showered Voltaire with attention, and Voltaire threw himself enthusiastically into the theatrical activity of the court. He soon discovered that Frederick's brother, Prince Henry, was a talented actor, and that Frederick's sisters were also eager performers: "Nous bâtissons icy des téâtres aussi aisément que leur frère aigné gagne des batailles et fait des vers," he informed d'Argental (D4241: "We are building theaters here as easily as their older brother wins battles and makes verses"). On a special stage built in the apartments of the king's sister, Princess Emily, Voltaire acted in his own *Rome sauvée,* playing a role that he had first played in his house in Paris and later played at the private theater of the duchesse du Maine at Sceaux. The part was that of Cicéron, and the play a *Gegenstück* to Crébillon's *Catilina* (1748). This performance at Frederick's court, with the newly arrived philosopher in the role of Rome's savior, seems to epitomize the expectations of both men. For the king, there is the opportunity to profit from the wisdom and erudition of Voltaire, to see him, both in the theater and in private suppers at Sans Souci, Frederick's new summer palace, as a kind of Cicero. For Voltaire, the freedom to act in his own play before the king betokened release from bondage to Louis XV, a larger freedom of action.

When Voltaire arrived in Berlin in 1750, he was already an experienced performer. The professional stage of Paris and the exclusive stage of the Petits Cabinets were closed to him, but he could perform at home and in *théâtres de société* less exalted than that of Madame de Pompadour. Primary among these was the theater at Cirey, where Voltaire lived, wrote, and acted in plays with Madame du Châtelet before his promotion to Gentleman of the Chamber. He and Madame du Châtelet had also performed at the theater at Sceaux, where the duchesse du Maine held sway over her own small court, and at the court theater of Stanislas Leczinski, king of Poland (Louis XV's father-in-law) at Lunéville.[32] He had even performed before Frederick before: on their first meeting, at Moyland Castle in 1740, he had read *Mahomet* to the young king.

Voltaire, according to Ronald S. Ridgway, specialized in two particular character types: "the sentimental patriarch and defender of the true faith," like Alvarez in *Alzire* or Lusignan in *Zaïre,* and "the champion of freedom and patriotic duty, exemplified by Brutus in *La Mort de César* and Cicero in *Rome sauvée.*" But above all, Ridgway concludes, these types tended to fuse into one role. Especially in the part of Cicéron, "Voltaire was playing himself, or rather an idealized version of himself."[33] Voltaire's identity with the role is celebrated in Condorcet's remarks on the play in the Kehl edition: "*Rome sauvée* fut représentée à Paris sur un théâtre particulier. M. de Voltaire y joua le rôle de Cicéron. Jamais, dans aucun rôle, aucun acteur n'a porté si loin l'illusion: on croyait voir le consul. Ce n'étaient pas des vers récités de mémoire qu'on entendait, mais un discours sortant de l'âme de l'orateur" ("*Rome sauvée* was performed in Paris in a private theater. M. de Voltaire played the role of Cicéron. Never, in any role, has any actor carried the illusion so far: it seemed that one actually saw the consul. What one heard were not lines recited from memory, but a speech that emerged directly from the soul of the orator").[34]

The performance of *Rome sauvée* at the house in the rue Traversière-Saint-Honoré to which Condorcet refers took place on June 8, 1750. From the very beginning, the entire production was under Voltaire's direct control. He read the script aloud to the actors, instructing them in the proper readings of their lines. He cast the play with care. Among the actors was a young jeweler's son who had already made a name for himself in one of the city's amateur acting troupes: Lekain would go on to become Voltaire's leading interpreter on the stage and his most important protégé. The stage itself was built to order. After the death of Madame du Châtelet in 1749, Voltaire had taken over the whole house which they had shared. The third floor was converted into a theater with movable scenery, seating about one hundred people on benches and permitting another twenty to watch the plays standing. Demand for admittance to the performances here was so great that tickets had to be printed. The costumes for *Rome sauvée* were borrowed from the Comédie Française, and were none other than those used for Crébillon's *Catilina*.[35]

Voltaire conceived the entire event as a vindication of the honor of the ancients against the moderns, and enlisted for this purpose the sponsorship of the duchesse du Maine. Whether she had actually requested it or not, *Rome sauvée* became her play. Writing eagerly to her on the day before the performance, June 7, Voltaire reports a dress rehearsal before an invited audience of churchmen, academics, and magistrates "qui savent leurs Catilinaires par coeur! Vous ne sauriez croire quel succez votre tragédie a eu dans cette grave assemblée" (D4154: "who know their Catilinarian orations by heart! You would not believe the success your tragedy has had before this grave assembly"). The project had been hers from the beginning: "Vous m'avez ordonné Catilina, et il est fait" (D3979: "You commanded Cataline of me, and it is done"), Voltaire wrote to her on August 14, 1749, although two days earlier he told d'Argental that he had written the play in a fit of possession: "le diable s'empara de moy et me dit: Vange Cicéron et la France, lave la honte de ton pays" (D3974: "The devil took hold of me and said, 'Avenge Cicéron and France, wash off the shame of your country'"). Voltaire also sought to enlist Frederick in his campaign, writing to him in detail about Crébillon's flaws. He circulated portions of Frederick's letters agreeing with his criticisms, and then was embarrassed when Crébillon circulated a letter from Frederick warmly praising *Catilina*.[36]

The enterprise became a vindication of France as well as of the ancients when it was presented to the duchesse du Maine. "La petite fille du Grand Condé, la conservatrice du bon goust et du bons sens avoit raison d'être indignée de voir la farce monstrueuse du Catilina de Crébillon trouver des aprobateurs," Voltaire continued in his August 14 letter. "Jamais Rome n'avoit été plus avilie, et jamais Paris plus ridicule" (D3979: "The granddaughter of the Great Condé, the preserver of good taste and good sense, was right to be angry to see the monstrous farce of Crébillon's Catilina receiving support and praise. Never has Rome been so degraded, and never has Paris been more ridiculous"). When the Great Condé wept at Corneille's *Cinna,* we recall, Voltaire described that as a key moment in the history of the human spirit. The whole of his *Siècle de Louis XIV,* which Voltaire was planning at this time, is related to *Rome sauvée* as another project of historical recovery or vindication. When it was finally published, it was perceived by many as a satire, holding up the past age as a contrast to the present, although Voltaire sought to defuse this application. The manner in which he attempted to do so, however, shows the same lack of tact that crippled his career in the French court. "Je crois surtout que madame de Pompadour pourait ne pas désapprouver la manière dont je parle de mesdames de La Valière, de Montespan et de Maintenon dont tant d'historiens ont parlé avec une grossièreté révoltante et avec des préjugez outrageants," he wrote to the duc de Richelieu (D4561: "I especially believe that Madame de Pompadour could not disapprove of the way in which I speak of Mesdames de La Vallière, de Montespan, and de Maintenon, of whom so many historians have spoken with a revolting coarseness and with outrageous prejudices").[37] In Voltaire's view, his history has become a vindication of the royal mistress by suggesting, without prejudice, that the position is a semiofficial office. By refusing to slander her predecessors, Voltaire feels that he has deserved Madame de Pompadour's favor.

In the context of this project of historical resuscitation, the duchesse du Maine becomes not just a conservative, whose taste and good sense are commendable in the current atmosphere of decline, but a reincarnation of her grandfather (just as, in a way, Madame de Pompadour has become a reincarnation of the previous royal mistresses). When Voltaire invokes "L'âme du grand Condé qui réside dans votre tête" (D4105: "The soul of the Great Condé living in your head"), he is not merely flattering the duchess. He is invoking a vision of past greatness, and urging the duchess to fulfill it. Similarly, he urged Madame de Pompadour to encourage both Crébillon and himself, as Henriette d'Angleterre had encouraged both Corneille and Racine; she declined, assuring Voltaire that she knew him incapable of malice against Crébillon (D3463). Voltaire then enlisted the duchesse du Maine, who held herself aloof from the court in her own establishment at Sceaux, dedicating to her his *Oreste* as well as treating *Rome sauvée* as her special tragedy. In the dedication of *Oreste,* he again invoked the vanished age of glory: "C'est dans ces temps illustre que les Condé, vos aïeux, couverts de tant de lauriers, cultivaient et en-

courageaient les arts; où un Bossuet immortalisait les héros, et instru-
isait les rois; . . . où les Racine, les Despréaux, présidaient aux belles-
lettres, Lulli à la musique, Le Brun à la peinture. Tous ces arts, madame, furent acuellis surtout dans votre palais" ("It was in those
famous times that the Condés, your ancestors, crowned with so many
laurels, nurtured and encouraged the arts; when Bossuet immortalized
heroes, and instructed kings; . . . when the Racines, and the [Boileau]-
Despréaux ruled over literature, Lulli over music, Le Brun over painting. All these arts, madame, were welcome especially at your palace").[38]
The nostalgia here again goes beyond conventional flattery. Voltaire
compares his status in Louis XV's court to that of Racine in Louis XIV's
court and, without directly complaining of the decline, links the house
of Condé, through its past sponsorship of Racine and its current sponsorship of Voltaire, to the true tragic spirit of the ancient Greeks.
Madame de Pompadour, despite her admiration of Voltaire's works and
her personal triumph in *Alzire,* could not be included in such an assessment: she equally admired the plays of Crébillon. As we have seen, the
idea of a reformed drama, restored to the purity of the ancients, is not
an idea in harmony with the practice of the Petits Cabinets.

Madame de Maintenon's and Racine's experiments with reformed
drama, however, have an ironic connection with Voltaire. Not only
did he feel driven to avenge the honor of Paris and the ancients by staging dramas without the "platte galanterie" that was the disease of the
times (D4105: "bland love talk"), but he was beset by other distorting
mirrors of the past. His *La Mort de César,* unsuccessful on the professional stage because it had no female roles, had been performed at a
Jesuit college. In June 1748, the order of the Visitandines de Beaune,
noticing its lack of a love interest, deemed the play appropriate for performance by the students at the convent. The girls staged it in honor
of their mother superior. One of the nuns involved was a near relation
of Madame du Châtelet, and she prevailed upon Voltaire to write a special prologue for the occasion.[39] Taking on the mantle of Racine
might not extend to special favor from the king and vindication over
the age's Corneille, Crébillon; but it did extend to the embarrassing
invitation to contribute some pious verses to a convent performance.

However much Voltaire preferred Racine to Corneille as a model,
however, in one particular area they agreed: tragedy required a subject
"plus mâle que l'amour" ("more masculine than love").[40] One of the
features of Crébillon's *Catilina* that Voltaire loathed was the invention

of Tullie, a daughter of Cicéron with whom Catilina is in love, and of a discarded mistress, Fulvie, who threatens to betray him. The plot oscillates between the two women's threats to Catilina's plans. Instead of the conflicts of love, jealousy, and filial duty that Crébillon added to his play, Voltaire sets his Catilina and Cicéron directly in conflict (although he does also create a female role in that of Catilina's wife, Aurélie). Love is of course not alien to the drama of Corneille, especially when it has political consequences, as the presence of Emilie in *Cinna* makes clear.

Both Crébillon and Voltaire, in fact, embarked upon their Roman conspiracy plays with *Cinna* as a famous precedent. Each playwright pays homage to the most famous lines in *Cinna,* the lines that Voltaire reported as reducing the Great Condé to tears: "Je suis maître de moi comme de l'univers; / Je le suis, je veux l'être." Crébillon's Catilina brings the first act to a thunderous close as he echoes Corneille's Auguste:

> Soutiens, Catilina, tes glorieux desseins:
> Maître de l'univers si tu l'es des Romains,
> C'est aujourd'hui qu'il faut que ton sort s'accomplisse,
> Que Rome à tes genoux tombe, ou qu'elle périsse.

> (Maintain, Catilina, your glorious schemes. Master of the universe if you are master of the Romans, today your destiny must be accomplished; Rome will fall at your knees or she will perish.)[41]

The allusion reveals that Catilina aspires to be another Auguste: but if mastery of Rome is mastery of the universe, what is missing in this echo of Corneille is the idea of an imperial self-mastery. Catilina's failure to recognize that aspect of rule is signaled by the incompleteness of the reference. As the chief of the conspirators, Crébillon's Catilina replays the role of Cinna, not that of Auguste. The Parisian audience, despite Voltaire's contempt of their enthusiasm for Crébillon, could recognize so famous an allusion. Auguste's words, inappropriately garbled in Catilina's mouth, hint at the inevitability of his failure.

Voltaire introduces the same allusion into *Rome sauvée.* Here Catilina proposes that César share with him in power after the overthrow of the republic. "On ne partage point la grandeur souveraine," César replies:

Va, ne te flatte pas que jamais à son char
L'heureux Catilina puisse enchaîner César.
Tu m'as vu ton ami, je le suis, je veux l'être;
Mais jamais mon ami ne deviendra mon maître.

(II.iii, p. 231–32: There is no sharing of sovereign greatness. Do not flatter yourself that the fortunate Catilina will ever chain César to his chariot. You have seen me your friend. I am, I wish to be. But never will my friend become my master.)

Voltaire uses the latter part of the allusion—"je le suis, je veux l'àtre"—and in selecting this more vulnerable part of Auguste's assertion, he is able to suggest a connection between César's desire to remain friends with Catilina and Auguste's clemency. "Soyons amis, Cinna," Auguste continues in Corneille; but the friendship will be on his terms. So too in *Rome sauvée:* César recognizes that there can be no sharing of absolute power. Thus Voltaire is able to hint that César is an anticipation of Corneille's Auguste. The play's portrayal of César as a cautious, manipulative self-server is in keeping with Voltaire's complex attitude toward the historical Augustus.

As Catherine Volpilhac-Auger has argued, Voltaire questioned the traditional identification of Louis XIV with Augustus by glorifying Louis at Augustus' expense. While Louis was a great patron of poets like Racine and Boileau, according to Voltaire, Augustus extracted praise and flattery from Horace and Virgil by bribery and covert threats. In his "Epitre à Horace," Voltaire contrasted Augustus not with Louis but with Frederick:

Je suis un peu fâché pour Virgile et pour toi
Que, tous deux, nés Romains, vous flattiez tant un roi.
Mon Frédéric du moins, né roi très légitime,
Ne doit point des grandeurs aux bassesses du crime.

(I am a little annoyed with Virgil and with you that both of you, born Romans, flattered a king so much. My Frederick, at least, born a king very legitimately, owes none of his greatness to the baseness of crime.)[42]

As a patron, Frederick is a Louis XIV, not an Augustus. César's willingness to be friends with Catilina is like Auguste's willingness to be friends with Cinna: the friendship is completely on his terms.

Voltaire's glorification of the age of Louis XIV draws much of its energy from his denigration of Augustan Rome; his glorification of Frederick draws its energy from the direct parallel between Frederick and Louis XIV. But the ironic historical perspective that informs Voltaire's assessment of Augustus does not transfer. There is no recognition of the difficulties of friendship between those who enjoy absolute power and those who do not. Or perhaps there is a willed obliviousness to the potential problem. Clearly, d'Argental had warned his friend about the peril of trusting in the generosity of kings, for Voltaire wrote to him in rebuttal on September 23, 1750:

> Mon cher et respectable amy, vous m'écrivez des lettres qui percent l'âme et qui L'éclairent. Vous dites tout ce qu'un sage peut dire sur des rois, mais je maintiens que mon roy est une espèce de sage. Il n'est pas un Dargental, mais après vous, il est tout ce que j'ay vu de plus aimable. Pourquoy donc me dira t'on, quittez vous monsieur d'Argental pour luy? Ah mon cher amy ce n'est pas vous que je quitte, ce sont les petites cabales, et les grandes haines, les calomnies, les injustices, tout ce qui persécute un homme de lettres dan sa patrie.

> (D4223: My dear and respected friend, you write me letters that pierce the soul and enlighten it. You tell me all that a sage can say about kings, but I maintain that my king is a kind of sage. He is no d'Argental, but next to you he is the most likable person that I have ever seen. Why, then, one will say, are you leaving Monsieur d'Argental for him? Ah, my dear friend, it is not you I am leaving, it is the little cabals, the great hatreds, the calumnies, the injustices, everything that persecutes a man of letters in his own country.)

When the king is a sage, the sage can trust the king. But in *Rome sauvée,* the two who would be kings are Catilina and César, and Cicéron saves Rome by playing the two against each other. César's eventual betrayal of the republic and of Cicéron remains in the play's future, hinted at in the very different kinds of caution practiced by both men. "Grands dieux! que ce héros soit toujours citoyen," Cicéron pleads at the end of the play: "Dieux! ne corrompez pas cette âme généreuse / Et que tant de vertu ne soit pas dangereuse" (V.iii, p. 267: "Great gods, let this hero always remain a citizen! Gods, do not

corrupt this generous soul, and let not so much virtue become dangerous!"). These final lines of the play are laced with a Virgilian irony, for
this plea, like Anchises' plea to the shade of Julius Caesar in the sixth
book of the *Aeneid,* will go unheeded.

For Voltaire in 1750, however, the play itself had become such an issue
that he disregarded its grim political message as he repeatedly staged it
at Frederick's court. *Rome sauvée* was densely involved in Voltaire's
decision to stay with Frederick and closely identified by him with the
Siècle de Louis XIV. In one of the most important letters of this period,
in which he attempted to justify his departure from France to the duc de
Richelieu, his former patron and sponsor, Voltaire promises to eschew
this nexus of associations: "Je ne vous parlerai cette fois ci ni de
l'ancienne Rome, ni de Cicéron, ni de Louis XIV" (D4206: "I will not
speak to you this time of ancient Rome, or of Cicero, or of Louis XIV").
As the letter continues, the promise is forgotten. Voltaire rehearses his
anxieties about the history of Louis and "malgré mes serments" ("in
spite of my vows") urges Richelieu, as "parrain" ("godfather") to the
play, to strive for its performance. He should show it to Madame de
Pompadour: "Il est bon que vous fassiez voir à Madame de Pompadour
qu'il y a du moins quelque différence entre un ouvrage bien conduit et
bien écrit, et la farce allobroge qu'elle a protégée" ("It would be good if
you could show Madame de Pompadour that there is at least some difference between a work that is well constructed and well written and the
crude farce that she has sponsored").

Frederick's sponsorship of *Rome sauvée* certifies his status as a sage,
and sets his court in contrast to the court of Louis XV, where the
clumsy work of Crébillon is honored (by this time, Voltaire has forgotten Frederick's own admiration of Crébillon). This contrast is fur-
thered by an identification of Frederick with Louis XIV that was total
and uncritical. When Voltaire arrived in Berlin, plans were under way
for a carousel, an outdoor royal entertainment with tournaments, fireworks, operas, and banquets like the *Plaisirs de l'île enchantée,* in
honor of the margrave and margravine of Bayreuth. On the first of
August, Voltaire wrote to the marquis de Thibouville (who had played
Catilina in the private performance of *Rome sauvée*) of "un carouzel
digne en tout de celuy de Louis 14" (D4178: "a carousel comparable in
every way to that of Louis XIV"). Credit for the wondrous transformation of the court of Berlin into a shelter for the arts goes to Frederick: "Il ne faut qu'un homme pour changer la triste Sparte en la bril-

lante Athenes" ("It takes only one man to change sad Sparta into brilliant Athens"). To the d'Argentals, after witnessing the spectacle, Voltaire wrote on August 28: "Il n'y a pas moyen de tenir au carrouzel que
je viens de voir. C'étoit à la fois le carrouzel de Louis 14, et la fête des
lanternes de Chine" (D4201: "There is no way to describe the carousel
that I just saw. It was at once Louis XIV's carousel and a festival of
Chinese lanterns"). The prince royal won a prize in the trials at arms;
"Il avoit l'air d'un héros des Amadis. On ne peut pas se faire une juste
idée de la beauté, de la singularité de ce spectacle, le tout terminé par
un soupé à dix tables, et par un bal. C'est le pays des fées. Voylà ce
que fait un seul homme" ("He was like a hero from Amadis. It is impossible to get the right idea of the beauty, the uniqueness of this spectacle, the whole affair capped with a supper of ten courses and with
a ball. It is fairyland. This is what one man has accomplished"). The
d'Argentals and the marquis de Thibouville were among those who
had warned Voltaire against his trip and who disapproved of his total
switch of allegiance to Frederick, so the letters have an air of salesman-
ship. In both, Voltaire is selling the uniqueness of Frederick; his spectacle is a demonstration not only of his power, but of his taste. Frederick, he assures the d'Argentals, would appear a hundred times greater
than Louis, were not Voltaire's heart broken by his distance from his
friends.

In the *Siècle de Louis XIV,* Voltaire takes a different line in his
account of the *Plaisirs de l'île enchantée* themselves. Louis XIV is the
hero of the narrative, because of what Voltaire portrays as an unremit-
ting sponsorship and support of Molière and *Tartuffe.* "Le roi voulut
voir ce chef-d'oeuvre, avant même qu'il fut achevé. Il le protégea
depuis contre les faux dévots" ("The king wanted to see this master-
piece, even before it was finished. He then protected it against the religious hypocrites"), Voltaire declares, although, as we have seen in the
previous chapter, the evidence suggests a more complex and difficult
relationship between king and playwright.[43] More importantly, Voltaire continues:

> La plupart de ces solennités brillantes ne sont souvent que pour
> les yeux et les oreilles. Ce qui n'est que pompe et magnificence
> passe en un jour; mais quand des chefs-d'oeuvre de l'art, comme
> le *Tartuffe,* font l'ornement de ces fêtes, elles laissent après elles
> une éternelle mémoire.

(Most of these brilliant festivities are often only for the eyes and ears. What is merely pomp and magnificence passes in a day; but when masterpieces of art, like *Tartuffe,* adorn these festivals, they leave behind them an eternal memory.)

The particular works of art that adorned Frederick's carousel at Charlottenburg and Berlin were comedies by d'Arnaud and Molière (*Le Médecin malgré lui*), the opera *Phaéton* by Quinault (in an Italian version that Voltaire did not like), Racine's *Iphigénie* in an operatic version, and a few short pieces. None of Voltaire's plays were performed. This could be, as Desnoiresterres suggests, because the preparations for such a magnificent event had to be well under way before Voltaire's arrival.[44] On this occasion, Frederick did not imitate Voltaire's idea of Louis XIV and protect a controversial work in progress, a potential *Tartuffe.*

Frederick had in fact protected Voltaire earlier, by praising *Mahomet,* which Voltaire saw as his own *Tartuffe.* When he was forced to withdraw the play from production in 1742, Voltaire wrote to Frederick: "Les hipocrites persécutèrent Moliere et les fanatiques se sont soulevez contre moi. J'ai cédé au torrent sans dire un seul mot. Si Socrate en eût fait autant, il n'eût point bu la ciguë" (D2647: "The hypocrites persecuted Molière and the fanatics have aroused themselves against me. I ceded to the torrent without saying a word: if Socrates had done the same, he would never have drunk hemlock").[45] Frederick's program at Charlottenburg and Berlin, however, was thoroughly conservative. Nonetheleess, Voltaire did have some reason to expect the king to support whatever controversial works he might write while in Prussia.

Rome sauvée, which had already been protected by Voltaire himself (with his own in-house production) and then by the duchesse du Maine, became in Voltaire's letters a play of just such a controversial order. Despite his plea to Richelieu to get the play staged, Voltaire also considered the play to be too severe, too Roman, for the French stage. On August 11, 1750, he wrote to Madame Denis that the news that the Comédie Française was planning a performance did not come to him as welcome:

> Rome sauvée ne me paraît point faite pour les jeunes et belles dames qui viennent parer vos premières loges, Je crois que notre élève le Kain jouerait très bien; mais le conjuration de Catilina

n'est bonne que pour messieurs de l'université qui ont leur Cicéron dans la tête, et peu de galanterie dans le coeur. Contentons nous de l'avoir vu jouer à Paris sur le théâtre de mon grenier, devant de graves professeurs, des moines, et de jurisconsultes.

(D4185: *Rome sauvée* does not seem to me at all appropriate for the young, beautiful ladies who come to adorn your front-row seats. I believe that our pupil Lekain would act very well; but the conspiracy of Catiline is suitable only for the gentlemen of the university who have their Cicero in their heads and little gallantry in their hearts. Let us be content that we saw it played in Paris in the little theater in my attic, before an audience of grave professors, monks, and judges.)

The social event for which tickets had to be distributed is forgotten, or evaded, here. Voltaire instead idealizes the dress rehearsal, as he did in his letter to the duchesse du Maine. There, however, he was laying the groundwork for the performance of the play at her theater; here he is arguing that his play is utterly unacceptable to the Parisian theater audience. Their coarseness is ingrained: "il y a toujours un reste de barbarie que le beau siècle de Louis XIV n'a put déraciner" ("there still remains a trace of barbarism that the beauteous age of Louis XIV could not uproot"), he explains to Madame Denis. To the select audiences at the rue Traversière-Saint-Honoré and at Sceaux, Voltaire would now add the courtiers at Sans Souci.

Because Frederick was both a philosopher and a king, this audience would be a fusion of two kinds of ideal audience: the audience of monks and professors who know their Cicero by heart *and* the royal audience of king, royal family, and innermost members of the court. Here at Sans Souci, a play unfit for the Parisian audience could be performed before an audience of the highest social and intellectual rank. Other playwrights could ridicule the performances of *Rome sauvée* at Paris and at Sceaux: "Il fait comme les pâtissiers qui, ne pouvant vendre leur pâtés, les mangent eux-même" ("he is behaving like a pastry-cook, who, unable to sell his pastries, eats them himself"), one rival had sneered.[46] Here at Sans Souci, Voltaire could truly achieve the enviable condition of eating his pastries and having them too. The dynamic of royal taking and mistaking, so troublesome to the playwright at court from the time of Shakespeare to Racine, does not obtain in this ideal world. Here the playwright can function as director and as actor, realizing the play in accordance with his vision, before an audience with whom his vision is as one.

Such, at least, is the impression given by Voltaire's letters home. Those who received the letters took some of his effusions with a grain of salt. "Il est vrai que le roy lui donnes des marques d'amitié et de distinction très fortes et vous sçavez le foible qu'a Mr de Voltaire pour la cour et pour les roys," Madame Denis wrote to Cideville, September 3, 1750 (D4211: "It is true that the king gives him very strong signs of friendship and distinction, and you know the weakness that M. de Voltaire has for the court and for kings").

Other observers, less intimately knowledgeable about Voltaire's private weaknesses, also noticed discrepancies between Voltaire's vision and the reality of court performance. "Pour nous, nous jouons icy Rome sauvée sans tracasserie, je gronde comme je faisois à Paris, et tout va bien," Voltaire wrote to d'Argental on September 14 (D4220: "As for us, we are playing *Rome sauvée* without fuss; I growl as I used to do in Paris, and everything goes well"). A famous anecdote was circulated about Voltaire's "growling." Collé described one rehearsal, at which the queen and the princess were present:

> Pour lui composer un Sénat, on lui avoit habillé plusieurs tailleurs et ouvriers de l'Opéra; un de ces drôles-là, qui le voyoit se démener comme un possédé, ne pouvant s'empêcher de rire, Voltaire lui dit en colère: *Mais f——, vous n'êtes pas ici pour rire!— Prenez donc garde,* lui dit quelqu'un, *vous êtes devant la reine!— Cela est vrai,* répondit-il, *je n'ai pas pris garde; mais tout est carême-prenant.*

> (To get together a Senate for him, they had dressed up a number of tailors and workmen from the Opera. One of these silly fellows, who was watching him behave like a madman, could not refrain from laughing. Voltaire said to him in a rage, "But f——, you aren't here to laugh." "Be careful," someone told him, "you are in the presence of the queen." "That's true," he replied, "I wasn't careful; but everything here is Carnival.")

Another version of the same story has the tailors replaced by soldiers, with Voltaire exclaiming "F——, j'ai demandé les hommes et on m'envoie des Allemands!" ("I asked for men and they send me Germans!").[47] Both stories reveal a harmony a little less than perfect between the philosopher and the philosopher-king's court. Voltaire's obscenity in both is unapologetic; in Collé's version, Frederick's court is transformed for an instant into a court of misrule in which the ordinary rules of discretion do not apply. No one will take offense at Voltaire's language here.

Among the visitors at Frederick's court that season was an English envoy, "qui sait par coeur les Catilinaires," Voltaire informed d'Argental (D4223: "who knows the Catilinarian orations by heart"). As we have seen in the letters to the duchesse du Maine and to Madame Denis, this is a precondition to being one of the ideal audience members for *Rome sauvée*. "But as some of His Polish Majestys Buffoons are Wits," Sir Charles Hanbury Williams wrote, reporting on his visit, "so most of His Prussian Majestys Wits are Buffoons. Voltaire is here in high glory." Williams went on to offer his responses to *Rome sauvée*:

> D4225: He has just wrote a Tragedy call'd Rome Sauvé founded on the story of Catilines Conspiracy. He has given it me to read. I dont like the whole But there is one scene in it between Caesar & Catiline that is delightfull. Both Characters unmask themselves and are well drawn. But the Catastrophe is intollerable & contradicts all History For Tully gives the command of the army against Catiline To Caesar: Who goes off the stage to take the command & comes back in five minutes to tell the senate that He has overcome Catiline. Since my reading this Play I have seen it acted & the part of Tully perform'd by Voltaire. He acts with great spirit. But the rest of the actors were designd by Nature to have nothing to do upon the stage but to snuff the Candles.

The anecdotes of Voltaire's explosion at rehearsal and the narrative of Williams paint a different picture from Voltaire's rosy letters. Surrounded by wooden German actors on a makeshift stage in a ludicrous court of misrule, Voltaire is transformed from sage to buffoon.

Despite its edge of satire, Williams's response is that of an educated Englishman, grounded in the Shakespearean tradition of historical drama. Thus he carps at the play's "intollerable" abuse of history. Voltaire, however, saw his version of the Catiline story as historically more accurate than Crébillon's, for his idea of what is historical does not extend to toleration of the leisurely, episodic dramaturgy of the chronicle form. Rather, what Voltaire saw as his achievement was to give to each of the leading figures in the drama a character appropriate to his historical role. Crébillon's version, in which Cicéron's machinations drive Catilina and Tullie to suicide, discovers a tragic dimension to the story. Catilina becomes a victim of his own ambition and his love. *Rome sauvée,* despite rejecting this kind of dramaturgy, fails to find a satisfactory alternative. Voltaire is unable to escape the need for a love interest, and Aurélie, Catilina's wife, finds herself forced to choose between a husband and a father.

The model of a kind of drama that can eschew such conflicts, the Roman plays of Shakespeare, had exercised a fascination for Voltaire ever since his first visit to England. But it was a horrified fascination. Voltaire had translated the first three acts of *Julius Caesar* into French and based a scene in his *La Mort de César* on Shakespeare's play. Yet Shakespeare's barbarisms, his offenses against good taste (especially in mingling comic with tragic scenes and verse with prose), testified to the barbarism of his age, and made his work excellent only in parts. As Thedore Besterman has pointed out, such an assessment of Shakespeare was also common among English critics in the eighteenth century.[48] The crudeness of Shakespeare's drama is ethical as well as aesthetic: Shakespeare failed to offer noble models of conduct for kings and for citizens. Here, of course, Crébillon also fails, for his play lavishes sympathy upon Catilina.

Rome sauvée was supposed to be a model of accuracy in that it could portray the characters of Cicéron, César, and Catilina in such a way that the moral superiority of Cicéron would be admirable to an audience. Cicéron, like Alzire, becomes the focus of all eyes. Madame de Pompadour, as we have argued, could take advantage of this feature of Voltaire's dramaturgy to present herself as a model of beauty and virtue to the court. In *Rome sauvée,* Voltaire as Cicéron takes the play's vindication of Rome and its reproach to France to another level: the play vindicates Voltaire himself. It epitomizes the decision he has made to transplant his allegiance from the French king to the Prussian king. The play is a gift from the playwright to the only royal audience that can understand it. Cicéron's virtue is placed at Frederick's service. Viewers who found Voltaire's conduct vain and overbearing and the play absurd did not appreciate the special relationship between the sage and the king.

The sources are mute about Frederick's response to the performances of *Rome sauvée.* He did not attend them all. The performance that Williams saw took place when the king was away: "Nous jouâmes pour nous réjouir" (D4223: "We played to cheer ourselves up"), Voltaire wrote to d'Argental. "Mes frères histrionnent" ("My brothers are playacting"), is Frederick's laconic comment on the theatrical activity of his court.[49] More dangerously, in the aftermath of Voltaire's embarrassing involvement in a black-market currency speculation, Frederick chided Voltaire in explicitly antitheatrical terms:

> Pour moi, j'ai conservé la paix dans ma maison jusqu'à votre arrivée; et je vous avertis, que si vous avez la passion d'intriguer et de cabaler, vous vous êtes très mal addressé. J'aime des gens doux et paisibles, qui ne mettent point dans leur conduite les passions violentes de la tragédie: en cas que vous puissiez vous résoudre à vivre en philosophe, je serai bien aise de vous voir; mais si vous vous abandonnez à toutes les fougues de vos passions, et que vous en vouliez à tout le monde, vous ne me ferez aucun plaisir de venir ici, et vous pouvez tout autant rester à Berlin.

> (February 24, 1751, D4400: As for me, I have kept my house at peace up until you arrived, and I warn you that, if you have a passion for intrigues and cabals, you have appealed to the wrong person. I like men who are docile and easy, who in no way conduct themselves with the violent passions of tragedy. If you can resolve to live like a philosopher, I will be happy to see you; but if you abandon yourself to all the ardors of your passions, and set yourself against everyone, you will do me no pleasure in coming here, and you can just as well stay in Berlin.)

Once again Voltaire found himself, as with Louis XV, cut off from the king—*his* king, who, as he assured the d'Argentals, was different from all the others. In this letter, Frederick draws a distinction between the philosopher and the actor. The philosopher is docile, quiet, easy. Voltaire is an actor, and as such a kind of Tartuffe: a disreputable, disruptive force in Frederick's house, wallowing in the passions of tragedy. The violent emotions Voltaire has stirred up offend the king. Frederick prefers, like Hamlet, the man that is not passion's slave for his company. The philosopher king demands that the philosopher stop playing tragedy and start behaving like a philosopher. But for Voltaire, striking poses, taking extravagant positions, and making audiences weep are essential to the philosopher's role.

"Mon mariage est donc fait," Voltaire wrote to Madame Denis on

October 13, 1750. "Sera-t-il heureux? Je n'en sais rien. Je n'ai pas pu m'empêcher de dire oui" (D4240: "My marriage is made. Will it be a happy one? I cannot tell. I couldn't stop myself from saying yes"). The marriage between the philosopher and the king did not last. For if the king could fuse those two persons in his one body, Voltaire, curiously, becomes unnecessary, and finds himself without a role to play. Frederick is a kind of virtuoso actor, successfully playing any number of roles. "C'est César, c'est Marc Aurèle, c'est Julien, c'est quelquefois l'abbé de Chaulieu, avec qui on soupe" (D4248: "It is Caesar, Marcus Aurelius, Julian, sometimes the abbé de Chaulieu with whom we take supper"), Voltaire enthused to Thibouville. But the more roles Frederick can fill, the more amorphous becomes Voltaire's status. Wooed and flattered by the king, Voltaire came to Frederick as to a marriage. But in this marriage, as the king forcefully reminded him, he was not an equal, and finally not even an acceptable partner. His tragic passions upset the tranquillity of the king's philosophic retreat.

Voltaire's passionate acting in *Rome sauvée,* the "great spirit" of his performance as Cicéron, anticipates his later alienation of the king through his emotional outbursts and embarrassing financial deals. In both instances, Voltaire is acting: throwing himself wholly into the part of Cicéron, he acts his anger against the French theater, against Louis XV, and against the enemies who tainted his career at the French court. In his violent misconduct in Prussia, Voltaire struggles to find a role to play, a way to express the uniqueness of his new situation, house philosopher to the philosopher king. His insistence that he and Frederick are friends, that their relationship is special, that this king is different from all other kings, involves creating an imaginary "paradis des philosophes" (D4248), in which he and the king function as equals, correcting each other's verses. But where the king can successfully play the role of *philosophe,* there is no role for the *philosophe* to play. When he described himself to Frederick after the suppression of *Mahomet* as a Socrates who does not drink hemlock, Voltaire unwittingly revealed the impossible contradiction within his own role. A Socrates who prudently declines the cup is no Socrates at all.

The Rome that is preserved in *Rome sauvée* is the republic. But Frederick's Prussia was not a republic, and Voltaire, attempting to define a new role in which he alone among the wits surrounding Frederick merits the king's love, is merely seen by the king as presumptuous. Voltaire's confused attraction to this king was in part a reaction

against the court of Louis XV and an idealization of Louis XIV revived
in Frederick. But it was also in part snobbery, as Madame Denis and
the d'Argentals noticed. To be an equal, an intimate, with Frederick
was to be a monarch too; a monarch of wit, ruling the civilized world
from the retreat at Sans Souci. Cicéron, in *Rome sauvée,* wonders if
the laconic César will remain a friend to the republic. Voltaire misread
the laconic Frederick as he enthused over the friendship which the
Prussian king had given him. Sparta had not been wholly transformed
into Athens; or if it had, it was into an Athens to which Socrates was
more trouble than he was worth.

The disillusionment that followed was mutual. Voltaire loved in
Frederick the man, not the king, he claimed; but the king responded
by reminding his friend that the king and the man were the same. Frederick admired in Voltaire the philosopher, not the histrionic prima
donna who disrupted his domestic peace. But just as Voltaire had
alienated Louis XV by asserting that he deserved his honors and pro-
motions, so he alienated Frederick by insisting that the king respond
to him on an emotional level as an equal, as a man.

IV

"Si Voltaire a échoué lorsqu'il gravitait autour d'un souverain," Jean
Sareil writes in his study of Voltaire's relationships with those in
power, "il a remarquablement réussi comme souverain. «Le roi Voltaire.»" ("If Voltaire failed whenever he gravitated to a monarch, he succeeded remarkably as a monarch himself: 'Le roi Voltaire'").[50] The
final phase of Voltaire's career, when, as the lord of his own estate at
Ferney, he received the visits of the great and presided over amateur
theatricals at his private theater, found him enjoying both the freedom
of action and the freedom of acting that he was denied in the courts
of Louis and Frederick. "Après avoir vécu chez les rois," he wrote, "je
me suis fait roi chez moi" ("After having lived with kings, I have made
myself a king in my own estate").[51] Part of living like a king was having a theater. "Tout ce que j'aprends des spectacles à Paris fait que je
ne regrette que Neuilly et mon petit téâtre" (D4180: "Everything I hear
about the shows in Paris makes me miss only Neuilly [their home] and
my little theater"), Voltaire wrote the d'Argentals from Potsdam. The
attempt to recreate this theater at Sans Souci failed. Before finally settling at Ferney, Voltaire initiated theatrical activity wherever he stayed.

For Voltaire, the freedom to stage his own plays and to act in them was an expression of autonomy, of full authority. It proclaimed not only his authorship of the specific texts performed, but also his total control over the conditions of performance themselves. There is no need to please a royal audience or to please the fickle, fashionable audiences of the town; no need to anticipate censorship or to fear misapprehension. When the playwright is also the actor and the owner of the theater and the patron of all its activities, his authority is absolute. Timothy Murray has recently portrayed the playwright Ben Jonson, the patron Cardinal Richelieu, and the theoretician of the theater the abbé d'Aubignac, as representatives of a general pursuit of the elusive goal of "theatrical legitimacy."[52] Voltaire's wholly self-validating theatrical industry takes this seventeenth-century problem and redefines it as theatrical autonomy. The fears that animate Shakespeare's rude mechanicals and the amateur playwrights of Charles I's court disappear in this new environment. The deference to the king's final authority that Molière's *Tartuffe* enacts becomes irrelevant at Ferney. Here playwright and actor are one, and there is no authority to challenge their union.

Before settling at Ferney in 1758, Voltaire encountered still other challenges to this idealized vision of theatrical autonomy. Forced to leave Frederick's kingdom and not permitted by Louis XV to return to Paris, he sought permission to live in Geneva. Extolling the virtues of this free republic, he purchased for himself an estate with lovely gardens, naming it Les Délices. Here he received among his first visitors the great actor Lekain; the leading citizens of Geneva, a city with no professional theater, were invited to attend special performances of *Zaïre*. The house was still topsy-turvy; renovations were in progress. Voltaire wrote to d'Argental on April 2, 1755 describing the visit:

> Le Kain a été, je crois, bien étonné: il a cru retrouver en moi le Père d'Orosmane et de Zamor, et il n'a trouvé qu'un maçon, un charpentier et un jardinier. Cela n'a pas empêché pourtant que nous n'ayons fait pleurer presque tout le Conseil de Genève; la plupart des ces messieur étaient venus à mes Délices, nous nous mîmes à jouer Zayre pour interrompre le cercle; je n'ai jamais vû verser plus de larmes; jamais des calvinistes n'ont été si tendres.
>
> (D6229: Lekain was, I think, quite surprised. He thought he would rediscover in me the father of Orosmane and Zamore, but

he found only a mason, a carpenter, and a gardener. However, this did not prevent us from making almost the entire Council of Geneva weep; most of these gentlemen had come to my *Délices,* and we set about to playing *Zaïre* to divert the group. I have never seen so many tears flowing; never have Calvinists been so tender.)

The witty shift from Voltaire as author—"father" to Lekain's famous roles—to Voltaire as builder highlights Voltaire's association of his theaters with his literary prestige. The joke about the weeping Calvinists, less fortunately, reveals what would make Les Délices impossible as a place in which Voltaire could exercise full autonomy. "C'est un audience que nous avions grande envie de plaire," Voltaire wrote on the same day to Jean Robert Tronchin. "Calvin ne se doutait pas que des catholiques feraient un jour pleurer des huguenots dans le territoire de Genève" (D6231: "It is an audience we have a great desire to please. Calvin would never have expected that Catholics would one day make Huguenots weep in the territory of Geneva"). Pleased as this audience might have been by the performance, theater was forbidden within the Calvinist confines of Geneva. On July 31, 1755, the council, taking note that Voltaire had installed in his house "un théâtre et des décorations" ("a theater and stage settings"[53]), urged him to cease and desist from theatrical activities.

The prohibition of theater in Geneva shortly became famous throughout Europe. D'Alembert, after visiting Voltaire in the summer of 1756, was delighted with Geneva and contributed an article on the republic to the *Encyclopédie.* Its clergy were worldly and its citizens enlightened; all it lacked was professional theater to polish the manners of the people and stimulate the production of literature. By such means, "Genève réuniront à la sagesse de Lacédémone la politesse d'Athènes" ("Geneva will reunite the wisdom of Lacedemon and the manners of Athens"), he enthused.[54] The response to this suggestion was Jean-Jacques Rousseau's vigorous antitheatrical tract, the *Lettre à M. D'Alembert sur les spectacles* (October 1758). The moral fiber of Geneva could only be corrupted by the admission of troupes of actors within its territory, Rousseau argued. The example of Athens could be turned another way: "c'est au théâtre qu'on y prépara l'exil de plusieurs grands hommes et la mort de Socrate; c'est par la fureur du Théâtre qu'Athènes périt, et ses désastres ne justifierent que trop le chagrin qu'avoit témoigné Solon aux premières représentations de Thespis" ("There at the theater they planned the exile of many great men and the death of Socrates; it was because of its rage for the theater that Athens perished, and her disasters served to justify only too well the trepidation to which Solon bore witness at the first performances of Thespis"). A republic like Athens, Geneva had no need for the institution that had caused its downfall. As for Voltaire's more republican plays, Rousseau made a slight exception: "Mais que M. de Voltaire daigne nous composer des Tragédies sur le modèle de la Mort de César, du premier acte de Brutus; et s'il nous faut absolument un Théâtre, qu'il s'engage à le remplir toujours de son génie et à vivre autant que ses Pièces" ("But let M. de Voltaire deign to create for us tragedies along the lines of *La mort de César* or the first act of *Brutus;* and if we must absolutely have a theater, let him commit himself to filling it always with his genius and to living according to his plays").[55] There is an unmistakable edge of personal malice here, as Rousseau counsels that Voltaire live as his plays preach. Geneva may have seemed to be an Athens to Voltaire, but its most famous citizen was revealing it to be a Sparta.

Retaining possession of Les Délices, Voltaire sought an environment friendlier to playacting. "M^r. Dalembert conseille à messieurs de Geneve d'avoir dans leur ville une trouppe de comédiens de bonnes moeurs. C'est ce que nous nous flattons d'être à Lausane," he wrote to Thieriot from Monrepos, his new home in Lausanne. "Ma nièce et moy nous avons de très bonnes moeurs dont j'enrage, mais il faut bien à mon âge avoir ce petit mérite" (January 21, 1758, D7596: "M. D'Alembert advises the gentlemen of Geneva to have in their city a troupe of actors with good morals. That's just what we flatter ourselves as having here at Lausanne. My niece and I have excellent morals, which frustrates me; but it is fitting at my age to have this small distinction"). Here Voltaire jokes about another idea which was of great importance to him. Rousseau's attacks upon the morals of actors clashed with Voltaire's lifelong defense of the dignity of the profession. The burial of Adrienne Lecouvreur in unhallowed ground in 1730 had inspired Voltaire to verses of "pain and rage," as Peter Gay has put it, comparing her treatment to the interment of the British actress Ann Oldfield in Westminster Abbey. Here London became the "rivale d'Athène" that put Paris to shame.[56] Later, when Mademoiselle Clairon sought, for the health of both her body and her soul, to retire

from the stage, she was summoned before the court for her disobedience to her royal patron. On May 1, 1765, Voltaire wrote urging her to
seize the opportunity to "déclarer que c'est une contradiction trop
absurde d'être au Fort-L'évèque si on ne joue pas, et d'être excom-
munié par l'évèque si on joue; qu'il est impossible de soutenir ce
double affront, et qu'il faut enfin que les Welches se décident"
(D12577: "declare that it is an utterly absurd contradiction be at Fort-
L'évèque [literally, the bishop's fort] if you do not act, and to be excommunicated by the bishop if you do act; that it is impossible to endure
this double affront, and that it is finally high time these 'Welshmen'
[barbarians] made up their minds"). "Il y a tantôt soixante ans que
cette infâme superstition me met en colère" (D12808: "For as many as
sixty years this infamous superstition has put me into a rage"), Voltaire wrote in July. Incensed at the "animals" who were making Mademoiselle Clairon's life difficult, Voltaire invited her that July to come
stay with him, and visit his doctor: "Plût à dieu que vous fussiez assez
riche pour quitter le théâtre de Paris, et jouer chez vous avec vos amis,
comme nous faisons dans un coin du monde où nous nous moquons
terriblement des sottises et des sots" (D12808: "Please God you will
become rich enough to leave the theater in Paris and act at your home
with your friends, as we do in a corner of the world where we make
terrible fun of foolishness and of fools").

Being rich enough is of course a key factor in Voltaire's later years,
as he sought his own perfect corner of the world. Early on, he had
skillfully transformed the substantial fortune he inherited from his
father into great wealth by speculating in Parisian municipal bonds (a
similar kind of speculation earned him Frederick's ire in Prussia). His
wealth permitted him autonomy, and made him the center of society
wherever he went. Edward Gibbon visited Voltaire's theater at Lausanne, and was impressed with what he saw:

> The highest gratification I derived from Voltaire's residence at
> Lausanne was the uncommon circumstance of hearing a great
> poet declaim his own productions on the stage. He had formed a
> troupe of Gentlemen and Ladies, some of whom were not desti-
> tute of talents: a decent theatre was formed at Monrepos, a coun-
> try house at the end of a suburb; dresses and scenes were provided
> at the expense of the actors, and the author directed the produc-
> tions with the zeal and attention of paternal love. In two succes-

sive winters his tragedies of Zayre, Alzire, Zulime and his sentimental comedy of the Enfant Prodigue were played at the Theatre of Monrepos, but it was not without much reluctance that the
envious bard allowed the representation of the Iphigenie of
Racine. The parts of the young and fair were distorted by his fat
and ugly niece, Madame Denys, who could not, like our amiable
Pritchard, make the spectators forget the defect of her age and
person.

For himself Voltaire reserved the characters best adapted to his
years—Lusignan, Alvarez, Benassar, Euphemon; his declamation
was fashioned to the pomp and cadence of the old stage, and he
expressed the enthusiasm of poetry rather than the feeling of
Nature. My ardour, which soon became conspicuous, seldom
failed of procuring me a ticket; the habits of pleasure fortified my
taste for French theatre, and that taste has perhaps abated my
idolatry for the Gigantic Genius of Shakespeare, which is incul-
cated from our infancy as the first duty of an Englishman.[57]

Gibbon paints a portrait of an autocrat, directing his own plays with
zeal and reacting like an "envious bard" when a play by Racine is proposed. A sign of his absolute control is the irrational preference of
Madame Denis for the leading female roles; "mieux que Gaussin" (February 9, 1757, D7152: "better than Gaussin") is one of Voltaire's many
enthusiastic judgments of her playing. Despite this absurdity, however, and despite Voltaire's old-fashioned declamatory style of acting,
Gibbon found acceptance within this exclusive social circle.

Monrepos, however, did not fully satisfy Voltaire. He purchased a
chateau at Tournay, on the French side of the border, where he again
set up a theater. On the fifteen minute trip here from Les Délices,
according to an anecdote told by Marmontel, Voltaire recalled his
days at Versailles and his friendship with Madame de Pompadour:
"«Elle vous aime encore," Marmontel reports himself as reassuring
Voltaire,

elle me l'a répété souvent; mais elle est faible, elle n'ose pas ou ne
peut pas tout ce qu'elle veut; car la malheureuse n'est plus aimée,
et peut-être elle porte envie au sort de madame Denis, et voudrait
bien être aux Délices. — Qu'elle y vienne, dit-il avec transport,
jouer avec nous la tragédie. Je lui ferai des rôles, et des rôles de
reines; elle est belle, elle doit connaître le jeu des passions. — Elle

connaît aussi, lui dis-je, les profondes douleurs et les larmes amères. — Tant mieux! c'est là ce qu'il nous faut, s'écria-t-il comme enchanté d'avoir une nouvelle actrice. Et en vérité on l'eût dit qu'il croyait la voir arriver. «Puisqu'elle vous convient, lui dis-je, laissez faire; si le théâtre de Versaille lui manque, je lui dirai que le vôtre l'attend.»

("She still likes you, she has often told me so. But she is weak, she dares not or cannot do everything she would want. Because the unhappy woman is not loved any more, and perhaps she is envious of the fortune of Madame Denis, and would herself like to be at Les Délices." "Let her come," he said with great emotion, "and play tragedy with us! I will write roles for her, roles of queens; she is beautiful, and well she must know the movement of the passions." "She knows also," I told him, "profound sorrows and bitter tears." "So much the better! That's exactly what we need!" he exclaimed, as though thrilled to have a new actress. And in truth one might have said that he believed he saw her arrive. "Since you can use her," I said to him, "let it be done. If the theater at Versailles fails her, I will tell her that yours awaits.")[58]

A better actress than Mademoiselle Gaussin, Madame Denis now becomes an object of Madame de Pompadour's envy. For the disappointments and intrigues of life at Versailles, Voltaire's little world offers stability. The idea of increasing his repertory company with the king's discarded mistress enthuses Voltaire in this tale. His theater is a rival to the theater at the Petits Cabinets, now no longer in operation. Madame de Pompadour, who never can forget that she is not a queen herself, will happily play the queen's part in Voltaire's new plays.

This anecdote (however credible) calls our attention to the degree to which Voltaire's idea of a perfect theater mirrors the court theaters in which his plays were applauded while his presence was forbidden. Here he can turn the tables on Versailles. Writing plays for Madame de Pompadour in which she can enact her sorrowful experiences of love, he transforms her from the powerful patroness who sponsored his court career into an aspiring actress dependent upon the playwright for suitable parts. The dynamic by means of which Madame de Pompadour could enjoy a personal triumph in *Alzire,* while the author of the play could be at the same time rudely snubbed, would be reversed. She would need him as he had once needed her. Madame de Pompadour's relationship to the king, once so precious to Voltaire, now is useful only in so far as it contributes to her range as an actor. Louis cannot make her a queen: Voltaire can do so as he writes the roles of queens especially for her.

Madame de Pompadour never took advantage of this opportunity. Once Voltaire's estate at Ferney, just across the French border from Geneva, was finished (extensive renovations, including a new theater, were required), the playing of tragedy at Les Délices came to an end. With homes in Switzerland and in France, Voltaire was able to choose his country from one day to the next. Plays, discouraged in Geneva, were the primary form of entertainment at Ferney. Visitors who described Voltaire's relations to the peasants of Ferney as those of a feudal lord found his conduct in the theater virtually autocratic. James Callandar, visiting in the summer of 1765, offers a particularly unkind account:

> Madame Clairon, perhaps the most distinguished actress that ever graced the boards of the French stage, was on a visit to Geneva during my residence there; and Voltaire, having a private theatre at Ferney, expressed his desire that his play of Lusignan should be performed. Some French actors were found to fill up the *dramatis personae,* reserving for himself the character of Lusignan, the hero of the piece. His appearance and costume were altogether the most preposterous it is possible to conceive. Only think of his tall gaunt figure, with a sword of corresponding dimensions, constantly getting between his legs. His coat was of the era of Louis XIV with a tiewig to correspond, the whole surmounted by a huge pasteboard helmet, in the most absurd and ridiculous taste. To resist a titter at the extreme awkwardness of his figure, was beyond all power of face; and it required no small exertion to smother the tendency of a general laugh, so as to hinder it from coming to an *éclat.* Next day it was a point of indispensable etiquette for the invited guests to pay their compliments at Ferney, and administer a *quantum sufficit* of adulation on the histrionic talents of the representative of Lusignan; for that was a point on which he was much more sensitive than on the poetical merits of the drama itself.

This morning visit Callandar dubs Voltaire's "levée": here the revival of the custom of the court of Louis XIV is as ridiculous as the antique costume Voltaire wears as Lusignan. Gibbon, too, rethought his previous admiration of Voltaire's acting on a later visit. "Either my taste is improved or Voltaire's talents are impaired since I last saw him," he wrote after seeing *L'Orphelin de la Chine* performed at Ferney in August 1763:

> He appeared to me now a very ranting unnatural performer. Perhaps indeed as I was come from Paris, I rather judged him by unfair comparison, than by his own independent value. Perhaps I was too much struck with the ridiculous figure of Voltaire at seventy acting a Tartar Conqueror with a hollow broken voice, and making love to a very ugly niece of about fifty. The play began at eight in the evening and ended (entertainment and all) about half an hour after eleven. The whole Company was asked to stay and set Down about twelve to a very elegant supper of a hundred Covers. The supper ended about two, the company danced till four, when we broke up, got into our Coaches and came back the Geneva, just as the Gates were opened. Shew me in history or fable, a famous poet of Seventy who has acted in his own plays, and has closed the scene with a supper and ball for a hundred people. I think the last is the more extraordinary of the two.[59]

Both Gibbon and Callandar describe events of regal pomp. In the first days at Berlin, when Voltaire could describe Prussia as a fairyland, he reveled in the entertainments, suppers, and balls. Now he presided over them.

Gibbon had found Voltaire's acting impressive eight years before; now it is an imposition upon his audiences. Callandar shows less sympathy, although what he had been permitted to see was an extraordinary event. Voltaire had remodeled his theater especially for Mademoiselle Clairon, expanding its capacity from fifty seats to over a hundred (it would eventually seat over two hundred), and the Genevans crowded into the small space in large numbers. "Mademoiselle Clairon a été reçue chez nous comme si Rousseau n'avait pas écrit contre les spectacles," Voltaire wrote to d'Alembert. "Les excommunications de ce père de l'église n'ont eu aucune influence à Ferney" (D12854: "Mademoiselle Clairon was received among us as though Rousseau had never written against the theater. The excommunications of that church father have had no influence at Ferney"). She acted in *Tancrède* and *Oreste:* in the latter play, Voltaire wrote d'Argence, "j'ai vu de la perfection en un genre pour la première fois de ma vie" (D12855: "I have seen perfection in one genre for the first time in my life"). This was a triumphant event, a vindication of the dignity of Clairon's craft close to the very heart of Rousseau's antitheatrical republic. In Callandar's version this becomes Voltaire's "play of Lusignan" with the author as "the hero of the piece."

Accounts of performances at Ferney veer strikingly between admiration and ridicule. At once the profession of theater is vindicated and rendered utterly foolish. If Voltaire was annoying as an actor, he was also an embarrassment as an audience member, correcting the actors if they missed their lines. John Moore wrote of his visit in July 1772:

> He sits on the stage, and behind the scenes; but so as to be seen by a great part of the audience. He takes as much interest in the representation, as if his own character depended on the performance. He seems perfectly chagrined and disgusted when any of the actors commit a mistake; and when he thinks they perform well, never fails to make his approbation with all the violence of voice and gesture.[60]

Once, at Lausanne, while watching a performance of *Zaïre*, Voltaire was drawn "par une sorte d'attraction magnétique" onto the stage as Orosmane drew his knife to kill Zaïre, distracting the actor and ruining the dénouement.[61] The total involvement of Voltaire in his theater testifies to a total identification. Swept away in the power of the event, the playwright ceases to make the appropriate distinctions, ceases to function in a proper role. A discreet audience member would hold his seat; a decent actor would be careful not to look ridiculous; a properly modest playwright would not weep openly or gasp with surprise at moments of emotion and turns of plot crafted by himself. But in his own theaters, Voltaire made the rules. There was no need here, as at Potsdam, to watch his language; here he, not Louis XV, was Trajan, perfectly within his own rights to pronounce himself content.

As Callandar suggests, it is as Lusignan that Voltaire most conspicuously excelled. A large, demanding role like that of Gengis Kan in *L'Orphelin de la Chine* was better suited to a young man, like Lekain, or as we shall see in the next chapter, Gustav III of Sweden. But Voltaire delighted in playing the patriarch, and Lusignan was a role that also suited his valetudinarian obsession with his fading health. The role is a short one, for Lusignan is not released from prison until the second act and is reported as dying offstage in the third. It is thus possible that all that Callandar saw at Ferney was the second act of *Zaïre,* which would truly be the "play of Lusignan." During this act, the old man is introduced to his two surviving children, Zaïre and Nérestan: he has not seen them since they were snatched away from him some twenty years before. Triggered by the cross that Zaïre wears, a tender recognition scene follows. Learning that Zaïre has been raised as a Muslim, Lusignan exhorts her, in a great speech, to recollect her Christian heritage:

> Ma fille, tendre objet de mes dernières peines,
> Songe au moins, songe au sang qui coule dans tes veines.
> C'est le sang de vingt rois, tous chrétiens comme moi;
> C'est le sang des héros, défenseurs de ma loi;
> C'est le sang des martyrs.

> (650–54: My daughter, tender object of my last sorrows, think at least, think of the blood that courses through your veins. It is the blood of twenty kings, all Christians like me; it is the blood of heroes, of defenders of my law; it is the blood of martyrs.)[62]

In this role, as in that of Euphémon in *L'Enfant prodigue,* Voltaire plays the long-suffering father of a prodigal child. As Zaïre begins to weep, he proclaims, "Je vois la vérité dans ton coeur descendue; / Je retrouve ma fille après l'avoir perdue" (685–86: "I see truth now descended into your heart; I recover my daughter who has been lost"). Even more than *Alzire, Zaïre* is a play that raises questions about religion. Zaïre is perfectly content to remain a Muslim at the beginning of the play; for her, religion is a matter of custom: "J'eusse été près du Gange esclave des faux dieux, / Chrétienne dans Paris, musulmane en ces lieux" (I.i.107–8: "Beside the Ganges I would have been a slave to false gods, a Christian in Paris, a Muslim here"). This relativism is close to Voltaire's own ideas: but playing Lusignan in the play, Voltaire must take the opposite tack. Despite how she has been raised, and despite having had no contact with her father throughout her childhood, Lusignan demands that Zaïre declare herself a Christian. As such she must reject Orosmane's offer of marriage and flee the seraglio with her brother, Nérestan. Orosmane's misinterpretation of her motives and of her relationship with Nérestan triggers his jealous rage and Zaïre's death at his hands.

Lusignan's rejection of the argument from custom forces Zaïre to take her place within the sequence of martyrs that is her family. As Voltaire repeatedly played this role in his private theaters, the martyrdom he forces upon Madame Denis is likewise a family destiny. The two stake out a special territory for themselves, a special martyrdom. *Les Scythes,* written at Ferney, has been seen by R. S. Ridgway as offering a "thinly disguised allegory" of Voltaire's wanderings in exile with his niece and their eventual independence and "simple life" at Ferney.[63] Of the cast of that play, Voltaire wrote to Richelieu "nous avons icy le meilleure troupe de l'Europe" and boasted of his own performance as Sozame: "surtout quand je me plaignais des cours, je puis me vanter d'avoir fait une impression singuliére" (May 27, 1767, D14202: "We have here the best troupe in Europe. . . . Especially when I complained about courts, I can boast of having made a profound impression"). Voltaire thought of his roles as reflections of his own feelings and circumstances. Lusignan's power over his daughter, his ability to persuade her in one speech of the truth of Christianity, elevates the role from that of "bonhomme" (as Voltaire frequently described it) to sage. The identification of Lusignan with twenty generations of Christian kings of Jerusalem pushes even further: Lusignan's power is that of God.

Full apotheosis for Voltaire had to wait, however. Like that of Charles and Henrietta Maria, or that of Louis XIV, Voltaire's apotheosis was a stage transformation. In March 1778, upon his return to Paris (permitted at last by Louis XVI after the previous king's death), Voltaire was crowned with laurels by the actors of the Comédie Française. He was crowned in person as he sat in his box, and then, between the two plays, the casts of *Irène,* the tragedy, and *Nanine,* the comic afterpiece, appeared on stage with a bust of Voltaire which was crowned as well, while Mademoiselle Clairon read a special poem written by Marmontel for the occasion. *Nanine* was then performed, and the bust, merely set to one side, was visible throughout the play.[64]

The disjunctive presence of the crowned bust during the comic play is of a piece with the disjunction between high ideals and clumsy execution that Voltaire's English visitors found ridiculous. The notion that an actor can be a kind of king, and a playwright a kind of god, has deep roots in Renaissance defenses of drama and inspires antitheatrical attacks upon the form's presumption. Where Renaissance dramatists, like Shakespeare and his Jacobean and Caroline successors, could incorporate this tension in the text of their plays, for the classic French playwrights, the notion has vitality in so far as it is vigorously forsworn. In *Tartuffe,* only the king can liberate the play from the actor's tyranny. Voltaire, however, lays claim to this absolute authority. Putting it into action, asserting a Cornelian mastery over self and universe, Voltaire pretended to equality with his kings, defying Louis and presuming upon Frederick's friendship.

Cinna's image of perfect absolutism lurks, as we have seen, in both Voltaire's and Crébillon's Roman plays. One more instance of its use, in *Zaïre,* throws into relief the mastery over self and universe that Corneille had envisioned as an ideal and that Voltaire had (perhaps not utterly unwittingly) parodied in his theaters at Monrepos, Tournay, and Ferney. Orosmane, in *Zaïre,* declares his desire to eschew the privileges of the harem in favor of marriage to Zaïre:

> Les soudans, qu'à genoux cet univers contemple,
> Leurs usages, leurs droits, ne son point mon exemple;
> Je sais que notre loi, favorable aux plaisirs,
> Ouvre un champ sans limite à nos vastes désirs;
> Que je puis à mon gré, prodiguant mes tendresses,
> Recevoir à mes pieds l'encens de mes maîtresses;
> Et, tranquille au sérail, dictant mes volontés,
> Gouverner mon pays du sein des voluptés.
> Mais la mollesse est douce, et sa suite est cruelle:
> Je vois autour de moi cent rois vaincus par elle;
> Je vois de Mahomet ces lâches successeurs,
> Ces califes tremblants dans leurs tristes grandeurs,
> Couchés sur les débris de l'autel et du trône,
> Sous un nom sans pouvoir, languir dans Babylone:
> Eux qui seraient encore, ainsi que leurs aïeux,
> Maîtres du monde entier, s'ils l'avaient été d'eux.

(I.ii.161–76: The customs, the rights of the sultans, whom the universe contemplates on its knees, are not my example. I know that our law, favorable to pleasure, opens a limitless field for our vast desires; that I can, for my own gratification, squandering my affections, receive the incense that my mistresses burn at my feet; and, at peace in my seraglio, dictating my will, govern my country from the bosom of voluptuousness. But softness is sweet, and its consequences are cruel: I see all around me a hundred kings vanquished by it. I see the feeble successors of Mahomet, the caliphs, trembling in their sorrowful greatness, reclining on the remains of altar and throne, with a name without power, languishing in Babylon: those who could have been, like their ancestors, masters of the whole world, if they had been masters of themselves.)

Orosmane's decision to marry Zaïre exclusively is thus analogous to Auguste's decision in *Cinna* to rule alone. He declares a self-mastery that defies the custom of the region and, in so doing, lays claim to empire. Voltaire here revises Corneille with a view to enhancing Orosmane's status and validating his claim upon Zaïre's love.

Where Voltaire and Crébillon revise Corneille, Frederick the Great, in a version of this passage, revised Voltaire. In the process, Frederick suggests something about the difference between a royal author and an author who aspires to define kingship. In "Variation d'un passage de *Zaïre*," the king rewrote the speech:

Tous les rois qu'à genoux cet univers contemple,
Leurs usages, leurs droits, ne sont point mon exemple.
Je pourrais, ainsi qu'eux, me livrant au plaisir,
Vivre tranquillement au sein d'un doux loisir,
Du trésor de l'État prodiguant des largesses,
Enrichir favoris, ministres, et maîtresses;
Du château de Potsdam dictant mes volontés,
Gouverner mon pays du sein des voluptés.
Mais je ne fus jamais l'ami de la paresse;
Malheur à tous ces rois vivant dans la mollesse,
Qui, montés sur le trône, se laissent gouverner
Sans avoir jamais su commander ni régner.

(The customs, the rights, of all the kings that this universe contemplates on its knees are not at all my example. I could, just like them, delivering myself to pleasure, live tranquilly in the bosom of a sweet leisure, squandering the treasury of the state with largesse, enriching favorites, ministers, and mistresses; from my chateau at Potsdam dictating my wishes, governing my country from the bosom of voluptuousness. But I have never been a friend to idleness; grief upon all kings living in softness, who, once they gain the throne, permit themselves to be governed without ever having known how to command or reign.)[65]

Frederick begins his paraphrase of the speech by, as the sultan does, asserting his uniqueness. But he quickly shows that his concerns are fiscal rather than moral: where Orosmane would not squander his "tendresses," Frederick will not squander his "trésor d'État." For the feeble caliphs, Frederick substitutes other, unspecified, kings who do not know how to command or to reign. Rather than a particularly sensual bondage — Orosmane is opposed to the custom of polygamy — Frederick opposes a more general failure of industry and application. Only kings who have studied command, who are foes to idleness, deserve to rule.

Like Orosmane, Frederick is eager to assert his seriousness. But where Voltaire's sultan, later in the play, succumbs to his passions and murders the one he loves, Frederick suggests that monarchs have more on their minds than sex. As we have seen, he accused Voltaire of succumbing to the passions of tragedy, of failing to play the role of *philosophe*. When Frederick plays the role of a monarch who has mastered his appetites, no one can challenge the actor and call the part miscast. When Voltaire plays Cicéron, the philosopher, Lekain himself felt that he had never seen anything "de plus vrai, de plus pathétique et de plus enthousiaste que M. de Voltaire dans ce rôle" ("more real, more pathetic, and more enthusiastic than M. de Voltaire in this role").[66] When Voltaire plays Lusignan or Gengis Kan, however, even in the safety of his own corner of the world, there is always someone in the audience to remark upon the poor fit between actor and role. As Voltaire plays the royal role, offstage as well as on, playing the tyrant over the other players and the audience, he becomes absurd. Yet his goal, the vindication of the dignity of theater, like his desire to vindicate the ancients and purge the stage of Paris, is a worthy one.

In order to achieve his goal, Voltaire challenged the traditional hierarchies of theater. He refused to defer to the power of his royal patrons, and he challenged the actors' control over the repertoire, their power over playwrights. But the new model of an entrepreneurial, bourgeois theater independent of royal patronage, where actor and playwright would in time defer to the authority of the director, remained in the future. It was Voltaire's habit to wear his costume all day when a play was planned for the evening: in this, as in his total involvement in every phase of his dramatic productions, he seems both to anticipate modern ideas about performance and to present himself as an object of ridicule.

The elements in his plays that have been called propaganda for the *philosophes*—their historical relativism, their skepticism about received truths, their pleas for tolerance—somehow do not manage to make themselves central to the plays.[67] In part, Voltaire's refusal to abandon the classical style and to concentrate on writing serious comedies in prose, as did Diderot and Beaumarchais, is to blame. But his fascination with the royal—his desire to educate kings, to dine with kings, and to play the king—makes this conservatism in matters of dramatic form comprehensible. The paragons of virtue, tolerance, and wisdom who populate his plays are antique, for they derive their being not from new ideas, but from old models. The model was old when Shakespeare dramatized it in Duke Theseus: that enlightened monarch, like Frederick, also claimed to be a philosopher as well as a king.

Throughout the journeys of his career, Voltaire continued to submit his plays to the paying audiences of Paris. But the sequence of audiences he dreamed of pleasing tells a story that is full of nostalgia. For all of his idealized audiences can be subsumed in his idealization of the age of Louis XIV. In that great age, as he described it, kings protected masterpieces from the assaults of hypocrites, and courtiers sponsored great poets. Denied such protection, and capable with his own fortune of sponsoring himself, Voltaire nonetheless continued to seek royal patronage and recognition. In the 1760s, when Catherine the Great sought his advice, his weakness for crowned heads again prevailed: in their correspondence, as Peter Gay puts it, "he stifled his critical judgment and gave his discerning taste a holiday."[68] In the Semiramis of the North, Voltaire had discovered a new Solon, a female Lycurgus. Only his advanced age prevented a replay of his adventures with Frederick.

The desire to imagine a perfect royal audience links Voltaire to his predecessors and separates him from the dramatists in his own period who were laying the groundwork for a drama that did not require kings as its patrons, in its audience, or as its protagonists. Looking back nostalgically to an idealized age of Louis XIV, Voltaire envisioned a theatrical world with the king at its center. Since he found no such world in the courts of Louis XV and Frederick, he was forced at last to invent one. His domestic theatricals point not toward revolution but to self-conscious retirement, to deliberate quaintness. The visitors who found Voltaire's theatricals at Ferney to be absurd noticed that in this area, at least, the most progressive of the age's thinkers was resolutely looking backward.

6

Player and King

Gustav III

~

I

"Hör konungen tala," wrote the court poet Carl Gustaf Leopold to the actor who would play the title role in his play *Oden* before Gustav III of Sweden. "Det är scholan. Imitera hans declamation: Se hans åtbörder, sätt dem i sitt spel" ("Listen to the king speak. There's your school. Imitate his declamation, watch his gestures: put them into your playing").[1] For the professional actor in the court of Gustav III, the king was not only a model, to be imitated in the preparation of a royal role, but also a competitor and colleague. His sponsorship of theater covered the whole range of theatrical activity, from acting in plays at court, through the writing of plays and scenarios for plays, to the founding of the Royal Dramatic Theater in 1788. Nephew to Frederick the Great and cousin to Catherine the Great, Gustav shared their interest in theater and their admiration of the dramas of Voltaire. Inspired by Voltaire's plays, especially those with medieval settings, Gustav supported the creation of a Swedish-language theater and wrote a number of plays nominally based upon Swedish history but clearly indebted to the plays of Voltaire and his contemporaries—Collé, de Belloy, Crébillon—for their plots.

As crown prince, Gustav received an education steeped in the tragedies of classical France. Early in his tutelage he declared to Baron
Scheffer, "son éducateur le plus sérieux" ("his most serious instruc-
tor"), the admiration he felt for Corneille's *Cinna*.[2] "Quand on voit la
belle tragédie de *Cinna*," Gustav wrote on February 17, 1760, at the
age of 14,

> on ne peut qu'être touché de la grandeur d'âme d'Auguste, on est
> extasié. Du moins pour moi, j'aurais voulu être dans le même cas
> pour avoir pu faire la même action. Vous souvient-il encore de ce
> beau vers *Auguste a tout appris et a tout pardonné*? L'effet que
> cette tragédie a produit sur Louis XIV est bien remarquable. Il dit
> en sortant de la comédie que si pendant le spectacle on lui avait
> demandé la grâce d'un seigneur (dont je ne me rapelle plus le
> nom) qu'il avait condamnait à mort et dont il avait refusé le par-
> don, il l'aurait accordé, tant qu'il etait touché de ce qu'il venait de
> voir.[3]

> (When one sees the beautiful tragedy of *Cinna*, one cannot help
> being moved by Auguste's greatness of soul, one is transported.
> For myself, at least, I would have wanted to be in the same situ-
> ation so that I could perform the same action. Do you remember
> that lovely line *Auguste has learned all and has pardoned all*?
> The effect this tragedy produced upon Louis XIV is certainly
> noteworthy. Upon leaving the play, he said that if anyone had
> asked him, during the performance, for mercy on a lord (whose
> name I don't remember) whom he had sentenced to death and
> had refused to pardon, he would have given it, so deeply had he
> been moved by what he had just seen.)

Where Leopold instructs the actor to observe the king's royal performance, the young prince's performance is itself governed by a highly
theatrical self-consciousness. In this letter, Gustav was responding to
an assigned reading: Rousseau's *Lettre à d'Alembert* (the correspondence between Gustav and Scheffer was primarily devoted to discussion of readings prescribed by Scheffer). The crown prince began with
a traditional defense of theater, but here he takes it a step further. He
makes it personal. He would like to be threatened with a hostile conspiracy himself, he assures Scheffer, so that he could display the magnanimity of Auguste. That is, the play offers a model for the king to

imitate. But Gustav's misquotation is revealing: Corneille's Auguste has not merely pardoned the conspirators ("*a tout pardonné,*" as Gustav cites the line), but he wills oblivion: "Auguste a tout appris, et veut tout oublier" (*Cinna,* V.iii.1780, the final line of the play). The idea of a royal pardon, rather than a harder-won oblivion, leads into the illustrative anecdote, intended to show the impact of theater upon a strong ruler like Louis XIV. Inadvertently Gustav reveals the difficulty of proposing such models: he cannot remember the name of the lord. And the lord was not pardoned; Louis felt tempted to pardon him during the play, but the mood passed.

The actor's preparation—watching and listening to the king—and the crown prince's education—emulating in spirit and acting out on the court stage the heroes of classical French tragedy—both point to an extreme identification of court with theater in the age of Gustav III. In part this identification was policy: the monarch's sponsorship of a national theater and a national opera was an aspect of his absolutist *coup d'état* of 1772, when Gustav seized power from the nobility, who had severely restricted the monarchy during his father's reign. Gustav's reforms had a theatrical dimension beyond his patronage of theater. He proposed legislation, never fully carried out, prescribing national dress (of his own design) for all classes of Swedish citizens. Most discomfited by this rule were the nobility, whose addiction to the latest fashions from France was its direct target. Gustav's complex interaction with the French model ran deeper than clothing, however. For just as the crown prince dreamed of imitating Corneille's Auguste, the king imitated Louis XIV, by planning his own palace modeled upon Versailles at Haga and establishing a Swedish Academy in emulation of the Académie Française in 1786.

The prefatory matter in the earliest edition of Gustav's works, edited by Jean-Baptiste De Chaux and published in Stockholm in French in 1804, proclaims still other royal models. Defending Gustav against the charge that he had devoted too much attention to theatrical activities, De Chaux insists upon the appropriateness of the first selection from Gustav's works that he chooses to publish—the scenario, in French, for the opera *Gustav Vasa* that was set into Swedish verse by Johan Kellgren. Gustav's "amusemens dramatiques" (as De Chaux terms them) would be open to the charge of idleness were they not aspects of a larger plan. Plays, De Chaux argues, support the agenda of the academy, and function as "l'exercice le plus propre à fixer la précision, l'élégance, et la pureté du langage" ("the most suitable exercise for establishing the precision, the elegance, and the purity of the language").[4] The choice of subject for the opera reveals a grander scheme of inspiring courage and ardor in the nation. "Rien n'était plus propre à produire cet effet que de remettre sous les yeux d'un peuple brave et généreux le spectacle de son affranchisement de la tyrannie" ("Nothing was so effective in producing this effect as setting before the eyes of a glorious and generous people the spectacle of their liberation from tyranny"). "Gustave III reproduisit sur la scène les héros dont il respectait le plus le mémoire," continues De Chaux. "Après y avoir représenté GUSTAVE VASA, le fondateur de la liberté suédoise, il ne pouvait manquer de rendre cet hommage à GUSTAVE ADOLPHE" (2:2: "Gustave III reproduced on the stage the heroes whose memory he respected most. After representing Gustav Vasa, the founder of Swedish liberty, he could not fail to offer the same homage to Gustav Adolph"). In a way, De Chaux is not misrepresenting chronology, although Gustav's two plays featuring Gustav II Adolph (*Gustav Adolphs Ädelmod* [*The Magnanimity of Gustav Adolph*] and *Gustav Adolph och* [*and*] *Ebba Brahe*) were both performed at court in 1783, while *Gustav Vasa* did not appear until its spectacular premiere at the opera in 1786. As Lennart Breitholtz has demonstrated, the idea of a play devoted to Gustav Vasa had occurred to Gustav in the 1770s. "Voissi un entreprise peut etre hasardee [:] un opperra sans amour sans touttes ces maximes de morales lubrique que Lulli rechauffa du feu de sa musique et qui ont ete adopte dans la suitte du tems commme une regle que forme la base de toutte operra," Gustav wrote ("This is an enterprise that might be worth risking: an opera without love, without all those lubricious moral maxims that Lulli reheats over the fire of his music and that have been adopted over the course of time as a rule forming the basis of all opera").[5] Since the plays on Gustav Adolph feature love plots, Gustav may be seen to have wavered in his intention during the intervening years.

The linkage between Gustav III and his two predecessors in name, Gustav I Vasa and Gustav II Adolph, is emphasized by De Chaux as he represents the king moving logically from first to second. And this movement is portrayed as theatrical: "Admirer un héros, apprécier les grandes vertues, célébrer celles de GUSTAVE ADOLPHE, c'est exprimer le désir de les imiter, et GUSTAVE III était digne de prendre GUSTAVE ADOLPHE pour modèle" (2:2: "To admire a hero, to appreciate great virtues, to celebrate the virtues of Gustav Adolph is to express the desire to imitate them, and Gustav III was worthy of taking Gustav Adolph as his model"). The integrity of Gustav III is demonstrated in his plays, in other words: his emulation of virtue constitutes his virtue. De Chaux' preface is apologetic; wishing to defend Gustav from the charge of vanity, he suggests that the greatness of the heroes of the past is infectious, and that Gustav III, as a player and king, became as great as the roles he wrote and acted.

The idea that performance in the theater can lead to active emulation of heroic behavior by the monarch and to the inspiration of noble, patriotic impulses in the audience is traditional in Renaissance defenses of theater. What made Gustav unique was his implementation of this principle as state policy. Theory and practice fused in Gustav's efforts to give life to the heroes he admired as a student. In addition to the two previous Gustavs and Louis XIV, Gustav found a monarch to idealize in the Henri IV of Voltaire's *Henriade*. One of his courtiers, Count von Creutz, reported Gustav's enthusiasm for the work to Voltaire himself. "Cet illustre vieillard versoit des larmes en aprenant que Votre Altesse Royale savoit la Henriade par coeur," von Creutz effused as he wrote of the encounter to the crown prince from Madrid in 1763. "Je l'avois bien composée, dit-il, dans l'idée de servir de leçon aux Roys, mais je n'esperoit pas qu'elle fructifiasse dans le Nord" ("This famous old man dissolved in tears as he learned that Your Royal Highness knew the *Henriade* by heart. 'I certainly wrote it,' he said, 'with the idea that it could serve as a lesson for kings, but I would never have expected it to bear fruit in the north'").[6] In the young Gustav, Voltaire again found the receptive audience he had idealized in Gustav's older relatives, Frederick and Catherine.

Or so von Creutz would like Gustav to believe. For both De Chaux, writing to celebrate Gustav's memory, and von Creutz, writing to the crown prince in terms that the crown prince would delight to read, the relationship is one of subject to monarch. Both urge their audiences, public or royal, to recognize the reconciliation of ideal with real, of theory and practice, in the person of Gustav himself. The king's active participation in theater and the highly theatrical nature of his death— assassination as he left a masked ball—have combined to perpetuate his image as *teaterkungen* or player-king.[7] While thoroughly ironized by modern historians, Gustav's idealistic role-playing has its roots both in the Renaissance humanist tradition of the prince's education and in Enlightenment programs of reform. Voltaire's *Henriade* and his tragedies, too, share this blend of the humanist ideal of emulation with the newer notion of liberation from the oppression of dead dogma, "l'infâme." For Gustav's immediate purposes, the oppressors were the nobility, from whom he seized power in 1772; his self-portrayal as a national liberator, as a ruler beloved by his people and scorned by the aristocracy, as a Gustav Vasa, a Gustav Adolph, a Henri IV, arose from his imaginative response to youthful indoctrination in the works of Voltaire.

This chapter will focus on two phases of Gustav's royal role-playing. First we will consider his participation as an actor in court theatricals, paying special attention to the Christmas holidays of 1775–76, when, from December 27 to January 10, Gustav played leading roles in five tragedies and took principal parts in five comic afterpieces as well. Proudly the king recorded the "Quantité de Vers, que J'ai sçue par coeur pour Le Theatre de Societe à Gripsholm 1775"—3,784 lines.[8] Among these plays, *Cinna* and *L'Orphelin de la Chine* are familiar from previous chapters. They take on new life and new potential meanings with a king in the roles of Cinna and Gengis-Kan.

After this theatrical Christmas, Gustav shifted his attention to plans for a Swedish language theater to challenge French domination of the professional and amateur court stage. Two of Gustav's historical dramas of intrigue, *The Magnanimity of Gustav Adolph* and *Gustav Adolph and Ebba Brahe,* were both performed at court in Swedish by amateurs in 1783. In these two plays we can see the idealization of Gustav II Adolph that De Chaux remarks upon; but Gustav, as playwright and impresario on these occasions, does not impersonate his hero himself. Rather, he has become the whole occasion of the play. Written by him and performed for him, featuring a hero-king who embodies all the royal virtues, the historical plays draw all their meaning from the delighted royal spectator. Gustav III's greatest theatrical achievement was the premiere of his opera *Gustav Vasa* in 1786. Originally planned to coincide with the unveiling of a monument in honor of Gustav II Adolph in 1772 (itself a commemoration of Gustav III's *coup d'état*), the opera sums up Gustav's idealization of his two predecessors and fully realizes his self-image as liberator, reformer, and hero.

II

The comtesse d'Egmont and Gustav had become regular correspondents after his visit to Paris in early 1771, referring to each other affectionately as "Euphémie" and "Bayard." The names are drawn from Pierre-Laurent de Belloy's tragedy, *Gaston et Bayard*, which had its premiere with the Comédie Française on April 24, 1771. Gustav himself, however, had played the role of Bayard with a group of Swedish courtiers early in 1770. On May 18, 1770, he wrote to his brother about a performance by the professional French players at Drottningholm, comparing the décor favorably to the amateur performance and criticizing the acting in some of the minor roles. In Paris, he participated with the comtesse d'Egmont in another amateur rendition of the play. On May 4, when the play had finally appeared at the Comédie Française, the Comtesse wrote: "On joue Bayard actuellement. Je ne puis rendre a V. M. l'émotion que j'ai éprouvée à cette tragedie, me rappelant que vous aviez choisi le rôle de ce vertueux chevalier, mon imagination me représentait comme vous rendiez sa noblesse et ses vertus franches et sublimes; tantôt je pensais que le rôle de Nemours vous convenait davantage" ("At present they are performing *Bayard*. I cannot report to Y[our] M[ajesty] the emotion I experienced at this tragedy, as I recalled that you had chosen the role of that virtuous knight, my imagination reminded me of the way you conveyed his nobility and his frank and sublime virtues; nonetheless I thought that the role of Nemours would have suited you better").[9] The comtesse refers to an amateur performance of the play that antedates its professional opening. According to Beth Hennings, the king had met de Belloy when the playwright was an actor in the late 1750s, a member of a troupe that played primarily in Russia but had also visited Sweden. De Belloy dedicated the first version of the play to Gustav.[10]

The comtesse's remarks point to one of the problems that courtiers would have in discussing plays in which the king chose to appear. She cannot report herself to have been greatly moved by the performances of the professional actors in Paris; her imagination has been filled by the king's performance instead. So vivid is her recollection of that triumph, that she muses that Gustave might well have taken the role of Gaston (Nemours) as well. The king, unlike a professional actor, can have any role he wants, and, the comtesse suggests, can fit it superbly. Both of the title roles in *Gaston et Bayard* can be his. The different requirements—that Gaston be youthful and Bayard a battle-hardened veteran—must yield to the king's skill.

In De Belloy's play, Gaston de Foix, duc de Nemours, viceroy of Milan, is the only character with royal blood. He has been given command over the armies of France in spite of his inexperience. "A combattre sous lui pouvez-vous vous contraindre?" the duc d'Urbin asks Bayard, "N'en rougissez-vous pas?" ("Can you force yourself to fight under him? Do you not blush at it?"). "Je n'ai point à me plaindre," responds Bayard, "Frère du roi d'Espagne et neveu de mon roi, / Nemours n'est-il pas né pour commander sur moi?" ("I have nothing to complain about. Brother of the king of Spain and nephew of my king, was Nemours not born to command over me?"). Gustav cast himself, as the comtesse points out, against type. Twenty-five years old in 1771, Gustav might better have taken the role of Gaston rather than the grizzled Bayard. Yet there is one advantage in the older part. On the threshold of becoming king, Gustav is able, as Bayard, to celebrate the potential of Gaston:

> Eh! que fait sa jeunesse,
> Lorsque de l'âge mûr je lui vois la sagesse?
> Profond dans ses desseins, qu'il trace avec froideur,
> C'est pour les accomplir qu'il garde son ardeur.
> Il sait défendre un camp et forcer des murailles,
> Comme un jeune soldat désirant les batailles,
> Comme un vieux général il sait les éviter.
> Je me plais à le suivre, et même à l'imiter;
> J'admire sa prudence, et j'aime sa courage.
> Avec ces deux vertus un guerrier n'a point d'âge.

(Eh! What does his youth matter, when I see in him the wisdom of ripe age? Profound in his plans, which he sketches out coldly, he saves his ardor for accomplishing them. He knows how to defend a camp and breach a wall; yearning for battles, like a young soldier, he knows, like an old general, how to avoid them. I am happy to follow him, even to imitate him; I admire his prudence, and I love his courage. With these two virtues, a warrior has no age.)[11]

By choosing the part of Bayard, Gustav assigns to himself a speech in praise of a young man whose skills have not yet been fully tested, a speech, in short, in praise of himself. The comtesse, seeing Gustav in Gaston rather than Bayard, shows her ability to recognize this complex effect. The king is always visible through the character; as the comtesse's letter suggests, no one who has seen the king in the play can see it plain afterwards. Even at the Comédie Française, her imagination fills both parts with the royal actor's presence.

The affectation of signing "Euphémie" to her letter further compounds the dependency of the comtesse's relationship to the king upon this play. In *Gaston et Bayard,* Euphémie has pledged her love in secret to Gaston, while her father has agreed to her marriage to Bayard. Wounded, Bayard withdraws his claim upon her; Gaston must command the armies in the field until he wins sufficient honors to win Euphémie, and Bayard remains behind, a friend, no longer a lover. Thus when the comtesse hints that she would welcome Gustav as Gaston on the stage, she seems also, flirtatiously, to be suggesting that their relationship could be a little less proper, a little less that of Bayard to Euphémie.

Such literary games were common among the courtiers of eighteenth-century Europe. It was less common to play such a game with a king. Gustav's penchant for playacting, his fondness for the plays of Voltaire, Corneille, and Racine as well as of second-rank playwrights like De Belloy, won him condemnation as well as praise. His versatility, celebrated by the comtesse, and his willingness to take on the roles of nonroyal heroes, could also be seen as frivolity. "H. M:t dinerade ofta på theatern och, efter representationens slut, kom Konungen, för att soupera, med hela hofvet, klädd uti sin theaterkostym," Axel Fersen, no enthusiast for such events, wrote, describing the Christmas festivities at Gripsholm in 1775–76. "Vi hafva sålunda sett honom utklädd såsom Radamiste, Cinna, och som öfverste prest i Jerusalems tempel; presenterande sig såsom ett föremål för åtlöje, vid sitt eget bord" ("H. M. dined often at the theater and, at the end of the performance, the king came to supper with the whole court dressed in his theater costume. So we have seen him dressed up as Rhadamiste, Cinna, and as the high priest of the Temple of Jerusalem; presenting himself as an object of ridicule at his own table").[12] Here, rather than being dignified by the roles he played, the king is coarsened and made ridiculous by his acting. His penchant, like Voltaire's, for wearing his costume offstage encourages derision. The disruption of the ordinary routines of court life represented by theatrical activity is another kind of casting against type. For the role the king should be playing is that of king, and the one role should be sufficient. A repellent incongruity, Fersen suggests, is the result when the king takes it upon himself to explore other possibilities.

While the king breaks down social barriers by taking on nonroyal roles, the converse, too, could happen. The pages during this visit to the palace, one observer reported, began writing verses and acting in plays: "Förstår du väl, hur svart det är att bedja dem om ett glas vatten eller att taga bort en tallrik" ("You can imagine how hard it was to ask them for a glass of water or to take away a plate"), Claes Ekeblad wrote. Another courtier reported that the pages had become so intolerable in their conduct that Lord High Chamberlain Liewen, who had himself been a page under Charles XII, described to the king the protocols of that court. The disruptions ceased: "konungen ej ville vara olik ettså glansande foredome, som den verldskunnige hjelten" ("the king did not want his own to be unlike so illustrious an era as that of the world-famous hero").[13] The valets, aping their betters, act out one kind of emulation; Gustav, imitating Charles XII this time, acts out another.

The comtesse's effusions and the courtiers' complaints represent wholly traditional attitudes about the theater. The first sees the enactment of virtues as inspirational; the language of emulation fills Renaissance defenses of theater. The second sees the performance of numerous roles as socially destabilizing; Fersen is another voice in the tradition of antitheatrical prejudice that Jonas Barish has traced back to Plato. For Fersen as for Plato, the virtuoso performer has no place in the state. While it might be appropriate for a crown prince, in the course of his education, to explore through theatrical activities the different roles a man might play, the role for a king is set. Fersen's argument from ridicule, augmented by an admonishment to the same effect from the French ambassador, was apparently effective. After January 1776, the king severely limited his own appearances on the stage.

Thus the orgy of role-playing over this Christmas season stands as the peak of Gustav's acting career. A manuscript of the repertoire of "la troupe de Societte a Gripsholm, 1775–76" in Gustav's hand, featuring the "Rolles du Roi," has survived:

Decembre	Athalie	Le Somnambule
26.	Joad	
28.	L'Orphelin de la Chine	Les fausses Infidelités
	Gengis Chan	Valvain
31.	Melanide	La Bohemienne
	Darviane	
Janvier	Rhradamiste et Zenobie	L'Impertinent
2.	Rhradamiste	Damis
4.	Adelaide du Guesclin	La Soirée a la Mode
	Vendome	
8.	Cinna	L'Anglois a Bordeaux
	Cinna	Milord

This list does not agree with the actual order of performances at Grips-holm as reported in the diary of Fredrik Sparre. *L'Orphelin de la Chine* was the first play performed, on December 28, followed by *Athalie* on December 30, *Adélaïde* on January 2, *Rhadamiste* on the third, *Cinna* on the fourth, and *Mélanide* on the ninth. Something of the spirit of the king's original list survived the rescheduling necessitated by the pressure of rehearsals: *Cinna* was reprised on the last night, January 10. *L'Orphelin* makes sense as the first play, for the court ama-teurs had just performed it on October 13, 1775.[14]

The order planned by the king places at the beginning and the end of the program plays by Racine and Corneille. The king in fact reprised the role of Cinna, the key play in this sequence, once more on November 3, 1776; while he had promised the French ambassador not to appear in any more comedies, he pointed out, tragedy was not in-cluded in the agreement.[15] This was, however, his final appearance on the stage. What it suggests, like the featured place of *Cinna* in the soci-ety performances at Gripsholm, is that Corneille's play retained for the king as he approached the age of thirty the fascination it had held for the crown prince of fourteen. But the crown prince had yearned to emulate Auguste, and the king now played the role of Cinna, the em-peror's rebellious, passionate, would-be assassin. As student prince, Gustav selected the royal role. As king and theatrical impresario, Gus-tav chose the best part.

The rest of the repertoire confirms the suspicion that the king cast himself, as in the case of *Gaston et Bayard,* not according to social rank but according to the more variable hierarchies of the theater.

From Joad the high priest to the English Milord in the final afterpiece, Gustav sketches out for himself a holiday in the theater, laying claim to the biggest, juiciest roles. The traditional idea of role-playing as educational gives way to the urge to show off. Gustav's role-playing, however, is constantly allusive to the fact of his kingship. The plays he chose and the roles he selected necessarily raise questions about the nature of monarchy. As Rhadamiste, made king of Armenia by the Romans, Gustav returns in disguise to Iberia, where his father tyrannically rules, vowing revenge and destruction. Seeing a king in costume playing a king in disguise complicates the court audience's experience of the play. As Joad, Gustav is guardian and educator of the true king of the Israelites; as Gengis-Kan he enacts the brutal tyrant, educated at last by virtue and love. Mastered by destructive passion as Vendôme, Gustav is prevented by chance from murdering his rival; in *Mélanide* he recovers a lost, noble father and concludes a successful courtship. In *Cinna* he sets before himself, and in conflict with his character, a model king. As Cinna learns to praise his clement emperor, Gustav's personal presence comes to dominate both roles. While Gustav the actor plays Cinna, the actor playing Auguste (Count Nils Barck over the Christmas holiday and Count Carl Fersen, a far more talented actor, in November) represents Gustav in his persona as ideal king. It is through the conception of the whole program that Gustav presents and represents himself.

Both the king's planned order of plays and the actual order in which the plays were performed trace a pattern that sketches out an ideal of enlightened monarchy. If the series of performances had begun with *Athalie,* the king as high priest and educator of the youthful monarch would, at the holiday's end, become his own opposite, Cinna overwhelmed by the clemency of Auguste. The actual order in fact heightens the sense of coherence between the first and last plays. *L'Orphelin de la Chine,* despite its exotic locale, is an education-of-a-prince play; and Gengis-Kan's clemency at the end is itself modeled upon that of Corneille's Auguste. "La conversion de Gengis-kan," according to Hippolyte Lucas, "imitée de la clémence d'Auguste, est malheureusement puérile" ("The conversion of Gengis-kan, imitated from the clemency of Auguste, is unhappily puerile"). "Écoutez-le," urges Henri Lion; "Vous croiriez entendre Auguste, à la différence des vers près" ("Listen to him. You would think you were hearing Auguste, with the exception of a difference in the lines").[16] The recognition that Voltaire's early critics experienced would be reversed for Gustav's audience. Listening to Auguste, they would recall the sudden change of Gengis-Kan.

The substitution of *L'Orphelin* for *Athalie* does not alter what appears to be a clear focus on royal education in Gustav's plan. Both plays, after all, feature a royal infant who must be hidden from a tyrant. In Voltaire's play, Gustav enacted the role of the tyrant; in Racine's, he played the wise priest. Juxtaposed in successive performances on December 28 and 30, the two plays reveal their similarities. The amateur actors would have been rehearsing *Athalie* not only on the twenty-ninth, but even as they prepared to revive *L'Orphelin,* which they knew much better. The two plays must have begun to inform each other. Fröken Uggla, who was the most talented of the ladies of the court, had to reverse the king's change of roles: where he moves from educable barbarian to high priest of divine kingship, she moves from the virtuous Idamé to the tryannical Athalie. *L'Orphelin* not only anticipates *Cinna,* the final play, but it also exists in a complementary relationship to *Athalie,* the play that follows it. Through the common plot element of hidden royal children, both plays promulgate a mystique of monarchy. The absolute devotion to the idea of the royal orphan embodied in Zamti (to the extent of attempting to placate Gengis-Kan by substituting his own son for the concealed prince) carries over into Joad's concealment of the boy king in the temple.

What might be understood in Voltaire's play to be "peinture des moeurs" ("moral portraiture") becomes at Gripsholm an exposition of the king's own principles. Zamti does not so much convert Gengis-Kan by his virtuous example as demonstrate his loyalty to a principle that the king, in the role of Gengis-Kan, cannot challenge. The flaws that Voltaire's critics pointed out in the play—that Gengis-Kan is not dangerous enough; that Zamti's patriotism and Idamé's maternal love are not really tested; that both the orphan and Idamé's son cease to be causes for an audience's concern after the third act, as it becomes clear that Gengis-Kan is not going to kill anybody—dovetail with the conditions of the Gripsholm production. If the king plays the role of Gengis-Kan, we must know that he will reform. He cannot be a full-blown barbarian. While it may be a problem in Voltaire's play that Gengis continually fails to follow through on his brutal threats, Gustav, because he is in fact the king and in fact not brutal, cannot be a convincing tyrant either. "C'est *Arlequin poli par l'amour,*" Voltaire wrote to d'Argental of Gengis; "C'est plutôt le Cimon de Boccace et de

La Fontaine, 'Cimon aima, puis devint honnête homme,' voilà le sujet de la pièce" ("He is 'Harlequin polished by love'; he is rather the Cimon of Boccaccio and La Fontaine: 'Cimon loved, then became a gentleman'; that is the subject of the play").[17] Voltaire's flippancy perhaps better suits the Gripsholm performance of this play than those in which he participated himself. For the king will appear as a polished, *honnête* lover later on during the short season. In the king's person, the roles are not incompatible.

Gengis invades the peaceful Chinese empire as a violent force of nature; at Gripsholm, repeated references to the Tartar emperor as a ruler from the north would be received with a slightly different irony from the presentation of Gustav as a fierce barbarian. "Ce roi des fiers enfants du Nord," Etan calls him, "Gengis-kan, que le ciel envoya pour détruire" ("This king of the proud children of the north, Gengis-kan, whom heaven sent as a destroyer"). The messenger characterizes his savage people:

Sa nation farouche est d'une autre nature
Que les tristes humains qu'enferment nos remparts:
Ils habitent des champs, des tentes et des chars;
Ils se croiraient gênés dans cette ville immense;
De nos arts, de nos lois la beauté les offense.
Ces brigands vont changer en d'éternels déserts
Les murs que si longtemps admira l'univers.

(I.iii, p. 307–8: His fierce nation is of another nature than the unhappy human beings closed in by our walls; they live in the fields, in tents, in carts; they would feel oppressed in this great city; the beauty of our arts, our laws, offends them. These brigands will transform into eternal wastelands the walls that the universe has admired for so long.)

For the sophisticated, French-educated courtiers of Sweden, these lines would evoke a complicated response. Certainly Gustav's nation is not inhuman in the way sketched out here, however northern and backward it may be to French eyes. The play's tension between Tartar crudeness and Chinese civilization becomes less a "peinture des moeurs" than a representation of the tension between Swedish and French cultures.

The Swedes were, in fact, sensitive to accusations of coarseness or barbarity. Gustav, upon taking the throne in 1771, had sent back to Paris the French professional actors whom his mother had invited to take up permanent residence in the 1750s. Discovering that the Swedish professional theater, run by Petter Stenborg, was inadequate to his dreams of a national theater, Gustav decided to found a national opera instead. The crude language and crude plays ("ohyfsadt teaterspråk och ohyfsade pjeser") of the native theater, Gustav explained, led him to conclude that Sweden was not yet ready for a theater on the model of the Comédie Française. He introduced Swedish language plays later, through amateur performances at court, but in the 1770s he divided his energies between sponsoring the Swedish Opera and performing in French plays himself. "To campaign for Swedish theatre in the capital, and then to enjoy French theatre in his leisure time," Michael Harvey argues, "seemed fickle even to those who admired and emulated the king."[18] The conflict in *L'Orphelin,* between a cultured and ancient civilization and a rude invader (who had previously been exposed to its culture as an exile) takes on a particular resonance. Gustav's ambition to make Sweden an equal in culture to France, and his mingled admiration and resentment of French theater and drama, informs Gengis's response to the Chinese. "Que dis-je?" muses Gengis:

> si j'arrête une vue attentive
> Sur cette nation désolée et captive,
> Malgré moi je l'admire en lui donnant les fers:
> Je vois que ses travaux ont instruit l'univers;
> Je vois un peuple antique, industrieux, immense.
> Ses rois sur la sagesse ont fondé leur puissance,
> De leurs voisins soumis heureux législateurs,
> Gouvernant sans conquête, et reignant par les moeurs.

(IV.ii, p. 336: What am I saying? If I fix an attentive gaze upon this desolate and captive nation, in spite of myself I admire her as I put her in chains. I see that her labors have educated the universe; I see an ancient people, industrious, vast. Their kings have based their power upon wisdom; happy legislators of their defeated neighbors, governing without conquest, and ruling through morals.)

In Gengis's attitude toward the Chinese we catch a glimpse of Gustav's attitude to the French. The very activity of rehearsing and performing this play at Gripsholm insists upon the civilizing force of French culture. When, at the end of the play, Gengis cedes his power to Zamti, the deference of the monarch of the north to the values of France is fully enacted. "Soyez ici des lois l'interprête suprême," Gengis declares,

> Rendez leur ministère aussi saint que vous-même;
> Enseignez la raison, la justice, et les moeurs.
> Que les peuples vaincus gouvernent les vainqueurs,
> Que la sagesse règne, et préside au courage:
> Triomphez de la force, elle vous doit hommage:
> Je donnerai l'exemple, et votre souverain
> Se soumet à vos lois les armes à la main.

(V.vi, p. 356: Be here the supreme interpreter of laws; make their administration as holy as yourself; teach reason, justice, and morals; let the conquered govern the conquerors; let wisdom rule, and preside over courage. Triumph over force, it owes you homage. I shall give the example, and your sovereign submits to your laws, bearing his arms.)

At Gripsholm, when the conqueror submits to a higher culture, the tribute reaches from Sweden to France. But if the role of Zamti was played, as is likely, by the king's brother Duke Charles, the gesture becomes one of solidarity between the two. Their shared enthusiasm for theater and for French culture plays itself in this moment.

The court stage offers a place for Gustav to align himself with the advanced ideas of the *philosophes* without threatening his royal position. His visit to Paris in 1771 brought him into social contact with "tous les philosophes," he wrote to his mother, "Marmontel, Grimm, Thomas, l'abbé de Morellet, Helvétius. Ils sont plus aimables à lire qu'à voir" ("all the *philosophes*. . . . they are more pleasant to read than to see"). The antimonarchical sentiments that shocked him in Paris could be safely parodied in the role of Gengis.[19] Equally well, as Joad in *Athalie,* Gustav could instruct the young Joas in the need to avoid the excesses of absolutism. "De l'absolu pouvoir vous ignorez l'ivresse," the high priest warns the boy king,

Et des lâches flatteurs la voix enchanteresse.
Bientôt ils vous diront que les plus saintes lois,
Maîtresses du vil peuple, obéissent aux rois;
Qu'un roi n'a d'autre frein que sa volonté même;
Qu'il doit immoler tout à sa grandeur suprême;
Qu'aux larmes, au travail le peuple est condamné,
Et d'un sceptre de fer veut être gouverné;
Que, s'il n'est opprimé, tôt ou tard il opprime:
Ainsi de piège en piège, et d'abîme en abîme,
Corrompant de vos moeurs l'aimable pureté,
Ils vous feront enfin haïr la verité,
Vous peindront la vertu sous une affreuse image.
Hélas! Ils ont des rois égaré le plus sage.

(IV.iii.1389–1402: You do not know the intoxication of absolute power and the siren voice of base flatterers. Soon they will tell you that the holiest laws, mistresses of the vile people, defer to kings; that a king has no curb but his own will; that all must be sacrificed to his greatness; that the people are condemned to tears and labor, and need to be ruled with an iron rod; that, if they are not oppressed they will sooner or later become oppressors themselves: thus, from trap to trap, pitfall to pitfall, corrupting the gentle purity of your morals, they will make you hate truth and paint you a horrid portrait of virtue. Alas! They have misled the wisest of kings.)[20]

The irony in Racine's play—that Joas will in fact grow up to foresake the God of his fathers and will have his friend Zacharie stoned to death in the court of the temple—is compounded here as the king takes the role of the prophet. As in *Gaston et Bayard,* Gustav here takes an opportunity to compliment himself. Unlike Joas, he has not become drunk with power. His revolution liberated the people from oppression by the nobility; his enlightened absolutism promulgates attractive, inspiring portraits of virtue. The performances at Gripsholm reinforce the claim that the king makes by casting himself as Joad. As high priest, he is as sadly aware of the pitfalls of power as Joas, the boy king, is ignorant.

Aristocrats of the previous generation in the audience, like Fersen and Liewen, might have added to their offense at the indecorums of the theater party a further offense at the recognition that, in playing

Joad, the king was playing themselves. The memories of Charles XII that could be invoked to curb the excesses of the pages could also be invoked to portray the excesses of an absolutist king. By acting the role of a wise advisor, a counselor inspired with prophetic wisdom, Gustav fuses in his person both the young king and old priest, for again his identity as king cannot be absorbed completely into the role he plays. The tensions between himself and the older generation of aristocrats, the tensions between his ideas of absolutism and the aristocratic party's fears of royal adventurism, animate Joad's fears that Joas will follow only too well in the ways of his fathers. By playing the prophet, the king manages to suggest that he will be different from previous generations of kings who ignore or kill their prophets (as Joas will kill Zacharie). Gustav's idealized self-image incorporates both wisdom and power.

Seeing the king parody tyrannical violence in Gengis and proffer wise counsel in Joad will have different meanings for different parts of the audience. While the older generation may be either reassured or discomfited by Gustav's reenactment of the principles of his revolution on the stage, the younger generation enjoyed the potential for ironic wit inherent in the situation. In a set of farewell verses, with explanatory notes, Johan Oxenstierna (who would later supervise the publication of Gustav's works in Swedish after his death) entertained the group on the final night. In *Athalie,* he reminds the "Troupe de Gripsholm," Gustav forgot some of his lines and substituted lines from other plays:

Oui, malgré des Talents qu'admire l'Univers,
Racine de son jeu fut souvent la Victime.
Il est vrai qu'à ses Loix il soumêtt jusqu'aux Vers,
Mais qui change un Etat peut changer une rime.

(Yes, in spite of talents that the universe admires, Racine was often the victim of his [Gustav's] acting. It's true that he obeys his [Racine's] laws to the letter; but whoever can change a state can change a rhyme.)[21]

Oxenstierna here makes witty play with ideas of royal life-and-death power over playwrights and play scripts. His joke is reminiscent of Davenant's witty prologue to *The Platonic Lovers,* or of Suckling's transformation of Aglaura into an Easter bride. But the idea of a royal prerogative to revise plays is also reminiscent of Molière's experiences with *Tartuffe:* in that case, the playwright was forced to include the wise, tolerant royal audience in his play itself. In Oxenstierna's version of this dynamic, the king challenges the author's empire of talent by the simple expedient of forgetting his lines. Racine is the victim, but his suffering is minor. Gustav's imperialistic attitude toward Racine's lines is analogized in Oxenstierna's verses to the revolution of 1772. The peril of a king who sets himself above the laws, delineated by Gustav as Joad in one of his longest speeches in the play, is subsumed into an inside joke. A king who can change governments can certainly alter his lines: even if the lines are lines about the limits of royal power.

Oxenstierna can comically portray the king's unlimited power by linking absolutism with forgetfulness. He also alludes to an incident of resistance to royal command. Fröken Uggla refused to dye her hair black to play Athalie. The loss to the play's dramatic impact, Oxenstierna ruefully submits, was incalculable:

La superbe Athalie au milieu de sa Gloire
N'a point assez deployé ses fureurs.
Une Once de Pomade Noire
Si elle eut daigné nous en croire
Auroit fait frémir tous les Coeurs.

(Proud Athalie, in the midst of her glory, did not adequately deploy her rages. An ounce of black pommade, if she would only have believed us, would have made all hearts quake.)

The poet allies himself with all the audience in mocking the actress's foolish vanity. The king as director, in this instance, is again portrayed as absolute: the black dye would have made all the difference. The joke, of course, is that it would not have made any difference at all. Athalie's glorious rage is dependent upon Fröken Uggla's acting skills, not upon the color of her hair. Forgetting lines, becoming trapped in minutiae of production: these hazards of the theatrical profession are portrayed by Oxenstierna as challenges to royal power. It is only by becoming an actor and a director that the king reveals the limits of his authority. Although he can change a political system, he cannot remember his lines; although he can rule a country, he cannot persuade a lady of the court to dye her hair. Backstage, the king becomes subject to the rules and pressures of the discipline of theater. He becomes, as Oxenstierna suggests, one of the company, one of "us."

Even the most powerful member of a repertory company, choosing the best parts for himself, is subject to the conditions of repertory theater. Joad is the only role in which Gustav cast himself against type. As we survey the parts he played over the holiday season, a personality emerges: like Gengis, Vendôme in *Adélaïde du Guesclin* is impetuous, violent, passionate (Lekain played both roles: Gengis at the premiere of *L'Orphelin* in 1755 and Vendôme in the successful revival of *Adélaïde* in 1765). Both characters set a pattern for Gustav's acting: they teeter on the verge of barbarism.

Where Gengis is restrained by his love and civilized by the virtue of the Chinese, Vendôme condemns his own brother, Nemours, to an ignominious death; the two are rivals for Adélaïde, who loves Nemours. Vendôme has taken Adélaïde prisoner, and has suborned Coucy to have Nemours executed. Coucy, "un très digne homme comme on n'en voit guère à la cour" ("a very worthy gentleman such as one hardly ever sees at court"), as Voltaire put it,[22] assents to Vendôme's horrid plan only to forestall it. As the cannon sounds announcing the death of Nemours, Vendôme is seized with remorse: Coucy then delivers him from his misery by presenting Nemours alive.

Vendôme's love for Adélaïde has stimulated his basest impulses: when Adélaïde urges him to serve France rather than England, he brutally rebuffs her. "Je deviendrai tyran," he snarls,

> mais moins que vous, cruelle:
> Mes yeux lisent trop bien dans votre âme rebelle;
> Tous vos prétextes faux m'apprennent vos raisons:
> Je vois mon déshonneur, je vois vos trahisons.

(II.v, p. 99: I shall become a tyrant, but less so than you, cruel one: my eyes read too well into your rebellious soul; all your false pretexts teach me your reasons: I see my dishonor, I see your treasons.)[23]

Vendôme's love makes him barbarous, and the index of that barbarism is his rejection of Adélaïde's political arguments as motivated by passion for his rival. The language of politics is wholly debased here. "Que m'importe l'Etat et mes vains alliés?" Vendôme barks when Coucy suggests that his reasons for wanting to kill Nemours are political, for the English seek his head (IV.v, p. 125: "What does the state matter to me? or my useless allies?"). His thwarted love drives him. Only at the end does he return to his senses: "Natur, je me rends; / Je ne veux point marcher sur les pas des tyrans" (V.ii, p. 130: "Nature, I return to you; I do not wish to walk in the footsteps of the tyrants"). "Je vois ce que je suis," he groans as he imagines that his repentance has come too late to save his brother, "et ce que je déteste" (V.iii, p. 130: "I see what I am, and what I detest"). But Coucy restores him to himself, to what he truly is: "Bon Français, meilleur frère, ami, sujet fidèle" (V.vi, p. 136: "Good Frenchman, better brother, friend, faithful subject"). Vendôme's abdication of himself to jealous tyranny becomes doubly forceful when we recall that the actor who plays it has just finished playing the role of Joad, and when that actor is himself a king. Although the New Year's holiday had intervened between *Athalie* and *Adélaïde,* the juxtaposition of the two roles is compelling.

Gustav played Vendôme on January 2 and Rhadamiste in Crébillon's *Rhadamiste et Zénobie* on the third. Again he is a character barely able to function in civilized society, a slave of passion, Joas rather than Joad. Rhadamiste, Zénobie tells her confidante at the beginning of the play, dragged her from the altar on the day of their wedding, stabbed her, and threw her into a river for dead. His jealous rage is comprehensible to her, because it emerges out of a nest of interlocking betrayals of the two young lovers by their fathers, who are brothers and neighboring kings. Zénobie finds herself now a prisoner in the court of Pharasmane, Rhadamiste's "père perfide, inhumain, et jaloux" (I.i, p. 145: "perfidious, inhuman, jealous father"), under the identity of Isménie, and beset by the love of Arsame, Rhadamiste's virtuous brother, and Pharasmane himself.[24] Rhadamiste, himself unknown as he appears on the scene in disguise as ambassador from the Roman empire, has sworn revenge against Pharasmane.

"Que sais-je, Hiéron?" he demands of his confidant, who has wondered aloud what his purpose might be,

> furieux, incertain,
> Criminel sans penchant, vertueux sans dessein,
> Jouet infortune de ma douleur extrême,
> Dans l'état où je suis, me connais-je moi-même?

(II.i, p. 154: What do I know, Hieron? Furious, insecure, a criminal without the inclination, virtuous without design, unlucky plaything of my extreme grief, do I recognize myself in the state I am in?)

He sees too close a resemblance between himself and his father, "père injuste et barbare" ("unjust and barbarous father"); Arsame, his brother, he finds remarkably different. In his soliloquy in act 3, scene 4, Rhadamiste contemplates his likeness to his terrible father and his difference from his virtuous brother: "Quel exemple pour moi!" (III.iv, p. 163: "What an example for me!"). Shame and self-disgust flood into him in his recognition scene with Zénobie: "Se peut-il que vos yeux puissent le méconnaître? / Oui, je suis ce cruel, cet inhumain, ce traître, / Cet époux meurtrier" (III.v, p. 165: "Could your eye possibly make a mistake? Yes, I am that cruel, that inhuman, traitor; that murderous husband"). "Barbare que je suis!" he howls in self-loathing as jealousy of his brother's love for Zénobie courses through him, "Quoi! ma fureur jalouse / Déshonore à la fois mon frère et mon épouse!" (IV.v, p. 173: "Barbarian that I am! My jealous rage dishonors at once my brother and my wife!"). Hurling himself into battle with his father, desperate to rescue Zénobie but careless of his own life, Rhadamiste dies at Pharasmane's hands. "J'ai reçu par vos mains le prix de mes forfaits," he declares. "Puissent les justes dieux en être satisfaits! / Je ne méritais pas de jouir de la vie" (V.vi, p. 181: "I have received at your hands the reward for my crimes. May the just gods be satisfied. I would not have deserved to enjoy life"). Father and son are reconciled at the end; Arsame is rewarded with Zénobie.

These barbarous roles testify to the energetic stage presence of Gustav. They also function as counterexamples to his own moderate style of rule: in the first four plays performed at Gripsholm, we find Gustav three times on the verge of disastrous, destructive excess and once, as the high priest, counseling a boy king of the danger of that verge. On January 4, Gustav followed these performances with his appearance as Cinna. This look at his other roles within the same brief period makes some sense out of what might otherwise merely enact a poignant historical irony. Gustav must have played Cinna with the same exuberance that his other roles demanded. His Cinna, youthful, passionate, eager, likewise teases the audience with the sense of potential monstrous transgression that is the keynote of Gustav's stage persona. Joad is the only exception to this rule, but in *Athalie* the only role that would have given Gustav an opportunity fully to indulge in the actor's freedom is that of the evil queen herself.

For his last three performances, on the fourth, the ninth, and the tenth, Gustav played essentially the same role: Cinna twice, and Dar-

viane in *Mélanide* on the ninth. Both are young lovers, essentially virtuous, but driven to extremes by their passions. Both Darviane and
Cinna threaten patriarchal authority figures: the emperor Auguste in
Corneille's play, and the marquis d'Orvigni, Darviane's rival and
father in Nivelle de la Chausée's. For the role of Darviane, the twenty-
nine-year-old king took on the challenge of playing an eighteen-year-
old with no family, no fortune, and no prospects. Unknown to him,
the woman Darviane assumes to be his aunt, Mélanide, is actually his
mother; the nobleman to whom his beloved, Rosalie, is promised is
actually his father. Confronted with the choice between fighting a duel
with or acknowledging his son, the marquis finally succumbs; Darviane, who has boldly reveled in his marginal social status, acquires a
family and a bride at the end.

Mélanide is a trifle compared to *Cinna;* but the order of the performances, placing the adolescent impetuousness of Darviane on a level
with the more complex passions of Cinna, may suggest that for the
original performers the two plays were not all that different in kind.
One of the pleasures the Gripsholm participants and audience members had over this holiday was that of seeing the king in unlikely situations. In *Mélanide,* Darviane undergoes a scolding that must have
been received as comic with the king in the role. Early in the play,
Mélanide finds herself forced to remonstrate with Darviane, and begins to sound like a mother, although it is not safe for her to reveal her
identity. "Un peu trop d'impetuosité" ("A little too much impetuousness") she confides to a friend, is Darviane's problem.[25] Shortly afterward, she takes him on herself:

> Vous avez dans l'esprit un feu séditieux
> Qui prend de plus en plus sur votre caractère:
> Le plus léger obstacle aussitôt vous altère;
> Vous ne supportez rien. N'apprendrez-vous jamais
> L'art de dissimuler, ou de souffrir en paix
> Les contrariétés dont la vie est semée?

> (I.ii, p. 127: You have a seditious fire in your spirit that is more
> and more taking over your character. The slightest obstacle dis-
> rupts you; you don't tolerate anything. Won't you ever learn the
> art of dissembling, or of suffering in silence the contrariness
> sown through life?)

For the courtiers in the audience and in the rest of the cast, a moment like this, in which the king receives a dressing-down about his impatience and haughtiness, is full of comic potential. Everyone, the younger as well as the older courtiers, like Fersen, had begun to repine at the constant obsession with theater during this visit to Gripsholm. For many of the actors, the rush of rehearsals, combined with cold rooms and inadequate sanitary facilities, led to complaints. But Gustav was indefatigable: "Utan att bekymma sig om tidens gång, eller om medspelarnas trotthet är han än 'père noble' än 'jeune premier,' men alltid régissör" ("Without taking any notice of the passage of time or of the fatigue of his fellow actors, he is now 'père noble' and now 'jeune premier,' but always the director"), wrote one visitor.[26] And a director whom it could be injudicious to defy.

"Pour être plus qu'un roi, tu te crois quelque chose!" ("For being more than a king, you think you're something!") Emilie barks contemptuously at Cinna, when he points out to her that even kings kneel down before the very slaves of Auguste (III.iv.990.) Emilie scorns Cinna, despising him at his word as a slave:

Pardonnez-moi, grands dieux, si je me suis trompée
Quand j'ai pensé chérir un neveu de Pompée,
Et si d'un faux semblant mon esprit abusé
A fait choix d'un esclave en son lieu supposé.

(1029–32: Forgive me, great gods, if I made a mistake when I thought I was in love with a nephew of Pompey, and if, abused by a false impostor, my wit chose a slave in his place.)[27]

With Gustav in the role, the ironies multiply. Emilie's disdain is showered not upon a hideous substitute, a slave mocking the greatness of Pompey, but upon the king costumed as a noble Roman. Cinna's struggle to find out who he really is, where his sympathies and loyalties truly lie, is itself made a mockery here, for Gustav's identity is well known. The close linkage affected between the roles of Cinna and Darviane further defuses both plays' querying of true origins and true nobility. We know the king is slumming; no change will result from his brief sojourn in these subversive parts.

The New Year's festivities at Gripsholm offered Gustav a chance to play out alternatives to his benign version of absolutism, to display to his audiences that he was not a tyrant, not a slave of passion, but a king who could master those impulses, who could be both Joad and Cinna at once. This elaborate process of self-modeling took place not in the public view, but before the select audience of the court, and functioned as a promulgation to the insiders of the secrets of the royal identity. By playing out barbarous and tyrannical impulses, the king revealed his capacity for tyranny: yet by doing so in the theater, he reassured his audience that these impulses were under control, that he was only acting. Directorial high-handedness, an imperious insistence that the whole company commit as much energy to the project as he did, was as close as Gustav came to the actual exercise of his royal prerogative during the holiday.

In the variety of roles he undertook, though, the king showed multiple sides to his personality. In one way, he revealed to the court his broad sympathy with others, with those not born to royalty. But in another way he showed, safely, a violent side to his personality, choosing role after role that demanded an actor capable of terrible brinksmanship. The sudden rages, the mad desires that Gustav permitted himself to express from the stage lay beneath the surface of daily life, as he played the role of the king. The riddle of Gustav is the riddle of all acting: How can we distinguish between the Gustav who plays the king and the king who plays the tyrant, the lover, and the high priest? How can we know the player from the king?

The comtesse d'Egmont offers a sidelight to this problem of the king's playing at Gripsholm. Again the subject of her letter is *Gaston et Bayard*. She writes to Gustav of a recent court performance before Louis XV:

> C'est un mouvement si vrai que l'autre jour, à la représentation de *Bayard,* à Versailles, j'aurai acheté de mon sang une larme du roi; mais, si vous aviez vu son air d'indifférence, l'ennui de M. le Dauphin, les rires de Mesdames à ce tableau si touchant des sentiments de notre nation pour nos rois, vous auriez partagé mon désespoir de voir une si charmante nation dénaturée, et des vertus si intéressants, si héroïques, devenues pour elle impossibles. . . . Après *Bayard,* exaltée par la pitié, irritée de la froideur des assistants, . . . je couru chez Madame de Bironne parler en liberté. Nous relûmes votre lettre et nous répétâmes mille fois: Voilà donc un roi qu'on peut aimer! Nous l'avons vu; il produirait des Bayards, il ferait revivre Henri IV; il existe, et ce n'est pas pour nous. Dites encore que nous sommes républicaines!

(It is so true a sentiment that the other day, at the performance of *Bayard,* I would have purchased a tear from the king at the price of my blood. But if you had seen his air of indifference, the boredom of the Dauphin, the laughter of the ladies at this moving tableau of the sentiments of our nation for our kings, you would have shared my despair at seeing so charming a nation so spiritless, and such interesting, heroic virtues now impossible for her. . . . After *Bayard,* exalted with pity, irritated by the coldness of the audience [especially when I compared their conduct with his, who played Bayard], I rushed to Madame de Bironne's, to speak with liberty. We reread your letter and repeated to ourselves a thousand times: There is a king one can love! We have seen him; he would produce Bayards; he would make Henri IV live again; he exists, but he is not for us. Now say again that we are republicans!)[28]

By playing who he is not, the king fulfills his destiny. The monarch who can play Bayard will never doze off during a performance of *Bayard.* The comtesse imagines an impossible scenario in which Gustav will appear on the stage of nations as a kind of scourge to the lazy Louis XV and the bored dauphin. His acting animates virtues that are both particularly French and particularly lacking among the French. Little did Voltaire dream that his *Henriade* would bear fruit in the north; the illustrious old man and the comtesse portray themselves as looking from a declining France to Gustav to fulfill their ideals. Here the player-king performs as an active corrective to the indolent king who merely sits in the audience.

In the most important eighteenth-century discussion of acting, Diderot's *Paradoxe sur le comédien* (1773), the kind of sentimental response that the comtesse reports is appropriate to audience members, but not to actors. Diderot insists that actors do not emotionally identify with the roles they play. Rather, they enact models that they have carefully and coldly studied. "Réfléchissez un moment ce qu'on appelle au théâtre *être vrai,*" Diderot urges his interlocutor in this dialogue:

Est-ce y montrer les choses comme elles sont en nature? Aucunement. Le vrai en ce sens ne serait que le commun. Qu'est-ce donc que le vrai de la scène? C'est la conformité des actions, des discours, de la figure, de la voix, du mouvement, du geste, avec un modèle idéal imaginé par le poète, et souvent exagéré par le comédien.

(Let us reflect for a moment upon what we call 'being real' in the theater. Is it showing things the way they are in nature? Not in the least. The 'real' in this sense would only be the commonplace. What then is 'the real' on the stage? It is the conformity of actions, of speech, of facial expression, of voice, of movement, of gesture to an ideal imagined by the poet and then exaggerated by the performer.)[29]

Characters are idealizations. "Etes-vous Cinna?" Diderot demands earlier. "Avez-vous jamais été Cléopatre, Mérope, Agrippine? Que vous importent ces gens-la? La Cléopatre, la Mérope, l'Agrippine, le Cinna du théâtre, sont-ils même de personnages historiques? Non. Ce sont les fantômes imaginaires de la poésie; je dis trop: ce sont des spectres de la façon particulière de tel ou tel poète" (p. 315: "Are you Cinna? Have you ever been Cleopatra, Mérope, Agrippina? What do these people mean to you? The Cleopatra, the Mérope, the Agrippina of the theater, are they even historical figures? No. They are imaginary phantoms of poetry; I'm going too far. They are phantoms in the particular manner of this or that poet"). "Mon ami," he concludes,

> il y a trois modèles, l'homme de la nature, l'homme du poète, l'homme de l'acteur. Celui de la nature est moins grand que celui du poète, et celui-ci moins grand encore que celui du grand comédien, le plus exagéré de tous. Ce dernier monte sur les épaules du précédent, et se renferme dans un grand mannequin d'osier dont il est l'âme; il meut ce mannequin d'une manière effrayante, même pour le poète, qui ne se reconnait plus, et il nous épouvante, comme vous l'avez fort bien dit, ainsi que les enfants s'épouvantent les uns les autres en tenant leurs petits pourpoints courts élevés au-dessus de leur tête, en s'agitant, et en imitant de leur mieux la voix rauque et lugubre d'un fantôme qu'ils contrefont.

(p. 376: My friend, there are three models: man in nature, man as imagined by the poet, man as portrayed by the actor. In nature, man is less great than in poetry, and he is less great than man as performed by the great actor, the most exaggerated of all. This last stands on the shoulders of his predecessor, and encloses himself in a wicker mannequin, of which he is the soul. He shakes this mannequin in a manner that is frightening, even for the poet, who doesn't recognize himself, and he scares us, as you put it so well, just as children scare one another by holding their little tunics up above their heads, shaking, and imitating as best they can the hoarse, lugubrious voice of the ghost they counterfeit.)

The image of children frightening each other does not belittle acting or theater, Diderot insists. Rather, it more accurately depicts the kind of emotions actors display than does the more conventional praise of total emotional identification.

While the *Paradoxe* was not published in final form until 1830, it was well known in the literary and theatrical circles that Gustav corresponded with in France. Its terms afford another means of approach to the phenomenon of Gustav's acting. Diderot's concern was with the extraordinary unflappability and coldness of the great professional actors: Lekain, Clairon, and the occasion of the *Paradoxe*, Garrick. Unmoved themselves, they moved their audiences: men of sensibility, Diderot claims, feel real grief, horror, and other emotions in the theater, while the actor, after his performance, feels only fatigue. During the performance, the great actors are sufficiently detached to kick aside an earring dropped during the previous scene or to mutter angry comments to each other during a love scene.

Gustav's status as a king among amateur actors creates a further paradox. The *modèle idéal* or phantom that Gustav imitates when he plays dangerous characters like Cinna or Rhadamiste is neither the poet's nor the actor's vision of those characters. Rather, what Gustav imitates is the great actor—or a model or phantom of great acting. What Gustav wants to demonstrate to his audience is his control over the emotions he depicts, his coldness, his mastery. By playing the great actor, Gustav reveals the qualities necessary to becoming a great king.

Gustav's audience's pleasure must derive, therefore, from their recognition of the disjunction between player and role. Unlike Diderot's men of feeling, they are not authentically moved by his performance. But in another sense, they can function like the audience that Diderot analogizes to children fleeing, screaming, from their companion playing the ghost. In both, the spirit of game, of play, is paramount. The analogy became concrete at Gripsholm: one night the guests were awakened by a specter, haunting the halls. No trace of the person who had played the role could be found, despite enthusiastic pursuit.

III

In succeeding years, once he had ceased playing on the court stage, Gustav sponsored more elaborate scenarios in which the whole castle became a kind of stage. His brother, Fredrik Adolph, returning from a trip to Italy, was menaced by ghosts and furies. He found himself cast in the role of heroic knight, called upon to brave numerous perils as he entered the castle and liberated a princess enchanted by Merlin. The exaggerated phantoms that Gustav played, the specters of a tryannical potential that he repudiated but simultaneously threatened, were in a way as appropriate to Gripsholm, a castle whose medieval antecedents and unrenovated Gothic decor appealed more to the king than to his grumbling courtiers, as these fantastic manifestations.

The years immediately after Gustav's retirement from active playing saw the king's attention devoted to staging tournaments and carousels; spectacular equestrian pageants were held out of doors not only at Gripsholm but also at Drottningholm and other royal residences. The new opera, too, engaged his interest. For the repertoire of French classic drama, in which the king had played his dangerous roles in the 1770s, professionals were engaged. By 1782, the king had rethought his decision to dismiss French actors from the court and had hired a new troupe led by Boutet de Monvel. Monvel's players opened the season at a remodeled Gripsholm theater with *Rhadamiste et Zénobie* on May 22, 1782, with the king now safely seated in the audience, watching a professional enact Rhadamiste's jealous rages.

Yet the king still refused to be relegated to a wholly conventional enactment of his royal role. Attending plays performed by professionals and participating in courtly tourneys are both utterly acceptable activities for a Renaissance prince. Inviting the bishop of the neighboring district to Gripsholm to view *Tartuffe* on New Year's day 1780, Gustav perhaps overplayed the conventional role of a wise monarch, with ironic reference to the all-seeing Louis XIV of the *Relation des plaisirs de L'île enchantée.* He greeted the bishop and priests by apologizing for the play selected: "Jag har ingen annan pièce at bjuda uppå, än Molières *Tartuffe,* som idag gifves, och jag kan tygt bjuda sådane prester, som ni ären, at se den samma, uta ni sjelfva eller någon annan dervid kan göra någon application" ("I have no other play to offer except Molière's *Tartuffe,* which is to be performed today, and I can certainly invite such priests as yourselves to see such a play without you or anyone else finding any applications").[30] Here the king reminds the divines that he, as royal censor, is the final arbiter of what is offensive or not. In the process, of course, he offers them a veiled challenge, daring them to see themselves reflected in the hypocrite before them. In the process, he created for the rest of the court audience a second comedy, as they watched the priests for signs of embarrassment and the monarch for signs of triumph in their discomfiture.

Not content with holding a mirror up to nature in this way, the king retired into his chambers during the Christmas holidays of 1782, accompanied only by his favorite, Baron Armfelt. The result of this private labor was not an important state paper or peace treaty, but instead was a play in Swedish on a Swedish historical theme, *The Magnanimity of Gustav Adolph*. The court amateurs were requested to act in the play, and were rewarded for their efforts by promotion to membership in the newly created Society for the Improvement of the Swedish Language, despite the fact, as Fersen noted, that not a single member of this society could be said to be fluent in the mother tongue.[31] There was insufficient rehearsal time, so the company performed instead *Birger Jarl och Mechtild,* a play in Swedish based upon a plot outline and a few scenes (in French) by Gustav, that they had performed in 1773 at the wedding of Duke Carl to Hedvig Elisabeth Charlotta. The king and Armfelt finished reworking the script of his new play; *The Magnanimity of Gustav Adolph* was staged a week later, January 11, 1783.

The first of Gustav's plays to deal with his great ancestor, the play presents to view a model monarch. It also incorporates opportunities for song and dance: the first act closes with a musical rehearsal for the wedding between Märta Baner and Lars Sparre; the whole play concludes with the wedding itself. In between, we learn that the Lars Sparre of the first act is in fact the lowborn Erik Johansen, and that the Erik of the first act is in fact Lars Sparre. They were exchanged at birth by their nurse, who, feeling that her mistress's son was about to die of a childhood illness, substituted her own in his place. The plot is not original: the king's play is wholly drawn from Voltaire's *Charlot* (1767). An invited audience of important diplomats, prominent residents of the nearby towns, and professional actors, both from Boutet de Monvel's troupe and from the Royal Opera, joined the courtiers in vying with one another in enthusiastic applause. Oxenstierna, formerly an ardent member of the court's theatrical set, found the whole event a bit much: "Jag går att se Gustaf Adolf och hela tyska kriget dansa chaconne. Jag måste tänka mig Westfalsika freden i scener och se ministrarna dansa lika som generalerna" ("I am going to see Gustav Adolph and the whole German war dancing the chaconne. I have to imagine the Peace of Westphalia on the stage, and see ministers dancing along with generals").[32] Oxenstierna's remarks are unfair: the play deals with a period well before Gustav Adolph's involvement in the Thirty Years' War. In fact, Gustav III's alterations to Voltaire's *Charlot* serve throughout to ground the romance in the specific details of his predecessor's early career.

The most significant alteration that Gustav made to *Charlot* is in fact the addition of the king to the main action of the play itself. In *Charlot,* the great monarch makes no appearance. At least that was the case when the play was first performed by Voltaire's own group of talented amateurs before the garrison of soldiers stationed at Ferney. In a later, revised edition of the play, Voltaire introduced Henri at the very end.[33] He enters in the final scene and summarizes his solution to the problem of mixed identities in a speech of fourteen lines. This great king has listened to the nurse, Madame Aubonne, and pardoned Charlot (who has here killed in self-defense the lowborn boy raised as a marquis). "Ce monarque adoré ne rebute personne; / Il écoute le pauvre, il est juste, il pardonne; / J'ai tout dit" (III.v, p. 382: "This beloved monarch never turns anyone away. He listens to the poor, he is just, he pardons. I told all"), Madame Aubonne tells the comtesse de Givry, who is unaware of the earlier substitution, and who believes her son to be dead. Henri arrives to announce that the "coup inouï" ("sudden shock") that has transformed sorrow into joy has provided him with a new soldier. The former Charlot, now elevated to comte de Givry, will accompany him into battle. "Adorons des Francais le vainqueur et le père," effuses the comtesse (V.vi, p. 383: "Let us adore the conqueror and father of the French"). The play celebrates Henri's common touch. He heeds the plea of the nurse, and he recognizes Charlot's essential goodness and innocence. The fact of his noble birth is as much a surprise to him as to the comtesse.

But in the first version of the play, the whole process is narrated at second hand by the duc de Belgarde. Madame Aubonne tells her story, as in the later version, and calls upon her husband, a good old soldier, as witness. The duc then tells of a "billet secret" ("secret letter") long concealed by the soldier; threatened with death and with tortures, the soldier sticks by the story. Presented with this "entière évidence," the king is not deceived: "On ne le trompe point; il sait sonder les coeurs: / Art difficile et grand qu'il doit à ses malheurs" (p. 387: "He cannot be deceived; he knows how to sound the depths of hearts, great and difficult skill that he owes to his misfortunes"). "Henri n'est pas le seul dont j'adore la loi" (p. 388: "Henri is not the only one whose law I adore"), Charlot, now a marquis, declares at the end, as offstage shouts of "Vive le roi!" conclude the play.

Early editions of Voltaire's works (such as the 1772 edition published in Lausanne by Grasset) print the earlier version of the play. Charlot's reminder that God's providence not be confused with the king's, the detail of the tortures threatened Mme Aubonne's husband, the king's own absence from the scene complicate a dénouement that Voltaire later simplified into a short moment of listening, confirming, and pardoning. Nor does the king at the end of the original *Charlot* invite the young man to join with him in seeking glory or promote him to the level of comte. Altogether, the second version presents a more magical dénouement and, by means of the king's physical appearance at the end, focuses the characters' (and the audience's) gratitude upon the figure of the monarch himself. Gustav III, however, is much more likely to have used the first version as his source.

By deleting the reference to the king's misfortunes, Voltaire made his play both less obviously historical and more obviously monarchical; the background of civil war is removed in the same gesture. Gustav's play, on the other hand, is filled with historical detail. Both plays open upon a scene in which some residents of the countess's estate discuss the king's impending arrival. A bailiff (comically pedantic in Gustav's play) is doing accounts. Voltaire's bailiff recalls a siege from the king's latest campaign: three peasants who had broken through the lines in search of food were sentenced to be hanged, but the king spared them. "Le bon roi! le grand roi!" the group exclaim together (I.i, p. 346). Far more circumstantial is the exposition in Gustav's play. Forty-seven years ago, the bailiff recalls, the countess left here with her late husband, Erik Stenbock: "Skrifva vi ej i dag den 23 Juni 1620? och det var tisdagen för Palmsöndagen 1573, som salig Herr Erik förde bort hennes Nåd" (237: "Isn't today June 23, 1620? And it was the Tuesday before Palm Sunday 1573 that blessed Lord Erik took her Grace away").[34]

Such detail, along with the discussion of the special dispensation necessary for the marriage, fixes the events of the play much more specifically in historical time.

Gustav Adolph's visit is a pilgrimage of peace. The countess's whole family was massacred by Gustav's father, Charles IX; she supported his enemy, the rival claimant Sigismund in the recent dynastic wars. "Hvad orsak skulle föra honom hit ut till mig, som han aldrig sett? hvars hela slägt blifvit uppoffrad af dess faders grymhet" (p. 244: "What cause can bring him here to me, whom he's never seen, whose whole family was sacrificed to his father's cruelty?"). Gustav is doing everything he can to help the families of his father's victims and to effect reconciliation. "Ack! Om jag kunde låta allt mitt blod rinna att bota dess sår!" he exclaims upon meeting the countess (II.vii, p. 270: "Oh! If only I could let all my blood flow to heal this wound!"). Where Voltaire, in the first version of *Charlot,* keeps Henri offstage, and in the second confines him to a final epiphany, Gustav introduces his idealized monarch in the middle of the second act. His attendance at the wedding is part of his grand scheme of reconciliation, and, more importantly, Gustav Adolph is aware of the true identities of the young men, as we learn immediately after his first appearance. His purpose in keeping the secret is to study them, and to put to the test Märta Baner's fidelity and love.

In *Charlot,* the king's attendance at the wedding is a happy coincidence. The focus in *The Magnanimity of Gustav Adolph* thus significantly shifts to the king from the two young men. Voltaire's play concentrates upon their rivalry; the lowborn Charlot's superior manners are contrasted to the crudeness of the marquis. In the person of the marquis, Voltaire is able to indict the high-handed conduct of the nobility (and, of course, by means of the revelation of the secret of the marquis' low birth, to defuse that indictment at the play's end). In both plays, the putative nobleman gives a servant a box on the ear. In *Charlot,* Guillot, the servant, explains to Babet, a serving girl, that the blow was caused by jealousy. Despite being engaged to Julie, the marquis is attracted to Babet, and Guillot complains:

Oh bien, il en veut donc avoir deux à la fois?
Ces jeunes grands seigneurs ont de terribles droits;
Tout doit être pour eux, femmes de cour, de ville,

Et de village encore: ils en ont une file;
Ils vous écrèment tout, et jamais n'aiment rien.

(I.ii, p. 350: Well, he wants both of them at once? These young
great lords have awful powers. Everything must be theirs: women
of the court, the city, and even the village; they have a whole line
of them. They skim off the cream of you, and never love any of
you.)

For womanizing, Gustav substitutes a less highly charged aristocratic
vice, hunting. Anders, the servant, is ordered by Sparre to take his gun
upstairs. Prudently, he asks if it is loaded. "Det vore en stor olycka om
en svinhund som du sköt ihjel sig: man får hundrade sådana igen,"
Sparre snarls (I.v, p. 249: "That would be just too bad if a dog like you
shot himself to death. There are hundreds more like you"). In both
plays, this crudeness excites comment. "Il a l'âme bien dure," Guillot
mutters aside, "Les mains aussi" (I.iv, p. 353: "He's got a hard soul;
hard hands, too"). In Gustav's play, the countess witnesses the blow
and directly scolds her son.

When she reminds him that he should prepare himself for marriage,
he is indifferent: "Välan! I afton, i dag, i morgon; det är så godt den
ena dagen som den andra" (I.v, p. 250: "Oh, well, this afternoon, today,
tomorrow; just as well one day as another"). Voltaire's young marquis
has to be persuaded to give up Babet for Julie. He learns from his
mother that she is rich: "Elle est riche? Tant mieux; / Marions-nous
bientôt" (I.iv, p. 355: "She's rich? So much the better. Let's get married
right away"). Märta Baner, aside, comments on her fiancé after she
hears his response: "Hvad han är plump!" (I.v, p. 250: "How crude he
is!"). Julie, fortunately, is not present at the corresponding moment to
hear the sentiments of the marquis. Despite their indifference, the two
false noblemen explode with jealous rage when they discover their
fiancées involved in musical tutelage with the supposed commoner.
The marquis makes lewd suggestions about the dancing lesson Charlot is giving Julie. After Sparre has interrupted a singing lesson for
Märta, Erik, no longer capable of controlling himself, confesses to
Lucia (whom he believes to be his mother) his hopeless passion for
Märta. Jealousy, in both plays, leads the two young men to the point
of violence.

In Gustav's play this dangerous energy does not lead to death.

Where Voltaire's Charlot is forced to kill the marquis in self-defence, Gustav's Erik is shot and wounded by the marquis. While Gustav Adolph explains to the countess that Erik is her true son and Sparre the nursemaid's boy, we see Sparre exit carrying his gun (which we know from its first act appearance to be loaded). Erik (the true Sparre) is shot, but only slightly wounded; he pleads for his would-be killer's life. Erik, who has already demonstrated his nobility in battle under the king's command, further demonstrates it here; the nobility of Charlot, on the other hand, has yet to be proved in battle.

"Glöm i denna stund att det är er Konung som ni ser; glöm ännu mer, att Carl IX:s son talar vid Gustaf Baners dotter. Men kom allenast ihåg, att Gustaf I:s sonson är eder närmaste frände, och att Gustaf Adolph är känd för att ömma svaghet och beskydda oskuld," Gustav Adolph addresses Märta Baner when they are alone together in the second act (II.x, p. 276: "Forget at this moment that it is your king you see; forget even further, that Charles IX's son is speaking with Gustav Baner's daughter. Bear only this in mind: that the grandson of Gustav I is your closest kinsman, and that Gustav Adolph is famed for his compassion for the powerless and protection of the weak"). Here the king, who in Gustav's play is the architect of all the play's events, finds it difficult to explain himself to Märta. In part, history is to blame: Charles IX has many sins to answer for, and Gustav is trying his best to eradicate his father's memory. Instead he invokes his blood tie with Märta, and, skipping a generation, urges her to remember not his father but his grandfather. But while urging her to forget that he is the king, he almost simultaneously urges her to remember his reputation for clemency and justice. Only in him, and not in the office, do the two coincide.

And not only in Gustav Adolph. The playwright-king, Gustav III, also wants to be recognized for who he is. Like the character in his play, Gustav III repudiates his father in favor of more glorious ancestors of his own choosing. Gustav II Adolph, Gustav I Vasa, are invoked to fill that space and to create a genealogy of nobility, clemency, and justice that skips the occasional generation. While Gustav III has no paternal crimes to expiate, he does have to reeducate his court in the meaning of monarchy, to educate a nobility used to limited monarchical prerogatives in the aesthetics as well as the politics of absolutism. In the suspenseful final moments of *The Magnanimity of Gustav Adolph,* the king's master plan seems about to unravel with the shots and the confused news of one death. These hints of possible failure suggest the delicacy of the enterprise. But luck is on the king's side: the false Sparre is a bad shot.

The king in the play is a playwright, staging a test for Märta and arranging for her to give a favor to Erik as he becomes a knight. He times his disclosure of the secret and is himself sole custodian of the letter that tells all. His timing almost fails. But the timing of the playwright who is also a king, the author, is flawless. Where Voltaire's Charlot can recall that there are two laws, the king's and God's, to which he owes his gratitude, in Gustav's play the laws of chance that circumscribe his hero-king are themselves subject to the monarch's royal authorship. Gustav III's ability to dramatize both the power and the limitations of Gustav Adolph's magnanimity testifies to his own mastery of more than merely that virtue.

"Henri IV est véritablement le héros de la pièce," Voltaire declared, explaining the king's absence from the play: "mais il avait déjà paru dans *la Partie de Chasse,* représentée sur le même théâtre; et on n'a pas voulu imiter ce qu'on ne pouvait égaler" (*Preface* to *Charlot,* p. 343: "Henri IV is the real hero of the play: but he had already appeared in *The Hunting Party,* performed on the same stage, and one did not wish to imitate what one could not equal"). Gustav felt no similar reluctance to imitate Charles Collé's popular play, *La Partie de chasse de Henri IV* (1774), any more than he was unwilling to admit his ideal monarch to the stage. On September 11, 1783, the Society for the Improvement of the Swedish Language performed a new play, *Gustav Adolph and Ebba Brahe,* before the court at the Drottningholm palace theater. The play, like Collé's, takes the form of a three-act comedy of intrigue in historical costume, a form which would be perfected several generations later by Scribe.

In the French play, the hunting party in question leads the king, lost in the woods, to the home of a humble miller. There he shares a simple meal, delights in the simple folk's country songs, and is overcome with emotion when they, all unaware of who sits at their table, urge him to join them in drinking the health of the king. "Je n'y puis . . . plus tenir. . . . Je suis prêt à verser des larmes . . . de tendresse et de joie," he confides, aside, as they press him (III.xiii, p. 179: "I can't . . . keep it up. . . . I am about to burst into tears . . . of tenderness and joy").[35] He flirts with the miller's charming daughter and helps to do the dishes. Agathe, a country girl who has been kidnapped and taken to Paris by the marquis de Conchini, interrupts the party: she has escaped and hurried here to rejoin her fiancé, the miller's son, Richard. Richard will have none of her; when the marquis and two other noblemen arrive, in search of the king, Henri is able to clear her reputation and expose the marquis as the sole author not only of her disgrace but also of attempting to engineer the fall of the king's loyal supporter, the duc de Sulli. The miller's son receives ten thousand francs to marry Agathe, and the daughter a like sum to marry her simple swain. Restored to favor, Sulli rises at the end to scold the king for his willingness to risk his life for the thrills of the hunt:

> Ah! mon cher maître, par ces traits de justice et de générosité, vous me ravissez. Vous venez d'en agir en roi et en père avec ces bons paysans, qui sont vos sujets et vos enfants, tout aussi bien que votre noblesse: mais, sire, vous devez aux uns et aux autres de ne point vous exposer votre vie à la chasse, comme vous faites tous les jours. . . . [*avec colère*] Permettez-moi de le dire à votre majesté, cela me met, moi, dans une véritable colère. . . . Vive Dieu, sire, votre vie n'est point à vous; vous en êtes comptable [*montrant le duc de Bellegarde*] à des serviteurs comme nous, qui vous adorent, [*montrant les paysans*] et au peuple français, dont vous voyez que vous êtes l'idôle.
>
> (III.xviii, pp. 190–91: Ah, my dear lord, you ravish me with these marks of justice and generosity. You have just acted as king and father to these good peasants, who are your subjects and your children, just as much as are your nobility. But, sire, you owe it to the one and to the other not to risk your life hunting, as you do every day. [*With anger*] Permit me to say to your majesty, this makes me, personally, really angry. May God be praised, sire, your life doesn't belong to you. You owe it to your servants like us [*pointing to the duc de Bellegarde*], who love you, and to the French people, who, you see [*pointing to the peasants*], idolize you.)

The assembled crowd of nobles and peasants cheers; Henri agrees to forgo dangerous pleasure in the future.

In the Swedish king's play, however, Gustav Adolph must forego much more. Court intrigue deprives him of his happiness, as Ebba Brahe, the woman he has loved and hoped to marry since childhood, is maneuvered, during his absence, into marriage with Count de la Gardie. The king's mother is behind the plot: Ebba, Gustav, and de la Gardie are all innocent victims. Gustav III uses Collé's device, the king's visit incognito with his ordinary subjects, but tranforms it into a proximate cause of the king's misery. Despite his mother's interception of his letters to Ebba (and her creative misinterpretation of the messages that do come through), Gustav is ahead of schedule on his way back to Kalmar, where Ebba awaits him, from the front. The fatal delay is caused when, waiting for a ferry to take him to Ebba, Gustav saves Erik, the ferryman's nephew, from drowning on his wedding day. Like Henri, Gustav Adolph hears his people praise him. When Johan, the ferryman, celebrates the king's victory, Gustav, like Henri, is deeply touched. "Hvad det är ljuft att se sig så älskad" (II.vii, p. 92: "How sweet it is to see oneself so beloved"), he confides aside. To Johan, he continues, "Far! Er glädje öfver segern och tillgifvenhet för er Kung skulle röra honom mycket, om han den såg . . . han vore derföre mycket erkänsam" ("Old man, your joy in the victory and your devotion to your king would move him greatly, if he could see it . . . he would be most appreciative"). When Gustav learns that Johan has a son named Sven, he almost betrays himself, for the same Sven saved his life in the battle.

The king is immediately given a chance to show his appreciation of this devotion, as Erik's boat founders. The king carries the unconscious lad into the hut; Sven, simultaneously, arrives. In Collé's play, the nobles' interruption leads to the recognition of the king; here Gustav is recognized by Sven, who acknowledges a reciprocity in their saving of lives. "Jag har då ej gjort mer än jag dig var sklydig; den minsta af mina undersåters lif är mig kärare än mitt" (II.ix, p. 97: "Then I have done no more than I owed to you; the life of the least of my subjects is dearer to me than my own"), the king tells him. Again, two couples of commoners are united with the king's help: Erik was betrothed to Sven's sister, Sven to Erik's. But where Henri merely gives the young people some money, Gustav Adolph will give up his happiness for them. "Ja, himmel! jag hoppas för mycket på din rättvisa, för att tro att den stund jag dröjt att uppfylla en Kungs, menniskas yppersta skyldigheter, att frälsa en undersåtes lif, att göra godt, skall störta min ofriga lifstid i sorg, och gifva döden åt mitt hjerta" (II.x, p. 99: "Oh, heaven! I expect too much from your justice to believe that the moment I have spent fulfilling a king's, any person's, highest duty, saving the life of a subject, doing a good deed, will ruin the rest of my life with grief and strike death to my heart"), the king prays as he sets forth again. But it is too late: the two peasant couples find their happiness, but the king finds Ebba Brahe already married.

Despite the fraudulence of the marriage, she refuses to divorce de la Gardie. Heaven has intervened; her suspicions, her susceptibility to the queen's cunning, her new resolve to remain faithful to de la Gardie, are all signs of the divine will. At length Gustav agrees to this view: "Uppfyllom Himmelens dom; Han har ej tillåtit min lycka. Han har ej velat vår förening, på det att mitt hjerta, lemnad endast åt fäderneslandet, skulle fara det endast troget" (III.vi, p. 116: "Let Heaven's judgment be fulfilled. He has not permitted my happiness. He has not permitted our marriage, so that my heart, entirely given over to my country, can be utterly faithful to it"), Gustav vows. The peasants, happier than he, enter; as they plead with him to live only for them, Gustav is deeply moved. "Gud! Hvad syn! hvad kärlek! Hvad rörande tafla! Hela min själ är deraf betagen" (p. 117: "God! What a sight! What love! What a moving tableau! My whole soul is overwhelmed"). "Quel spectacle divin!" (III.xviii, p. 191; "What a divine spectacle!"), Henri exclaims aside as the peasants plead with him to give up hunting. By making the brief visit with the peasants a matter of life and death, by making Gustav's good deed incorporate the forfeit of his happiness, Gustav III transforms the hunting party into a royal apotheosis. Collé's earthy monarch is a man of the people; Gustav's idealized Gustav Adolph is a man chosen for greatness by God.

Both of the plays about Gustav Adolph, like their source plays, end with loud praise of the king. But in the Swedish plays, as in neither Voltaire's *Charlot* nor Collé's *La Partie de chasse,* the king takes a moment to acknowledge the applause. The Countess offers the people's gratitude, love, and devotion to Gustav Adolph at the end of *Magnanimity,* and the king accepts: "Det är en god Konungs största belöning" (V.xii, p. 301: "That is a good king's greatest recompense"). "Varen tillfreds," Gustav Adolph tells the peasants at the end of *Ebba Brahe,* "det är er lycka, er kärlek och mitt folks väl, som skall trösta mig och utplåna minnet af min sorg" (V.vii, p. 119; "Be content: your happiness, your love, and the well-being of my people shall comfort me and wipe out the memory of my sorrow"). Gustav III, in these endings, makes explicit that the people's love of the king is a kind of compensation, in the one instance for being magnanimous and in the other for personal loss. As the plays end, this notion of reward within the plot transfers from the monarch on the stage to the monarch who has written and staged the entertainment. The applause that accompanies these stirring last lines is applause that celebrates the playwright-king, that in effect compensates him for his endeavors, his sacrifices, in creating the play.

The audience's applause thus becomes identified with the love of the people that is glorified within the plays' plots. The original audience to *The Magnanimity of Gustav Adolph* clearly recognized themselves mirrored onstage in the countess and the grateful lovers (played on that occasion by Armfelt and his fiancée). The playbill issued for the occasion announced a drama in five acts, "applaudissementer tillåtas och Piecen äfven får siffleras" ("applause is permitted, and the play may even be hissed"). "Les applaudissements sont permits," Oxenstierna wrote to a friend. "Vous sentez qu'ils ne manqueront pas" ("Applause is permitted. You can be sure that there will be no lack of it"). According to Fersen's report of the occasion, lackeys and chambermaids, who had been invited to watch the performance from recessed vantage points in the domed ceiling of the playhouse, were loud in their approval. "Hofmännen täflade om hvem skulle kunna klappa händerna starkast, och alla blefvo hofmännen," he grumbled ("The courtiers competed for who could clap the loudest, and everyone became a courtier").[36] The coy "permission" of applause worked perhaps too well.

When the plays of Gustav III moved from the court stages where they received their premieres into the professional theater, applause became an even more explicit political statement. As Levertin points out, members of the royal family were greeted with applause as they entered the theater. The idealized portraits of kings, not only in Gustav's plays but also in the rest of the repertoire permitted on the professional stage, encouraged audiences in extending the identification. All kings in Gustavian drama fuse into a single figure, "Gustaf III, den folkkäre härskaren, som genom ett oblodigt statsstreck gjort slut på 'frihetstidens fördömda partianda'" ("Gustav III, the people's beloved sovereign, who with a bloodless coup had brought to an end the 'damned party politics of *frihetstiden*'").[37] The king's popularity was at its height in Stockholm, and when his opera, *Gustav Vasa,* was first performed, its reception was marked with effusions of loyalty and praise.

Johan Kellgren set *Gustav Adolph and Ebba Brahe* into verse after its first performance, working apparently from the king's Swedish draft. *Gustav Vasa,* on the other hand, was a project in which Kellgren was involved from the very beginning. Almost from the very moment of his *coup d'état* in 1772, Gustav III had planned an opera based upon the great liberator of his country. The project was also closely connected with Gustav Adolph: at that time, Karl Fredrik Adelcrantz, the king's architect, had begun work on a statue of Gustav Adolph for the square that bore his name. Adelcrantz had designed theaters for Gustav's mother both at Ulriksdal (the Confidence) and at Drottning-holm, and had renovated the Drottningholm theater for Gustav in the 1780s; he became an obvious choice to build Gustav III's new opera house. Located on Gustav Adolphs Torg (Square), the building was begun in 1775 and finished in 1782. Work on the opera itself likewise proceeded slowly. Kellgren reported that he had almost finished the libretto in 1782; J. G. Naumann composed the music during a visit to Sweden in 1782–83. In 1784, Gustav invited the French scene designer, Louis-Jean Desprez, to Sweden. "Nous ne sommes en Suède que deux à avoir de la fantaisie: Desprez et moi," he is said to have proclaimed ("We are the only two in Sweden who have any imagination, Desprez and I".)[38]

With a German composer, a French designer, and a libretto based upon a French translation of an English play (Henry Brooke's *Gustavus Vasa, or, the Father of his Country,* 1739), *Gustav Vasa* was a project truly European in its scope. The large, state-of-the-art stage at the opera house permitted ambitious scenic effects impossible in the smaller court theaters. Fersen reported that the king was devoting extraordinary atten-tion to design: "Konungen arbetade med en utomordentlig trägenhet, tillsammans med sin dekorationsmålare Desprès, för att påhitta the-ater-effekter; han ville låta kavalleri synas och strida på theatern; använder metallkanoner för att dermed skjuta brèche på tornet af Christiern tyrans slott i Stockholm; han ville med ett ord omöjligheter" ("The king worked with extraordinary diligence, together with his scene painter Desprez, inventing theater effects. He wants the cavalry to appear and do battle on the stage; he is using metal cannons to blast a breach in the tower of Christiern the tyrant's castle in Stockholm. In a word, he wants impossibilities").[39] In place of the modest settings and amateur premieres of the Gustav Adolph plays, the new opera house offered magnificent scene changes and professional voices.

Gustav III and Kellgren, working together on the script, followed Gustav's original plan for an opera without a love interest. Where Brooke's play (the first play to be suppressed under England's licensing act of 1737) was full of stirring speeches on the theme of "Liberty," the mainspring of its plot was an amorous rivalry between Gustav Vasa and Christiern (*sic* in both English and Swedish texts) of Denmark. This persists (or is emphasized even more strongly) in the French version of the play by Du Clairon (1766).[40] In the Swedish opera, however, Gustav Vasa is motivated solely by the love of his country. The emotion that reinforces his patriotism is revenge.

Both Brooke's play and the opera begin underground. Brooke opens with a scene in the copper mines of Dalarna, where Gustavus, incognito, awaits the time to rise up and deliver his people from bondage. The opera, however, opens upon the dungeon in Christiern's castle in Stockholm, where Gustav's mother and sister are kept prisoner. The focus has clearly shifted from Gustav's own strategic difficulties to the plight of Christiern's victims. The sizeable chorus of widows and orphans, crying out to heaven for justice and dreaming of Gustav's return, represents the plight of the whole country. Rather than seeing a hero gathering up his strength, we begin by seeing Sweden groaning in its chains.

Christiern demonstrates his tyranny not, as in the English play, by threatening Gustav's beloved, but by sending Gustav the message that if he persists in his siege of Stockholm, his mother and sister will be put to death. Gustav consults his soldiers: "Om man fordrade af någon ibland eder, att försaka fosterlandets beskydd, eller att förlora en maka, en syster eller moder, hvad blefve edert svar?" (II.iv, p. 24: "If it were demanded of any of you to yield in the protection of your native land or to lose a wife, a sister, or a mother, what would your answer be?"). The voices build as one soldier after another (joining into a quartet) reminds Gustav of the sacrifices they have made already, and vow, in chorus, striking their swords on their shields, to follow Gustav to victory or death. Norrby, Christiern's ambassador but himself of noble nature and moved by this sight, hastens to return this answer to the tyrant.

The operatic form provides a new dimension in Gustav III's drama, for now the people's effusions of loyalty can become fully integrated into the spectacle, orchestrated and choreographed. Shouts of praise and tears of gratitude, set to inspiring music, become an essential part of the experience. The audience's applause, sought after by the endings of the Gustav Adolph plays yet slightly annoying when offered up throughout, is an acceptable response to every aria, every choral high point in the opera. In the conventions of this form, applause is not merely "permitted" but *de rigueur*. Despite the individual fame of each of Gustav's collaborators, this applause redounds primarily to the credit of the royal impresario himself.

Opera also permits the introduction of supernatural elements. While characters in the Gustav Adolph plays invoke divine providence for aid in their confusion, providence remains indirect in its action, working through the magnanimity and prudence of the king. Royal apotheosis, in *Gustav Vasa,* on the other hand, comes about through the direct manifestation of Sweden's guardian angel. The night before the assault on Stockholm, Gustav Vasa prepares himself sadly for sleep, not daring to hope for his mother's life. The angel urges him to trust in victory and departs, invoking "glada drömmar" ("pleasant dreams") for Gustav's sleep and "fasansfulla drömmar" ("horrible dreams") to torment the sleep of Christiern the tyrant (II.vii, p. 27.) The dreams enter: Honor crowns Gustav with laurels, Victory lays a trophy at his feet. Meanwhile, Treachery approaches the bed where Christiern lies sleeping and presents him with a crown and a shield with the Swedish coat of arms; Conscience torments him with snakes; Hatred shakes a torch over his head, while Revenge crushes his crown and, seizing the shield, presents it to the spirit of Pallas, who together with Victory, hangs the shield over Gustav's head. The scene changes, to show Gustav the promise of his victory; another scene change, and the Temple of Immortality appears, where Honor, Victory, and Pallas crown Gustav with flowers. The second act ends as Gustav awakens, comforted and inspired by these visions; the third act opens upon a badly shaken Christiern, fighting to regain control of himself and reject the troubling voice of conscience.

The transformations that had characterized court masque in the era of Inigo Jones had become, by the eighteenth century, the characteristic stock-in-trade of opera.[41] Gustav III deploys the full range of scenic effects here; the allegorical spectacle must inspire not only Gustav Vasa but also the audience. To make sure of that effect, the act break facilitates an interruption for sufficient applause. The second act ends upon Gustav's awakening; for the response of Christiern to his nightmares, the audience must wait for the beginning of the third act.

This is a significant alteration from what has generally been recognized as the source for the scene: the visit of the ghosts to the tents of Richard III and his challenger, Richmond, at Bosworth Field in Shakespeare's *Richard III*. In Shakespeare's play, each ghost delivers a message—of despair to Richard, of hope to Richmond—to each in turn. Richard's panicky awakening precedes Richmond's tranquil one. In *Gustav Vasa,* each king receives a separate allegorical masque, and the audience is only allowed to see Christiern's panic after the musical climax of Gustav Vasa's apotheosis has garnered their applause. The balance struck in Shakespeare's split staging shifts, as Christiern's fears become the prologue to his defeat rather than the result of his dreams.

Nor is Christiern tormented, as Richard is, by the ghosts of his victims. Rather, he is taught the same lesson that the masque that visits Gustav Vasa teaches: that tyranny is self-defeating. Throughout the opera, Christiern's tyrannical behavior is exaggerated, overdone. Ruling through fear, craving revenge, forcing Gustav to choose between his mother and his country, Christiern is a Gengis-Kan. The similarity extends to the degree to which these tyrants are allowed to be dangerous: where Gustav III, playing Gengis-Kan, both arouses and assuages his audience's fears, Christiern is doomed from the start. The opera's insistence on historical inevitability (we know before even seeing the first scene in the prison that Sweden will be liberated) is compounded by the celebratory nature of its performance.[42] Christiern is a demon to be exorcised, a model (a straw man, as Diderot suggests?) of tyrannical absolutism to be deplored and ridiculed in Gustav's enlightened realm. His final appearance is on a stage machine, as the scene changes to the harbor of Stockholm and he and his Danes sail away from the victorious Swedes. Engulfed by scenery in this way, Christiern loses whatever status he enjoyed early in the opera as Gustav's opponent.

Dramatic tension that would fully explore the issues raised by *Gustav Vasa* is not, of course, its royal author's goal. Whatever is Shakespearean about the opera, it is not to be found in a demand for complexity of response from its audience.[43] The audience applauds the vision of national unity under a hero-king that materializes in the opera's spectacular transformations. But where Ben Jonson and Inigo Jones broke because of their dispute over who could be deemed the proper author of the masque's transformations, Gustav III is *Gustav Vasa*'s author in the fullest sense. Everything—the writing, the composing, the scene painting, the casting, the acting, the singing—associated with this production issues from and returns to the king. Gustav Vasa's apotheosis is a small triumph compared to the full mastery of the created world enjoyed by Gustav III.

If Gustav as king represents the antithesis to social mobility, as actor his career describes another kind of arc. From player (as crown prince and king) he moves on to become actor-manager at Gripsholm and then to take the part of collaborative playwright and *régissör* in his Swedish-language plays. With *Gustav Vasa,* his royal apotheosis (through his great ancestor) coincides with a theatrical triumph of corresponding totality. When Inigo Jones and Ben Jonson squabbled over who, designer or poet, was to be considered the "inventor" of a court masque, we can glimpse the beginnings of the modern idea of the director. This function, undertaken by Shakespeare or Molière in his company—as by Peter Quince in his—comes to overrule both designer and poet in Gustav's theater.

Under threat from an unruly nobility, the king expresses his absolutist fancy in an opera in which king and people fuse as one and expel the tyrannical intruder. Politically it was important for Gustav to cement relations with the citizens of Stockholm and the Swedish peasantry, and the Gustav Adolph plays and *Gustav Vasa* can be seen as part of this strategy. Yet the myth that they perpetuate, of a monarch misunderstood and misled by his courtiers but beloved by his people, is a myth that reaches back through Collé's *Partie de chasse de Henri IV* to Shakespeare's *Henry V* and beyond. The people's love embarrasses a disguised monarch like the duke in *Measure for Measure.* Through his use of the disguised-monarch motif, Gustav actively seeks it.

In the process he embraces the idea of king as actor-on-display that so disconcerted his English predecessors, Elizabeth and James. Rather than seeing Gustav's desire for applause as an expression of futile flight into a theatrical cloud-cuckoo-land, we can see it as another, powerful, example of the persistence of the analogy between player and king that is liberating, not demeaning. The special vitality of Michael Goldman's idea of the actor's freedom lies in the challenge the actor poses to established orders of being and codes of conduct. Gustav indulges this freedom, trying out various alternative roles at Gripsholm, from the crazed, tryannical Rhadamiste and Vendôme to the wise high priest of Jerusalem. In his more subtle reflections of himself in Gustav Adolph and Gustav Vasa, he continues to express an actorly freedom from his place as director and impresario, and the models of royal sacrifice and popular adoration that he presents win him the actor's reward of applause.

IV

Sir Henry Wotton, describing the production of Shakespeare's *Henry VIII* that caused the Globe theater to burn in 1613, found the staging excessively glorious. The play was "set forth with many extraordinary circumstances of Pomp and Majesty . . . sufficient in truth within a while to make greatness very familiar, if not ridiculous," Wotton complains.[44] The complaint is itself familiar: putting the splendor of rule onstage somehow degrades it. There is no novelty, Castiglione reminds us, for a prince to play a prince; and if he does so, he risks spreading the perception that what he must do in earnest is itself merely play. Wotton and Castiglione express the same fear of the actor's freedom that Axel Fersen experienced when he showered Gustav with ridicule for appearing at supper dressed as Rhadamiste. What is threatening is not that acting and splendid costume make the difference between real regal authority and its counterfeits disappear; rather it is that the difference between kings and subjects is revealed as the same as the difference between actors and audience members. What the aristocrats chafe against is their own relegation to the passive ranks of common spectators.

Henrietta Maria had to promise the authorities at Oxford that the costumes and sets for *The Royal Slave* would not find their way into the possession of common players who would borrow them at Hampton Court. When Madame de Maintenon had *Athalie* performed at Saint-Cyr, she sought to correct the excesses of *Esther* by requiring the girls to play in their regular class uniforms. Both feared contamination, just as Wotton appears to do. For Antonin Artaud, the theater *is* the plague: the worry of Henrietta Maria and Madame de Maintenon suggests that it is for them as well. The university officials worry that the taint of common playing might somehow rub off on the Oxford costumes; Madame de Maintenon tries to blame the costumes themselves for the refusal of *Esther* to remain simple, pure, and innocent of more than one meaning. In August 1664, Samuel Pepys went to the theater to see the Earl of Orrery's new play, *Henry V*. He enjoyed the "noble play," found in it "raptures of wit and sense." But he did not mention in his diary the costumes, which were especially fine. Edward Downes, however, did mention them: "This Play was Splendidly Cloath'd," he reported; "The King, in the Duke of York's Coronation Suit; Owen Tudor, in King Charles's; the Duke of Burgundy, in the Lord of Oxford's, and the rest all New."[45] The very idea that actual coronation garb could be used on the professional stage reveals the vast distance between Charles II and Henrietta Maria, his mother. The audience, however, took this innovation in stride. For neither Pepys nor Downes, apparently, does the risk of infection suggest itself. The English Restoration audience avoids noticing, as it did so many other problems that would return to haunt it, a reduction of greatness to familiarity that would have been shocking to previous and to subsequent generations.

Gustav's conduct is shocking in another, related way. Like Voltaire, he finds in his acting and in his proprietary role in the theater a freedom denied to him in his ordinary life. But where Voltaire arrogates to himself the freedom to play the king and to conduct himself as an equal to kings, the role that Gustav finds confining is that of king. What he prefers to play is the part of the master actor, Diderot's wicker man. Criticism of Shakespeare's *Richard II* has long found an index of Richard's ineffectuality in his theatricality: Shakespeare's king begins to play the role of king with great conviction only after he has lost all kingly power. Yet Bolingbroke too is himself a player: the facile distinction between player and king does not hold in the case of Gustav III any more than it does in the case of Richard II.

Playing the king neither thoroughly demystifies nor thoroughly mystifies being the king. The monarch in the audience is, no less than the actor playing the monarch on stage, open to the audience's attention, vulnerable, exposed. Yet the actor knows that the monarch in the audience has the power to end his performance, as Claudius does that of Lucianus and the Player King in *Hamlet,* by crying out for light and storming away, or, as Louis XIV ended the performances of *Tartuffe* for five years, by permitting a less easily readable suppression. In the play, it is when Tartuffe aspires to the royal role, playing out the king's "juste violence" before the hapless family, that the patient Exempt recognizes his cue and reveals the true identity of the notorious convict. The actor is forcibly returned to the social niche he would occupy without the king: prison.

By enacting the king's sacrifice, by playing out the tragic split of his two bodies or the comic union of them, actors can avoid prison and remind the king of their mutual dependence. This dependence has been examined here in plays performed at court, beginning with works of Shakespeare and ending with the plays of Voltaire and his royal imitator, Gustav III. The mutual dependence of king and actor in this period, I have argued, is a matter of such moment to playwrights, actors, and monarchs, that concern about it is central to the scripts of plays written when court performance is a mere possibility, just as it is central to the occasion of court performance itself. The wide range of materials collected here offers a wide range of attitudes toward the dynamic of royal performance. As Thomas Rymer noticed, the scrutiny turned upon the royal role in English seventeenth-century drama was extraordinary for its acuity and its skepticism. A similar complexity of perspective, if not a similar treatment of kings as "*Dogs*," can be found in the French drama. Corneille, Molière, and Racine do not merely hymn the absolutist ideal; they explore its potential for dramatic conflict, creating complex figures of opposition in Cinna, Tartuffe, and even the innocent Esther. For Voltaire, the royal role is one of spreading enlightenment, of transforming Sparta into Athens: when Louis XV and Frederick the Great fall short of the role, he discovers (as he had always suspected) that it was a role best suited to the monarch of wit. Excited by Voltaire's ideas, Gustav III emulated his hero's heroes, Louis XIV and Henri IV. His theater is so inextricably tied in with his policies that his agenda of liberation finds no better expression that *Gustav Vasa*.

Sponsoring theater does not mean, for the monarchs of the seventeenth and eighteenth centuries, sponsoring the means of their own embarrassment, exposure as a fraud, and debasement to the level of the common player. Nor did the French Revolution reduce Europe's monarchs to a crowd of posturing figureheads. Rather theater glorifies monarchy as no other institution can, for the actor can play out models of autonomy, forbearance, wisdom, and generosity that the monarch in the audience can aspire to, can even emulate. Or the actor can play the tyrant, the horrible opposite to the king in the audience. As court theater narrows its choice of potential participants to the innermost circles of the court (as at Madame de Pompadour's Petits Cabinets or at Gustav III's Gripsholm), the dynamic of royal performance persists, despite the exclusion of the common player. As we have seen, in the professional actor's absence, the idea of professional-ism becomes of special importance, as Madame de Pompadour demands that her performance exceed that of Mademoiselle Gaussin, and as Gustav expects high praise for his virtuosity, if not his royal virtue.

When kings and royal mistresses desire to be actors, when the greatest poet of the age, Voltaire, expects his guests to enjoy his playing as much as they admire his plays, acting can certainly be said to have achieved a status undreamed of by Puck, even as he promises to make amends. Shakespeare distinguishes his professional company from the bumbling mechanicals, but at the same time he suggests that a monarch should be as forbearing to professionals as to amateurs in the area of offense. One of the things that Lucio exposes in *Measure for Measure* is the duke's inadequacy as a playwright and an actor, his dependence upon the ridiculous coincidental death of Ragozine. Yet the duke's authority survives this momentary embarrassment, and Lucio is firmly put in his place. That the actor's place in the royal household is a fluid one, however, is clear enough in these plays. The fluidity of this relationship, first sketched out by Shakespeare, has been the object of our examination throughout this study.

Being the king and playing the king, the actor suggests, are not essentially different activities. Nor are they essentially the same. Rather, they are mutually dependent activities, sharing a dynamic doctrine of two bodies. When the king sits in the audience, watching the actor play the king, two bodies, not necessarily those of the political theory, appear before an audience's eye. Sometimes, as we have suggested to be the case in the court of Charles I, double vision can ensue. A royal couple, or, as in the case of *Esther,* another king in the audience can complicate both the decorum of the occasion and the meaning of the play. The royal role the actor strives to play is neither the same as nor different from the role the monarch plays: there is infinite variety in the model. What remains constant is the dynamic of royal performance, the exchange of energy the audience can witness as rivalry or as presumption. Unlike masques and courtly entertainments like carousels, plays that come to court come as much as interlopers as guests. Even in the most controlled environments, in the Petits Cabinets or at Gripsholm, plays bring with them complicated institutional histories and associations that persist to complicate a royal audience's or actor's experience.

Plays are written for actors at least as much as for audiences; in fact, the actor is the playwright's most important reader. Without the actors' approval of a play for performance, its submission to a royal censor becomes a matter of no moment. The actors' objections, not those of Duke Theseus and Hippolyta, cripple Peter Quince's play. That their objections anticipate negative responses from the royal audience testifies to a kind of self-censorship. Royal performance places the actor's authority and freedom into comparison with the king's authority and freedom. A discourse of rivalry, as we have seen, characterizes discussion of such performances. King and actor struggle for control over the event itself; distinctions between theatrical and political power blur. Normal decorums of both worlds are challenged. The orderly separation of audience from actor in the professional theater, each with its own clear responsibility, breaks down as the king demands his place in the audience's eye at court. The normal panegyric dynamic of court entertainment also breaks down when the entertainment is a play written for the scrutiny of actors, to survive the test of multiple professional performances, rather than a piece written to royal order for a single occasion.

For kings and actors, the end of the eighteenth century marks the end of a long tradition of institutional cooperation with the end of direct royal patronage of national theaters. Such patronage has nominally persisted, variously redefined, in the continued presence of the Comédie Française and in such recent innovations as the Royal Shakespeare Company and the Royal National Theatre. The royal mystique continues to lend respectability to acting. Conversely, the custodian of the royal mystique continues to be the actor. Despite radical changes in institutional structure, the actor and the king, in the mutual dependence of their two bodies, carry on the traditions of royal performance.

Notes

1 *Royal Performance,*
A Midsummer Night's Dream, *and a Royal Progress*

1. All citations from Shakespeare in the text are from William Shakespeare, *The Complete Works,* ed. Alfred Harbage (Baltimore: Penguin Books, 1969).

2. Baldesar Castiglione, *The Book of the Courtier,* here quoted from Sir Thomas Hoby's Elizabethan translation, Everyman's Library (London: J. M. Dent, 1928), pp. 99–100. See also Charles S. Singleton's translation (Garden City, N.Y.: Doubleday, 1959), pp. 103–4.

3. *The Poems and Letters of Andrew Marvell,* ed. H. M. Margoliouth, 3d ed., rev. Pierre Legouis and E. E. Duncan Jones (Oxford: Clarendon Press, 1971), 1:92. Among those who have discussed the theatricality of Charles's death in relationship to the demystifying powers of theater are: Anne Barton, "'He That Plays the King': Ford's *Perkin Warbeck* and the Stuart History Play," in *English Drama: Forms and Development, Essays in Honour of Muriel Clara Bradbrook,* ed. Marie Axton and Raymond Williams (Cambridge: Cambridge University Press, 1977), 69–93; Franco Moretti, "'A Huge Eclipse': Tragic Form and the Deconsecration of Sovereignty," and Stephen Orgel, "Making Greatness Familiar," both in *The Power of Forms in the English Renaissance,* ed. Stephen Greenblatt (Norman: University of Oklahoma Press, 1982). David Scott Kastan, "'Proud Majesty Made a Subject': Shakespeare and the Spectacle of Rule," *Shakespeare Quarterly* 37

(1986), 459–75, lays special stress upon theater as a demystifying institution; Nancy Klein Maguire, "The Theatrical Mask/Masque of Politics: The Case of Charles I," *Journal of British Studies* 28 (1989), 1–22, documents the persistence of the royal mystique through the Interregnum. For a discussion of *Henry V* itself in this context, see Christopher Pye, *The Regal Phantasm: Shakespeare and the Politics of Spectacle* (London: Routledge, 1990), 13–42.

4. *Regicide and Revolution: Speeches at the Trial of Louis XVI,* edited with an introduction by Michael Walzer, trans. Marian Rothstein (Cambridge: Cambridge University Press, 1974), pp. 85–86.

5. John Selden, *Table Talk,* ed. Frederick Pollock (London, 1927), p. 61; quoted from Walzer, *Regicide and Revolution,* p. 16.

6. Franco Moretti, *Signs Taken for Wonders: Essays in the Sociology of Literary Forms,* trans. Susan Fischer, David Forgacs, and David Miller (London: Verso, 1983), p. 68.

7. The doctrine's full dimensions are described in Ernst H. Kantorowicz, *The King's Two Bodies: A Study in Mediaeval Political Theology* (Princeton: Princeton University Press, 1957). See also Jean-Marie Apostolidès, *Le Prince sacrifié* (Paris: Minuit, 1985) for a discussion of the king as martyr or scapegoat.

8. William Davenant, *The Fair Favourite,* in *The Dramatic Works of Sir William D'Avenant* (Edinburgh: William Paterson, 1872–73), 4:211.

9. Michael Goldman, *The Actor's Freedom: Toward a Theory of Drama* (New York: Viking, 1975) speaks of the actor's power as "terrific": "Whatever primitive images he may suggest," and among them are those of the shaman and the year-king, "the energy he projects by being other-than-himself is fundamental to his art" (pp. 8, 10–11). This "otherness" is common to kings and actors. See also Mendel Kohansky, *The Disreputable Profession: The Actor in Society,* Contributions in American Studies 72 (Westport, Conn.: Greenwood Press, 1984): "Thus the actor assumes the social role of the sacrificial goat who takes upon himself the spectator's uncommitted sins. As such he inspires both gratitude for lifting the burden of sin off the spectator's shoulders, and for assuming it the revulsion one feels towards the sinner" (p. 5).

10. Anne Righter [Barton], *Shakespeare and the Idea of the Play* (London: Chatto and Windus, 1962), p. 104.

11. Keith Sturgess, *Jacobean Private Theatre,* Theatre Production Series (London: Routledge and Kegan Paul, 1987), p. 25.

12. E. K. Chambers, *The Elizabethan Stage* (Oxford: Clarendon Press, 1923), 3:224–25. *The Tempest, The Winter's Tale, Julius Caesar, Othello, 1 and 2 Henry IV,* and *Much Ado About Nothing* (twice) were the Shakespeare plays selected for this occasion. For the full list, see Yoshiko Kawachi, *Calendar of English Renaissance Drama, 1558–1642* (New York: Garland Press, 1986), p. 159.

13. The quotation is from Charles Carlton, "Three British Revolutions and the Personality of Kingship," in *Three British Revolutions: 1641, 1688, 1766,* ed. J. G. A. Pocock (Princeton: Princeton University Press, 1980), p. 194; but similar quotations can be found almost anywhere.

14. See Daniel Arasse, *The Guillotine and the Terror,* trans. Christopher Miller

(London: Allen Lane, Penguin Press, 1989), especially part II, "Mechanical Effects," pp. 31–73.

15. Sir Philip Sidney, *The Defence of Poesy,* in *Sir Philip Sidney,* The Oxford Authors, ed. Katherine Duncan-Jones (Oxford: Oxford University Press, 1989), p. 230.

16. The word *director* in this sense is anachronistic, but in this study this word will describe the function. Someone has to tell the actors where to stand and control their jockeying for stage space and audience attention. One of Gustav's contemporaries refers to him as a *régissör,* an obvious borrowing into Swedish of a French word that still means "director" in the modern theatrical sense.

17. For a summary of the vicissitudes of this play, see Marvin Carlson, *The Theatre of the French Revolution* (Ithaca: Cornell University Press, 1966), pp. 1–6.

18. Such as, for example, George Steiner, *The Death of Tragedy* (London: Faber and Faber, 1961) and Maurice Valency, *The Flower and the Castle: An Introduction to Modern Drama* (New York: Macmillan, 1963).

19. *Antitheatrical* is used here, and throughout this study, in the sense fully developed by Jonas Barish in *The Antitheatrical Prejudice* (Berkeley and Los Angeles: University of California Press, 1981). Goldman, *The Actor's Freedom,* pp. 8–9, refers to Barish's idea of the "ontological subversiveness" of the actor.

20. *An Apology for the Life of Mr. Colley Cibber,* ed. Robert W. Lowe (London: John C. Nimmo, 1889), 2:213–15.

21. Herbert Blau, *The Audience* (Baltimore: Johns Hopkins University Press, 1990), p. 49. Blau prefaces this observation with the comment that "perhaps too much has been made of this by recent scholarship." Much new historicist criticism, especially the work of Stephen Greenblatt, has focused attention upon the serious question of power in the theater, but often with the effect of portraying the institution as monolithic and disregarding the complexity of performance.

22. In the prefatory material to the First Folio, quoted from Robert S. Knapp, *Shakespeare: The Theater and the Book* (Princeton: Princeton University Press, 1989), p. 3.

23. J. L. Styan's *Modern Drama in Theory and Practice,* 3 vols. (Cambridge: Cambridge University Press, 1981) offers a model of performance-oriented criticism. Harry Berger, *Imaginary Audition: Shakespeare on Stage and Page* (Berkeley and Los Angeles: University of California Press, 1989), attacks the limitations of performance-oriented criticism of Shakespeare, offering itself as "an attempt to recuperate standard features of armchair practice while maintaining a fairly strict focus on the drama of theatrical and interlocutory relations" (p. 45).

24. John G. Sweeney, *Jonson and the Psychology of Public Theater: To Coin the Spirit, Spend the Soul* (Princeton: Princeton University Press, 1985); Timothy Murray, *Theatrical Legitimation: Allegories of Genius in Seventeenth-Century England and France* (New York: Oxford University Press, 1987).

25. James L. Calderwood, *Shakespeare and the Denial of Death* (Amherst: University of Massachusetts Press, 1987), p. 180.

26. Philip C. McGuire, for example, calls for a "Different Paradigm" of criticism of play texts that would be to conventional literary analysis what quantum physics was to Newtonian; see McGuire, *Speechless Dialect: Shakespeare's Open Silences*

(Berkeley and Los Angeles: University of California Press, 1985), pp. 122–50.

27. Lynn Hunt, "History as Gesture; or, the Scandal of History," in *Consequences of Theory: Selected Essays from the English Institute, 1987–88*, New Series no. 14, ed. Jonathan Arac and Barbara Johnson (Baltimore: Johns Hopkins University Press, 1991), p. 103.

28. On the topic of the actor's status, see especially Jean Duvignaud, *L'Acteur: Esquisse d'une sociologie du comédien* (Paris: Gallimard, 1965), pp. 39–118.

29. Goldman, *The Actor's Freedom*, p. 55.

30. Thomas Rymer, *The Tragedies of the Last Age Consider'd and Examin'd*, with a preface by Arthur Freeman (New York: Garland Publishing, 1974), pp. 29–30.

31. For an account of this transformation, see Laura Brown, *English Dramatic Form, 1660–1760: An Essay in Generic History* (New Haven: Yale University Press, 1981).

32. Foucault's epistemes—Renaissance, Classical, and Enlightenment—mark radical discontinuities; they are delineated in Foucault, *The Order of Things*, trans. A. Sheridan (New York: Random House, 1970). On the architectural continuity of the stage, see Marvin Carlson, *Places of Performance: The Semiotics of Theatre Architecture* (Ithaca: Cornell University Press, 1989).

33. Unlike Ben Jonson, Shakespeare never went to jail; while there is evidence of the censors' attention to a number of Shakespearean texts, none created a scandal on the level of *Eastward Ho*, George Chapman's *Byron* plays, or Thomas Middleton's *A Game at Chess*. See Annabel Patterson, *Censorship and Interpretation: The Conditions of Writing and Reading in Early Modern England* (Madison: University of Wisconsin Press, 1984); Steven Mullaney, *The Place of the Stage: License, Play, and Power in Renaissance England* (Chicago: University of Chicago Press, 1988).

34. *Entertainments for Elizabeth I*, ed. Jean Wilson (London: Woodbridge, 1980), p. 42

35. Paul A. Olson, "*A Midsummer Night's Dream* and the Meaning of Court Marriage," *ELH* 24 (1957), 102. See also Nicholas Grene, *Shakespeare, Jonson, Molière: The Comic Contract* (London: Macmillan, 1980), p. 65; Joseph H. Summers, *Dreams of Love and Power* (Oxford: Clarendon Press, 1984), p. 20.

36. "Now, for the poet, he nothing affirms, and therefore never lieth" (Sidney, *The Defence of Poesy*, p. 235).

37. McGuire devotes a chapter to Hippolyta's silence: *Speechless Dialect*, pp. 1–18.

38. René Girard, "Myth and Ritual in Shakespeare's *A Midsummer Night's Dream*," in *Textual Strategies*, ed. Josué V. Harari (Ithaca: Cornell University Press, 1979), p. 212.

39. George Gascoigne, who wrote the play, says it was not performed because of "lack of opportunity and seasonable weather," but he also published the palliative play he was asked to put on instead, the queen "hasting her departure from thence." John Nichols, *The Progresses and Public Progressions of Queen Elizabeth* (1823; rpt. New York: Burt Franklin [1966]), 1:514, 515. See also Lisa Hopkins, *Elizabeth I and Her Court* (London: Vision Press, 1990), p. 147.

40. Thomas Churchyard, *A Discourse of the Queenes Maiesties entertainement in Suffolk and Norffolk: with a description of many things then presently seene* (London, 1578); the copy quoted in the text is the microfilm version of the Huntington Library copy. There is a transcription of Churchyard in Nichols, *The Progresses and Public Processions of Queen Elizabeth,* 2:179–215.

41. Louis Adrian Montrose, "'Shaping Fantasies': Figurations of Gender and Power in Elizabethan Culture," *Representations* 1:2 (1983), 61–94; quotations from pp. 61, 85, 77.

42. Alvin Kernan, *The Playwright as Magician* (New Haven: Yale University Press, 1979), p. 77.

43. It is not possible to ascertain whether Elizabeth saw the play or, if she did, whether the occasion was an important wedding. As Annabel Patterson complains, that Elizabeth did see the play at a wedding has become an unsubstantiated "fact": "Despite the difficulty that critics experience in finding an appropriate marital occasion in 1595–6, and an uneasy recognition that the play seems rather to *problematize* than celebrate marriage, it is somewhat alarming to see how readily this hypothesis has been absorbed as fact into texts designed for students" (Annabel Patterson, *Shakespeare and the Popular Voice* [Cambridge, Mass.: Basil Blackwell, 1989], p. 58). See John W. Draper, "The Queen Makes a Match and Shakespeare a Comedy," *Yearbook of English Studies* 2 (1972), 61–67, for one particularly recondite attempt to place Elizabeth on the scene of a premiere performance of *A Midsummer Night's Dream.*

44. Joel Fineman, "Fratricide and Cuckoldry: Shakespeare's Doubles," in *Representing Shakespeare: New Psychoanalytic Essays,* ed. Murray M. Schwartz and Coppélia Kahn (Baltimore: John Hopkins University Press, 1980), p. 73.

45. See, for an example of such solidarity, Germaine Greer, "Love and the Law," in *Politics, Power, and Shakespeare,* ed. Frances McNeely Leonard (Arlington: Texas Humanities Resource Center, 1981): "The people who do not change, the people who are constant, the people who are natural votaresses of Diana, are the two women, Helena and Hermia" (p. 39).

46. William A. Ringler, Jr., "The Number of Actors in Shakespeare's Early Plays," in *The Seventeenth-Century Stage: A Collection of Critical Essays,* ed. Gerald Eades Bentley (Chicago: University of Chicago Press, 1968), p. 133. In Peter Brook's famous 1971 production of the play the fairies were hefty stagehands.

47. Patterson, *Shakespeare and the Popular Voice,* p. 58.

2   "I love the people, but . . ."
Royal Performance and Royal Audience in the Court of James I

1. Quoted from J. E. Neale, *Elizabeth I and Her Parliaments* (New York: St. Martin's Press, 1958), 2:119.

2. "Elizabeth wanted [Mary] secretly killed, done away with in the old style," says Michael Walzer, "so that she could publicly repudiate the act. The horror she would have expressed (and perhaps even felt) on hearing of the assassination was the tribute she wanted to pay to sacred kingship, to Mary's regality and her own" (*Regicide and Revolution: Speeches at the Trial of Louis XVI,* edited and with an

introduction by Michael Walzer, trans. Marian Rothstein [Cambridge: Cambridge University Press, 1974], p. 50).

3. James I, *Workes* (1616; rpt. New York: G. Olms, 1971), p. 141.

4. Quoted from *James I by His Contemporaries,* ed. Robert Ashton (London: Hutchinson, 1969), p. 64.

5. *Regicide and Revolution,* p. 23.

6. Jean-Christophe Agnew, *Worlds Apart: The Market and the Theater in Anglo-American Thought* (Cambridge: Cambridge University Press, 1986), p. 148.

7. Josephine Waters Bennett, *"Measure for Measure" as Royal Entertainment* (New York: Columbia University Press, 1966).

8. Jonathan Goldberg, *James I and the Politics of Literature* (Baltimore: Johns Hopkins University Press, 1983), p. 235. See also Robert S. Knapp, *Shakespeare: The Theater and the Book* (Princeton: Princeton University Press, 1989), where *Measure for Measure* is characterized as "the one Shakespearean comedy that self-consciously situates itself as post-Elizabethan" (p. 215). Leah S. Marcus also discusses the issue of the play's apparent topicality (*Puzzling Shakespeare: Local Reading and its Discontents* [Berkeley and Los Angeles: University of California Press, 1988]), where she finds allusions to Hapsburg Vienna and the Treaty of London in the play. These allusions, however, shift in and out of focus: "What Shakespeare accomplished through the play's restlessly oscillating topicality was the initiation of a theatrical event which could be taken as Stuart propaganda or as the expression of a contemporary nightmare, or most likely as both together" (p. 200).

9. Richard Levin, *New Readings vs. Old Plays* (Chicago: University of Chicago Press, 1979), pp. 171–93.

10. Knapp, *Shakespeare,* p. 217.

11. Darryl G. Gless, *"Measure for Measure," the Law, and the Convent* (Princeton: Princeton University Press, 1979), p. 152.

12. Anne Barton, "The King Disguised: Shakespeare's *Henry V* and the Comical History," in *The Triple Bond,* ed. Joseph G. Price (University Park: Pennsylvania State University Press, 1975), pp. 92–117; Leonard Tennenhouse, "Representing Power: *Measure for Measure* in Its Time," in *The Power of Forms in the English Renaissance,* ed. Stephen Greenblatt (Norman: University of Oklahoma Press, 1982), pp. 139–56.

13. Gless, *"Measure for Measure,"* p. 245.

14. Goldberg, *James I,* p. 236.

15. Harriett Hawkins, *Measure for Measure,* Twayne New Critical Introductions to Shakespeare (Boston: Twayne, 1987), p. 113. The fullest discussion of the friar disguise in contemporary plays is Rosalind Miles, *The Problem of Measure for Measure* (London: Vision Press, 1976), pp. 167–75. Mary Ellen Lamb, "Shakespeare's 'Theatrics': Ambivalence toward Theater in *Measure for Measure,*" *Shakespeare Studies* 20 (1990), 129–45, argues that different interpretations of the duke's disguise issue from different attitudes toward the power of theater in the play, and so the question of whether duke's role-playing will have good or ill effect is unresolved.

16. Jonathan Dollimore, "Transgression and Surveillance in *Measure for Mea-*

sure," in *Political Shakespeare,* ed. Jonathan Dollimore and Alan Sinfield (Ithaca: Cornell University Press, 1985), p. 78.

17. The other "sheep-biter" in Shakespeare is Malvolio (*Twelfth Night,* II.v.5). The *OED* cites that line in support of the definition "a malicious or censorious fellow" (2a); of some interest in this context is definition 4: "One who runs after 'mutton'; a woman-hunter, whoremonger," precisely the reputation the duke seeks most to dodge.

18. For the argument that the duke does become a better ruler, see especially Cynthia Lewis, "'Dark Deeds Darkly Answered': Duke Vincentio and Judgment in *Measure for Measure,*" *Shakespeare Quarterly* 34 (1983), 271–89.

19. G. P. V. Akrigg, *Jacobean Pageant, or The Court of King James* (New York: Atheneum, 1967), pp. 232–33.

20 James I, *Workes,* p. 168.

21. Dollimore, "Transgression and Surveillance," p. 83.

22. Richard Monette, as Lucio in the production of *Measure for Measure* directed by Robin Phillips at Stratford, Ontario, in 1975, physically functioned as an intermediary with the audience, spending much of his time just between stage and auditorium, sharing with the audience his skepticism about the duke's enterprise: this was a Lucio who early on glimpsed the duke beneath the cowl.

23. Alfred Harbage, *Shakespeare and the Rival Traditions* (New York: Macmillan, 1952), p. 98.

24. Francis Osborne quoted from Goldberg, *James I,* p. 143.

25. Richard P. Wheeler, *Shakespeare's Development and the Problem Comedies: Turn and Counter-Turn* (Berkeley and Los Angeles: University of California Press, 1981), p. 133.

26. Marcia Riefer, "'Instruments of Some More Mightier Member': The Constriction of Female Power in *Measure for Measure,*" *Shakespeare Quarterly* 35 (1984), 167. In Philip C. McGuire's discussion of the play's ending, there is a veritable chorus of silences: see McGuire, *Speechless Dialect: Shakespeare's Open Silences* (Berkeley and Los Angeles: University of California Press, 1985), pp. 63–96.

27. Steven Mullaney, *The Place of the Stage: License, Play, and Power in Renaissance England* (Chicago: University of Chicago Press, 1988), p. 115.

28. Philip J. Finkelpearl, "'The Comedians' Liberty': Censorship of the Jacobean Stage Reconsidered," *English Literary Renaissance* 16 (1986), 125; quotation from John Melton, p. 135.

29. Keith Sturgess, *Jacobean Private Theatre,* Theatre Production Series (London: Routledge and Kegan Paul, 1987), p. 25.

30. Ibid.

31. C. F. Tucker Brooke, "The Royal Fletcher and the Loyal Heywood," quoted from J. F. Danby, *Poets on Fortune's Hill* (London: Faber and Faber, 1952), p. 184.

32. Michael Neill, "'The Simetry, Which Gives a Poem Grace': Masque, Imagery, and the Fancy of *The Maid's Tragedy,*" *Renaissance Drama,* n.s. 3 (1970), 125.

33. E. K. Chambers, *The Elizabethan Stage* (Oxford: Clarendon Press, 1923), 3:223–25. See also Yoshiko Kawachi, *Calendar of English Renaissance Drama, 1558–1642* (New York: Garland Press, 1986), p. 159.

34. Sarah Sutherland, *Masques in Jacobean Tragedy* (New York: AMS Press, 1983), 69–71. Jerzy Limon has recently discussed the complex intertextuality of masque "cycles" over the long term of an event like the wedding celebrations for Elizabeth and Frederick; he analyzes the entertainments of February 1613 in *The Masque of Stuart Culture* (Newark: University of Delaware Press, 1990), pp. 125–69.

35. All quotations in the text are from *The Dramatic Works in the Beaumont and Fletcher Canon,* ed. Fredson Bowers, vol. 2 (Cambridge: Cambridge University Press, 1970) for *The Maid's Tragedy* and *A King and No King;* vol. 1. (Cambridge: Cambridge University Press, 1966), for *Philaster.*

36. Jonson's masques are quoted in the text from *Ben Jonson,* ed. C. H. Herford, Percy and Evelyn Simpson, vol. 7 (Oxford: Clarendon Press, 1963).

37. David Lindley, "Embarrassing Ben: The Masques for Frances Howard," *English Literary Renaissance* 16 (1986), 345. "Viewed with the knowledge of hindsight," Cyrus Hoy argues, "masques like *Hymenaei* and *A Challenge at Tilt*—wherein all the powers of virtuous love are invoked to celebrate the two marriages of Lady Frances Howard—seem almost too blatant examples of idealism come unhooked from the occasions it was intended to inform" (quoted by Sutherland, *Masques,* p. 70).

38. Akrigg, *Jacobean Pageant,* p. 181.

39. Neill, "'The Simetry,'" p. 114; William Shullenberger, "'This for the Most Wrong'd of Women': A Reappraisal of *The Maid's Tragedy,*" *Renaissance Drama,* n.s. 13 (1982), 140, 146–47.

40. Lee Bliss, *Francis Beaumont* (Boston: Twayne, 1987), p. 103.

41. Peter Davison, "The Serious Concerns of *Philaster,*" *ELH* 30 (1963), 14; quotation from James I, *Workes,* p. 3.

42. See Lee Bliss, "Three Plays in One: Shakespeare and *Philaster,*" *Medieval and Renaissance Drama in England* 2 (1985), 153–70; in addition to *Othello,* Bliss discusses echoes of *Hamlet* and *Twelfth Night* in the play.

43. Bliss, *Francis Beaumont,* p. 86.

44. Michael Neill, "The Defence of Contraries: Skeptical Paradox in *A King and No King,*" *Studies in English Literature* 21 (1981), 321.

45. Ibid., p. 332; Danby, *Poets on Fortune's Hill,* pp. 17, 161, 165.

46. Danby, *Poets on Fortune's Hill,* p. 201.

47. *Calendar of State Papers: Venetian, Vol. 16, 1619–21,* ed. A. B. Hinds (London: H. M. Stationery Office, 1910), p. 111.

48. Harbage, *Shakespeare and the Rival Traditions,* first sketched such a view of the Blackfriars audiences. Ann Jennalie Cook, *The Privileged Playgoers of Shakespeare's London* (Princeton: Princeton University Press, 1981), has challenged many of Harbage's conclusions. William C. Woodson, "The Casuistry of Innocence in *A King and No King* and Its Implications for Tragicomedy," *English Literary Renaissance* 8 (1978), 313, 327.

49. Mullaney, *The Place of the Stage,* 113; Richard Burt, "'Licensed by Authority': Ben Jonson and the Politics of Early Stuart Theater," *ELH* 54 (1987), 554.

50. Sir Francis Bacon, *The Essayes or Counsels, Civill and Morall,* ed. Michael Kiernan (Cambridge, Mass.: Harvard University Press, 1985), pp. 117, 118.

51. *The Chamberlain Letters,* ed. Elizabeth McClure Thomson (New York: G. P. Putnam's Sons, 1965), p. 75.

52. Bacon, *Essayes,* p. 118.

53. *Calendar of State Papers: Venetian, vol. 15, 1617–19,* ed. A. B. Hinds (London: H. M. Stationery Office, 1909), pp. 111, 113–14.

54. *James I by His Contemporaries,* pp. 243–44.

3   The King in Love
The Union of the King's Two Bodies in the Court of Charles I

1. Edward Hyde, Earl of Clarendon, *The History of the Rebellion,* ed. W. D. Macray (Oxford: Oxford University Press, 1888), 2:37–38.

2. John Miller, *Bourbon and Stuart: Kings and Kingship in France and England in the Seventeenth Century* (New York: Franklin Watts, 1987), pp. 111, 115.

3. See especially Stephen Orgel and Roy Strong, *Inigo Jones: The Theatre of the Stuart Court* (London: Sotheby Parke Bernet, 1973), 1:49–75.

4. Stephen Orgel, *The Illusion of Power* (Berkeley and Los Angeles: University of California Press, 1975), pp. 52, 89.

5. Quoted by Suzanne Gossett, "'Man-maid begone!': Women in Masques," *English Literary Renaissance* 18 (1988), 98.

6. Charles Carlton, "Three British Revolutions and the Personality of Kingship," in *Three British Revolutions: 1641, 1688, 1776,* ed. J. G. A. Pocock (Princeton: Princeton University Press, 1980): "At the group level the Court acted out its fantasies in plays, especially the elaborate Christmas masques it rehearsed for months. . . . This courtly cloud-cuckoo-land reached its apogee in the Twelfth Night masque for 1640, the year that saw Charles's personal rule come crashing down" (p. 189). Carlton apparently resents not only the performances, but the time spent in rehearsals. For Jennifer Chibnall, the masques are also a delusive waste of time, not only for the royal audience but for the aristocracy, "which defined itself as the ultimate order of earthly achievement" (see Chibnall, "'To that secure fix'd state': The Function of the Caroline Masque Form," in *The Court Masque,* The Revels Plays Companion Library, ed. David Lindley [Manchester: Manchester University Press, 1984], p. 82). Stephen Kogan, *The Hieroglyphic King: Wisdom and Idolatry in the Seventeenth-Century Masque* (Rutherford, N.J.: Fairleigh Dickinson University Press), finds that the Caroline masques convey the idea that Charles "and his queen were inherently divine and that the court was a perfect world all its own" (p. 127). For the view that Caroline masque was less intellectually sophisticated than Jacobean masque, see Graham Parry, *The Golden Age Restor'd: The Culture of the Stuart Court, 1603–42* (Manchester: Manchester University Press, 1981).

7. Kevin Sharpe, *Criticism and Compliment: The Politics of Literature in the England of Charles I* (Cambridge: Cambridge University Press, 1987). For the view that opposition to the court was not necessarily antitheatrical, and that a significant body of theater was critical of Stuart policies, see Margot Heinemann, *Puritanism and Theatre: Thomas Middleton and Opposition Drama under the Early Stuarts* (Cambridge: Cambridge University Press, 1980); Martin Butler, *Theatre*

and Crisis, 1632–1642 (Cambridge: Cambridge University Press, 1984). See also R. Malcolm Smuts, *Court Culture and the Origins of a Royalist Tradition in Early Stuart England* (Philadelphia: University of Pennsylvania Press, 1987).

8. The attitude toward *préciosité* in the criticism of the drama has tended toward contemptuous dismissal. See, for example, G. F. Sensabaugh, "Love Ethics in Platonic Court Drama, 1625–1642," *Huntington Library Quarterly* 1 (1937–38), 277–304. A recent and forceful objection to Sensabaugh can be found in Erica Veevers, *Images of Love and Religion: Queen Henrietta Maria and Court Entertainments* (Cambridge: Cambridge University Press, 1989). See also René Bray, *La Préciosité et les Précieux de Thibaut de Champagne à Jean Giraudoux* (Paris: Nizet, 1945), especially pp. 143–66.

9. *The Dramatic Records of Sir Henry Herbert,* ed. Joseph Q. Adams (1917; rpt. New York: B. Blom, 1964), p. 57.

10. *The Plays and Poems of William Cartwright,* ed. G. Blakemore Evans (Madison: University of Wisconsin Press, 1951), p. 253. All subsequent quotations from *The Royal Slave* and from Evans's reproduction of materials relevant to the play are from this edition and are cited in the text.

11. *Dramatic Records of Sir Henry Herbert,* p. 76. Alfred Harbage, *Cavalier Drama* (New York: Modern Language Association, 1935), p. 112.

12. Quoted from *The Dramatic Works of Sir William D'Avenant* (Edinburgh: William Paterson, 1872), 2: 3–4; all quotations from Davenant's plays are from this edition and are cited by act and page number in the text. *The Unfortunate Lovers* is in vol. 3 (1873); *The Fair Favourite* in vol. 4 (1873).

13. Philip Bordinat and Sophia B. Blaydes, *Sir William Davenant* (Boston: Twayne, 1981), p. 54. See also Veevers: "Court audiences of 1635 required something more French, more feminine, an art of talking about love moulded by Platonic idealism or the niceties of pastoral and romance" (*Images of Love and Religion,* p. 54).

14. For a full account of this literary fashion, see, in addition to Veevers, *Images of Love and Religion,* Ian Maclean, *Woman Triumphant: Feminism in French Literature, 1610–1652* (Oxford: Clarendon Press, 1977).

15. Kathleen McLuskie, in Philip Edwards, Gerald Eades Bentley, Kathleen McLuskie, and Lois Potter, *The Revels History of Drama in English, Volume IV, 1613–1660* (London: Methuen, 1981), p. 158, notices the echoes of *The Maid's Tragedy.*

16. G. E. Bentley reads the lines here as suggesting that "the play was written on order (presumably the Queen's)" (*Jacobean and Caroline Stage* [Oxford: Clarendon Press, 1941–68], 3:212), but it seems clear in the context that the commission alluded to was one in the past.

17. Edwards, et al., *Revels History of Drama,* 4:13.

18. Thomas Carew, "In Answer to an Elegiacal Letter (from Aurelian Townsend) upon the Death of the King of *Sweden:* inviting me to write on that subject," in Carew, *Poetical Works,* ed. J. W. Ebsworth (London: Reeves and Turner, 1893), p. 115. Joanne Altieri discusses the poem in connection with Carew's court masque, *Coelum Britannicum,* in her "Responses to a Waning Mythology in Carew's Political Poetry," *Studies in English Literature* 26 (1986), 107–24. See also

Kogan, *Hieroglyphic King,* pp. 128–37; Sharpe, *Criticism and Compliment,* pp. 145–48.

19. Gossett, "'Man-maid begone,'" p. 111. Miller, *Bourbon and Stuart,* p. 117. Selden quoted from Smuts, *Court Culture,* p. 200. Sharpe, *Criticism and Compliment,* pp. 67–88, discusses the gulf between ideal and real conduct in the play. 67–68.

20. Mary Edmond, *Rare Sir William Davenant,* The Revels Plays Companion Library (New York: St. Martin's Press, 1987), p. 59.

21. Sharpe, *Criticism and Compliment,* p. 67; J. B. Fletcher, "Précieuses at the Court of Charles I," *Journal of Comparative Literature* 1 (1903), 195. Cynical speculation reaching beyond Sharpe's to the level of general principle can be found in Sensabaugh, who argues that the platonic love cult "placed a halo of purity around mental adultery and incest" ("Love Ethics," p. 291).

22. Bentley, *Jacobean and Caroline Stage,* 3:220–21, 4:34–36. John Lough, *Paris Theatre Audiences in the Seventeenth and Eighteenth Century* (London: Oxford University Press, 1957), p. 29.

23. Keith Sturgess, *Jacobean Private Theatre,* Theatre Production Series (London: Routledge and Kegan Paul 1987), pp. 44–47, discusses the use of artificial lighting in this period.

24. *Dramatic Works of D'Avenant,* 2:313.

25. Butler, *Theatre and Crisis,* p. 55.

26. See Butler's discussion of the masque, ibid., pp. 29–31. In standard versions of neoplatonic love, "will" should be guided by reason, but according to *préciosité* the reversal of this priority is not uncommon. Sensabaugh equates this reversal of values with a "lawlessness" that "helped fan the flame of the coming rebellion" ("Love Ethics," p. 304).

27. Butler, *Theatre and Crisis,* p. 55.

28. *Dramatic Records of Sir Henry Herbert,* p. 76.

29. Butler, *Theatre and Crisis,* pp. 58–59.

30. Veevers, *Images of Love and Religion,* p. 68.

31. Maclean discusses the extraordinary influence of this novel (*Woman Triumphant,* pp. 156–71).

32. Philip Edwards, "The Royal Pretenders in Massinger and Ford," *Essays and Studies* 2 (1974), 36.

33. Albert H. Tricomi, *Anticourt Drama in England, 1603–1642* (Charlottesville: University Press of Virginia, 1989), p. 153.

34. Sharpe, *Criticism and Compliment,* p. 50.

35. *Dramatic Records of Sir Henry Herbert,* p. 57.

36. Bentley, *Jacobean and Caroline Stage,* 3:134–41, also prints the materials here quoted from Evans's edition of Cartwright.

37. Butler, *Theatre and Crisis,* p. 46.

38. Allardyce Nicoll, *Stuart Masques and the Renaissance Stage* (New York: Harcourt, Brace and Co., 1938), pp. 138–40.

39. Anne Barton, "He that plays the king: Ford's *Perkin Warbeck* and the Stuart History Play," in *English Drama: Forms and Development,* Essays in Honour of Muriel Clara Bradbrook, ed. Marie Axton and Raymond Williams (Cambridge:

Cambridge University Press, 1977), p. 92. Butler, *Theater and Crisis,* p. 49; Sharpe, *Criticism and Compliment,* p. 50. Veevers also notices that Barton and Butler use the same evidence to arrive at opposite conclusions (*Images of Love and Religion,* p. 72).

40. Smuts, *Court Culture,* p. 249.

41. Garrard quoted from Bentley, *Jacobean and Caroline Stage,* 5:120; *Aglaura* quoted from *The Works of Sir John Suckling,* vol. 2, *The Plays,* ed. L. A. Beaurline (Oxford: Clarendon Press, 1971); all subsequent references are cited in the text.

42. Harbage, *Cavalier Drama,* p. 111.

43. Sharpe, *Criticism and Compliment,* passim; Butler, *Theatre and Crisis,* p. 56.

44. Quoted from Edmond, *Rare Sir William Davenant,* p. 88.

45. William Davenant, *The Shorter Poems and Songs from the Plays and Masques,* ed. A. M. Gibbs (Oxford: Clarendon Press, 1972), p. 139.

4 "Je suis maître de moi comme de l'univers . . ."
In Search of Absolutism in the Court of Louis XIV

1. Jean Racine, *Phèdre,* in *Oeuvres complètes: Volume I, Théâtre et poésies,* Bibliothèque de la Pléiade, ed. Raymond Picard (Paris: Editions Gallimard, 1964), p. 799. All subsequent quotations from works of Racine are cited in the text from this edition.

2. See Judd Hubert, *Essai d'exégèse racinienne: Les secrets témoins* (Paris: Librairie Nizet, 1956), p. 206: "Comme Vénus, il sort de l'écume de la mer" ("Like Venus, it emerges from the foam of the sea"). See also Martin Turnell, *Jean Racine: Dramatist* (London: Hamish Hamilton, 1972), pp. 270–73.

3. Nathan Gross, *From Gesture to Idea: Esthetics and Ethics in Molière's Comedy* (New York: Columbia University Press, 1982), p. 15n.

4. Nancy Klein Maguire, "The Theatrical Mask/Masque of Politics: The Case of Charles I," *Journal of British Studies* 28 (1989), 19.

5. This account of the court of Louis XIV derives from several sources, chief among them Jean-Marie Apostolidès, *Le Roi-machine: Spectacle et politique au temps de Louis XIV* (Paris: Minuit, 1981).

6. Voltaire, *Le Siècle de Louis XIV,* in Voltaire, *Oeuvres complètes,* ed. Louis Moland, 52 vols. (Paris: Garnier Frères, 1877) 14:548. The speech is from act 5, scene 3 of *Cinna,* here quoted as transcribed by Voltaire.

7. Henry Carrington Lancaster, *A History of French Dramatic Literature,* 5 pts. in 9 vols. (Baltimore: Johns Hopkins Press, 1929–42), dates the first performance of *Cinna* in "the latter part of 1640 . . . or early in 1641" (Pt 2, *The Period of Corneille, 1635–51,* 1:312). This is the generally accepted date, although Georges Mongrédien, in *Recueil des textes et des documents du XVIIe siècle rélatifs à Corneille* (Paris: Éditions du Centre National de la Recherche Scientifique, 1972), p. 94, accepts a later date of summer 1642. For the rationale supporting a later date, see René Pintard, "Autour de *Cinna* et de *Polyeucte,*" *Revue de l'Histoire Littéraire de la France* 65 (1965), 377–413.

8. Mongrédien, *Corneille,* p. 62.

9. John Lough, *Seventeenth-Century French Drama: The Background* (Oxford: Clarendon Press, 1979), p. 39.

10. See Timothy Murray's analysis of the opening night of the Salle de la Comédie in his "Richelieu's Theater: The Mirror of a Prince," *Renaissance Drama*, n.s. 8 (1977), 275–98, and also Timothy Murray, *Theatrical Legitimation: Allegories of Genius in Seventeenth-Century England and France* (New York: Oxford University Press, 1987), especially pp. 111–30. Lancaster, *History of French Dramatic Literature*, pt. 2, 1:20, describes the two theaters at the Palais Cardinal.

11. Corneille, *Théâtre complet: Tome premier, oeuvres théoriques, pièces de Mélite à Cinna*, Edition du Tricentenaire, ed. Alain Niderst (Rouen: Publications de l'Université de Rouen, 1984), 2:635. *Cinna* is cited from this edition, 2:767–824; all subsequent references appear in the text.

12. Pierre Mélèse, *Le Théâtre et le public à Paris sous Louis XIV: 1659–1715* (Paris: Droz, 1934), p. 425.

13. Georges Mongrédien, *Recueil des textes et des documents du XVIIe siècle relatifs à Molière*, 2d ed., 2 vols. (Paris: Éditions du Centre National de la Recherche Scientifique, 1973), 1:111.

14. Maurice Rat alludes to this tradition in his edition of the play: Corneille, *Théâtre complet* (Paris: Garnier Frères, 1966), p. 719. So also does Gustav III of Sweden; see chapter 6, below.

15. Murray, *Theatrical Legitimation*, p. 244.

16. Jacques Scherer, *Le Théâtre de Corneille* (Paris: Nizet, 1984), pp. 62, 63; Mitchell Greenberg, *Corneille, Classicism, and the Ruses of Symmetry* (Cambridge: Cambridge University Press, 1986), p. 88.

17. Napoleon quoted from Robert Abirached, *La Crise du personnage dans le théâtre moderne* (Paris: Bernard Grasset, 1978), p. 79. Whether Napoleon's *Cinna* is congruent to Corneille's intentions, Abirached points out, is not to the point; rather, this is how theater works.

18. Closer relationships to topics of contemporary interest have been sought by a number of critics. Georges Couton, *Corneille* (Paris: Hatier, 1958), p. 68, summarizes the most popular topical readings of the play and concludes, "Nous nous contenterions de dire, d'une façon plus générale, que *Cinna* présente une conspiration du style Louis XIII" ("We will content ourselves with saying, in a more general way, that *Cinna* presents a conspiracy in the style of the period of Louis XIII"). Pintard adds to these conspiracies—the "Va-nu-pieds" uprising in Normandy and the "Conspiration des Dames" of 1626—the rebellion of Cinq-Mars, an allusion made possible by his later date for the play ("Autour de *Cinna*," pp. 404–13). André Stegmann, *L'Héroïsme cornélien: Genèse et signification* (Paris: Armand Colin, 1968), concentrates on Machiavellism as a contemporary issue throughout Corneille's career; for *Cinna*, see especially 2:587.

19. Livie's role has provoked much discussion. For Paul Ginestier, she is the key to Auguste's change: "la clémence d'Auguste résulte d'une intuition de sa femme, pure et gratuite, justifiée en suite sur le plan politique par l'analyse raisonnable d'une décision déjà prise" ("Auguste's clemency results from his wife's intuition, pure and gratuitous, justified later on the political level by rational analysis of a decision that has already been made") (Ginestier, *Valeurs actuelles du théâtre clas-*

sique, Collection d'études (Paris: Bordas, 1975), p. 68. For Antoine Soare, on the other hand, Livie's counsels are Machiavellian, based on arguments from success: "*Cinna* ou la clémence au deuxième degré," in *L'Image du souverain dans le théâtre de 1600 à 1650,* Actes de Wake Forest, ed. Milorad R. Margitic and Byron R. Wells (Paris: Papers on French Seventeenth Century Literature, 1987), p. 117. Soare argues that Auguste must transcend this first, politically motivated, degree of clemency and arrive on his own at a second degree. See, however, Solange Guenoun's response to Soare in the same volume, pp. 161–66. Odette de Mourgues discusses Auguste's change of attitude toward Livie's advice as only an apparent incoherence of characterization ("Coherence and Incoherence in *Cinna*", in *Form and Meaning: Aesthetic Coherence in Seventeenth-Century French Drama,* ed. William D. Howarth et al. [Avebury: Avebury Publishing Company, 1982], pp. 51–62).

20. Jean-Marie Apostolidès, *Le Prince sacrifié: Théâtre et politique au temps de Louis XIV* (Paris: Editions de Minuit, 1985), p. 66.

21. See Catherine J. Spencer, "*Cinna:* Un crayon imparfait . . . ?" *Romanic Review* 78 (1987), 420–31, for an extended rhetorical analysis of Cinna's speech.

22. D'Aubignac quoted from Mongrédien, *Corneille,* p. 95; Corneille, *Théâtre complet,* 1:778. T. E. Lawrenson discusses duplicity of place in *Cinna* in his *The French Stage and Playhouse in the Seventeenth Century: A Study in the Advent of the Italian Order,* 2d ed. (New York: AMS Press, 1986): "In other words, one room in a palace was used, and this defined the stage as either 'chez Emilie' or 'chez Auguste'" (p. 151).

23. Serge Doubrovsky, *Corneille et la dialectique du héros* (Paris: Gallimard, 1963), argues that Cinna is a monarchist from the start, and that his oration to the conspirators is disingenuous (pp. 191–93).

24. Greenberg, *Corneille,* p. 156. Louis Marin, *Portrait of the King,* translation of *Le Portrait du roi* by Martha M. Houle (Minneapolis: University of Minnesota Press, 1988), p. 8.

25. In this way, *Cinna* seems to anticipate Corneille's dramas written during the regency of Anne of Austria: see Alain Niderst, "La Royauté sans roi dans le Corneille de la régence," in Margitic and Wells, *L'Image du souverain,* pp. 49–58.

26. André Félibien's *Relation des plaisirs de l'île enchantée* quoted from Molière, *Oeuvres,* ed. Eugène Despois and Paul Mesnard (Paris: Hachette, 1878), 4:98. Subsequent references are cited in the text as *Plaisirs.* For a full analysis of the festival itself, see Apostolidès, *Le Roi-machine,* pp. 93–113; the quest for pleasure and the necessity to transcend pleasure is, for Apostolidès, the theme of the event (p. 98). As Ruggiero, Louis can experience and overcome temptations that would otherwise endanger the state. "Après chaque fête," Apostolidès continues, "les gazetiers rassurent le public sur l'efficacité de ce vaccin: les divertissements du roi l'aident à accomplir son métier" (p. 99: "After each festival, the gazetteers reassure the public of the effectiveness of this vaccine: the king's entertainments help him to do his job").

27. *Plaisirs,* pp. 230–31. See also Mongrédien, *Molière,* 1:215.

28. *Gazette* entry and *L'Homme glorieux* quoted from Mongrédien, *Molière,* 1:216, 220–21.

29. Apostolidès, *Le Roi-machine,* p. 97. See also *Tartuffe, Dom Juan, Le Misan-*

thrope, ed. Georges Couton (Paris: Gallimard, 1973), p. 12: "Son costume suffisait pour que, dès son entré, le premier Tartuffe se trouvât catalogué: un postulant aux bénéfices ecclésiastiques, un homme d'Église ou qui en sera" ("His costume was enough to classify the first Tartuffe according to type at his first entrance: a postulant for church orders, a man of the cloth or one who would become one"). All quotations from *Tartuffe* are from this edition, and are cited in the text.

30. Mongrédien, *Molière* 1:214. See also Gustave Michaut, *Les Luttes de Molière* (Paris: Hachette, 1925), p. 65.

31. Jacques Scherer, *Structures de* Tartuffe (Paris: Société d'Edition d'Enseignement Supérieure, 1966) notices that the *Relation* in La Grange's 1682 edition of Molière's works declares the play to have been unfinished, awaiting reading by "gens capables d'en juger" ("people capable of judging it") (p. 48); see also the notice in *Plaisirs,* pp. 270–365.

32. The phrase *hors d'oeuvre* is from Lancaster, *History of French Dramatic Literature,* pt. 3 (Baltimore: Johns Hopkins Press, 1936), 2:622; see the discussion of *Tartuffe* in W. G. Moore, *Molière: A New Criticism* (Oxford: Clarendon Press, 1949).

33. Michael Spingler, "The King's Play: Censorship and the Politics of Performance in Molière's *Tartuffe,*" *Comparative Drama* 19 (1985–86), 240–57.

34. See especially Scherer, *Structures de* Tartuffe, and Alvin Eustis, *Molière as Ironic Contemplator* (The Hague: Mouton, 1973), p. 214.

35. Spingler, "The King's Play," p. 252.

36. Jacques Guicharnaud, *Molière: Une Aventure théâtrale* (Paris: Gallimard, 1963), p. 163.

37. English verse translation by Donald M. Frame from *Tartuffe and Other Plays* (New York: Signet Classics, 1967). For a discussion of the problem of order in Molière's comic households, see Karolyn Waterson, *Molière et l'autorité: Structures sociales, structures comiques* (Lexington, Ky.: French Forum, 1976).

38. Judd Hubert, "Molière: The Playwright as Protagonist," *Theatre Journal* 38 (1982), 366.

39. Susan Tiefenbrunn, *Signs of the Hidden: Semiotic Studies* (Amsterdam: Rodopi, 1980), p. 165.

40. Jonas Barish, *The Antitheatrical Prejudice* (Berkeley and Los Angeles: University of California Press, 1981), pp. 99–126.

41. Quoted by Georges Couton, "Réflexions sur *Tartuffe* et le péché de l'hypocrisie, 'Cas réservé'," *Revue d'Histoire Littéraire de la France* 69 (1969), 410.

42. Quoted and translated by Emanuel S. Chill, "*Tartuffe,* Religion, and Courtly Culture," *French Historical Studies* 3 (1963), 156.

43. Quoted by Henry Phillips, *The Theatre and Its Critics in Seventeenth-Century France* (New York: Oxford University Press, 1980), p. 145. Phillips discusses the problem of *Tartuffe* on pp. 145–50.

44. Guicharnaud, *Molière,* p. 77.

45. For the notion of "stripping" Tartuffe, see Marcel Gutwirth, "*Tartuffe* and the Mysteries," *PMLA* 92 (1977), 33–40.

46. Michael Goldman, *The Actor's Freedom* (New York: Viking Press, 1975), p. 55.

47. Ralph Albanese, Jr., "Une Lecture idéologique du dénouement de *Tartuffe*," *Romance Notes* 16 (1974–75), 623–35.

48. Ibid., p. 627.

49. For the worldly cynics, see John Cairncross, "*Tartuffe, ou Molière hypocrite,*" *Revue d'Histoire Littéraire de la France* 72 (1972), 890–901.

50. "Tartuffe is discovered as a result of *past* crimes, and Orgon is excused because of *past* favors rendered to the King during the Fronde," concludes Myrna Kogan Zwillenberg, "Dramatic Justice in *Tartuffe,*" *MLN* 90 (1975), 588.

51. Apostolidès, *Le Prince sacrifié,* notes the parallel but sees in *Tartuffe* an inversion: "Alors qu la fin de *Cinna* montrait l'ascension du monarque dans le monde des dieux, celle de *Tartuffe* présente le mouvement inverse: il redescend parmi les hommes, réinstaure l'ordre privé, efface le trouble provoqué par les frictions avec le domaine de l'histoire" (p. 176: "While the ending of *Cinna* showed the ascension of the monarch into the world of the gods, that of *Tartuffe* presents an inverse movement: he redescends among men, reinstates private order, erases the turmoil provoked by these discords with the rule of history").

52. Madame de Sévigné, *Lettres,* Bibliothèque de la Pléiade (Paris: Gallimard, 1963), 3:311. Subsequent references are to this volume of this edition, and appear in the text.

53. "La pièce serait uniquement pour Saint-Cyr et ne serait nullement connue du public," she wrote; quoted in Théophile Lavallée, *Madame de Maintenon et la maison royale de Saint-Cyr (1686–1793),* 2d ed. (Paris: Henri Plon, 1862), p. 84. Subsequent references to this book appear in the text as Lavallée.

54. René Jasinski, *Autour de l'*Esther *racinienne* (Paris: Nizet, 1985), p. 187.

55. Marie Marguerite de Valois de Vilette de Murçay, comtesse de Caylus, *Souvenirs de Madame de Caylus,* ed. Bernard Noël (Paris: Mercure de France, 1965), p. 92. Subsequent references appear in the text as Madame de Caylus.

56. Raymond Picard, *La Carrière de Racine* (Paris: Gallimard, 1956), pp. 411–13. Phillips points to the revocation of the Edict of Nantes in 1685 as a key moment in providing encouragement to antitheatrical gestures: "The growing moral austerity of his reign after 1680 was more than matched by a regeneration of the Church's hostility to drama, and the all-embracing exclusion of theatrical personnel from the sacraments in the ritual of Metz (1713) was a fitting conclusion to the debate in the king's lifetime" (*The Theater and Its Critics,* p. 15).

57. Jean Pommier, *Aspects de Racine* (Paris: Nizet, 1954), pp. 47–85, engages the issue of the so-called "silence de Racine," the period between *Phèdre* and *Esther.* Louis Racine's *Mémoires* are quoted from Jean Racine, *Oeuvres,* p. 46.

58. Jean Orcibal, *La Genèse d'*Esther *et d'*Athalie (Paris: Librairie Philosophique J. Vrin, 1950); see also Marin, *Portrait,* pp. 105–17.

59. Pommier, *Aspects de Racine,* p. 84.

60. The phrase is from Leah S. Marcus, *Puzzling Shakespeare: Local Reading and Its Discontents* (Berkeley and Los Angeles: University of California Press, 1988).

61. See, for example, the poem by the baron de Bretagne appended by Voltaire to his edition of the *Souvenirs de Madame de Caylus* (Madame de Caylus, p. 189).

62. "La plus brillante" (Lavallée, p. 94). See also Philippe de Courcillon, marquis de Dangeau, *Journal du Marquis de Dangeau* (Paris: Librairie de Firmin-Didot, 1854), who felt that with Madame de Caylus "la pièce n'avait mieux réussi" (3:323: "the play had never been more of a success"). Dangeau attended most of the performances. "Madame la comtesse de Caylus joua le rôle d'Esther et s'attira l'admiration de tout le monde" ("Madame de Caylus played the role of Esther and attracted the admiration of everyone"), wrote the marquis de Sourches; quoted by Mélèse, *Le Théâtre et le public*, p. 389. The sole dissenting voice was that of Madame de Lafayette, who felt that "the girls of Saint-Cyr did not really throw 'de la poudre aux yeux de la Chammelay, de la Raisin, de Baron et des Monfleury'"; quoted by Lancaster, *History of French Dramatic Literature*, pt. 4, *The Period of Racine, 1673–1700* (Baltimore: Johns Hopkins Press, 1940), 1:299.

63. Duc de Saint-Simon, *Mémoires: Extraits*, ed. Auguste Dupouy (Paris: Bibliothèque Larousse, 1960?), 1:169–70. Saint-Simon was only thirteen at the time of the performances of *Esther;* what he retails here must be seen as the common gossip of the court in the years after Madame de Caylus's premature retirement from the stage.

64. "Sans théâtre, sans pompe, sans décorations, dans la classe bleue" (Lavallée, p. 113). Occasionally, the girls would be invited to perform at Versailles, before small, select audiences, in the king's private apartments.

65. Quoted by Mélèse, *Le Théâtre et le public*, p. 390.

66. Dangeau, *Journal*, 3:291, 305, 310, 323, 324, 330, 331, 333.

67. Quoted in Lancaster, *History of French Dramatic Literature*, pt. 4, 1:294.

68. Barbara L. Woshinsky, "*Esther:* No Continuing Place," in *Re-Lectures Raciniennes: Nouvelles approches du discours tragique,* ed. Richard L. Barnett (Paris: Papers on French Seventeenth Century Literature/Biblio 17, 1986), p. 257.

69. Judd Hubert, *Essai d'exégèse racinienne: Les Secrets Témoins* (Paris: Nizet, 1956), p. 228.

70. In addition to Marin, *Portrait*, pp. 8–14, see Louis Marin, *Food for Thought,* trans. Mette Hjort (Baltimore: Johns Hopkins University Press, 1989), 189–217, and Marin, "Le Tombeau de la représentation tragique: Notes sur Racine historien du roi et de Port-Royal," in Barnett, *Re-lectures raciniennes,* 99–111.

71. Apostolidès, *Le Roi-machine*, pp. 66–79, discusses the process of "Mythistoire" by which Louis became Louis-Auguste.

72. Apostolidès, *Le Prince sacrifié*, p. 181.

5 Le Roi Voltaire
The Monarch of Wit in the Courts of Louis XV and Frederick the Great

1. Quoted by P. M. Conlon, *Voltaire's Literary Career from 1728 to 1750*, Studies on Voltaire and the Eighteenth Century, 14 (Geneva: Institut et Musée Voltaire, 1961), p. 321.

2. Peter Gay, *Voltaire's Politics: The Poet as Realist,* 2d ed. (New Haven: Yale University Press, 1988), 233.

3. Arsène Houssaye, *Le Roi Voltaire* (Paris: Michel Lévy, Éditeurs-Libraires, 1858), p. 1.

4. Clifton V. Cherpack, "Gold and Iron in Voltaire's *Alzire*," *MLN* 74 (1959), 629.

5. Voltaire, *Oeuvres Complètes*, ed. Louis Moland, 52 vols. (Paris: Garnier Frères, 1877–85), 3:272.

6. Voltaire, *Correspondance*, ed. Theodore Besterman (Geneva: Institut et Musée Voltaire, 1968–77), letter no. D3089. Subsequent references to the correspondence will be incorporated in the text by D-number only.

7. Quoted in John Lough, *Paris Theatre Audiences in the Seventeenth and Eighteenth Century* (London: Oxford University Press, 1957), pp. 231–32.

8. Duc de Luynes, *Mémoires sur la cour de Louis XV*, ed. L. Dussieux and E. Soulie (Paris: Firmin Didot Frères, 1862), 7:132. Subsequent references to this edition will appear in the text as de Luynes.

9. Conlon, *Voltaire's Literary Career*, p. 298; Conlon argues, on the basis of a police report of December 26, 1745, that Voltaire did in fact address the king. Voltaire's nineteenth-century biographers were of the opinion that this anecdote was a malicious calumny; see Gustave Desnoiresterres, *Voltaire et la société au XVIIIᵉ. siècle*, 2d ed. (Paris: Didier, 1871), 3:30–35. Desnoiresterres sees the king's silence as typical of his shyness in company (p. 33).

10. Quoted by Conlon, *Voltaire's Literary Career*, p. 292. Conlon points out that Madame d'Etioles could hardly have helped Voltaire in this fashion at that time, as she was barely beginning her own career as the king's mistress.

11. For a full discussion of this trend throughout Europe, see Marvin Carlson, *Places of Performance: The Semiotics of Theatre Architecture* (Ithaca: Cornell University Press, 1989), pp. 51–60.

12. Adolphe Jullien, *La Comédie à la cour: Les Théâtres de société royale pendant le siècle dernier* (Paris: Firmin-Didot, [1883]), p. 141.

13. Danielle Gallet-Guerne, *Madame de Pompadour, ou le pouvoir féminine* (Paris: Fayard, 1985), p. 63.

14. The full bill of statutes is reproduced in Jullien, *La Comédie à la cour*, p. 148.

15. Ibid., p. 155.

16. Emmanuel, duc de Croÿ, *Journal inèdit, 1718–1784*, ed. le vicomte de Grouchy and Paul Cottin (Paris: Flammarion, 1906), 1:81.

17. Gallet-Guerne, *Madame de Pompadour*, pp. 62–63.

18. This version is quoted from Jullien, *La Comédie à la cour*, p. 171. Voltaire, *Oeuvres complètes*, 10:531, prints a later, revised version of the poem which is slightly less offensive (for example, in place of "Que votre amour soit éternel" ["Let your love be eternal"] it reads "Qu'un sort si beau soit éternel" ["Let so beautiful a destiny be eternal"]). Conlon argues that Voltaire was "probably" present at the theater on this occasion, on the basis of a letter to Cideville in which Voltaire complains of being snubbed upon finally being admitted to the Petits Cabinets (*Voltaire's Literary Career*, pp. 306–7).

19. Jullien, *La Comédie à la cour*, p. 192.

20. De Luynes, 10:222; Madame de Pompadour quoted from Jullien, *La Comédie à la cour*, p. 220; from Gallet-Guerne, *Madame de Pompadour*, p. 59.

21. See, for example, Jack Rochford Vrooman, *Voltaire's Theatre: The Cycle*

from Oedipe *à* Mérope, Studies on Voltaire and the Eighteenth Century, 25 (Geneva: Institut et Musée Voltaire, 1970), pp. 124–25.

22. R. S. Ridgway, *Voltaire and Sensibility* (Montreal: McGill-Queen's University Press, 1973), p. 183.

23. For a fuller discussion of this moment and its implications in terms of Renaissance ideas of acting, see William B. Worthen, *The Idea of the Actor: Drama and the Ethics of Performance* (Princeton: Princeton University Press, 1984), pp. 27–29.

24. Cherpack, "Gold and Iron," p. 632.

25. Eva Jacobs, "Tragedy and Didacticism: The Case of Voltaire," in *Voltaire and His World: Studies Presented to W. H. Barber,* ed. R. J. Howells, A. Mason, H. T. Mason, and D. Williams (Oxford: Voltaire Foundation at the Taylor Institution, 1985), pp. 51–65.

26. Alain Niderst, "Tragique Voltaire," in *Le Siècle de Voltaire: Hommage à René Pommeau,* 2 vols., ed. Christiane Mervaud and Sylvain Menant, (Oxford: Voltaire Foundation, 1987), 2:705.

27. Conlon, *Voltaire's Literary Caree,* p. 314.

28. Although it was printed: see Voltaire, *Oeuvres complètes,* 4:485n, for a full account.

29. Quoted from Jullien, *La Comédie à la cour,* p. 220. According to Jullien, Voltaire sent this poem to Madame de Pompadour the day after the first performance; Desnoiresterres, *Voltaire,* 3:380, places it the day after the second.

30. Quoted from Desnoiresterres, *Voltaire,* 4:379.

31. Christiane Mervaud, *Voltaire et Frédéric le Grand: Une Dramaturgie des lumières, 1736–1778,* Studies on Voltaire and the Eighteenth Century, 234 (Oxford: Voltaire Foundation at the Taylor Institution, 1985), quotes this letter as an epigraph to this extensive and detailed study of the twists and turns of the relationship.

32. This account is based upon R. S. Ridgway, "Voltaire as an Actor," *Eighteenth-Century Studies* 1 (1968): 261–76.

33. Ibid., 265, 267.

34. Voltaire, *Oeuvres complètes,* 5:203; cited also by Ridgway, "Voltaire," p. 267. Subsequent citations from *Rome sauvée* are from vol. 5, and are incorporated in the text by act, scene, and page number.

35. Desnoiresterres, *Voltaire,* 3:372–77. See also Jean-Jacques Olivier, *Voltaire et les comédiens, interprètes de son théâtre* (Paris: Société Française d'Imprimerie et de Librairie, 1900), for a full account of Voltaire's relationship with Lekain.

36. Mervaud, *Voltaire et Frédéric le Grand,* p. 176. Frederick, in fact, had celebrated Crébillon's play in a verse epistle to Maupertuis, which Voltaire had received with approval in early 1749. There Frederick praised Crébillon for his characterization of Cicéron:

Plus loin, aux bords de l'Hippocrène,
On voit l'amant de Melpomène,
Son *Catilina* dans les main,
Faisant haranguer sur la scène
Le Démosthène des Romains.

(Further off, by the shores of the Hippocrene, we see the lover of Melpo-
mene, his *Catilina* in his hand, causing the Demosthenes of the Romans to
make his speeches on the stage.)

Frederick II, King of Prussia, *Oeuvres de Frédéric le grand* (Berlin: Rodolphe
Decker, 1849), 11:49.

37. Jean Sareil, *Voltaire et les grands* (Geneva: Librairie Droz, 1978) quotes this
letter (p. 120). Sareil offers a full discussion of Voltaire's relations with Madame de
Pompadour (pp. 103–34).

38. Voltaire, *Oeuvres complètes,* 5:79.

39. Desnoiresterres, *Voltaire,* 3:191–92.

40. Pierre Corneille, "Premier Discours sur le poème dramatique," in *Writings
on the Theatre,* ed. H. T. Barnwell (Oxford: Basil Blackwell, 1965), p. 8.

41. Prosper Jolyot de Crébillon, *Théâtre complet,* ed. Auguste Vitu (Paris:
Librairie Garnier Frères [1923]), p. 242.

42. Catherine Volpilhac-Auger, "Auguste et Louis XIV: Les Contradictions de
Voltaire devant le pouvoir absolu," in *La monarchie absolutiste et l'histoire en
France,* Colloque tenu en Sorbonne les 26–27 mai 1986 (Paris: Presses de l'Uni-
versité de Paris-Sorbonne, 1987), 197–215. "Epitre à Horace" quoted from 210.

43. Voltaire, *Oeuvres complètes,* 14:440.

44. Desnoiresterres, *Voltaire,* 3:437.

45. See Voltaire, *Oeuvres complètes,* 4:97–100; and Sareil, *Voltaire,* pp. 47–48,
for fuller discussion of the suppression of *Mahomet.*

46. Nivelle de La Chaussée, quoted by Jullien, *La Comédie à la cour,* p. 126.

47. Both versions are quoted from Desnoiresterres, *Voltaire,* 4:98.

48. *Voltaire on Shakespeare,* ed. Theodore Besterman, Studies on Voltaire and
the Eighteenth Century, 54 (Geneva: Insitut et Musée Voltaire, 1967), pp. 24–26.

49. Quoted from Desnoiresterres, *Voltaire,* 4:100.

50. Sareil, *Voltaire,* p. 13. The title itself was conferred upon Voltaire by Arsène
Houssaye. Jean Orieux also uses the image in his *Voltaire: ou la royauté de l'esprit*
(Paris: Flammarion, 1966); see, for example, p. 377: "En ce temps-là l'Europe avait
deux rois: le roi de Prusse et le roi Voltaire" ("In those days, Europe had two kings:
the king of Prussia and King Voltaire").

51. Quoted from *Voltaire,* Collection Génie et Réalités, ed. François Bluche et
al. (Paris: Hachette Réalités, 1978), p. 193.

52. Timothy Murray, *Theatrical Legitimation: Allegories of Genius in Seventeenth-Century England and France* (New York: Oxford University Press, 1987).

53. Desnoiresterres, *Voltaire,* 4:122

54. Jean Le Rond d'Alembert, *Oeuvres complètes* (Paris: Belin, 1822), 4:417.

55. Jean-Jacques Rousseau, *Lettre à M. D'Alembert sur les Spectacles,* ed. M.
Fuchs (Geneva: Librairie Droz, 1948), p. 163. The two plays that Rousseau men-
tions here went on to become among the most popular plays of Voltaire during the
French Revolution. See Phyllis S. Robinove, "Voltaire's Theater on the Parisian
Stage, 1789–99," *French Review* 32 (1958–59), 534–38. *Brutus* was performed 144
times during this period, *La Mort de César* fifteen times in the summer of 1792,

during the trial of Louis XVI. By contrast, during this decade, *Rome sauvée* received four performances.

56. Gay, *Voltaire's Politics,* pp. 62–63.

57. Quoted from Gavin de Beer, "Voltaire's British Visitors," Studies in Voltaire and the Eighteenth Century, 4, ed. Theodore Besterman (Geneva: Institut et Musée Voltaire, 1957), pp. 14–15.

58. Quoted from Desnoiresterres, *Voltaire,* 5:394–95.

59. Both Callandar and Gibbon quoted from de Beer, "Voltaire's British Visitors," pp. 63–64, 31.

60. Ibid., p. 111.

61. Desnoiresterres, *Voltaire,* 5:304.

62. Voltaire, *Zaïre,* ed. Eva Jacobs (London: Hodder and Stoughton, 1975). Subsequent citations from this edition are in the text.

63. Ridgway, "Voltaire," p. 272. See also Ronald S. Ridgway, *La Propagande philosophique dans les tragédies de Voltaire,* Studies on Voltaire and the Eighteenth Century, 15 (Geneva: Musée et Institut Voltaire, 1961), pp. 203f., for a fuller discussion of *Les Scythes.*

64. Olivier, *Voltaire et les comédiens,* pp. 347–50.

65. Frederick II, *Oeuvres,* 14:177.

66. Ridgway, "Voltaire," p. 267.

67. In addition to Ridgway, *La Propagande philosophique,* see Robert Niklaus, "La Propagande philosophique au théâtre au siècle des lumières," Studies on Voltaire and the Eighteenth Century, 29 (Geneva: Institut et Musée Voltaire, 1963). Vrooman also notes the disjunction, but views it more favorably: "While clinging to an aristocratic form, Voltaire inserted an essentially bourgeois ideal" (*Voltaire's Theatre,* p. 181).

68. Gay, *Voltaire's Politics,* p. 171.

6   Player and King
Gustav III

1. Quoted from *Bref rörande teatern under Gustaf III, 1788–1792,* ed. Eugène Lewenhaupt (Uppsala: Akademiska Boktryckeriet, 1894) p. 141. See also Kjell Stromberg, "La Tragédie Voltairienne en Suède," *Revue d'Histoire Littéraire de la France* 23 (1916), 118.

2. Michel Launay, "J-J Rousseau et Gustave III de Suède," *Revue de Littérature Comparée* 32 (1958), 498.

3. *Gustave III par ses lettres,* ed. Gunnar von Proschwitz, vol. 8 of *Svenska Akademiens Handlingar från år 1986* (Stockholm: Norstedt, 1986), p. 27. Von Proschwitz notices the misquotation without comment.

4. *Collection des écrits politiques, littéraires, et dramatiques de Gustave III, roi de suède, suivie de sa correspondance,* ed. Jean-Baptiste De Chaux, 4 vols. (Stockholm: Charles Délen, 1804), 2:1. Subsequent references to this edition will be incorporated in the text.

5. Lennart Breitholtz, *Studier i Operan "Gustaf Wasa"* (Uppsala: Uppsala Universitets Årsskrift, 1954), p. 100. Breitholtz reproduces Gustav's unique spelling.

6. Quoted from ibid., p. 118.

7. The study of Gustav III published in honor of the two hundredth anniversary of the Swedish Academy in 1986 is entitled *The Great Role: Gustav III as Played by Himself:* see Erik Lonnroth, *Den Stora Rollen: Gustaf III som sin Själv,* vol. 1 of *Svenska Akademiens Handlingar från år 1986* (Stockholm, Norstedt, 1986). August Strindberg's historical drama, *Gustav III* (1902), utilizes metatheatrical conceits throughout.

8. Quoted from Michael Lance Harvey, "The History of the Gripsholm Castle Theater during the Reign of Gustav III of Sweden" (Diss., University of Minnesota, 1969), p. 84. Agne Beijer points out that 2,456 of these lines are tragic alexandrines, "Gustavianskt teaterliv på Gripsholm," in *Gripsholm: Slottet och dess Sammlingar, 1537–1937* (Stockholm: Nordisk Rotogravyr, 1937), p. 93. In this chapter, discussion will be confined to Gustav's serious roles, although the comic afterpieces are also of some interest.

9. *Gustave III par ses Lettres,* pp. 75–78; Gustav refers to a planned performance of *Gaston et Bayard* in September 1770 at Ulriksdal in honor of the visit of Prince Henry of Prussia, Frederick the Great's histrionic brother (p. 88).

10. Beth Hennings, *Grevinnan d'Egmont och Gustave III* (Stockholm, 1920), pp. 174–75.

11. *Gaston et Bayard* quoted from *Chefs d'oeuvre[s] dramatiques de De Belloy, Répertoire du théâtre français (2ème. ordre),* vol. 28 (Paris: P. Didot, 1822), I.iv, p. 191.

12. Fredrik Axel von Fersen, *Historiska Skrifter,* 8 vols. (Stockholm: Norstedt, 1869), 3:213.

13. Quoted from Harvey, "Gripsholm Castle Theater," pp. 53–54.

14. Oscar Levertin, *Teater och Drama under Gustaf III,* 2d ed. (Stockholm: Bonniers, 1911), reproduces the king's list on pp. 68–69; Beijer provides Sparre's report of the actual order of plays, "Gustavianskt teaterliv," on p. 93.

15. See Harvey, "Gripsholm Castle Theater," p. 99.

16. Lucas quoted from the editors' notes to *Oeuvres complètes de Voltaire* (Paris: Garnier Frères, 1877), 5:356. Henri Lion, *Les Tragédies et les théories dramatiques de Voltaire* (1895; rpt. Geneva: Slatkine Reprints, 1970), p. 228.

17. Quoted from Lion, *Tragédies de Voltaire,* p. 231.

18. Gustav quoted from Levertin, *Teater,* p. 9. Georg Nordensvan, *Svensk Teater och Svenska Skådespelare från Gustav III till våra dagar,* 2 vols. (Stockholm: Bonniers, 1917), 1:3–4, recounts the audition performance of Stenborg's company before the court. Harvey, "Gripsholm Castle Theater," p. 189.

19. Quoted from *Gustave III par ses lettres,* p. 107; Launay, "J-J Rousseau et Gustave III de Suède," describes Gustav as "choqué par le républicanisme" (p. 509).

20. Jean Racine, *Athalie,* ed. Henri Maugis (Paris: Classiques Larousse, 1933). Subsequent references to this edition are in the text.

21. Harvey, "Gripsholm Castle Theater," pp. 213–17, prints Oxenstierna's verses in their entirety. Quotations here are from pp. 213–14.

22. Quoted from Lion, *Tragédies de Voltaire,* p. 90.

23. Voltaire, *Oeuvres Complètes,* 3:99; subsequent references to *Adelaïde du Guesclin* are from this volume, and appear in the text.

24. *Rhadamiste et Zénobie* quoted from Prosper Jolyot de Crébillon, *Théâtre Complet*, ed. Auguste Vitu (Paris: Garnier 1923). Subsequent references are in the text.

25. *Mélanide* quoted from *Chefs d'oeuvre[s] dramatiques de Nivelle de la Chausée, Répertoire du théâtre français, (2ème ordre)*, vol. 21 (Paris: Didot, 1822), p. 124. Subsequent references are in the text.

26. Letter from Pierre de Luz, quoted by Harvey, "Gripsholm Castle Theater," p. 82.

27. *Cinna* quoted from Pierre Corneille, *Théâtre complet: Tome premier, oeuvres théoriques, pièces de* Mélite à Cinna, Édition du Tricentenaire, ed. Alain Niderst (Rouen: Publications de l'Université de Rouen, 1984).

28. Quoted from Auguste Geffroy, *Gustav III et la cour de France* (Paris: Didier, 1867), 1:239-41. Hennings has published a Swedish translation of the same letter (*Grevinnan d'Egmont*, pp. 218-19), which contains the phrase omitted in Geffroy: "Jag var ännu upprörd över stycket och vredgad över åskådaras likgiltighet, i synnerhet när jag jämförde deras sätt med den, som spelat Bayard" ("I was still upset about the play and angry about the audience's indifference, especially when I compared their conduct with his, who played Bayard"). The comtesse could be referring equally here to the actor in the court performance or to Gustav.

29. Denis Diderot, "Paradoxe sur le comédien," *Oeuvres esthétiques de Diderot*, ed. Paul Vernière (Paris: Garnier, 1965), p. 317. Subsequent references are in the text.

30. Quoted from Harvey, "Gripsholm Castle Theater," p. 129.

31. "Ehuru det icke fanns en enda af hela sallskapet kunne tala, än mindre modersmålet felfritt" (Fersen, *Historiska Skrifter*, 5:133).

32. Quoted from Harvey, "Gripsholm Castle Theater," p. 167.

33. *Charlot, ou la comtesse de Givry* quoted from Voltaire, *Oeuvres complètes*, vol. 6. All references are in the text. Voltaire, *Oeuvres* (Lausanne: Grasset, 1772), vol. 21: *Théâtre Complet, v. 8* has also been consulted for the early version.

34. In the interest of consistency, Gustav III's plays are quoted from the most readily available edition, *Konung Gustaf III:s Dramatiska Skrifter*, vol. 1 (Stockholm: Expeditionen af Konversations-Lexikon, 1857). This is essentially a reprint of Oxenstierna's Swedish edition of Gustav's *Skrifter* (Stockholm: Charles Délen, 1806), which itself appears to be based upon the De Chaux edition (see n. 4, above). The complex bibliographical relationships among these published texts and the extant manuscripts of Gustav's plays are discussed in Oskar Levertin, *Gustav III som dramatisk författare*, 2d ed. (Stockholm: Bonnier, 1911). With regard to *Gustav Vasa*, Lennart Breitholtz disagrees with many of Levertin's conclusions. Swedish verse versions of the plays by Johan Kellgren have also been consulted: Johan Kellgren, *Samlade Skrifter*, vol. 1 (Orebro: N. M. Lindh, 1860).

35. *La Partie de chasse de Henri IV* quoted from *Chefs d'oeuvre[s] dramatiques de Collé et Favart, Répertoire du théâtre français (2ème ordre)*, vol. 30 (Paris: Didot, 1824). Subsequent references are in the text.

36. Playbill quoted from Levertin, *Teater*, p. 74; Oxenstierna, from Levertin, *Gustav III*, p. 71; Fersen, *Historiska Skrifter*, 5:137.

37. Levertin, *Teater*, p. 180.

38. Barbro Stribolt, "Louis Jean Desprez," in *The Drottningholm Theatre Museum* (Borås: Drottningholm Theatre Museum, 1984), p. 38. See also Beth Hennings, *Gustav III: en biografi* (Stockholm: Norstedt, 1957), p. 202.

39. Quoted from Breitholtz, *"Gustaf Wasa,"* p. 92.

40. See ibid., pp. 96f. for a full discussion of the opera's relationship to these two plays.

41. See, for a full account of this development in England, Robert Etheridge Moore, *Henry Purcell and the Restoration Theatre* (Cambridge, Mass.: Harvard University Press, 1961).

42. See Herbert Lindenberger, *Historical Drama: The Relation of Literature and Reality* (Chicago: University of Chicago Press, 1975), for discussion of the way opera can function as a "magnification" of history (pp. 60–64). See also Lindenberger, "The History in Opera: *La Clemenza di Tito, Khovanshchina, Moses und Aron,*" *The History in Literature: On Value, Genre, Institutions* (New York: Columbia University Press, 1990), pp. 85–108.

43. Fersen originally spotted the imitation of Shakespeare: "Konungen hade för denna sin opera imiterat engelska tragedien Richard III" ("The king had for this opera of his imitated the English tragedy *Richard III*") (*Historiska Skrifter*, 6:64). Breitholtz and Levertin disagree on which French version of Shakespeare's plays Gustav might have used: see Breitholtz, *"Gustaf Wasa,"* pp. 113–14. He did not know the play in English.

44. Quoted from William Shakespeare, *King Henry VIII,* The Arden Edition, ed. R. A. Foakes (London: Methuen, 1957), p. 180. See also Phyllis Rackin, *Stages of History: Shakespeare's English Chronicles* (Ithaca: Cornell University Press, 1990), p. 223n.

45. Pepys and Downes quoted from *The London Stage, 1660–1800: Part One, 1660–1700,* ed. William Van Lennep, with a critical introduction by Emmett L. Avery and Arthur H. Scouten (Carbondale: Southern Illinois University Press, 1965), p. 80.

Index

Designed by Martha Farlow

Composed by A. W. Bennett, Inc., in Sabon with Adobe Minion display

Printed by Thomson-Shore, Inc., on 50-lb. Glatfelter Eggshell
and bound in Rainbow Linique